SOCIAL POLICY IN A COLD CLIMATE

Policies and their consequences since the crisis

Edited by

Ruth Lupton, Tania Burchardt, John Hills,
Kitty Stewart and Polly Vizard

First published in Great Britain in 2016 by

Policy Press
University of Bristol
1-9 Old Park Hill
Bristol
BS2 8BB
UK
+44 (0)117 954 5940
pp-info@bristol.ac.uk
www.policypress.co.uk

North America office:
Policy Press
c/o The University of Chicago Press
1427 East 60th Street
Chicago, IL 60637, USA
t: +1 773 702 7700
f: +1 773-702-9756
sales@press.uchicago.edu
www.press.uchicago.edu

British Library Cataloguing in Publication Data
A catalogue record for this book is available from the British Library

Library of Congress Cataloging-in-Publication Data
A catalog record for this book has been requested

ISBN 978 1 44732 771 4 hardcover
ISBN 978 1 44732 772 1 paperback
ISBN 978 1 44732 775 2 ePub
ISBN 978 1 44732 776 9 Mobi

Cover design by Hayes Design
Front cover image: www.alamy.com
Printed and bound in Great Britain by CMP, Poole
Policy Press uses environmentally responsible print partners

Contents

List of tables, figures and boxes

Tables

Figures

Boxes

List of acronyms

5A*-C EM	5A*-C grades at GCSE, including English and maths
ACRA	The Advisory Committee on Resource Allocation
ADL	activity of daily living
AEI	Average Earnings Index
AHC	after housing costs
ALMP	active labour market policies
ASB	Adult Skills Budget
BERR	Business, Enterprise and Regulatory Reform
BHC	before housing costs
BIS	Department for Business, Innovation and Skills
BRES	Business Register and Employment Survey
BSF	Building Schools for the Future
CASE	Centre for Analysis of Social Exclusion
CCG	clinical commissioning group
CPI	consumer prices index
CQC	Care Quality Commission
CSA	Child Support Agency
DCLG	Department for Communities and Local Government
DCSF	Department for Children, Schools and Families
DDA	Disability Discrimination Act
DEL	departmental expenditure limit
DfE	Department for Education
DfES	Department for Education and Skills
DFLE	Disability free life expectancy
DH	Department of Health
DHP	Discretionary Housing Payment
DIUS	Department for Innovation, Universities and Skills
DWP	Department for Work and Pensions
E-Bacc	English Baccalaureate
ELSA	English Longitudinal Survey of Ageing
EMA	Educational Maintenance Allowance
ESA	Employment and Support Allowance
EU	European Union
EUROMOD	tax-benefit microsimulation model for the European Union
FE	further education
FSM	free school meals

FTE	full-time equivalent (working hours)
GCSE	General Certificate of Secondary Education (public exam mainly taken at 16)
GDP	gross domestic product
GHQ-12	General Health Questionnaire score of 12 or more
GHS	General Household Survey
GVA	gross value added
HBAI	Households Below Average Income
HE	Higher education
HEFCE	Higher Education Funding Council for England
HSCIC	Health and Social Care Information Centre
IADL	instrumental activity of daily living
ICOF	Independent Commission on Fees
ICT	information and communication technology
IDACI	Index of Deprivation Affecting Children
IFS	Institute for Fiscal Studies
IMD	Index of Multiple Deprivation
LEP	Local Enterprise Partnership
LGA	Local Government Association
LHA	Local Housing Allowance
LSC	Learning and Skills Council
LSOA	lower super output area (ONS small area geography of about 1,400 people)
MSOA	Middle layer Super Output Areas (ONS Medium area geography of 7,200 people on average)'
NAO	National Audit Office
NCVO	National Council of Voluntary Organisations
NDPB	non-departmental public body
NEET	not in education, employment or training
NEST	National Employment Savings Trust
NHS	National Health Service
NIC	National Insurance Contribution
NICE	National Institute for Health and Care Excellence
NOMIS	National Online Manpower Information System, ONS labour market statistics data service
NRF	Neighbourhood Renewal Fund
NRU	Neighbourhood Renewal Unit
NSNR	National Strategy for Neighbourhood Renewal
OBR	Office for Budget Responsibility
OECD	Organisation for Economic Co-operation and Development
ONS	Office for National Statistics

PAYE	Pay as You Earn
PCT	primary care trust
PESA	Public Expenditure Statistical Analysis
PFI	private finance initiative
PRU	Pupil Referral Unit
PVI	private, voluntary or independent
QIPP	Quality, Innovation, Productivity and Prevention Initiative
RDA	Regional Development Agency
ROSSI	Inflation index that uprated benefits based on the September increase in the all-items RPI, excluding rent, mortgage interest, Council Tax and housing depreciation
RPA	Raising the Participation Age
RPI	Retail Prices Index
S2P	State Second Pension
SEAL	social and emotional aspects of learning
SEN	special educational needs
SFA	Skills Funding Agency
SNP	Scottish National Party
SSC	Sector Skills Council
TME	Total Managed Expenditure
TUC	Trades Union Congress
UK	United Kingdom
UKCES	UK Commission on Employment and Skills
ULF	Union Learning Fund
UMBR	unadjusted means-tested benefit rate (LSE CASE construct, indicating poverty level)
UTC	university technical colleges
VAT	value added tax
WCA	Work Capability Assessment
WHO	World Health Organization
YPLA	Young People's Learning Agency

Notes on editors and contributors

Editors

Ruth Lupton is a professor of education at the University of Manchester. She was previously principal research fellow and deputy director at the Centre for Analysis of Social Exclusion (CASE), London School of Economics and Political Science (LSE), where she is now visiting professor.

Tania Burchardt is associate professor of social policy at LSE and deputy director of CASE. Her research interests include theories of social justice, including the capability approach, employment, welfare and exclusion, and equality and inequality in Britain.

John Hills is Richard Titmuss Professor of Social Policy, director of CASE and co-director of the International Inequalities Institute at LSE. His interests include the welfare state, social security, pensions, income and wealth inequality, and social policy and the life cycle.

Kitty Stewart is associate professor of social policy at LSE and a research associate at CASE. Her research interests include child poverty, early childhood education and care, and the relationship between financial resources and other dimensions of well-being.

Polly Vizard is an associate professorial research fellow at CASE, LSE. Her research focuses on inequality and deprivation, the capability approach, rights-based approaches and social and public policy.

Contributors

Jack Cunliffe obtained his doctorate at LSE and is a lecturer in quantitative methods and criminology at the University of Kent.

Paola De Agostini is senior research officer at the Institute for Social and Economic Research, University of Essex.

Amanda Fitzgerald was research officer at CASE for the Social Policy in a Cold Climate programme while completing her PhD at the University of Cambridge.

Emily Jones is a graduate of LSE and joined CASE as part of the LSE Graduate Internship Scheme.

Abigail McKnight is an associate professorial research fellow at CASE, LSE.

Polina Obolenskaya is research officer at CASE, LSE.

Holly Sutherland is research professor and director of EUROMOD at the Institute for Social and Economic Research, University of Essex.

Stephanie Thomson is a postdoctoral research fellow at the Department of Social Policy and Intervention, University of Oxford.

Rebecca Tunstall is Joseph Rowntree Professor of Housing Policy and director of the Centre for Housing Policy Studies, University of York.

Lorna Unwin is professor of vocational education and deputy director of LLAKES Research Centre, UCL Institute of Education.

Acknowledgements

The Social Policy in a Cold Climate programme, of which this book forms the final output, was funded by the Joseph Rowntree Foundation and the Nuffield Foundation, with London-specific analysis supported by the Trust for London. We are very grateful for all the financial and other support and guidance they have generously offered throughout the programme, including through the joint advisory group, but any opinions expressed are those of the authors and not necessarily those of the funders.

This book could not have been completed and published without the support for the entire programme from Jane Dickson (CASE centre manager), but also especially from Bert Provan (knowledge broker) and Cheryl Conner (CASE administration and knowledge exchange assistant), who have co-ordinated its production and preparation for publication, as well as of the research reports and working papers that underlie it. We have benefited greatly from the research assistance of Emily Jones, Su Sureka, Simone Marino, Alexander Roberts, and Liz Vossen, as well as Tom Smith and his team at OCSI for support on data presentation. We have been ably and efficiently supported throughout the process of publication the team at Policy Press including Emily Mew, Laura Vickers and Laura Greaves.

We are also particularly grateful to Howard Glennerster, not just for his wise advice throughout the programme, but also for reading and commenting on an earlier draft of the whole book, saving us from a number of errors.

Chapter Two draws on earlier papers for which we received very helpful advice, comments and support from Fran Bennett, Chris Goulden, Rachel Takens-Milne, Ben Richards, David Utting and Sharon Witherspoon. The authors of Chapter Three would like to thank Alison Garnham, Leon Feinstein, Naomi Eisenstadt, Eileen Munro, Jane Lewis, Rachael Takens-Milne, Sharon Witherspoon and Harriet Waldegrave for taking time to comment on the papers on which this chapter is based, and Shirley Allen and Ludovica Gambaro for useful discussion of developments around childcare and early education. The authors of Chapter Four are very grateful to Amanda Fitzgerald for her editorial work, Alex Roberts for his help with data collection and colleagues at the DSCF, DfE and HM Treasury who kindly responded to their queries. Their thanks also go to their many colleagues at the Centre for Analysis of Social Exclusion (CASE), and in the wider educational research community who took the time to read and comment on the work underpinning this chapter. The authors of Chapter Five are very grateful to Amanda Fitzgerald for her editorial work, and to Julian Gravatt and Kitty Stewart for their comments on earlier versions of the chapter. Their thanks also go to their many colleagues at the CASE and in the wider educational research community who took the time to read and comment on the work underpinning this chapter. The author of Chapter Six would like to thank Conor D'arcy for comments on the earlier research paper on which the chapter is based; and Timo Long and Andrew Keep at HM Treasury for assistance with the PESA data series. The author of Chapter Seven would like to thank Ruth Lupton and Bert Provan for comments and suggestions on drafts of the chapter. The authors of Chapter Eight would like to thank Howard Glennerster, Julian Le Grand and John Appleby for comments and suggestions on the earlier research reports on which the chapter is based; and Ellie Suh for her work on mental health data using Health Survey for England. The authors of Chapter Nine are very grateful to Holly Holder and Richard Humphries for invaluable comments on an earlier version. The authors of Chapter Ten are indebted to Dan Edmiston and John Hills for sharing with them their spreadsheets and thoughts from the previous iteration of the exercise to track the changing boundaries of public and private welfare, and to Howard Glennerster, Bert Provan and Polly Vizard for insightful comments on the approach. The authors of Chapter Thirteen are very grateful to Bert Provan for his advice and his work on the Indices of Multiple Deprivation and Alex Fenton for contributions to earlier work underpinning this chapter. The authors also thank Neil Lee for his useful comments on some of the underlying work for this chapter. They also thank colleagues at numerous government departments who kindly responded to their queries, and Howard Glennerster, Polly Vizard, Rebecca Tunstall, John Hills and other colleagues at CASE who commented on drafts or gave advice and comments as the chapter developed.

Several chapters draw on Office for National Statistics (ONS) statistics which are subject to Crown copyright and are reproduced under the Open Government Licence v.3.0. For the analysis presented in Chapters Eleven and Twelve we are very grateful to Mike Daly at the Department for Work and Pensions (DWP) and to Elaine Chamberlain at the ONS for providing the access to the data from the HBAI dataset and the Wealth and Assets Survey respectively, and to Alex Barton at DWP and Alan Newman at ONS for conducting the analysis and their subsequent excellent communications in clarifying the details of those results. Several chapters draw on data from the Labour Force Survey and Family Resources Survey, deposited in the UK Data Archive. Figure 11.5 is Crown Copyright and is reproduced under Class Licence C20060001 by kind permission of the Office for Public Sector Information (OPSI) and the Queen's Printer for Scotland.

ONE

Introduction

Ruth Lupton, Kitty Stewart, Tania Burchardt, John Hills
and Polly Vizard

In June 2007, when Gordon Brown took over from Tony Blair as Labour leader and Prime Minister of the UK, the climate for social policy-making in the UK was decidedly warm. The country was enjoying a sustained period of economic growth, the current budget deficit and public sector net debt were both lower than when Labour came to power, and the electorate was broadly supportive of the government's expansive social spending and the improved public services they had delivered.

Our own assessment of Labour's decade under Blair highlighted a complex and nuanced story, but one which indicated a shift towards a more equal society in several important respects (Hills et al, 2009). Inequality at the very top and the very bottom of the income distribution had continued to rise, as had absolute gaps in wealth and a range of measures of inequality in health outcomes. But there had been notable reductions in child and pensioner poverty, improvements in the relative position of disadvantaged neighbourhoods, narrowing gaps in educational achievement between children from lower-income families and others, and narrowing gaps in employment, education and incomes between some minority ethnic groups and the majority white population. The significant increases in the 'social wage' delivered through education and healthcare spending had had a substantial equalising effect. Looking at a range of official *Opportunity for all* indicators, trends had improved from 1997 compared to the decade before for nearly half of them, although they had deteriorated for a quarter. Where significant policy initiatives had been taken – and many were – we concluded that outcomes had generally moved in the right direction, if not always as rapidly as policy-makers and other observers might have hoped.

The period that followed, until the election of the Conservative government in May 2015, was an extraordinary one in British economic and political history. As has been well documented

1

elsewhere, the global financial crisis that began to unfold in the summer of 2007 and culminated in the banking collapses and bail-outs of autumn 2008 plunged the UK, like many other countries, into their worst recession since the 1930s, and punched a large hole in the public finances (see, for example, Gregg et al, 2014; Riley and Chote, 2014). Public sector net debt rose from 36.7 to 49.0% of GDP and the current budget deficit from 0.6 to 3.4% of GDP in a single year between 2007/08 and 2008/09. At the same time, pressures on the public purse seemed set to increase, as the number of very elderly people continued its long-term upward trend, and a new baby boom signalled additional demand for early years education and primary school places in the short term.

Labour's initial response, to continue to expand spending on public services in order to stave off the worst of the economic downturn, was strongly criticised by the Conservatives in the run-up to the 2010 General Election, with a strong narrative emerging that Labour's public spending had caused the country's indebtedness. The inconclusive election, and the intense political negotiations that followed, eventually produced a Conservative/Liberal Democrat coalition (the UK's first since the Second World War) committed to the diametrically opposed strategy of rapid debt reduction to be achieved primarily through spending cuts. While the results of the British Election Study in 2009/10 (see www.bes2009-10.org/) do not reveal any great appetite for 'austerity', neither do they show any appetite for increasing taxation in order to finance sustained social spending. Two-thirds of those polled favoured either the status quo in terms of tax and spend (56%), or cutting taxes and spending less (10%). The climate for the design and delivery of social policy was now distinctly cold. Moreover, the new government committed itself to a programme of fundamental restructuring of the welfare state that aimed to shift significant responsibility from state to private providers, citizens and the community, thus leading to permanently lower spending, lower debt and market-led growth (Taylor-Gooby, 2012).

This book documents the changes (and continuities) in social policy and social spending, and their effects, during this extraordinary period. As such, it is a sequel to two earlier books by members of the same editorial team examining the social policies of the Labour governments under Blair: *A more equal society? New Labour, poverty, inequality and exclusion* (Hills and Stewart, 2005) and *Towards a more equal society? Poverty, inequality and policy since 1997* (Hills et al, 2009). Like those volumes, this book is intended as a wide-ranging yet detailed reference guide for students of social policy, policy-makers and opinion formers and 'ordinary voters' who want to look behind the claims and counter-claims made through the media to gain a fuller understanding of the actual policies pursued and their consequences. Like these earlier books, this, too, has a particular focus on the effects of policies on poverty and economic inequality, and on the distribution of spending, policy effort and outcomes between different groups in society. We understand the achievement of a more equal distribution of opportunities and outcomes than market forces would deliver to be an implicit goal of social policy. Our aim is to assess the extent to which both Labour and the coalition succeeded in protecting the most vulnerable, sharing the burden of deficit reduction fairly, and delivering more equal access to services and more equal outcomes, against the challenging post-2007 backdrop.

In principle, this approach opens up the possibility that we may be judging one government but not the other on its own desired terms. In practice, both Labour and the coalition expressed a clear commitment to a fairer and more equal society. In Gordon Brown's first conference speech as Prime Minister in September 2007, he described himself as standing for 'a Britain where everyone should rise as far as their talents can take them and then the talents of each of us should contribute to the well being of all.' In *Budget 2008*, the government's economic objectives were stated to be 'a strong economy and a fair society, where there is opportunity and security for all' (HM Treasury, 2008, p 1). The coalition government declared on taking office that its most urgent task was to tackle the country's debts. But it also insisted that fairness would lie at the heart of its decisions, 'so that those most in need are most protected' (HM Government, 2010, p 7). In the October 2010 Spending Review, George Osborne declared that those with the 'broadest shoulders should bear the greatest burden', having already promised in the June 2010 Budget that the better-off would be expected to 'pay more than the poorest, not just in terms of cash, but as a proportion of income as well.' Beyond deficit reduction, the coalition set a goal of improving social mobility and creating a society where 'everyone, regardless of background, has the chance to rise as high as their talents and ambition allow them' (HM Government, 2010, p 7). It may have had different intentions about how to achieve these goals than its predecessor, pledging to deliver 'radical reforming government, a stronger society, a smaller state and power and responsibility in the hands of every citizen' (HM Government, 2010, p 8). There may also have been differences in the conceptualisation and measurement of relevant indicators for assessment: the coalition declared itself committed to reducing child poverty, for example, but consulted on changing the child poverty measures, proposing downgrading the income and material deprivation measures included in Labour's Child Poverty Act in favour of a wider set of indicators of 'life chances'. Nevertheless, we think the broad terms of our assessment cover goals that neither Labour nor the coalition would reject.

The first part of this book, from Chapters Two to Nine, follows a topic-by-topic approach. We look in turn at different areas of social policy, from taxes, benefits and pensions to early years policy, health, education, employment, housing and social care. For each area, we describe the policies enacted, trends in spending, and the results in terms of inputs and outputs (for example, services delivered, buildings built or staff employed) and outcomes (for example, qualification rates, mortality rates or levels of poverty). These chapters draw on, and update, a set of much longer and more detailed papers separately examining Labour's record from 1997 to 2010 and the coalition's from 2010 to 2015.[1] Readers interested in further facts, figures and analysis in specific areas are strongly recommended to visit these accounts.

The limitation of the topic-by-topic approach is, of course, that the *a priori* decisions and political principles that affect all areas of policy can be given less visibility than they deserve. By this we mean decisions about the role of the state versus that of individual citizens, charities or employers in social welfare provision, about the role and power of the central state versus the local state in its different forms, and about the broader goals that governments are trying to pursue – fairness, equality, social cohesion or social mobility, for example. We also mean decisions about the overall level of public spending, the scale and speed of deficit reduction, and the priority that is given to different policy areas. The coalition's social policies in specific areas, described in Chapters Two to Nine, were all heavily influenced by three key decisions made at the time of the Emergency Budget in June 2010: to achieve more than three-quarters of budget savings from spending cuts rather than tax increases; to protect health and schools (two very large spending areas) from substantial cuts; and to make savings within the social security budget from benefits for working-age households, not from pensions. These decisions meant that whatever ambitions ministers had for reform and improvement, they were carried out in an overall environment of budget reduction, and that some areas were much more severely affected than others.

In the second part of the book, Chapters Ten to Thirteen, therefore, we look across and beyond the specific policies described in Chapters Two to Nine and address some of the broader considerations that have preoccupied politicians, academics and other commentators. To what extent has the welfare state become 'privatised'? What have been the combined effects of the economic crisis and the policies pursued on poverty and inequality? Which social and demographic groups have been winners and which losers? Have different areas of the country pulled further apart in social and economic terms, or have their characteristics and fortunes started to converge? We conclude in a final chapter by drawing together some of the key cross-cutting themes from our analysis of the individual policy areas.

Like any collection, this one has limits to its scope. An important limitation, given the economic context, is that this is a book about social policies, evaluating them in the context of the possibilities and constraints open to the government at the time. We do not engage in detailed discussion of Labour or coalition governments' management of the public finances, nor the extent to which they have been successful in putting the country on a sound economic footing. Nor do we engage in discussion of the underlying politics that produced the policies we describe: the tensions between Blairite and Brownite wings of the Labour party, for example, or the fascinating politics of coalition. These are covered in other texts (see, for example, Chote et al, 2010; Rawnsley, 2010; Wren-Lewis, 2013, 2015; Emmerson and Tetlow, 2015; Hazell and Yong, 2015; Seldon and Finn, 2015).

A second limitation is that, in seeking to cover policies, spending, inputs, outputs and outcomes, our coverage of the detailed development of policy is inevitably brief. In addition to the fuller background papers, readers interested in this aspect might consult the volume edited by Bochel et al (2016). Third, for reasons simply of scale, we do not cover *all* social policies. Children's social care is omitted, for example, as is much of higher education policy, although we include policies relating to funding of and access to higher education (HE) in Chapter Five, since they are so central to questions of social mobility, as well as being so publicly contested during the period in question. Other policies which are of interest to many and which clearly affect our welfare in its broadest sense are also omitted – for example, policies relating to transport, migration or criminal justice. The book does, however, cover all the major areas of social policy and those that absorb the vast majority of social spending.

The increasing divergence of social policies between the constituent countries of the UK has been one of most striking developments of the period since New Labour was first elected in 1997, and perhaps particularly since 2007 (with the Scottish National Party [SNP] forming its first minority government in Scotland, with Labour still in office in Westminster) and then 2010 (with the Conservative-Liberal

Democrat coalition in Westminster and the SNP continuing in power in Scotland, with a majority government from 2011). Discontent in Scotland and Wales with Westminster policies played a prominent part in the 2015 General Election and in debate since, prompting a fresh lobby for 'English votes for English laws', and for devolution of powers within England itself. However, despite its obvious interest, a full four-country comparison of social policies is well beyond the scope of this book as it would require analyses of four different sets of policy documents, spending figures and statistical datasets. We cover the UK for areas in which policy is not devolved (for example, personal taxes and cash benefits) and England for areas in which it is. We recommend readers to other texts in which some of these cross-country comparisons may be found (see for example Connolly et al, 2011 and Bevan et al, 2014 on health and Alcock and May (2014) on a range of social policy areas including social care and education).

A final limitation is unavoidable. While this book was written in 2015, and completed after the election in May of a new Conservative government, it can only really be seen as an interim report on the effects of the coalition. In some cases, policies have been fully implemented and we can already see the results. This is the case for university tuition fees, for example. However, in many cases, policies have only recently been put in place, or are still being rolled out, and their effects cannot yet be seen in the data that is currently available. In part this is simply a problem of lagged data. The most up-to-date statistics in this book relate to 2014/15, but in some cases data are only available up to 2013/14. We do two things to address this problem. In the case of taxes and benefits, we project forward the changes that have been announced, to see what effect they will have on people's incomes in future years. In other areas, we draw on qualitative evidence and commentaries from practitioners and experts on the ways in which the changes are unfolding and some of the emerging or possible effects. This is necessarily more speculative: people will adapt and systems will evolve in unpredictable ways. We aim to give as up-to-date and balanced a picture as possible of what is happening and what the likely effects will be.

While these approaches help in relation to service delivery and the immediate impact of tax-benefit changes, the assessment of outcome variables raises further challenges, exacerbated by but not limited to lags in the publication of data. The long-term and cumulative ways in which many policies have an impact mean it may take years for the full effects of cuts and reforms to play out. Data on educational attainment at 16, or the share of young people not in education, employment or training (NEET), or even child development at age five, all reflect policies and inputs starting many years earlier. It is tempting to treat 2010 as a clear demarcation between one government and another, but in reality even the most recent data included in this book on some outcomes probably tell us more about the effects of Labour government policy than about the coalition. All we can do about this problem is to advise caution in interpreting existing outcome data, and to note that it may be worthwhile to revisit the coalition's record further down the line.

Finally, in all chapters, and particularly in our conclusion, we reflect on the early policy announcements of the new Conservative government. Do these represent new directions, or the continuation of a coalition strategy? What do they indicate for future trends in poverty, inequality and social mobility? And to what extent do they promise to address the challenges facing the government in a continued climate of austerity? As always, understanding the situation we are now in – and the choices now being made – requires an understanding of where we have come from. We hope this book will contribute to that.

Note
[1] All working papers, summaries and reports from the Social Policy in a Cold Climate research programme are available at http://sticerd.lse.ac.uk/case/_new/research/Social_Policy_in_a_Cold_Climate.asp. The underlying data for much of the project is available at www.casedata.org.uk

Part One

TWO

Benefits, pensions, tax credits and direct taxes

John Hills, Paola De Agostini and Holly Sutherland

What is now often referred to as 'welfare' is the most contentious, but often least understood, part of social policy. At its broadest, 'welfare' could mean the whole welfare state – including the two-thirds of public spending that goes on healthcare, education, housing and personal social services, as well as cash social security benefits, including pensions. At its narrowest – following US terminology, and often accompanied by similar stigmatisation – it could mean cash payments to working-age people who are not in work (about a twentieth of public spending). In between, it could refer to what are, for clarity, described here as 'cash transfers' – social security benefits (including state pensions) and tax credits.[1]

A popular perception is that the 1997-2010 Labour government greatly increased spending on benefits and tax credits, particularly for those out of work, creating much of the deficit by the time it left office, and in some versions causing the financial and economic crisis itself. The coalition government coming to office in May 2010 set reducing the deficit as its highest priority, and argued that the 'welfare budget' should make a major contribution – albeit with state pensions largely protected. Some of the resultant cuts became among its most controversial policies.

This chapter examines what actually happened to cash transfers in the period since the crisis started, looking at policies in the final years of the Labour government[2] from 2007/08 and under the coalition, levels of public spending, benefit levels and the distributional effects of policy change (including direct taxes) since 2010. These form part, alongside other developments, such as in the labour market (see Chapter Six), of what drove the changes in poverty and inequality discussed later in this book, in Chapter Eleven.

The situation on the eve of the crisis

Labour's aims for poverty and inequality were selective. Child and pensioner poverty were key priorities, alongside wider objectives for life chances and social inclusion. Equality was discussed in terms of 'equality of opportunity', not of outcomes, with little emphasis on inequalities at the top.

Correspondingly, Labour's spending increases concentrated on families with children and pensioners. Its emphasis for the working-age population was on education, training, 'making work pay' (including the first National Minimum Wage), and support into work. A major reform was to transform means-tested cash benefits for working families with children, first, from 1999 into a more generous Working Families' Tax Credit, and then, from April 2003, into Child Tax Credit (going to families in and out of work in an integrated system) and Working Tax Credit (for the first time going to those without children). Both were designed to mimic Income Tax, being adjusted after the end of the year to reflect income changes over the year. An explicit aim was to reduce the stigma attached to claiming in-work benefits through the changes in name and administration, reinforcing the 'making work pay' message, but with the side-effect of often requiring unpopular clawbacks from tax credits paid the following year. For pensioners, the initial strategy was based on improving means-tested minimum incomes.

Spending on working-age cash transfers unrelated to having children *fell* in real terms between 1996/97 and 2007/08 (see Figure 2.2) and as a share of GDP. Despite more generous treatment of families with children and pensioners, overall spending on cash transfers was the same 10% share of national income in 2007/08 as in 1996/97 (see Figure 2.1 later in the chapter). This is far from the caricature that Labour greatly increased 'welfare spending' in advance of the crash, especially on 'handouts' to those who were out of work.

The results matched Labour's priorities and spending. By 2007/08, child poverty had fallen by 4 percentage points since 1996/97 before allowing for housing costs (3 points after allowing for them). Given the difficulty of making progress against the 'moving target' of a relative poverty line over a decade with strongly rising overall living standards, this was an achievement, but was far short of Labour's target of halving child poverty by 2010, let alone 'eliminating' it by 2020.[3] Pensioner poverty had fallen faster – by 3 percentage points before housing costs (BHC) or 10 points (two-fifths) after them (AHC).[4] On the other hand, relative poverty for working-age adults was unchanged, and indeed rose for those without children.

Taken as a whole, Labour's tax and benefit policies had redistributed modestly (if compared to the system it inherited adjusted for income growth) from the top half of the income distribution to the bottom half,[5] although Labour avoided the use of the word 'redistribution'. This, and its other policies, kept income inequality across the *bulk* of the population (as measured by the '90:10 ratio') roughly constant before housing costs between 1996/97 and 2007/08 (with a small rise after housing costs). But it was not enough to stop a significant rise in inequality across the *whole* population, allowing for rapidly rising incomes at the very top (as measured by the Gini coefficient); see Figure 11.3 in Chapter Eleven.

Policies since 2007

Labour under Gordon Brown

In many ways the most important policy for cash transfers followed after the crash, with Gordon Brown as Prime Minister from June 2007, was to continue to increase them with inflation (generally measured by the retail price index [RPI]). The coalition did the same initially. The macroeconomic – and political – arguments against cutting real transfers during a recession are outside the scope of this book. But this protection in bad times was consistent with working-age adult benefits *not* increasing during the preceding good times when real incomes for those in work rose. As wages – and with them net incomes for those in work – fell in real terms during the recession, this policy of protecting incomes at the bottom acted to reduce relative poverty and inequality.

Combined with increases in tax credits for children in 2008/09 and the effects of rising unemployment, real spending on cash transfers as a whole rose and, with GDP falling, the share of national income going on cash transfers rose faster, by 2 percentage points between 2007/08 and 2009/10 (see Figures 2.1 and 2.2 later). This is what would be expected from a system designed to stabilise incomes in hard times.

Labour's major structural reforms for non-pensioners were already in place before Gordon Brown became Prime Minister, implemented while he was Chancellor. But its main pension reforms came following the recommendations of the independent Pensions Commission in 2005 (see Evandrou and Falkingham, 2009). Through the Pensions Acts of 2007 and 2008 Labour improved the future value of state pension rights, including widening rights to a full pension, improving its value for lower earners, and returning to linking pension values to earnings (planned from 2012), but with the State Pension Age due to rise from 65 after 2024. It also introduced 'automatic enrolment' of employees into employer pension schemes or a new low-cost National Employment Savings Trust (NEST), but with the right to opt out. The reforms were designed to halt the growth of means-testing in old age that would otherwise have occurred, giving clearer incentives to save for retirement and a lower-cost way of doing so.

A controversial change to Income Tax early in the period was the abolition from 2008/09 of Labour's own reduced starting '10p band' at the same time as the main rate was cut to 20%. The combination of the two left some low earners who were not entitled to (or did not receive) tax credits as losers, even after an emergency increase in the general level of tax allowances the following autumn. Just before it left office, Labour made revenue-raising changes to direct taxes. From April 2010 the tax-free Income Tax personal allowance was tapered away from those with incomes above £100,000, and a new top rate of 50% was applied to slices of income above £150,000 per year. Labour also announced that National Insurance Contribution (NIC) rates would rise from April 2011.

Coalition aims and goals

It is striking how coalition policy was dominated by the inclusion in the initial coalition agreement and subsequent *Programme for government* (HM Government, 2010) of two key – and expensive – Liberal Democrat aims, a £10,000 tax-free allowance for Income Tax, and the basic pension increasing with a 'triple lock' from 2011 (the higher of price inflation, earnings growth or 2.5%). At the same time, other benefits for pensioners would be protected, as promised by the Conservatives, such as Winter Fuel Payments, free bus passes and free TV licences for older people. The promise to raise the annual tax-free Income Tax personal allowance to £10,000 was a huge pledge at a time of fiscal crisis.[6] As only a minority of the tax measures proposed to finance it were implemented, finding other savings to balance its cost became crucial.

The coalition maintained the goal of 'ending child poverty in the UK by 2020' (HM Government, 2010, p 19), but tax credits would be cut back for higher earners, and their administration reformed 'to reduce fraud and overpayments'. Otherwise comparatively little was initially agreed on working-age benefits. However, after the election, Iain Duncan Smith was appointed as Secretary of State for Work and Pensions, bringing with him plans from the Centre for Social Justice, which he had established in 2004, to unify means-tested benefits and tax credits in what became the coalition's centrepiece Universal Credit.[7]

This longer-term reform would, however, come after a series of specific cuts and reforms to working-age benefits. These smaller reforms, alongside decisions on how to uprate benefits from year to year, dominated what happened to cash transfers and their distributional effects up to 2015/16. Box 2.1 gives a timeline of these reforms.

Coalition policies

The coalition's policies towards cash transfers and income distribution can be grouped into five:

- personal tax changes, including the commitment to increasing the Income Tax personal allowance to £10,000
- decisions on how social security benefits should be adjusted from year to year, differing markedly between pensions and other benefits
- cuts and reforms to specific benefits
- continuing but adding to Labour's pension reform programme
- merging six working-age benefits into Universal Credit.

Personal tax changes

The Income Tax allowance was increased in stages from £6,475 in 2010/11 to reach £10,600 by April 2015. Compared to adjustment in line with consumer price index (CPI) inflation, this was worth £700 per year for basic rate taxpayers, although adjustments to the higher rate threshold meant that the best-off taxpayers did not benefit from the increases (until the final year). At the same time, the extra 'age allowance' was phased out, so many pensioners gained little from these changes. From 2015/16 single-earner married couples are able to transfer £1,060 of an unused tax allowance to a spouse (worth £212 per year). NICs were increased in 2011/12, as planned by Labour. The coalition also retained the withdrawal of the personal allowance from those with incomes above £100,000, brought in some tighter limits on higher-rate pension contribution tax relief, and introduced changes that tapered away the value of Child Benefit from families containing an individual with annual taxable income of over £50,000. But from 2013/14, the 50% marginal rate on incomes above £150,000 inherited from Labour was cut to 45%.

Box 2.1: Benefits, pensions, tax credits and direct taxes policy timeline

2008	2009	2010	2011	2012	2013	2014	2015
Initial 10% Income Tax rate abolished; Basic rate cut to 20%; Personal allowance increased		Top Income Tax rate to 50%; personal allowance (PA) withdrawn above £100,000	Increase Income Tax PA above inflation (with reduction in higher rate threshold) →		Reduce top tax rate from 50% to 45%		PA £10,600, higher rate threshold raised
			Index some direct tax thresholds in line with CPI inflation instead of RPI →				
	Benefit and tax credit rates still uprated with RPI →						
	Basic State Pension indexed by highest of earnings, prices (CPI) and 2.5% (known as 'triple lock') →						
				Uprate most benefits by CPI rather than RPI/Rossi	Increase most benefits by 1% for 3 years	Increase most working-age benefits by 1% only instead of CPI →	
Tax credits for children increased above inflation					Freeze Child Benefit in cash terms for 3 years; Cash freeze in basic and 30 hours elements of WTC	Increase Child Benefit by 1% only →	
			Increase in main VAT rate from 17.5% to 20% and main National Insurance Contribution rates up by 1%	Cash freeze in couple and lone-parent element of WTC	Replace CTB with local support (cut for working-age claimants)		Introduce transferable PA for married couples without a higher rate taxpayer
			Council Tax freeze for 2 years (3 in Scotland)	Taper Child Benefit away from families with anyone with taxable income over £50,000	Introduce benefit cap		Introduction of tax-free childcare for two-earner families paying formal childcare costs
			Increase withdrawal rate of tax credits and baby element of CTC abolished		Replace DLA with PIP, reassessing all ICB claimants		
			Child Trust Funds abolished		Cut HB for under-occupied social housing ('bedroom tax')		
			Tighter maximum rents for private tenant HB				

CPI – Consumer Prices Index; CTB – Council Tax Benefit; CTC – Child Tax Credit; DLA – Disability Living Allowance; HB – Housing Benefit; PA – Personal Allowance; PIP – Personal Independence Payment; RPI – Retail Prices Index; VAT – Value Added Tax; WTC – Working Tax Credit

Uprating benefits

As discussed above, a critical initial 'non-decision' of both Labour and the coalition was to continue uprating benefits in line with RPI inflation up to 2012/13. The effect was to shield some of the poorest initially from the effects of the 2008 financial crisis. What has happened since presents a marked contrast between pensions and other benefits. The basic pension (and the future amalgamated 'single tier' pension described below) is 'triple-locked'. But for most working-age benefits, default indexation was switched to the CPI, rather than the RPI (or a related index). The CPI generally increases more slowly. And for three years from April 2013 working-age benefits were increased by only 1%, aiming to reduce their real value (although in the event, inflation was low in any case). The coalition agreed on a two-year cash freeze from April 2016. In the long term, benefit levels will be constrained by a new overall 'welfare cap', putting a cash limit on aggregate spending (excluding state pensions and Jobseeker's Allowance). If the cost of or numbers receiving one benefit rise, spending will have to be cut elsewhere to keep within the cap.

Specific benefit and tax credit reforms

Specific benefit and tax credit reforms included:

- A cap of £26,000 a year on the total amount of benefits most working-age families could receive.
- Tighter limits on Housing Benefit for private tenants, and cuts for working-age social housing tenants deemed to have spare bedrooms (the so-called 'bedroom tax') (see Chapter Seven).
- Child Benefit was frozen in cash terms for three years from 2011/12, and then increased by 1% in 2014/15, representing a significant real terms cut. The 'family element' of Child Tax Credit was also frozen.
- Abolition of Labour's Child Trust Funds from early 2011.
- Council Tax was frozen for most households, but Council Tax Benefit reforms meant many low-income households paying more or paying part of the tax for the first time.
- Reforms to tax credits (such as abolition of the extra 'baby tax credit' and a faster rate of withdrawal as income increased) made them less generous, although the 'per child' element was increased.
- Tighter conditions and tougher administration arrangements for disability and incapacity benefits. These were intended to reduce the overall spending, although this was not achieved, despite

controversial effects as individual payments were cut or delayed (OBR, 2014, chart 4.5; Gaffney, 2015).

• Abolition of most of the Social Fund that gave emergency grants and loans to people with low incomes. Councils were given responsibility for organising local support, but with a lower budget.

• Stricter administration of many out-of-work benefits, including much greater use of 'sanctions' imposed on unemployed and other claimants for not meeting particular job search requirements.[8]

Pension reform

Alongside continuing Labour's pension reforms and the 'triple lock' for uprating, the coalition further reformed state pensions. This included amalgamating the two elements of state pensions into a flat-rate 'single tier' pension to be paid to those retiring from 2016. This will benefit many women and self-employed people, but its zero net cost means that others will receive less than they would have done. Increases to state pension age were accelerated, with the increase to 66 brought forward to 2020, and plans announced to accelerate a further increase to 67. A separate surprise major reform was removal from April 2015 of the requirement to convert accumulated funds into a regular income for life (retirement annuities). In the long run this may have substantial effects on whether people actually reach their later years of retirement with any income beyond the state pension.

Universal Credit

Universal Credit will replace six means-tested benefits and tax credits (including Housing Benefit) for those in and out of work. It removes overlaps in means-testing and taxes that can mean some benefit claimants lose 90% or more of additional income (although effective marginal tax rates will increase for others). The new credit is paid monthly, instead of weekly or fortnightly. Entitlement is calculated in 'real time', based on actual income reported by employers, without later adjustment. Its introduction was much slower than planned, with only 65,000 people receiving it by May 2015, compared to the 2 million originally planned by October 2014 and the 7.5 million households expected to receive it by 2017.[9] In Figure 2.6 below, we look at the distributional effects that the coalition's design of Universal Credit would have if fully in place by 2020/21, alongside their agreed benefit and tax indexation arrangements.

Spending on social security and tax credits

Levels of spending on cash transfers after the crisis reflected a collision between policies designed to restrain spending growth after the coalition was elected, and the pressures on the system from rising unemployment as the recession struck, higher rents and an ageing population. Table 2.A1 (at the end of this chapter) presents a long-term time series for spending divided between that going to pensioners, to families because they have children, and other working-age benefits and tax credits.[10] Figure 2.1 shows how this spending broke down between that aimed at the three groups as a share of national income each year since 2006/07 (and in 1996/97). Figure 2.2 shows the cumulative changes in real terms between 1996/97 and each financial year from 1997/98 onwards.

On the eve of the crisis, in 2006/07, total spending on cash transfers was £171 billion (at 2014/15 prices), or 10.1% of GDP. This was 34% higher in real terms than in 1996/97, but the same share of GDP. By Labour's last complete year, 2009/10, total spending had grown to £201 billion and 12.1% of GDP. The following year, as the coalition took office, with benefit and tax credit rules as set in April 2010, real

Figure 2.1: Social security benefits and tax credits as a percentage of GDP, 1996/97 and 2006/07 to 2014/15, Great Britain

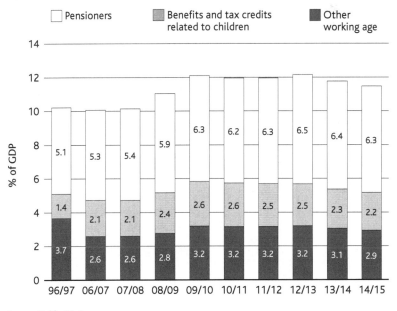

Source: Table 2A.1

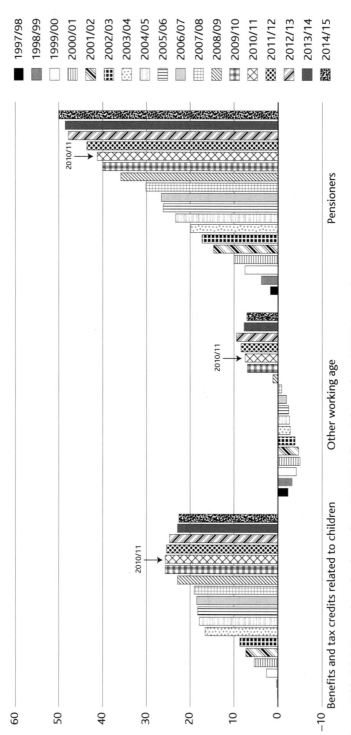

Figure 2.2: Real change in spending on social security and tax credits since 1996/97, Great Britain (£ billion at 2014/15 prices)

Legend:
1997/98, 1998/99, 1999/00, 2000/01, 2001/02, 2002/03, 2003/04, 2004/05, 2005/06, 2006/07, 2007/08, 2008/09, 2009/10, 2010/11, 2011/12, 2012/13, 2013/14, 2014/15

Benefits and tax credits related to children   Other working age   Pensioners

Source: Table 2 A.1. Figures show the change from 1996/97 in financial years from 1997/98 onwards.

spending rose to £203 billion, but fell slightly to 12.0% of GDP. In the coalition's final year, 2014/15 spending had reached £208 billion, falling further to 11.5% of GDP.

For working-age benefits unrelated to children, spending in Labour's first 10 years fell from £46 to £44 billion in 2006/07, before jumping with the recession to £53 billion in 2009/10. Under the coalition it peaked at £55 billion in 2012/13, falling back to £53 billion in 2014/15. As a result, this spending fell over the Labour period as a whole, from 3.7% of GDP in 1996/97 to 3.2% in 2009/10, and further over the coalition period to 2.9% of GDP by 2014/15. In contrast to public perceptions (Hills, 2015b, chapter 9), under both governments such transfers fell in relation to both total public spending and national income.

By contrast, spending related to children rose rapidly under Labour but fell under the coalition. With more generous tax credits, child-related transfers more than doubled in real terms under Labour to reach nearly £44 billion in 2009-10, but were reduced to £41 billion by 2014/15 (at 2009/10 prices). They rose from 1.4 to 2.6% of GDP over the Labour years, but fell to 2.2% of GDP by 2014/15.

Spending on pensioners rose under both governments. In real terms, pensioner benefits rose from £64 billion in 1996/97 to £104 billion in 2009/10 and £114 billion in 2014/15. In the coalition period, pensioner benefits continued to grow, while other benefits and tax credits fell back. As a share of national income, transfers to pensioners rose from 5.1% of GDP in 1996/97 to 6.3% in 2009/10, and were at the same figure in 2014/15 (but down from a peak of 6.5% in 2012/13).

In summary, looked at in relation to national income, the coalition continued Labour's pattern of increased spending on pensioners, but partly reversed Labour's increased spending on children. Working-age benefits unrelated to having children fell under both governments, despite the effects of the economic crisis.

Benefit levels and generosity

To give some long-term context to the trends over the coalition period, Figure 2.3 presents Office for Budget Responsibility (OBR) figures for the real and relative values of average awards made for state pensions and unemployment benefits (now Jobseeker's Allowance) since 1983/84. Recipients may also have been receiving other benefits related to housing costs, children or other means-tested top-ups. Today it seems remarkable that, with elements such as earnings-related additions, unemployment

Figure 2.3: Real and relative values of average state pension and unemployment benefit awards, 1983/84 to 2014/15 (£/week, 2013/14 prices and % of GDP per adult)

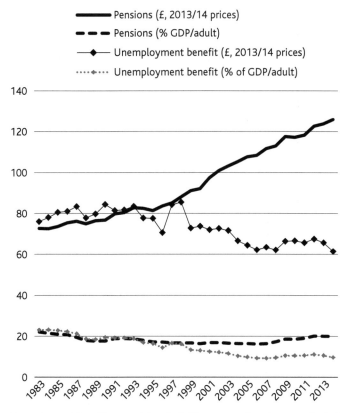

Note: Unemployment benefit covers Jobseeker's Allowance and predecessors (including Income Support for unemployed people, but not allowances for children).

Source: OBR (2014, figures 5.1 and 8.1)

awards were greater than average pension awards, at 23% compared to 22% of national income per capita in 1983/84. But by 2010/11, the real value of unemployment awards had fallen and more than halved in relation to incomes. By contrast, average state pensions had risen by more than 60% in real terms (including state second pensions), although were now only 19% of income per capita. Over the coalition period to 2014/15 this divergence continued. The average pension award rose to £126 per week and back to 20% of average incomes, but unemployment awards fell further to £61 per week, less than 10% of incomes. From exceeding state pensions, unemployment benefits are now less than half as generous.

The dominant feature of cash transfers affecting poverty rates (discussed later in Chapter Eleven) is the value of means-tested minimum incomes at the bottom of the income distribution relative to middle (median) incomes. Up to 2012/13 most pensions, benefits and tax credit rates were still increased regularly in line with inflation (as measured by the RPI). But after 2008/09 real wages fell in the wake of the crisis, and with them net household incomes. Table 2.1 gives one indication of the effects of this. It presents the state's minimum income levels (what used to be Income Support) for nine different family types as a percentage of the official poverty line (as given by 60% of median incomes AHC) since 1997/98.

The notable feature over the Labour period was the sharp difference between family types. Minimum income for pensioner couples rose from 83% of the poverty line to 96% by 2010/11, and from 93% to 110% for single pensioners. With more generous benefits and tax credits for children there were increases, too, for working-age couples with children and single parents, although to levels still short of the official poverty line. But for single people and couples without children, minimum incomes fell further below this poverty line, to less than half of it for single people under 25.

Table 2.1: State minimum income levels as a percentage of poverty thresholds 1997/98 to 2013/14, by family type

	1997/98	2008/09	2010/11	2013/14
Single, 18-24, no children	52	40	42	40-42
Single 25+, no children	65	51	52	51-53
Couple working age, no children	60	46	48	47-49
Couple, 1 child aged 3	67	66	69	69-70
Couple, 2 children aged 4, 6	67	75	78	79-81
Couple, 3 children aged 3, 8, 11	71	82	85	86-87
Single parent, 1 child aged 3	81	81	84	84-86
Pensioner couple (aged 60-74)	83	94	96	98
Single pensioner (aged 60-74)	93	108	110	111

Notes:

The poverty threshold used is 60% of median equivalised household incomes (AHC) in that year from Shale et al (2014) and earlier equivalents.

Minimum income levels are income-related Jobseeker's Allowance, Child Tax Credit and Child Benefit for working-age families and Pension Credit for pensioners (with Winter Fuel Payments) and earlier equivalents. The bottom end of the 2013/14 range is for people with the local authority giving 80% maximum Council Tax support (using English average Council Tax, band A for single people, B for one-child families and C for larger families). The top of the range assumes full Council Tax support.

Source: Sefton et al (2009, table 2.4), extended and updated

Over the first three years of the coalition minimum income levels grew slightly in relation to the poverty line for nearly all of the family groups shown, *if* in an area where full Council Tax support remained available. This reflected the fall in real median net incomes (and hence relative poverty line), while these benefit levels were generally price-inflation protected. However, for working-age people without children living in areas where full Council Tax support was no longer available, minimum income levels fell further relative to the poverty line. By contrast, for pensioner couples, minimum incomes remained close to the poverty line, and for single pensioners they had reached 111% of it.

Redistribution

Understanding the distributional effects of changes in cash transfer and tax policies requires analysis that models their effects on representative samples of the population. Such analysis also allows us to focus on the effects of these *policy* changes, abstracted from other economic changes. The discussion below looks at results from the University of Essex EUROMOD (tax-benefit microsimulation model for the European Union [EU]) for the changes under Labour from 2008/09 to May 2010 and then over the coalition period to May 2015.[11] The results show the effects of changes to direct taxes (not indirect taxes), benefits and state pensions.

Changes under Labour from 2008/09 to 2010/11

Compared to its tax-benefit system in 2008/09, if it had been adjusted in line with *price* inflation, Figure 2.4 shows that the changes made by the time Labour left office had progressive effects, but with only a small contribution to deficit reduction. Because benefits and tax credits were increased with (earlier) changes in the RPI (faster than the concurrent change in the CPI), as well as some specific tax credit increases, lower-income groups gained on average compared to a CPI-linked base, while the highest-income ones lost from Income Tax increases. An alternative way to look at how tax-benefit systems have changed is to compare the actual 2010/11 system with a situation in which the 2008/09 values of benefits and tax thresholds and brackets had been adjusted in line with *earnings* growth (as measured by the Average Earnings Index, AEI).[12] As real earnings fell over this period, the value of benefits rose even faster compared to an earnings-linked base, and the overall effect was a small cost to the public finances, despite the increases in Income Tax at the top.

Figure 2.4: Net percentage change in household disposable income by income group due to policy changes, 2008/09 to 2010/11 (compared to price-indexed and earnings-indexed systems)

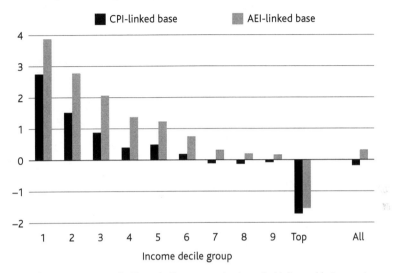

Notes: Observations are ranked into decile groups using household disposable income in 2008 equivalised using the modified OECD equivalence scale.

Source: Authors' calculations using EUROMOD G2.35

Changes under the coalition

Figure 2.5 gives a more detailed breakdown for the coalition period of average gains or losses from changes made to six broad parts of the direct tax and benefit systems by May 2015 compared to the system inherited in May 2010 if it had been uprated by price (CPI) inflation.[13] The solid line shows the net effect of all of them together, combining the various negative and positive effects. For the components, negative effects (downward pointing parts of the bars) are due to increases in tax and contribution liabilities, or to reductions in benefit and pension entitlements (for those receiving them), and positive effects to tax and contribution cuts or benefit increases. The results are shown for each twentieth ('vingtile') of individuals.

A first observation is that, on average (shown in the right-most bar), households *gained* from the changes, by around 1% of incomes. Means–tested benefits and tax credits were cut, compared to a price-indexed system, but people paid less net Council Tax (as cuts of what was Council Tax Benefit were more than offset by Council Tax being frozen), and some gained from reduced Income Tax liabilities (with the increased personal allowance), and from state pensions rising faster

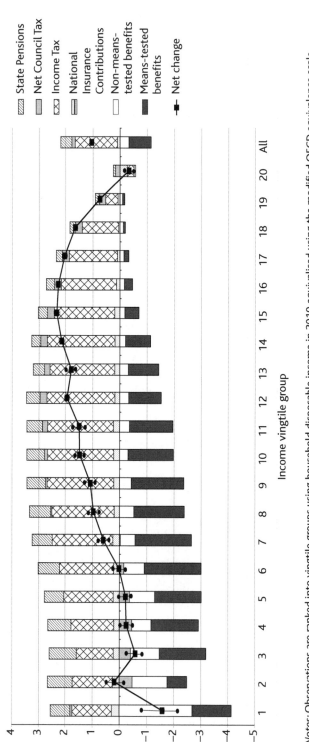

Figure 2.5: Percentage change in household disposable income by income group due to policy changes 2010/11 to 2015/16 (compared to base policies uprated using CPI)

Notes: Observations are ranked into vingtile groups using household disposable income in 2010 equivalised using the modified OECD equivalence scale. The net change is shown with a 95% confidence interval, calculated using bootstrap.

Source: De Agostini et al (2015), based on analysis using EUROMOD G2.35.

than CPI inflation. Remarkably, given that this was a time of austerity, the net effect of the reforms (not including indirect tax increases) was a *cost* to the public finances. Savings from benefits and tax credits becoming less generous in real terms were more than offset by the cost of increasing the Income Tax personal allowance and pensions.

The gains were not equally distributed, however. Overall, the poorest twentieth lost nearly 2% of their incomes (even before allowing for increased indirect taxes), and three of the next four twentieths also lost. But with the exception of the top twentieth, the income groups in the top half of the distribution were net gainers on average. From the bottom to four-fifths of the way up, the changes were regressive, hitting those lower down hardest as a share of their incomes.[14] Benefit reductions were greater for the bottom half than their gains from lower Income Tax. But rising through the top fifth of the distribution, the gains from higher Income Tax allowances were increasingly offset by other changes, so that those in the penultimate twentieth broke even, and the top twentieth made a small loss on average (but within this some of the best-off gained from the cut in the top tax rate). On this basis, coalition reforms had the effect of making an income transfer to the richer half of households, partly financed by some of those in the poorest third (and some of the very richest), while making no contribution to deficit reduction.[15]

Looking at the population divided in other ways (see De Agostini et al, 2015, section 5), lone-parent families were losers on average, while those with two earners or with elderly members were the biggest gainers. Families with children, particularly those with more than two, did worse than the average. Looked at by age, those in their fifties and early sixties gained most, and children aged under 10 (and their parents) gained least. Those in their twenties gained more from higher tax allowances than they lost from reduced benefits, offsetting part of the sharp deterioration in their labour market position that we discuss later, in Chapter Twelve. Londoners were, on average, less favourably affected than people in other regions (as more of them have very high and very low incomes, and because Housing Benefit limits had more impact in the capital).

Longer-term effects of reforms agreed by the coalition

Some of the coalition's most important policy changes were designed to take effect after the May 2015 General Election. Several of these have been changed (and intensified) by the incoming Conservative government, but to understand the lasting impact of the coalition,

Figure 2.6 shows what the effects of their plans *would have been* if they had been sustained to 2020/21. This allows for the planned introduction of Universal Credit and the new basis for uprating pensions, benefits and tax credits from year to year (CPI indexation for most, the triple lock for state pensions, but with some working-age benefits frozen for two years from 2016/17). It shows the total net effects of direct tax and benefit changes by comparison with the May 2010 system uprated by either price inflation or by earnings growth. Because real earnings are now expected to grow between 2015 and 2020, the two comparisons show rather different results.

Compared to the May 2010 system uprated for price inflation, the results are generally similar to those shown in Figure 2.5, with a small increase in the net gain to households as a whole, and a regressive pattern across most of the income distribution, excluding the bottom and top tenths, and some increases to the gains for those in the middle of the top half. To consider effects on inequality and relative poverty, the comparison with an earnings-linked base is more appropriate, however. In these terms, by 2020/21, the overall position would

Figure 2.6: Net percentage change in household disposable income by income group due to policy changes, 2010 to 2020/21 (compared to 2010 policies uprated by prices and by earnings)

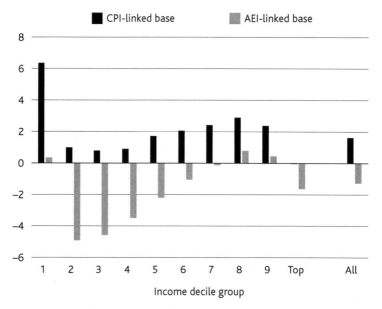

Notes: Observations are ranked into decile groups using household disposable income in 2010 equivalised using the modified OECD equivalence scale.

Source: De Agostini, Hills and Sutherland (2015), figure 7.1, using EUROMOD G2.35

be considerably less favourable for households than that reached in 2015/16, with an average loss of 1.2% of income compared to the 2010 system. Households would have paid the same Income Tax under the 2020/21 system as in an earnings-uprated May 2010 system, with the tax reductions from 2010 to 2015/16 offset by the effects of fiscal drag in the later period. Overall losses in the relative value of benefits would have been further increased beyond those up to the 2015/16 period, despite the introduction of Universal Credit. Looked at on this basis, the changes would have strengthened the regressive pattern for the bulk of the population between the second and the eighth decile groups, with the second poorest group losing 5% of its income overall, but the eighth group still gaining by approaching 1% of its income.[16]

However, right at the bottom, the picture is different, with a net gain of 6% compared to a price-linked base and 0.3% compared to an earnings-linked base for the bottom tenth by 2020/21. This reflects the effects of introducing Universal Credit, which in this modelling is simulated to lead to large gains for some households that do not currently receive all of the benefits that it replaces. It assumes that a household that currently receives *any* of the benefits that it replaces would then claim Universal Credit. This is one of the main advantages claimed from consolidating payments and claims processes. However, this could go the other way if, for instance, Universal Credit becomes more stigmatised than some of the benefits people previously claimed, or if increased conditionality or changes in how it is paid put off claimants. When Universal Credit is fully introduced, its effects will depend critically on such behavioural differences, which makes its overall effects hard to forecast.

Conclusion

Cash transfer policies between 2008 and the May 2015 General Election can be divided into three phases. First, in the immediate aftermath of the economic and financial crisis, both under Gordon Brown as Prime Minister and in the first years of the coalition, the most important feature was that the real values of benefits, tax credits and pensions were protected, even as real incomes in work fell. Some tax credits were even increased in value in 2008/09, while the most prominent cuts under the coalition took effect from 2013/14 onwards. Spending on cash transfers rose from 10% of national income in 2007/08 (the same level as Labour had inherited) to a peak of more than 12% in 2012/13. As we will see later in Chapter Eleven, this coincided with sharp falls in inequality and relative poverty in the election year, 2010/11, and then little change in the first years of the coalition.

In the second phase, from 2013, the cuts and reforms designed by the coalition began to take effect. These included a sharp difference between the way pensions and other benefits were to be adjusted from year to year, with pensions benefiting from the new 'triple lock', protecting their relative value, while working-age benefits are linked to the CPI measure of inflation (and below that in some years). While Labour had increased transfers for pensioners and families with children (but not other working-age benefits), the coalition continued to improve pensions, but started cutting back support to families with children. They also made a series of specific cuts with large effects on particular groups, including to disability benefits, Council Tax support and Housing Benefit, as well as much greater use of sanctions, cutting off benefits entirely from increasing numbers of people. These coincided with increasing reports of hardship in individual cases, and rapidly rising numbers using food banks.

This all coincided with the coalition's large increases in the value of the tax-free personal Income Tax allowance. Looked at together, the effect of changes in direct taxes and cash transfers was progressive in the last two years of the Labour government, but was regressive across most of the income distribution under the coalition. Those with incomes in the bottom half lost more from the coalition's cuts in benefits and tax credits than they gained from tax cuts, but for most of the top half (outside the top tenth) the reverse was the case.

For the longer term, the coalition left two specific legacies. One was the introduction of Universal Credit. If it succeeds in one of its original aims, improving benefit take-up through simplifying working-age benefits, it could result in higher incomes for some of those who are currently amongst the poorest, because they are not receiving all the separate benefits to which they are entitled. But if it is stigmatised regardless of who it is going to, the reverse could be the case. With its introduction taking much longer than the coalition planned, this, and other aspects of its operation, remain uncertain.

There is also uncertainty over the long-run effects of the coalition's pension reforms. There will be some clear gainers from the 'single-tier' pension reforms for those reaching state pension age from April 2016, although these will be balanced by losses to others. But the biggest long-run effects may come from deregulating the use of pension pots. For some, it may mean they can use and invest their retirement resources in the ways that best meet their needs. But it also opens the door to substantial 'mis-selling', and to people running down their savings quickly in a way they later regret. Without constraints on how pension savings are used, the reforms throw into doubt the whole meaning and purpose of 'pension savings', and the substantial tax privileges it attracts.

But the most important legacy of the coalition may turn out to be the overall direction it set for policy, to be continued and reinforced by its successor Conservative government. These rest on further cuts to 'welfare' spending, accompanied by tax cuts through increases in the personal allowance. With much deeper cuts to working-age benefits and future tax credits brought in by the Conservatives' post-election budget, the already regressive effects of that combination seen in the period up to 2015/16 are likely to be repeated and intensified.

Appendix

Table 2A1: Benefit and tax credit spending, 1996/97 to 2014/15, Great Britain, overleaf.

Table 2A1: Benefit and tax credit spending, 1996/97 to 2014/15, Great Britain

	£ billion, 2014/15 prices				% TME				% GDP			
	Total	Children	Other WA	Pensioners	Total	Children	Other WA	Pensioners	Total	Children	Other WA	Pensioners
96/97	128.1	18.0	46.0	64.1	26.8	3.8	9.6	13.4	10.2	1.4	3.7	5.1
97/98	127.6	18.1	43.7	65.8	26.7	3.8	9.1	13.7	9.9	1.4	3.4	5.1
98/99	128.9	18.3	42.8	67.8	26.6	3.8	8.8	14.0	9.7	1.4	3.2	5.1
99/00	134.0	20.5	41.9	71.6	26.9	4.1	8.4	14.4	9.7	1.5	3.0	5.2
00/01	138.5	23.3	41.1	74.1	26.8	4.5	7.9	14.3	9.7	1.6	2.9	5.2
01/02	145.4	25.3	41.4	78.7	26.7	4.6	7.6	14.5	9.9	1.7	2.8	5.4
02/03	150.2	26.6	42.2	81.4	26.2	4.7	7.4	14.2	10.0	1.8	2.8	5.4
03/04	161.8	34.6	43.3	83.9	26.6	5.7	7.1	13.8	10.3	2.2	2.7	5.3
04/05	166.7	35.8	43.4	87.4	25.9	5.6	6.8	13.6	10.4	2.2	2.7	5.5
05/06	170.1	36.2	43.6	90.2	25.6	5.5	6.6	13.6	10.3	2.2	2.6	5.4
06/07	171.3	36.5	44.1	90.7	25.2	5.4	6.5	13.4	10.1	2.1	2.6	5.3
07/08	176.4	37.0	45.2	94.2	25.2	5.3	6.5	13.5	10.1	2.1	2.6	5.4
08/09	187.9	40.8	47.2	99.9	25.4	5.5	6.4	13.5	11.0	2.4	2.8	5.9
09/10	200.8	43.6	53.0	104.2	26.5	5.8	7.0	13.7	12.1	2.6	3.2	6.3
10/11	202.5	43.7	53.5	105.3	26.7	5.8	7.0	13.9	12.0	2.6	3.2	6.2
11/12	205.4	43.4	54.5	107.6	27.6	5.8	7.3	14.4	12.0	2.5	3.2	6.3
12/13	210.0	42.7	55.4	111.9	28.1	5.7	7.4	14.9	12.2	2.5	3.2	6.5
13/14	207.1	40.8	53.7	112.5	28.2	5.6	7.3	15.3	11.8	2.3	3.1	6.4
14/15	207.6	40.5	53.1	114.0	28.2	5.5	7.2	15.5	11.5	2.2	2.9	6.3

Notes: Spending on non-pensioner benefits is divided between items aimed at children – mainly Child Benefit, Child Tax Credit and Working Tax Credit for families with children (and their earlier equivalents, such as Family Credit and Working Families' Tax Credit) – and other transfers for the working-age population (which includes items such as the adult parts of Income Support or Jobseeker's Allowance, including for parents, as well as maternity benefits, Housing Benefit for working age families, and Working Tax Credit for non-parents). Working Tax Credit divided between parents and non-parents using data from Her Majesty's Revenue and Customs (HMRC) (2015) (with 2013/14 proportions applied to later years).

TME is total managed expenditure. WA = working age.

Source: Derived from DWP (2015c)

Notes

[1] This matches what is covered by the Office for Budget Responsibility's (2014) *Welfare trends report*.

[2] For a detailed account of the Labour period up to 2008, see Evandrou and Falkingham (2009) and Sefton et al (2009). See Hills (2013) for an analysis of the whole Labour period.

[3] Defined as 'being amongst the best in Europe' (DWP, 2003, p 20).

[4] Using a relative poverty line based on 60% of median income. See Figure 11.5 in Chapter Eleven.

[5] See Sefton et al (2009, Figure 2.5), covering policy change from 1996/97 to 2008/09.

[6] Originally costed at £16.8 billion in their election manifesto (Liberal Democrat Party, 2010, p 100).

[7] See Timmins (2015) for a discussion of the idea's origins and the Centre for Social Justice (2009) for the original proposals.

[8] In the year to March 2014, the number of Jobseeker's Allowance recipients sanctioned for breaching conditions and having benefits suspended for one to three months (or longer) was 800,000, compared to 200,000-300,000 per year in the decade up to 2008 (MacInnes et al, 2014, pp 94-5; figures for Great Britain).

[9] For a more detailed discussion, see Hills (2015a, pp 19-21) and Finch (2015). Implementation of Universal Credit in Scotland may in future differ from elsewhere, including in its treatment of housing costs and the way in which it is paid.

[10] This uses the Department for Work and Pensions' (DWP) calculations of past spending using current definitions (for instance, excluding payments in the past made for Council Tax Benefit). See the notes to Table 2A.1 for how working-age spending is divided between payments related to children and other amounts. The figures are for Great Britain (as social security in Northern Ireland is separately administered), with tax credits spending adjusted by the DWP from UK figures.

[11] See Sutherland and Figari (2013) for a description of the model. The results do not allow for any behavioural change induced by the policies – for instance, if working patterns are changed or people arrange to move reported incomes between tax years in response to pre-announced changes in the highest income tax rates. They allow for partial take-up of benefits by some entitled to them. See Sefton et al (2009) for the effects of Labour's reforms

up to 2008. The discussion here of the coalition period draws heavily on De Agostini et al (2015).

[12] This is helpful for understanding the effects of reforms on inequality and on relative poverty, for instance.

[13] Because changes in prices and earnings over this period as a whole were close to one another, the picture compared to an earnings-linked base was similar and is not shown here; for a comparison, see De Agostini et al (2015, Figure 7.1). Some differences between the two are noted below.

[14] Other analysis using different methods and assumptions, by the Institute for Fiscal Studies (see Adam et al, 2015, Figure 1) and HM Treasury (2015b), has some differences but confirms the general picture that across the bulk of the population, between the second and seventh or eighth of the distribution, the changes were regressive. See De Agostini et al (2015, section 6) for a detailed discussion of the reasons for differences between the analyses.

[15] If the comparison is with the base system uprated in line with average earnings (De Agostini et al, 2015, Figure 4.1[b]), which fell in real terms, the net gain to households was a little more, an average of 1.5% of disposable income. The overall distributional pattern was similar to that shown in Figure 2.5, but with only the bottom twentieth losing by comparison with the earnings-linked base.

[16] The Conservative's July 2015 Budget added to this effect through announcements of £12 billion further cuts to benefits and tax credits beyond those agreed by the coalition, and through extension of the freeze on most working-age benefits to four years, rather two, but discussion of this and the details of how they plan to achieve the cuts is beyond the scope of this book.

THREE

Young children

Kitty Stewart and Polina Obolenskaya

The situation on the eve of the crisis

Until 1997, early childhood sat on the periphery of government concern in the UK. With the exception of health check-ups and universal Child Benefit, the state largely stepped out of a baby's life after birth, and only stepped back in when the child arrived at primary school more than four years later. While some inner-city local authorities provided free nursery education, for the most part nurseries, playgroups and toddler groups were organised by the voluntary or independent sector. Maternity leave provision was among the least generous in Europe, and state spending on childcare almost non-existent.

By 2007 the landscape for young families looked very different. Investment in early childhood had been a key feature of the Labour administration for a decade, promoted by a constellation of Labour politicians because it promised to further a number of policy goals at once. Centre stage was the goal of eradicating child poverty in 20 years, which required both higher family incomes in the immediate term and a focus on early child development, with an eye on giving the next generation of parents a fighting chance of non-poverty wages. Policies that made it easier and more financially viable for mothers (and fathers) to combine work and family responsibilities were also recognised to be key to furthering growth, promoting gender equality and reducing gender pay gaps.

Between 1997 and 2007 spending on cash benefits for families with children in the UK nearly doubled. Most of the increase came from the expansion of targeted in-work benefits under the tax credit system, but benefits to out-of-work families with children were also made more generous. Poverty fell steeply for some household types, and especially for children living with a lone parent working part time (Stewart, 2009). Poverty also fell much more quickly in families with a child under five than for those with older children, reflecting a series of changes to benefits favouring these households: Income Support allowances for children under 11 were increased in line with those for older children, and there were new benefits for babies, including the near-universal baby tax credit and the £500 Sure Start Maternity Grant for low-income families (Stewart, 2013). Maternity leave was lengthened, and although it continued to be paid at a relatively low flat rate, the median leave taken had doubled to 39 weeks by 2008, with policy change appearing to make the biggest difference to lower-skilled and lower-paid women (Chanfreau et al, 2011; Stewart, 2013).

Meanwhile, spending on early years services in England increased by a factor of 3.5. Free part-time nursery places were extended to all three- and four-year-olds, with near universal take-up. The childcare element of Working Tax Credit greatly increased the affordability of childcare for eligible parents, and the share of lone parents in employment rose from 45% to 56%. Employer childcare vouchers were introduced, providing a small subsidy to parents not eligible for childcare support through tax credits. Sure Start children's centres were being extended across the country, with a stronger emphasis on provision of childcare and early education, in response to early evaluation of Sure Start local programmes that had found no positive (and some negative) effects on developmental outcomes for disadvantaged children (NESS, 2005). Children's centres were also at the heart of attempts to improve the integration of services around the child, following on from the 2003 *Every Child Matters* framework (HM Treasury, 2003).

Despite these achievements, a series of challenges faced the government as Gordon Brown took over as Prime Minister in the summer of 2007, before the financial crisis hit. Most obviously, in terms of cash support, there were questions about how sustainable the tax credit route was as a way to continue bringing poverty down (Hirsch, 2006). Indeed, after good progress in the first two Labour Parliaments, progress on child poverty had slipped: poverty rose between 2004/05 and 2007/08. In terms of services, there were tensions in reconciling the different policy goals of promoting child development and facilitating parental employment: many free nursery places were either too low in quality or too inflexible to further both goals at once. The number of childcare places had increased substantially, but questions over both quality and affordability (the latter particularly for middle- and higher-income families) remained. There were also questions about whether children's centres would be able to maintain their offer as roll-out continued: funds were being increased overall, but stretched more thinly across the growing number of centres.

Policies, 2008-15

Labour's response to the crisis

As Chancellor, Gordon Brown was credited with much of the progress towards meeting Blair's child poverty pledge, and spoke frequently of the moral obligation to address child poverty. During the Brown Premiership, Child Tax Credits were increased annually above inflation: the 2008 Budget included the largest increases to Child Tax Credits since 2004. As the scale of the financial crisis became clear, the 2009 Budget emphasised the need to 'support vulnerable groups through the downturn' (HM Treasury, 2009a, p 91). A new Health in Pregnancy Grant was introduced in April 2009 as planned, bringing the start of Child Benefit forward to cover the last 12 weeks of pregnancy; an increase in Child Benefit was brought forward to January 2009; entitlement to childcare support became protected for four weeks if families lost qualifying hours; and a Take-Up Taskforce was established to improve the coverage of tax credits and benefits.

At the same time, the steady extension of conditionality for lone parents continued, affecting under-fives for the first time: from 2008, all lone parents were required to attend a six-monthly work-focused interview, regardless of the age of their youngest child.

In relation to services, the government continued with changes set out in the Childcare Act 2006, including the full introduction in 2008 of the early years foundation stage curriculum, which imposed a single quality framework across all providers, from childminders to reception classes. Early years professional status was introduced – a graduate role for those leading children's centres and full day care settings, based loosely on the concept of the Scandinavian pedagogue, but without equivalent pay or status with teachers. The Graduate Leader Fund financed early years professionals and other aspects of workforce development from 2008, building on the earlier Transformation Fund. Free part-time nursery places were piloted for two-year-olds from disadvantaged backgrounds.

In a final significant move, the government enshrined the child poverty targets in law, passing the Child Poverty Act in March 2010. Four child poverty targets for 2020/21 were established, along with requirements for UK governments to publish a regular child poverty strategy and annual progress reports, and to set up an advisory child poverty commission. The Act was passed with cross-party support, although the Conservatives argued that the targets (all income or material deprivation-based) were too narrow, and said that a Conservative government would aim to 'build up targets which are more likely to address the underlying causes of poverty' (Kennedy, 2014).

The coalition

Early childhood did not feature strongly in the election manifestos of either of the coalition parties. But there were early encouraging signs of government interest in the early years, driven by an emphasis on social mobility for which the constraints introduced by the Child Poverty Act may have been partly responsible. The Act was amended by the coalition in 2012 to require a social mobility as well as a child poverty strategy, broadening the government's remit in this area while diluting the focus on household income.

In the foreword to the new government's first social mobility strategy, Deputy Prime Minister Nick Clegg declared 'improving social mobility [to be] ... the principal goal of the Coalition Government's social policy' (Cabinet Office and ODPM, 2011, p 3). Like the amendments to the Child Poverty Act, both the child poverty and social mobility strategies underlined a move away from what was termed Labour's 'narrow focus on income measures' (p 8), and indicated a greater focus on services: 'Our aim is to improve the life chances of children in lower-income families, and we believe that the most sustainable way to do this is to invest in the public services which they use, and to monitor the progress of those children more closely' (DfE, 2011, p 48). Under the government's framing, then, the coalition would increase opportunity through services rather than income alone. In light of the evidence on Labour's record on social policy, outlined briefly above and in more detail elsewhere, this might alternatively be characterised as a shift from a dual strategy – investment in household income and services – to a focus on services alone (Lupton et al, 2013b; Stewart, 2013).

To some extent, the call for a stronger focus on services was backed up by a series of independent reviews, each commissioned by the government early in Parliament: Labour MPs Frank Field (2010) on poverty and life chances and Graham Allen (2011) on early intervention; Dame Clare Tickell (2011) on the early years foundation stage; Professor Cathy Nutbrown (2012) on the early years workforce; and Professor Eileen Munro (2011) on child protection. Between them, these reports made a powerful case for more investment in services and support for young families.

However, as documented earlier in Chapter One, two key early decisions shaped coalition policy in practice: to cut the deficit predominantly by reducing spending and not increasing taxes; and to protect spending on schools, health and pensions. Together these decisions left unprotected spending areas carrying a disproportionate burden of deficit reduction. This included social security benefits for households of working age, and also services provided by local authorities, among them – despite the rhetoric – the key services aimed at under-fives and their parents.

In relation to cash benefits, the coalition administration can be split into two time periods. Between 2010 and 2013, numerous cuts and reforms were made to child-contingent benefits, as documented in Box 3.1, contrasting with Labour's policy of increasing support to families in the face of the downturn. A number of the cuts specifically affected households with a baby: 2011 saw the abolition of the Health in Pregnancy Grant, the baby tax credit, and restrictions to the Sure Start Maternity Grant. However, at the same time, most benefits continued to rise in line with inflation, even while real earnings fell. As noted in Chapter Two, this 'non-decision' was in practice crucial in continuing to shield many families from the worst effects of the recession. In addition, the child element of Child Tax Credit continued to be increased above inflation in both April 2011 and April 2012, compensating low-income families for the freeze in the less targeted family element and in Child Benefit.

From April 2013 there were three significant changes. First, most working-age benefits (including maternity leave) began to be uprated by 1% annually rather than with inflation, meaning an annual squeeze in real terms as the economy started to grow. Second, a range of Housing Benefit reforms took effect, among them the 'bedroom tax'. Third, an annual cap on benefits per household was imposed, hitting those with high Housing Benefit receipt or many children (or both). Unlike earlier reforms, these changes were not targeted specifically at households with children, but they affected children too, and the welfare cap disproportionately so: 94% of households whose benefits had been reduced because of the cap by February 2015 were families with children; 35% had five children or more (DWP, 2015a).

In relation to services, the key factor was the substantial cut in local authority funding. This was greater in more deprived authorities, with a fall of around one-third in real terms in London and other large cities between 2009/10 and 2013/14 (Hastings et al, 2013; Fitzgerald et al, 2014). Against this backdrop, the coalition pursued one main expansionary policy, rolling out Labour's pilot early education places

Box 3.1: Young children policy timeline

Timeline spanning 2008–2015

2008
- Early years professional status introduced
- Early years foundation stage curriculum, single quality framework for all providers
- Free part-time nursery places for two-year-olds piloted

2009
- All lone parents required to attend a work-focused interview (age of youngest child no longer relevant)
- Take-Up Taskforce established to improve coverage of tax credits and benefits
- Childcare entitlement protected for 4 weeks if families lost qualifying hours
- Budget contained largest increases to Child Tax Credit since 2004
- Health in Pregnancy Grant child benefit in last 12 weeks of pregnancy

2010
- Child poverty targets in law

2011
- Free early education extended from 12.5 to 15 hours per week (as Labour plan); more flexibility introduced (a minimum of 2 days rather than 3)
- Health in Pregnancy Grant and Child Trust Fund abolished. Sure Start Maternity Grant restricted to first child only. Requirement lifted for children's centres in most disadvantaged areas to offer childcare and early education and to employ a teacher
- Child element of Child Tax Credit increased above inflation

2012
- Baby Tax Credit abolished; Sure Start Maternity Grant restricted to first child only.
- Increases in withdrawal rate for tax credits from 39% to 41%.
- Earnings disregard for tax credits reduced from £25,000 to £10,000.
- Threshold for receiving full family element of Child Tax Credit (CTC) reduced from £50,000 to £40,000.
- Maximum repayment under childcare element of CTC cut from 80% to 70% of costs.
- Child Benefit and family element of CTC frozen for 3 years, switch to benefit uprating using CPI.
- Early years single funding formula introduced to improve transparency and fairness of funding to different providers (as Labour plan) (essentially removing subsidy from maintained settings)

2013
- Increase in the Working Tax Credit working hours requirement for couples with children from 16 to 24
- Removal of a separate threshold for receiving the family element of CTC (effectively removing tax credit from one-child families on £26,000 and four-child families on £45,400)
- Introduction of a £2,500 tax credit disregard for when income falls
- Child Benefit withdrawn from families with at least one earner on more than £60,000 (withdrawal starts when one earner reaches £50,000)
- Free early education extended to 20% most disadvantaged two-year-olds

2014
- Below inflation uprating in tax credits and benefits (1%), including maternity and paternity benefits, earnings disregard for tax credits reduced from £10,000 to £5,000
- 1% increase in Child Benefit
- Free early education extended to 40% most disadvantaged two-year-olds; change to statutory guidance to local authorities, removing local authority role in supporting quality improvements (Ofsted becomes 'sole arbiter of quality')

2015
- More flexibility to share parental leave was introduced, with only the first 2 weeks (rather than 20 weeks) reserved exclusively for mothers
- Planned (launch expected 2017): tax-free childcare scheme introduced, covering up to 20% of childcare costs for parents earning up to £150,000 each; early years Pupil Premium introduced

to the most disadvantaged 20% (and later 40%) of two-year-olds. It also pledged to expand the Family Nurse Partnership (providing intensive support for teenage parents), and to increase the number of health visitors. But while these policies were protected, other aspects of provision for under-fives were not: the ring-fence around Sure Start funding and the (small but positively evaluated) Graduate Leader Fund were removed. It remained a statutory requirement to provide free early education places, but non-statutory services now had to compete with other local services in the context of a much tighter overall budget.

However, spending cuts are not the full story of coalition policy on services. The government also pursued a number of reforms to the design and delivery of services for young children. First, there were several attempts to achieve better value for money: by trialling 'payment by results' in children's centres (abandoned after the pilot stage); by requiring more targeting of Sure Start services on more vulnerable families; and by establishing the Early Intervention Foundation (as recommended by the Allen Review) to improve the evidence base and to raise investment for effective interventions from non-government sources, potentially using social impact bonds.

Second, there were changes that affected the quality of early education. Most of these had no cost implications but few were clearly beneficial to quality. The requirements for children's centres in disadvantaged areas to provide childcare and early education and to employ a teacher were lifted. Local authority responsibility for supporting improvements in childcare quality was removed, making Ofsted (the Office for Standards in Education) 'the sole arbiter of quality'. New qualifications were introduced, including the title of 'early years teacher', but without conferring the pay and status of qualified teacher status, despite the recommendations of the Nutbrown review (2012). More clearly beneficial, the government pledged in 2014 to extend the Pupil Premium (extra funds for disadvantaged children) down to early years settings.

Finally, there was a significant shift away from a focus on broader child development and wellbeing towards a concern with narrower educational goals, for young as well as school-age children. The Department for Children, Schools and Families (DCSF) was renamed the Department for Education (DfE), while Labour's *Every Child Matters* framework, with its five broad outcomes, was quietly dismantled in favour of the language of 'achievement'; for example, the delivery team for the two-year-old offer was labelled 'Achieving Two-Year-Olds'. Concerns were raised that new measurement checks, such as a baseline school assessment for four-year-olds planned for 2016, failed to capture child development in its broadest sense, and would inevitably lead to early years settings narrowing their focus (see, for example, Messenger and Molloy, 2014).

Spending, 2008-14

Figure 3.1 shows what happened to public spending on early education, childcare and Sure Start in England after the onset of the crisis, in the context of spending since 1997. This does not include all relevant services: in particular, age-specific expenditure on health is not readily available. In addition, the need for caution should be noted in relation to Sure Start spending figures, which come from local authority Section 251 returns since the removal of the central ring-fence on Sure Start funding in 2010. There are concerns about the consistency of local authority reporting in these returns (Freeman and Gill, 2014), but they remain the only source available for Sure Start spending.

It is clear, first, that spending on young children's services continued to rise in real terms between 2007/08 and 2009/10 at a similar rate to the earlier boom years. Only the childcare element of Working Tax Credit levelled out in real terms between 2008/09 and 2009/10,

Figure 3.1: Spending on Sure Start, early education and childcare in England, 1997/98 to 2013/14 (£ million, 2014-15 prices)

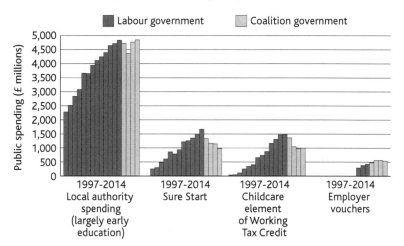

Sources: Main sources are Public Expenditure Statistical Analysis (PESA) for early education; Section 251 returns for Sure Start (most recent data published in DfE (2014f); HMRC (2015) and early equivalents for the childcare element; Hansard records for employer childcare vouchers (see Stewart and Obolenskaya 2015, Table 2)

as the number of lone-parent claimants stopped rising for the first time since the credit was introduced in 2003. Because expenditure on these services taken together continued to rise while GDP was falling, spending increased as a share of GDP in Labour's last years in office, from 0.44% in 2007/08 to 0.51% in 2009/10.

Equally clear is the sharp fall in spending after the change in government. Spending on early education benefited from the relative protection of education funding overall. In real terms it was the same in 2013/14 as it had been in 2009/10.[1] Nevertheless, in per capita terms this represents a substantial reduction in resources, not only because of the growing numbers of young children (the population under five grew by 6% in England between 2010 and 2014), but also because by 2013/14 this budget was also covering the targeted two-year-old places. It appears that additional funding dedicated to these new places was effectively cancelled out by reductions in spending on three- and four-year olds. There are several reasons this could have happened. First, early education was vulnerable within the Dedicated Schools Grant because until 2013/14 the annual per capita Minimum Funding Guarantee applied only to maintained schools and not to private and voluntary settings (attended by more than one-third of three- and four-year-olds).[2] Second, some local authorities had opted to top up early education spending from other parts of the budget, for example, offering 25 hours to four-year-olds, rather than the statutory 15. Their ability to do this was severely tested by the wider context of local funding cuts.

This context also contributed to the dramatic drop in Sure Start spending once its ring-fence was lifted — a real terms fall of 41% between 2009/10 and 2013/14. Caution about the precision of Sure Start spending figures has been noted, but this appears to be a swingeing cut, perhaps harsher than that facing any other public service. Meanwhile, the childcare element of Working Tax Credit fell by a third, reflecting both the fall in reimbursement from 80 to 70%, and changes to the rules around tax credit entitlement that reduced the number of qualifying households.

Overall, spending on the four areas shown in Figure 3.1 fell by 13% in real prices. Per capita, the drop was about one-fifth, down from a peak of £2,572 per child under five in 2009/10 to £2,121 in 2013/14, taking per capita spending back to just below the level in 2005/06. As a share of GDP, spending fell from 0.51% in 2009/10 to 0.42% in 2013/14.

Figure 3.2 shows spending on child-contingent cash transfers in the UK (covering all children up to age 18). Labour's increase in cash

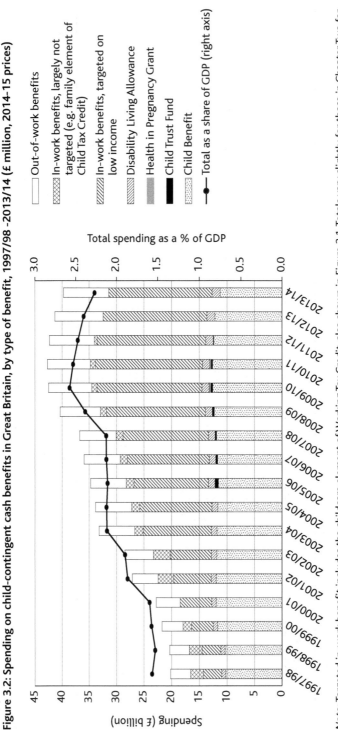

Figure 3.2: Spending on child-contingent cash benefits in Great Britain, by type of benefit, 1997/98 -2013/14 (£ million, 2014–15 prices)

Note: Targeted in-work benefit includes the childcare element of Working Tax Credit, also shown in Figure 3.1. Totals vary slightly for those in Chapter Two for definitional reasons.

Sources: Tax credit data from HMRC (2015) and earlier equivalents. Child Benefit, Child Trust Fund, Disability Living Allowance and Health in Pregnancy Grant from DWP benefit expenditure and caseload tables. For further details see Stewart and Obolenskaya (2015, Table 3).

support for families against the backdrop of recession shows up in the rapid rise in spending between 2007/08 and 2009/10 after several years of slower growth. The increase was of a similar magnitude – around one-fifth – for both out-of-work benefits and in-work means-tested benefits. As a share of declining GDP, spending on all child-contingent cash transfers rose steeply, having remained steady between 2003/04 and 2007/08.

After 2009/10, spending on cash transfers started to fall slowly. Spending on benefits for out-of-work families was 5% higher in 2013/14 than in 2009/10, but there was a 7% cut in support for in-work families and an 11% cut in Child Benefit, as well as the abolition of the Health in Pregnancy Grant and Child Trust Fund. Overall, real spending on child-contingent cash transfers fell by 7% between 2009/10 and 2013/14.

Inputs and outputs, 2008-14

How did these spending trends affect the level of services provided? Spending in 2013/14 had fallen back to around the level of 2005/06: were services cut accordingly? Or were government attempts to introduce better value for money effective in protecting the extent of provision?

Early education

The number of three- and four-year-olds accessing places grew steadily between January 2008 and January 2015, rising by 4-5% between 2008 and 2010, and by 11% between 2010 and 2015 (DfE, 2010, 2015). This is slightly faster than the estimated rise in the number of children in this age group, pushing take-up rates up from 92% to 94% of three-year-olds and from 98% to 99% of four-year-olds. As in previous years most of the growth, particularly for three-year-olds, was in the private, voluntary and independent (PVI) rather than state maintained sectors. Between 2008 and 2010, two-thirds of new places created for three-year-olds were in PVI settings, while between 2010 and 2015, virtually *all* new places (around 99%) were PVI. For four-year-olds, state reception class provision expanded to provide the majority (more than six in ten) of new places, but the PVI sector grew most quickly in percentage terms: reception class places grew by 17% and PVI places by 32%.

Part-time places for the most disadvantaged 20% of two-year-olds were rolled out from September 2013, and for the most disadvantaged

40% a year later, but DfE estimates show only 58% of eligible children accessing a place in January 2015. More than 80% of these children attended private or voluntary sector day nurseries and playgroups, with 6% in local authority day nurseries, 4% in state maintained nursery schools or classes, 1% in Sure Start children's centres and 3% with childminders (DfE, 2015, Table 7).

Given the strength of evidence that early education provision needs to be high quality if it is to promote child development, and that qualified (especially graduate) staff play a key role in raising quality (see e.g. Waldfogel, 2006; Gambaro et al, 2014), the concentration of places in PVI settings is a potential concern. Staff qualification levels have been and remain lower in PVI than in maintained settings. In January 2015 only 45% of two-year-olds accessing a free early education place had a qualified graduate working with them at any point in the week (DfE, 2015). On the positive side, there has been a steady improvement since 2008 in the percentage of graduate staff working with young children, as illustrated in Figure 3.3. Nevertheless, the gap between PVI and maintained sector provision remains wide. Furthermore, improvements between 2008 and 2013 are likely to reflect the impact of funding sources such as the Graduate Leader Fund (2008-11) that have now been lost.

Figure 3.3: Percentage of paid staff that have a relevant Level 6 qualification (a degree), Childcare and Early Years Providers Survey

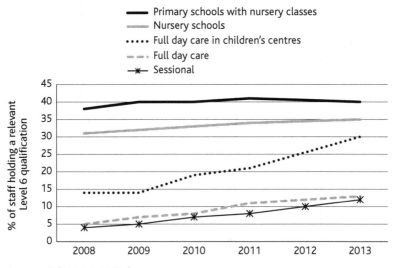

Source: DfE (2014b, Table 7.1)

Childcare

There is some evidence from Ofsted registration data of a small fall in the number of childcare providers from 2009, after a steady increase over the course of a decade (Stewart and Obolenskaya, 2015). However, the number of places in non-domestic settings held up, indicating that smaller settings may be closing while larger ones expand. Childminder numbers fell steadily, continuing a long-run trend.

Meanwhile, affordability became increasingly challenging, with the price of a nursery place for a child under two in England rising by an average of 5% annually between 2008-10 and by 6% annually between 2010 and 2015, easily outstripping growth in both wages and other prices (author's calculations based on data from the Family and Childcare Trust annual childcare cost surveys; see, for example, Rutter, 2015). At the same time, the support on offer through tax credits fell: as Figure 3.4 shows, after a steady increase in previous years, both the number of families receiving support and the average weekly award fell from 2009/10, with the sharpest fall between 2010/11 and 2011/12, reflecting the 2011 changes to qualifying conditions for tax credits and the simultaneous cut in maximum reimbursement. As a share of rising childcare costs, the generosity of support deteriorated rapidly: the average weekly award covered 79% of the average cost of 25 hours' nursery care for a child under two in 2007/08, 75% in 2009/10 and 51% in 2013/14 (author's calculations). Take-up of formal childcare

Figure 3.4: Families receiving childcare element of Working Tax Credit, and average weekly award

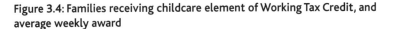

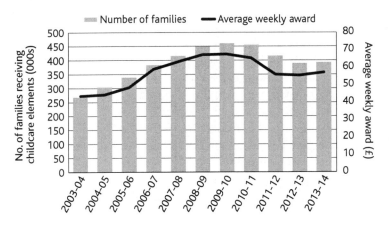

Note: Price adjustment made using annual CPI.

Source: HMRC (2015) and earlier equivalents

for those aged 0-2 was stable between 2007 and 2010, and fell slightly, from 39% to 37%, between 2010 and 2012 (Kazimirski et al, 2008; Smith et al, 2010; Huskinson et al, 2014).

Sure Start

The number of Sure Start children's centres fell after the coalition took office, down from 3,631 in April 2010 to 3,019 in June 2014, although the government argued that most of the fall reflected 'mergers' between centres rather than outright closures. In regard to the reach and quality of services in centres that remained, several points stand out. First, local authority responses to budgetary pressures varied considerably, with Sure Start carrying a much heavier burden in some areas than others. Fitzgerald et al's (2014) study of three London authorities found Camden largely protecting services for under-fives while cutting provision for young people and the elderly, while in Brent, children's centres had experienced a budget cut of more than 50%. In the annual census conducted by 4Children, two-thirds of centres reported a decrease in budget between 2012 and 2013, while 52% expected a decline in 2014, a majority but not a universal experience (4Children, 2013, 2014).

Second, there is evidence of many centres showing impressive resilience in the face of budget reductions, keeping services going with a number of strategies, including increased workloads, stretched management roles, reliance on volunteers and a 'thinner', less frequent, service offer (Tanner et al, 2012; Goff et al, 2013; Fitzgerald et al, 2014; Sylva et al, 2015). These approaches have cushioned families from the full impact of the budget squeeze, and might be seen as improving value for money in the short run. But it is not clear how far they will be sustainable, particularly in the face of further cuts. The Evaluation of Children's Centres in England found staff reporting that their capacity was already overstretched, and that they felt under-resourced to meet expectations on them, particularly in relation to families with complex needs (Sylva et al, 2015).

Third, changes in provision reflected not only cuts but also new thinking under the coalition about what centres should be doing, summed up by David Cameron in 2010: 'It can't just be a service that everyone can jump into and get advantage out of. It really is there for those who are suffering the greatest disadvantage' (*The Telegraph*, 2010). Following revisions to children's centres' core purpose, there was a shift to more targeted provision, an increase in evidence-based parenting programmes and decreases in more universal, open access activities such as 'stay and play' and 'messy play' (Goff et al, 2013; 4Children, 2014; Sylva et al, 2015). Between 2012 and 2014 affluent families were those most likely to have stopped using children's centre services, and low-income and non-working families least likely, suggesting success in this strategy (Maisey et al, 2015). But staff fear that targeting may lead to services being stigmatised, and they worry about denying services to families who have less complex needs but who are still living in poverty (Sylva et al, 2015).

The other major change in guidance for children's centres was the removal of the requirement to provide early education and childcare: the numbers doing so fell sharply in response, from 800 in 2010 (already down from a peak of 1,000 in 2009) to just 450 in 2013 (DfE, 2014b). A tiny share of overall childcare provision (just 3% at the peak, now 2%), this fall is nevertheless significant because childcare in children's centres has generally been both higher quality than elsewhere (see Figure 3.3 above), and more likely to cater to children with disabilities.

Household financial support

Figure 3.5 shows the sharp fall in the number of in-work families in receipt of tax credits when more restrictive rules were introduced in April 2011 and April 2012, a drop of 40% in two years. Assessing what happened to the real value of tax credits for in-work families

Figure 3.5: Numbers of families in receipt of tax credits, 2003/04 to 2013/14 (000s)

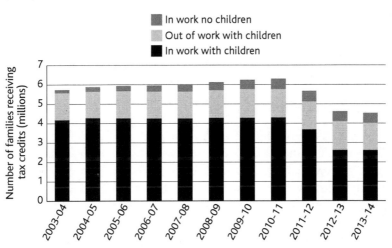

Source: HMRC (2015)

continuing to receive them is difficult because of the changing make-up of recipient families (families losing entitlement were largely those higher up the distribution receiving smaller awards). For out-of-work families, however, it is clear that tax credit support rose steadily until 2012/13: the average payment increased by an average of 5% annually in real terms in the two years to 2009/10, and by an average of 2% in the following three years. The April 2011 rule limiting benefit rises to a nominal 1% changed the trend: the real value of out-of-work tax credits fell by 1% between 2012/13 and 2013/14.

Low-income families with a baby, however, were less well protected from 2010 onwards. Together, the Health in Pregnancy Grant, baby tax credit and Sure Start Maternity Grant provided an income boost of £1,230 between the sixth month of pregnancy and a baby's first birthday. Their abolition or restriction meant that non-working households having a second young child in 2013/14 received 12-13% less in real financial support than similar families in 2009/10 (Stewart and Obolenskaya, 2015, Table 6). As these households were below the poverty line to begin with, this change will not have affected headcount poverty measures, but it will have increased poverty depth.

In combination, restrictions in in-work Child Tax Credits, the removal of additional support for babies, as well as the affluence testing of Child Benefit, meant children under five were the age group least advantaged by the coalition's tax-benefit reforms. This is shown in Figure 3.6, from De Agostini et al (2015), which compares the coalition package of reforms to a hypothetical alternative in which the 2009/10 system was simply uprated in line with average earnings. For households with young children, cuts in financial support outweighed the effects of a higher personal Income Tax allowance, leaving children as a group neither better nor worse off overall. In contrast, households without dependent children were substantial net *gainers* overall, as reflected by the U-shaped age profile for adults in Figure 3.6.

Outcomes, 2008-14

It is very early to assess the impact of these changes on children's outcomes. The short time frame is exacerbated by the fact that many useful data are available only with a lag, and by changes in measurement methodology that create breaks in trend over time. Nevertheless, we present the picture to date for one each of three types of outcome: income poverty (an outcome measure in its own right, as well as a factor affecting child development), early child health, and cognitive and social/behavioural development.

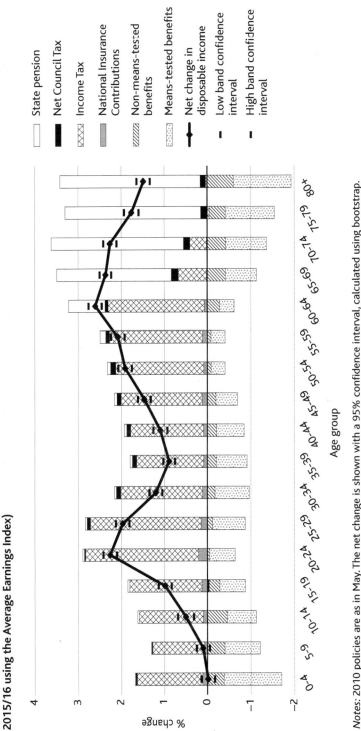

Figure 3.6: Percentage change in household disposable income by age group due to policy changes, 2010-2015/16 (2010 policies uprated to 2015/16 using the Average Earnings Index)

Young children

Notes: 2010 policies are as in May. The net change is shown with a 95% confidence interval, calculated using bootstrap.

Source: De Agostini et al (2015, Figure 5.1), using EUROMOD

Child poverty

The rate of relative child poverty fell until 2010/11, then remained stable until 2013/14 (the last data available at the time of writing). This is true whether poverty is measured before or after housing costs (BHC or AHC), and reflects both the decline in median living standards and the protection of financial support in real terms until 2013. Against a fixed income line, child poverty was also broadly stable over this timeframe. (See Chapter Eleven for figures and further discussion.)

As Figure 3.7 illustrates, the overall child poverty figures mask very different trends for children of different ages. Children under five saw much more rapid progress than older children during the Labour years; indeed, poverty rates for younger and older children converged to 2010/11, as poverty remained stable or even rose in households where the youngest child was over 11. Since 2010/11, the trend has reversed: poverty has risen only for children in households with a baby and (as before) in households where the youngest child is 16 or over. In these households, poverty rose against both a relative and a fixed income line, and whether income is measured BHC or AHC.

Figure 3.7: Percentage of children living in households below the poverty line (AHC), by age of the youngest child in the household, Great Britain

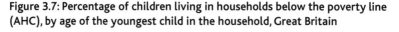

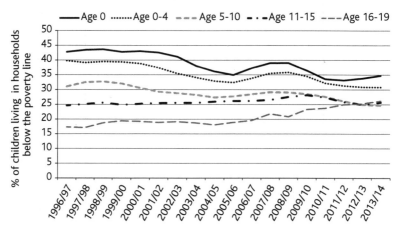

Note: Poverty line defined as 60% median equivalised income AHC. Poverty rates are presented as three-year averages because of small cell size. The year on the x-axis indicates the last of the three averaged years.

Source: Institute for Fiscal Studies calculations using the Family Resources Survey

Early child health

Low birth weight is an important indicator of later health outcomes that has also been linked to delays in cognitive and social development. As Table 3.1 shows, the percentage of babies born at low birth weight to parents classified as doing routine or manual jobs or as long-term unemployed fell substantially between 2005 and 2009, while the rate for higher social classes (managerial, professional or intermediate) flatlined, meaning a steady reduction in the social class gap, whether measured in absolute or percentage terms. The trend thereafter is less positive. The rate for professional and managerial groups fluctuated between 2009 and 2013, while that for routine and manual groups fell slightly between 2009 and 2011, and then rose sharply between 2012 and 2013. As a result the social class gap also fluctuated and then rose. In 2013, both the rates of low birth weight themselves and the relative and absolute gap were back to where they had been in 2007.

Early child cognitive and social development

Figure 3.8 shows improvements in the proportion of five-year-olds achieving 'a good level of development' at the end of reception

Table 3.1: Percentage of babies born weighing less than 2500g, by combined occupational class, 2005-13, England and Wales (all live births)

Year	Social classes 1-4 (most advantaged)	Social classes 5-8 (least advantaged)	Absolute % point gap	Relative gap (absolute gap as a % of the rate for classes 1-4)
2005	6.4	8.6	2.2	34.4
2006	6.6	8.2	1.6	24.2
2007	6.4	7.7	1.3	20.3
2008	6.4	7.8	1.4	21.9
2009	6.4	7.3	0.9	14.1
2010	6.1	7.2	1.1	18.0
2011	6.6	7.1	0.5	7.6
2012	6.0	7.1	1.1	18.3
2013	6.4	7.7	1.3	20.3

Notes: Social classes 1-4: where the most advantaged of either parent's occupation is classified as managerial, professional or intermediate. Social classes 5-8: where the most advantaged of either parent's occupation is classified as routine and manual occupations, never worked or long-term unemployed. Social class classified using the National Statistics Socioeconomic Classification (NS-SEC rebased on the SOC2010). The breakdowns of socioeconomic classification are based on a 10% sample grossed up to agree with known totals.

Source: ONS (2015h)

Figure 3.8: Percentage of children achieving a 'good level of development' at age 5 (early years foundation stage), by FSM status

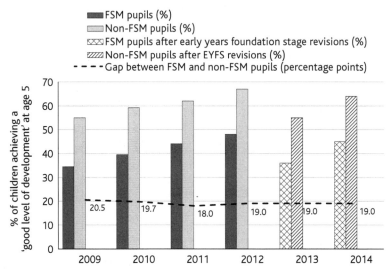

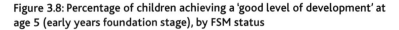
- FSM pupils (%)
- Non-FSM pupils (%)
- FSM pupils after early years foundation stage revisions (%)
- Non-FSM pupils after EYFS revisions (%)
- - - - Gap between FSM and non-FSM pupils (percentage points)

Source: Compiled from annual reports from the DfE, 'Early years foundation stage profile attainment by pupil characteristics in England' '(DfE (2014e) and earlier equivalents)

class, as judged against the indicators in the early years foundation stage curriculum, which include measures of cognitive, social and behavioural development. The revisions to the early years foundation stage introduced in 2012 created a break in the series, so 2013 and 2014 data are not comparable with those for earlier years. Under the new 2013 measure there was an initial drop to 52% achieving a good level, although this was back up to 60% in 2014.

Until 2011, improvement was very slightly faster for pupils eligible for free school meals (FSM) than for others, leading to a small narrowing of the FSM gap. Between 2011 and 2012 the gap widened, and there appears to have been no further progress since then. This is consistent with the picture for the gap between children in the 30% most deprived areas and others, which narrowed steadily between 2007 and 2011, from 17 percentage points to 12, and then stalled (see Stewart and Obolenskaya, 2015, Table 9).

Analysing change and the relationship between policies and outcomes

Government policy towards young children after the financial crisis splits clearly into two periods. Between 2007 and 2010 the Brown administration protected, and further invested in, both family benefits and services for young children. Child Tax Credits were increased annually above the rate of inflation, and Child Benefit was extended into the last three months of pregnancy. Additional Sure Start children's centres were opened, and the Graduate Leader Fund was established to support investment in more qualified childcare staff.

From 2010 to 2015, under the coalition government, a very different set of decisions was made. Some specific services were prioritised – the Family Nurse Partnership and the roll-out of free part-time nursery places to disadvantaged two-year-olds – but against a background in which young children's services were heavily squeezed overall by cuts in local authority funding settlements. Spending on early education, childcare and Sure Start fell by around one-fifth per child between 2009/10 and 2013/14, compared to a cut of less than 3% in public spending overall (HM Treasury, 2015c). At the same time, a series of reforms and cuts to benefits and Child Tax Credit reduced the financial support available to families with children. Until 2013 these largely reduced support for middle-income households, as well as for all families with a baby; from 2013, the effects will have been felt most sharply at the bottom of the distribution, by those dependent on social security benefits for more of their income.

It is too early to judge the impact of these policy choices for children's outcomes, but not too early to be concerned. We know very well from wider research that both family income and high-quality services are crucial to children's development (Waldfogel, 2006; Cooper and Stewart, 2013). The record of the Labour government provides further evidence: its dual strategy (addressing income poverty while investing in services) delivered narrowing socioeconomic gaps in infant mortality, low birth weight and child development measured against the early years foundation stage curriculum (Stewart, 2013). Labour's record also reminds us that policies can take time to bed in and show effects. Sure Start local programmes, for example, showed few positive results at the time of their first evaluation, but later rounds found significant effects on the quality of parenting and the home environment that were still there when the children were seven (NESS, 2005, 2008, 2012). Social class gaps in low birth weight and the infant mortality rate remained stubbornly high during the early Labour years, only narrowing substantially from 2005 onwards. The gap in early child development between children from disadvantaged areas and others did not respond immediately to the roll-out of free early education between 1999 and 2004, but started to fall from 2007, probably reflecting steady improvements in the quality of provision, including the development of the early years foundation stage curriculum and investment in more highly qualified staff.

If investment in benefits and services reaped rewards, but took time to do so, the opposite is also likely to be true. Dismantling services and cutting benefits seems certain to make it more difficult for young families in disadvantaged circumstances to ensure that their children will thrive, but the effects may take time to show up in full. There are early indicators of what reduced services will mean: Fitzgerald et al (2014) find families in their case study authority of Brent, for example, identifying an effect of Sure Start cuts on their own levels of stress and their children's behaviour and development. Some outcome measures are also already raising early warning signs of negative consequences. Whether the recent widening in the social class gap in low birth weight is a blip or a more persistent new trend is something that should be monitored closely.

In assessing Labour's record in 2013, we pointed to the immense difficulty of untangling the effects of different aspects of Labour's policy agenda, and highlighted the danger that crucial parts of the strategy might consequently be unravelled (Stewart and Obolenskaya, 2015). This seemed particularly pertinent in light of the apparent shift from a two-pronged approach to improving children's life chances to one more heavily reliant on services, with less focus on the role of income poverty. In practice, even aspects of service provision that were subject to robust evaluation, and showed positive results, were squeezed or dismantled under the coalition (Sure Start, the Graduate Leader Fund). The danger turned out not to be the absence of research evidence, but either a lack of interest or faith in this evidence, or simply the prioritisation of other goals in spite of it.

Conclusion

There is an irony in the way in which policy for young children has developed since the 2007 financial crash. On the one hand, early childhood has come of age, accepted in principle as a legitimate – and essential – area for government intervention by the coalition parties as well as the previous Labour government. Yet, on the other hand, since 2010, families with young children have been asked to carry perhaps the heaviest burden of austerity measures. The rolling back of benefits and services for young children comes just at the point that policies appeared to be beginning to deliver convergence in outcomes between disadvantaged children and their peers. The double blow experienced by families with young children also contrasts with the situation of other groups. School-age children were negatively affected by tax-benefit reforms, but spending on schools was protected, and the Pupil Premium channelled more of those resources to poorer children, as will be discussed in Chapter Four. People above working age experienced budget cuts for key services such as adult social care, but their pension income was protected (see Chapters Two and Nine).

Looking forward, the outlook for young children is not bright. The election of a majority Conservative government in 2015 heralds further cuts in both services and benefits. The squeeze on local authority budgets is likely to continue, meaning increasingly difficult choices for local authorities looking to protect Sure Start services and to promote the quality of childcare. In the July 2015 Budget the government set out its intention to remove tax credits for third and subsequent children, a move that will seriously affect the wellbeing of children in families affected. Additional proposed cuts to tax credits were abandoned after a revolt in the House of Lords in late 2015, but similar cuts will nevertheless be implemented as part of Universal Credit when it is rolled out. Changes announced in the official child poverty measures have gone further than expected in completely dropping income as a poverty measure, meaning that the government will not consider itself accountable for the effects of this or other tax-benefit reforms on income poverty. This is despite strong evidence of the importance of income for children's outcomes, and near universal support for keeping income at the heart of poverty measurement in responses to the coalition government's consultation on the issue (Cooper and Stewart, 2013; Roberts and Stewart, 2015). Early education places are being extended to a full school day for working families, after a pledge made during the 2015 General Election, but as a consequence lone parents will be required to look for work (and to take up the full day place) when their youngest child is three, which is not obviously in the interest of all these children. Further, there is uncertainty about funding for the longer day: if not adequately funded, the pledge will have a negative effect on the quality of existing provision.

Of all the people who might be held responsible for the 2007 financial crash, it is difficult to think of a group with cleaner hands than children not even born when the coalition took office in 2010. Yet the decisions taken by the coalition have left these children paying the heaviest price, despite what we know about the consequences not only for the quality of their childhood, but also for their life chances. It is hard to see this as anything other than deeply unfair. For any government concerned about economic growth, social mobility, or both, it seems also extremely short-sighted.

Notes

[1] The reason for the lower figure in 2011/12 is unclear. Note also that in earlier PESA publications, the amount for 2012/13 was similar to that for 2011/12, suggesting a downward trend, as reported in Stewart and Obolenskaya (2015). In PESA 2015, the 2012/13 figure has been revised upwards without explanation.

[2] From 2013/14 an MFG (Minimum Funding Guarantee) was applied to all early years funding, including in private, voluntary or independent (PVI) settings, but only covered the 'base rate' of funding and not additional supplements for quality or disadvantage (DfE, 2012, para 125).

FOUR

Schools

*Ruth Lupton, Stephanie Thomson
and Polina Obolenskaya*

The situation on the eve of the crisis

Throughout this book, 2007 is referred to as the last year of the 'warm climate' for social policy that Labour enjoyed. In schools policy, it also represents a turning point, with Ed Balls taking over as Secretary of State for Education and beginning to take policy in new directions.

The Labour programme for schools up to 2007 had four key themes. The main policy emphasis was on pushing up standards of teaching and learning. National Strategies were introduced to provide teachers with standardised materials and guidance, supported by advisers. The government set 'floor targets' for minimum performance, naming and shaming schools that did not reach them, and forcing some to close and reopen with new leadership. Teachers' salaries were increased, and performance pay introduced. Teacher training was reformed and a new workforce agreement was signed, designed to cut down the time teachers spent on administration, resulting in a large increase in the number of support staff.

Curriculum and assessment was a second theme, but a much less prominent one initially. Indeed, a key decision was made not to accept the recommendations of the 2004 Tomlinson report, which proposed new 14-19 diplomas in place of GCSEs, A-levels and vocational qualifications. However, a wider range of vocational courses, deemed equivalent to GCSEs, was introduced. A third theme was structural reform – again something less strongly emphasised initially, when David Blunkett pledged that his priority would be standards, not structures. In practice, Conservative policies of choice and diversity were extended. Schools were encouraged to develop specialisms, and from 2002 academy schools were introduced to replace struggling schools in disadvantaged areas. The way was paved for subsequent coalition reforms through decisions to give parents the right to request new schools, move local authorities into commissioning roles, and encourage schools to join together in federations.

Fourth, there was a prominent focus on addressing socioeconomic inequalities, partly through the academies programme, but also through the 'Teach First' programme (which brought top graduates into teaching in the most disadvantaged schools), an increasingly redistributive school funding formula, and targeted area-based schemes such as Excellence in Cities and the London Challenge. Labour's Building Schools for the Future (BSF) programme, designed to renew the entire secondary school building stock in 15-20 years, was also initially targeted on the most disadvantaged areas.

One result of these policies was a large increase in spending. Spending on secondary schools was up 64% from 1997/98 to 2006/07 (51% per capita), and on primary schools, 49% (62% per capita). Capital spending rose by a factor of 3. There was clear evidence of improvement in attainment according to national tests, and of a reduction in socioeconomic inequalities. At the end of primary school (Key Stage 2), overall attainment rose sharply between 1997, when around[1] 62% of pupils were achieving the expected level, and 1999, and gradually thereafter, reaching around 78% in 2007. The gap between the attainment of those on free school meals (FSM) and those not, measurable from 2002, fell from 26 percentage points to 21 in English by 2007 and from 23 points to 20 in maths. The proportion of students achieving five A*-C grades at GCSE increased steadily at a rate of between 1 and 2 percentage points each year until 2004, and more sharply thereafter, reaching 59.9% in 2007, compared with 45.1% at the start of the period. The sharp upturn in results coincided with the introduction of a wider range of equivalent vocational qualifications. The FSM gap at GCSE 5 A*-C fell slightly, from 30.7 percentage points in 2002 to 28.3 in 2007.

Thus the 'warm climate' from 1997-2007 had enabled substantial investment, expansion and improvement. Balls inherited a relatively healthy situation, but also a policy regime criticised both from the Right in terms of 'dumbing down', 'grade inflation' and over-centralisation, and from the Left in terms of creeping marketisation, over-testing, over-centralisation and the large gaps in attainment that still persisted between children born in different socioeconomic groups.

Labour policies, 2007-10

In some respects, the three years of Labour policy up to 2010 may be seen as a period of stability. There were no major reforms of school structure, no overhauls of the curriculum and examination system or of the teaching profession. However, Balls' period in office can also be seen as the beginning of new directions in policy that would have had very different implications for the school system had Labour won the 2010 General Election, and which were notable for their focus on addressing inequalities.

Chief among these was the broadening of the role of the school. From 2007, the former Department for Education and Skills (DfES) was renamed the Department for Children, Schools and Families (DCSF) as the skills and universities briefs were moved to the new Department for Innovation, Universities and Skills (DIUS). Building on Labour's earlier *Every Child Matters* (ECM) agenda, *The Children's Plan* of 2007 signalled a vision of a 21st-century school that was not just about cognitive attainments, but 'actively contributes to all aspects of a child's life – health and wellbeing, [and] safety ... because they help children achieve, but also because they are good for children's wider development and part of a good childhood' (DCSF, 2007a, p 146). The change in terminology and the interagency working that followed, in combination with existing initiatives on social and emotional aspects of learning (SEAL), extended schools, vocational qualifications and work-based learning, encouraged schools to see achievement in a broader sense, to offer a wider range of learning opportunities in order to promote engagement, and to work with other agencies to support achievement, particularly for the most disadvantaged. New inspection arrangements required schools to assess how they were contributing to children's wellbeing, not just their cognitive attainments.

The late 2000s also saw an increasing focus on individual pupils who were falling behind and on those facing disadvantage, partly in recognition of the fact that research showed more advantaged pupils benefiting most from programmes targeted at schools. Three specific programmes – Every Child a Reader, Every Child a Writer and Every Child Counts – were developed and rolled out under the auspices of the National Strategies, thus retaining the centrally driven approach that had characterised earlier Labour policies. The City Challenge approach adopted in London was extended to Greater Manchester and the Black Country.

In 2007, the DCSF also funded a two-year Narrowing the Gap research and development programme to work out how better to narrow gaps (on all the *Every Child Matters* outcomes, not just attainment) between disadvantaged and vulnerable children and their peers by strengthening institutional arrangements between schools and children's services, improving leadership and governance, and engaging parents and carers. A programme of support for leadership and teaching in schools facing challenging circumstances was succeeded in 2008 by the Extra Mile project, designed to help struggling schools implement the successful practices of other schools that appeared to 'buck the trend' with highly disadvantaged intakes. Provision for pupils educated outside of mainstream schooling in Pupil Referral Units (PRUs) or other settings was subject to a major review, with the 2008 *Back on track* White Paper (DCSF, 2008) announcing measures to establish a core educational entitlement for young people, and to improve planning, commissioning and accountability.

Last, post-2008, Labour made some moves to relax control of the curriculum and to reduce the prominence of testing. In 2008/09 it commissioned Sir Jim Rose to conduct an independent review of the primary curriculum with the aim of reducing prescription and content in order to give schools more flexibility over how to teach and how best to supplement the basic curriculum in order to meet local and individual needs. Rose's recommendations for a slimmer national entitlement were adopted in 2009, but had not been implemented by the 2010 General Election. The government rejected a critical report on 'teaching to the test' by the House of Commons Children, Schools and Families Committee (2008) that recommended decoupling assessment from school accountability. Nevertheless it abolished Key Stage 2 tests in science, and piloted a system of 'single tests' with children being entered when teachers thought they were ready rather than at a specific age. National tests at Key Stage 3 (age 14) were scrapped in 2008, partly to do with problems with their delivery, but also to enable a greater focus on learning rather than on testing in the early years of secondary school.

Coalition policies, 2010-15

Labour's policies were radically changed when the coalition was elected in 2010. Two important points must preface detailed discussion of the new government's approach. First, in a climate of austerity and with cuts of up to one-third being made in the spending of some departments, the coalition made an early decision to protect spending on schools. Thus, schools were insulated from the worst effects of the 'cold climate'. Second, the coalition's high-level aims were the same as those of its predecessor: to increase attainment and to reduce inequalities. The focus on addressing inequalities played a prominent part in Michael Gove's campaigning while in opposition, and was a notable and perhaps unexpected position for a government of the Centre-Right.

Yet the government's means of achieving these goals marked a radical departure from what had gone before, with sweeping reform in every major area of the school system. The end of Ed Balls' wider vision for schools was immediately signalled by another renaming of the department, this time to the Department for Education (DfE). Reversing the previous government's promotion of curriculum breadth, vocational qualifications and personal learning, and its tentative withdrawal from some aspects of testing, the coalition set in train a major overhaul of curriculum and assessment with more emphasis on traditional subjects, fewer vocational equivalents and a different approach to assessment with more emphasis on end-of-course examinations. The notion of an English Baccalaureate (e-Bacc), consisting of GCSEs in English, maths, two sciences, history/geography and a language, was introduced and began to be measured, although it was not introduced as a formal qualification. A major change from 2014 was that the number of vocational qualifications counting towards school performance tables was reduced, and each would only count as equivalent to one GCSE. Schools were also no longer allowed to include the results from exam 're-sits' in performance tables. Other curriculum and assessment reforms included:

- a new national curriculum for primary and secondary schools from 2014, with a more traditional emphasis that demanded greater knowledge and skills at earlier ages;
- a different baseline assessment during primary school reception year;
- a new test (a phonics screening check) at the end of Year 1, as well as new internally assessed tests for seven-year-olds;
- a new test in grammar, punctuation and spelling at age 11;
- a switch at GCSE to assessment wholly or mainly by final examination, rather than partly on the basis of course work;
- an overhaul of GCSE programmes placing more emphasis on acquiring factual knowledge;
- reforms of A-levels, including decoupling them from AS-levels.

The coalition also stepped back from Labour's centrally driven approach to school improvement, discontinuing the National Strategies and other central programmes including those targeted at disadvantage. Instead, it set about plans to create a system of autonomous schools. At the heart of this strategy was a new academies programme, allowing outstanding or good schools to convert to academy status (and thus moving the focus away from struggling schools in disadvantaged areas) and introducing new 'free schools' run by parents, charities or other local organisations, including studio schools and university technical colleges (UTCs). Academy status was also extended to primary schools. By January 2014, over half (61%) of secondary schools were academies, and 15% of primary schools.

Academies have freedoms to vary teachers' pay and conditions, and may employ unqualified teachers – one of a number of moves made by the coalition to reform the teaching profession. Others included expanding Teach First and radically changing the system of initial teacher training so that it could be provided by schools directly, weakening the role of universities. While Labour drove improvements in teaching and learning through the National Strategies, the coalition encouraged experienced headteachers to become National or Local Leaders of Education, supporting other schools. At the same time the government changed the inspection regime to make it narrower and tougher. From 2012, schools could no longer be graded 'satisfactory'. If neither 'good' nor 'outstanding', they were deemed to 'require improvement'. A wider range of performance measures was introduced to strengthen school accountability, and floor standards were raised.

Like its predecessor, the new government believed that its overall education reforms would result in better standards of education for disadvantaged students, helping to close the attainment gap. For example, extending Teach First would bring more top graduates into high-poverty schools, and reforms to school performance tables would ensure a closer focus on progress and attainment of children eligible for FSM throughout the attainment range rather than exclusively on the overall numbers reaching expected levels. However, it also tackled this issue through a new flagship policy, the Pupil Premium, a per capita grant to schools for disadvantaged pupils to be spent directly on raising their attainment. The grant started at £488 per pupil, but increased rapidly each year, rising to £1,300 for primary school pupils and £935 for secondary school students by 2014/15, with eligibility widened in 2012/13 to anyone eligible for FSM during the previous six years. Additional premia were available for children of armed services personnel and those in local authority care. Schools were given responsibility for deciding how best to use the Pupil Premium and required to account for their decisions via their websites and through Ofsted inspection. To support school decisions, the government set up an Education Endowment Foundation to identify 'what works' in closing socioeconomic attainment gaps. In contrast to Labour's approach, the Pupil Premium therefore brought the attainment of disadvantaged children more prominently to the attention of all schools, rather than only those in the poorest areas. It emphasised individual rather than school-wide approaches, and classroom and school interventions rather than child poverty and multiagency action. The coalition also discontinued BSF and replaced it with a smaller capital programme targeting schools in the worst physical condition, rather than those in poor areas, and enabling the building of new free schools and academies. Box 4.1 presents a policy summary.

Spending

The effects of these policies on the public purse was that school spending continued to rise in real terms under Labour following the economic crisis, and then was broadly stable under the coalition, rising slightly or falling slightly depending on the definition used (see the following section).

Data from the Public Expenditure Statistical Analysis (PESA) dataset shows that primary school spending in England rose from £20 billion (real terms 2014/15 prices) in 2006/07 to £22.1 billion in 2009/10 (a rise of 10%), and secondary school spending from £29.4 billion to £32.8 billion (up 12%). Under the coalition to 2013/14, primary school spending continued to rise, to £22.4 billion (up 2%), but secondary school spending fell to £30.9 billion (down 6%). The net effect was a slight fall of 3% in overall schools spending between 2009/10 and 2013/14. As a percentage of UK GDP, school spending in England fell from 3.3% of GDP in 2009/10 to 3.0% in 2013/14, although this is a function of the recovery of GDP, and not the small change in school funding.

More salient is the data for per capita spending. As Figure 4.1 shows, while spending rose under Labour between 2006/07 and 2008/09, pupil numbers in state primary and secondary schools declined slightly. However, the coalition encountered a situation of rising primary school numbers, up by a considerable 8% between January 2010 and January 2014. Secondary numbers continued to fall. The result of this was that while per capita spending for both primary and secondary pupils rose under Labour, under the coalition, primary spending per capita fell 6% (from £5,566 per head to £5,240), while secondary spending fell 3% (£10,003 to £9,715). These figures include current and capital spending. They also include a broad definition of school spending, including central functions, and not just direct spending going to schools. In our earlier paper on the coalition (see Lupton and Thomson, 2015a) we used DfE accounts from 2009/10 to 2013/14, which isolate spending going to schools. This remained

Box 4.1: Schools policy timeline

Timeline years: 2007 | 2008 | 2009 | 2010 | 2011 | 2012 | 2013 | 2014 | 2015

2007: Department for Children, Schools and Families created

2011: Department renamed Department for Education

E-bacc introduced (2011)

Increased efforts to target disadvantage through 'Every Child a Reader', 'Narrowing the Gap' and other programmes

Pupil Premium implemented with extra funding schools for each FSM pupil, but discontinuation of other programmes aimed at reducing disadvantage

'City Challenge' approach extended from London to Greater Manchester and the Black Country

Academies Act enables 'converter' Academies and Free Schools

- New degree requirement for new recruits to teaching
- Teaching Schools and Schools Direct
- Pupil Premium criterion changed to 'ever 6'
- Year 1 Phonics screening check

'National Challenge' increased floor standard for schools with threats of closure

- Rose Review signals slimmer and more flexible primary curriculum
- Partial withdrawal from testing (Key Stage 2 science and Key Stage 3 tests)

- Pay reforms
- Only 'outstanding' universities allocated initial teacher training places
- Tests in grammar, punctuation and spelling replace writing at Key Stage 2

- Pupil Premium loaded to primary
- First performance tables reflecting reduced vocational offer and revised equivalences
- New national curriculum

Children's plan signals wider role for schools

New GCSE syllabus for English and maths and other subjects to follow

Figure 4.1: Spending on primary and secondary schools against total pupil numbers, 2007/08 to 2014/15, England (real terms 2014/15 prices)

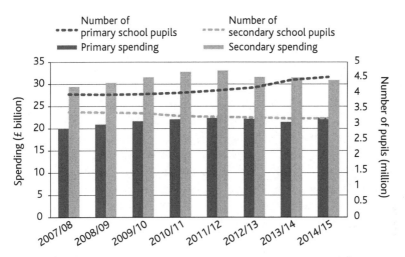

Notes: Expenditure by country and sub-function of education in PESA is available for five-year intervals on a consistent basis. Here PESA 2015 has been used for 2009/10 to 2013/14 and PESA 2012 for 2006/07 to 2008/09. For this reason expenditure on primary and secondary education for the period between 2006/07 and 2008/09 is not strictly comparable to 2009-10 to 2013-14 but these data offer the best broad view of education spending.

Sources: Spending data is from PESA 2012 (HM Treasury, 2012) and 2015 (HM Treasury, 2015b); pupil numbers are from 'Schools, pupils and their characteristics' (DfE SFR 16/2015) (DfE 2015c)

broadly constant (a rise of 1%). Sibieta (2015) reports a rise of 3% over the period 2010/11 to 2014/15 (0.6% on a per capita basis). The PESA dataset is used here to provide a consistent time series spanning both governments, but the slightly different picture that it shows compared with what is typically thought of as 'the schools budget' or 'day-to-day school spending' needs to be borne in mind.

A key point of debate has been whether the coalition's Pupil Premium actually increased the budgets of schools with the most disadvantaged intakes, given that many of the other grants to these schools were cut, and that the coalition also simplified the system by which local authorities distribute funding to schools, which will have had variable local effects. Labour's various grants and funding rule changes had also amounted, in effect, to a Pupil Premium, significantly increasing the loading to schools with poorer intakes within the funding system (Sibieta et al, 2008). Our analysis of these data, which is set out more fully in Lupton and Thomson (2015b), shows that it was not until 2013/14 that the Pupil Premium exceeded the value of the grants it replaced. However, it did have redistributive effects. Figure 4.2 shows the percentage change in school-level grant income per capita, splitting primary and secondary schools into groups based on their proportion of pupils eligible for FSM in 2013/14.

The least deprived group of secondary schools experienced real terms losses in income of around 0.1%, while more deprived schools had real terms increases (of around 4.3% for the most deprived schools). For primary schools, the least deprived schools (about 40% of all primary schools) experienced a small increase in grant funding (of around 3.2%), while the most deprived schools experienced a larger increase (of around 11.2%).[2] Estimates from the National Audit Office (NAO) for the period 2010/11 to 2014/15, and using a different classification of schools, show smaller increases and larger decreases, but broadly the same redistributive pattern (NAO, 2015). Both our own and NAO analysis also show that a more complex picture underlies these headline results. Within each band, the range is very wide and some schools have seen significant losses. Thus, although the Pupil Premium has had a positive effect for disadvantaged schools as a whole, its effect has not been uniform. Moreover, at around 3% of the overall school budget,

Figure 4.2: Changes in school-level income per pupil by FSM band, 2009/10 to 2013/14, England

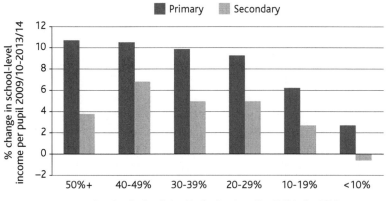

Bands of schools by % of school pupils eligible for FSM

Notes: Maintained schools here means those schools maintained by the local authority and so does not include academies. Data for academies is not directly comparable to that for maintained schools. Schools with unrepresentative funding (for example those in the process of closing at the time of financial reporting) have been excluded from calculations. Another version of this analysis, in 2009/10 prices, appears in earlier publications (see Lupton and Thomson, 2015a).

Sources: Authors' calculations from consistent financial reporting data for maintained schools (2009/10 and 2013/14) and GDP deflators (HM Treasury, 2015c)

it can by no means be regarded as a panacea for the problem of wide socioeconomic attainment gaps.

Inputs and outputs

Given the relative stability in spending under the coalition, there is less to say about the effect on system resources than in some of the other chapters in this book, where large changes in spending played out in significant changes to the services provided. For schools, broadly speaking, the data show that the main period of system transformation (extra staff, reduced class sizes and so on) coincided with increased spending during Labour's second term in the early 2000s (for a more detailed account, see Lupton and Obolenksaya, 2013), with more gradual change in the later period of Labour government. Under the coalition, the broad picture is one of stability, although with some signs of increasing pressure as funding was held constant and pupil numbers grew.

We show some of the detail here. As Figure 4.3 shows, there were very substantial increases in the school workforce under Labour, far exceeding the increase in the number of pupils, and with the biggest increase coming in the numbers of support staff rather than the number of teachers. The number of full-time equivalent (FTE) teachers grew by 11% between 1997 and 2010, an extra 48,000 teachers, with 8,700

Figure 4.3: Trends in numbers of teachers and teaching assistants, 1997-2014, England

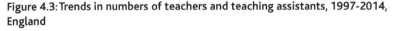

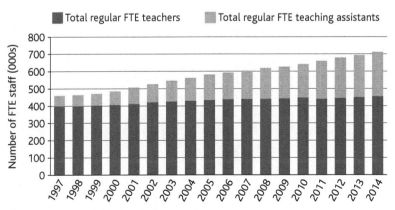

Note: Figures are for January for the period 1997-2010 and November thereafter (see Note 3).

Sources: Data from 'School workforce in England' (DfE SFR 21/2015, DCSF SFR 23/2009, DCSF 29/2007 (DfE 2015b, DCSF 2009, DCSF 2007b))

of these being added between January 2007 and January 2010. The number of FTE teaching assistants more than trebled (1997-2010), with the addition of 134,000 extra FTE staff, and 30,000 of that number added between January 2007 and January 2010).[3] Under the coalition, FTE teacher numbers increased by 2% to 2014, and FTE regular teaching assistants by 31%, additions of around 7,000 and 61,000 respectively.

These increases in the number of teachers (January 2010-15) were slightly lower than increases in the number of pupils, at 4%, but not sufficiently so to increase overall pupil-teacher ratios and pupil-adult ratios, which stabilised having been on a declining trajectory under Labour. Primary class sizes, however, did start to rise. As Figure 4.4 shows, this increase started in 2009 and continued under the coalition. Meanwhile the opposite trend occurred for secondary schools. By 2015, the average class size in primary schools had risen to its highest point (27 pupils), while the average in secondary schools was at its lowest (20.1 pupils).

The proportion of primary school pupils taught in large classes also started to rise in some areas, particularly Outer London, as teacher numbers failed to keep pace with the growing primary age population. Keeping primary school classes small had been a priority of the Labour government elected in 1997, and there were very substantial reductions in the proportions of children taught in large classes in all regions in the early 2000s, especially in London. These trends continued

Figure 4.4: Average class sizes of primary and secondary schools, 1997-2015, England

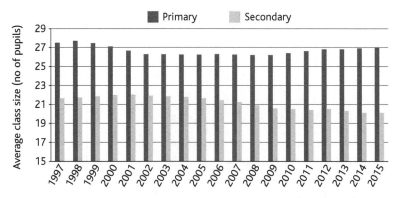

Source: Data from 1997 to 2001 are from 'Schools in England 2001' (HMSO 2001)); data from 2002 to 2005 are from 'Schools and pupils in England 2005' (DfES SFR 42/2005) (DfES 2005); data from 2006 to 2010 are from 'Schools, pupils and their characteristics 2010' (DfE SFR 09/2010)(DfE 2010b) and data for 2015 are from 'Schools, pupils and their characteristics 2015' (DfE SFR 16/2015) (DfE 2015b)

under Labour from 2007 to 2010, but in a number of regions, a slight increase in the proportion of pupils in large classes was seen between 2010 and 2015 (see Table 4.1). The proportion of inner London pupils educated in large classes is strikingly low in all years, a factor perhaps worthy of further investigation in accounts of London's relative educational success.

Estimates of system quality are harder to make for two reasons. First, the notion of quality in education is a contested one, as academic and public debate over reforms to teaching and examinations show. There is a widely held view, cited by the House of Commons Children, Schools and Families Committee (2010), that the current generation of teachers are the 'best yet', with high standards of training and professional practice (that is, we have higher quality teaching). We also see continuing evidence of increased attendance at school. Absence rates fell steadily during the 2000s and continued to fall under the coalition, as did the rate of permanent exclusions (for further details, see Lupton and Obolenskaya, 2013; Lupton and Thomson, 2015a). However, critics also argue that teachers' work has become increasingly defined by routinised preparation of pupils for standardised tests, and thus, that the depth of knowledge and quality of pedagogical relationships has diminished (that is, we have lower quality education despite higher quality teaching staff) (for one recent example, see Hutchings, 2015). Educationalists are also divided over

Table 4.1: Percentage of primary pupils (in one teacher classes) in a class of 31 or more, English regions

	2001	2007	2010	2015
North West	26	17	13	15
East Midlands	25	18	14	15
South West	24	18	14	13
Yorkshire and the Humber	23	17	15	16
South East	22	16	13	14
West Midlands	21	13	11	12
East of England	19	13	10	11
North East	19	12	11	8
Outer London	18	8	8	10
Inner London	6	3	3	2
England	21	14	12	12

Source: Data from 1997 to 2001 are from 'Schools in England 2001' (HMSO 2001)); data from 2002 to 2005 are from 'Schools and pupils in England 2005' (DfES SFR 42/2005) (DfES 2005); data from 2006 to 2010 are from 'Schools, pupils and their characteristics 2010' (DfE SFR 09/2010)(DfE 2010b) and data for 2015 are from 'Schools, pupils and their characteristics 2015' (DfE SFR 16/2015) (DfE 2015b)

whether allowing access to many vocational options is better because it increases engagement, confidence and success, or worse because it tracks predominantly working-class pupils into options that have lower labour market value. These kinds of wider questions are beyond the scope of our current work, which is limited to the quantitative measures available.

Second, although there are data on school quality (the findings of Ofsted inspections), these are hard to compare over time, since the framework for inspection is regularly changed. It appears that there was a genuine improvement between 2005/06 and 2009/10, when the Ofsted framework was stable, with a halving of the percentage of secondary schools deemed inadequate (from 13% to 6%), and a doubling of the proportion deemed outstanding, from 10% to 22% (Francis, 2011) Ofsted's 2014 annual report suggests that the quality of schools also improved under the coalition. In 2014, 81% were rated 'good' or 'outstanding' compared with 66% in 2009. However, it is harder to be sure about this because the grading system moved from a five-point to a four-point scale. Ofsted also noted in 2014 that secondary schools' performance had 'stalled': the proportion of secondary schools rated 'inadequate' had risen in the last year, from 3% to 6% and from 5% to 11% in the most deprived fifth of areas. The proportion of secondary schools rated as having 'inadequate' leadership almost doubled between 2012 and 2014. At the same time, there was a series of high-profile cases of financial mismanagement in some academies and concerns about the oversight of teaching and learning in others.

This highlighted the difficulties of managing an autonomous school system and led to critical reports from the NAO, Public Accounts Committee and House of Commons Education Committees about the lack of oversight in the new system and its implications for school quality (NAO, 2012; House of Commons Committee of Public Accounts, 2015b; House of Commons Education Committee, 2015). Separate concerns also emerged about the impact of the coalition's teaching reforms. Although it remains the case that the vast majority of teachers are qualified, the percentage of lessons taught by teachers with a relevant qualification fell in all subjects between 2010 and 2013 (88.4% to 84.8% in English, 83.6% to 82.7% in maths and 89.1% to 87.6% in science). Teacher unions and the School Teachers Review Body also started to highlight the potential for teacher shortages, due to lack of take-up of the new teacher training routes, reforms to teachers' pay, high workloads, high professional risk for headteachers and falling morale, as well as to the economic recovery, which will tend to diminish the relative attraction of teaching.

Outcomes

Last, we look at the outcomes of policy in terms of achievements up to the age of 16.[4] We look first at overall attainment, then at socioeconomic inequalities as measured by gaps between pupils eligible for FSM and others, and briefly at a wider range of outcomes, so far as is possible. A critical issue in reading all of these data is their possible relationships to policy. Most of the coalition's major reforms to curriculum and assessment had not come into effect at all by the time the tests reported here were taken. Some at GCSE level had come into effect by 2014, a point that we explore closely. Moreover, the effects of policy on education results are always hard to assess, since education is cumulative. Improving results in GCSEs, for example, may be due to better prior knowledge and skills of the cohort coming through, due to earlier primary school policy changes, as much as they are to do with policy or practice in the GCSE phase.

The overall pattern is that attainments in standard tests rose during the period covered by this book and were higher at the end than at the start. However, tests at the end of primary school (Key Stage 2) show different trends than those at age 16, and there are differences in trends between subjects and depending on which measures are used.

Key Stage 2 results in maths appeared to plateau between 2007 and 2010 after rising steadily since 2000. They then rose from 2010, with a particularly sharp rise in 2012. In 2014, 86% of children reached the expected level in Key Stage 2 maths. In reading, results actually fell between 2008 and 2010, before rising again under the coalition.[5] In 2014, 89% of children reached the expected level, after a slight dip in 2013.

At GCSE level, as Figure 4.5 shows, there was a very marked improvement between 2007 and 2010. This was most pronounced in the 5 GCSE A*-C measure (which rose from 59.9% to 75.6%) but was also evident in the 5 GCSE A*-C measure including English and maths (hereafter 5 A*-C EM). Possible explanations include the effects of the secondary National Strategies and other school improvement initiatives, the higher attainments of children entering GCSE cohorts and the effect of the National Challenge, announced in 2008, which put immediate pressure on 638 schools below the floor standard to raise their attainments or face closure, as well as providing additional support. On the other hand, Jerrim (2012) notes that achievements of English students in international tests did not show the same improvement over this period, adding weight to claims that the GCSE results reflect greater success in getting pupils through exams or more channelling into vocational equivalents in response to school performance pressures.

Under the coalition, until 2013, the upward trend in both measures continued. However, in 2014, GCSE results fell – by a drop of 17.5 percentage points in the proportion passing 5 GCSEs at A★-C (from 83% to 65.5%), and 4 points on the 5 A★-C EM measure (from 60.6% to 56.6%). As a result, the proportion gaining 5 A★-C in 2014 was 10.5 percentage points lower than it had been in 2010, while the proportion gaining 5 A★-C EM was 1.5 percentage points higher.

In 2014 the coalition made changes to the counting of vocational qualifications and early entries, introduced linear GCSEs and removed speaking and listening from the assessment of the English GCSE. Perhaps the key point to note is that the dramatic drop in results at 5 A★-C took that measure back to its 2008 level, indicating that the increase since that time had nearly all been driven by vocational entries and exam re-sits. However, this is not the whole story. The broad-dashed line in Figure 4.5 shows the results re-calibrated to include everything in 2014 that would have been included in 2013. This allows a like-for-like comparison. As is shown, results at 5 A★-C also fell in 2014 on this basis, although the same trend is not evident when English and maths are included (5 A★-C EM). Thus it appears that the changes to the assessment of GCSEs have resulted in genuinely lower

Figure 4.5: Trends in Key Stage 2 and GCSE attainment, 1997-2014, England

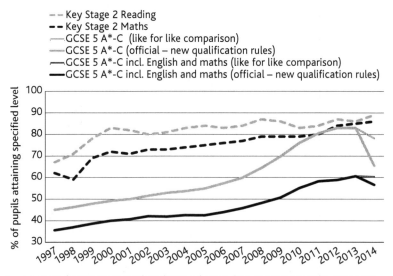

Sources: Data for Key Stage 2 is from 'National curriculum assessments at Key Stage 2 in England, 2014 (revised)' (DfE SFR 50/2014) (DfE 2014d); GCSE data is from 'Revised GCSE and equivalents results in England, 2013-2014' (DfE SFR 02/2015) (DfE 2015c)

attainment for some of those young people working at the lower end of the attainment spectrum.

In terms of socioeconomic inequalities, we see a similar pattern of improvement (narrowing gaps) at primary level, and also at secondary level until 2013, but with gaps widening in 2014 (see Table 4.2). We pay particular attention here to the GCSE results. Three points are notable. One is that both under Labour and the coalition, only very modest progress was made in closing the gap at 5 A*-C EM, which stood at 28 percentage points when Ed Balls took office, 27.7 points when Michael Gove took over, and 27 points in 2014. This is despite the considerable political priority and spending devoted to narrowing educational inequalities. Second, there is no evidence of a Pupil Premium effect in either of the GCSE measures. This is not surprising, given that it was not until 2013/14 that the Pupil Premium represented extra funding for schools overall, and that any policy could be expected to take time to bed down, but nevertheless salient to recall given the strong claims made about the importance of this policy. Third, the genuine falls in attainment in 2014 referred to above seem to have been experienced by poorer (FSM-eligible) students more than others (non-FSM-eligible). Table 4.2 shows the results and FSM gaps in 2014, both according to the new counting rules (the official results) and the old rules (the like-for-like comparison so that any underlying changes can be seen). At 5 A*-C, the gap between poorer and other pupils (the FSM gap) widened between 2013 and 2014 under the new rules by 12 percentage points, but by less than 1 point at 5 A*-C EM. This indicates the importance of vocational equivalents and early entries for lower-attaining FSM pupils in particular. Moreover, the like-for-like comparison also shows a widening gap at 5 A*-C, from 16 to 19.8 percentage points. Further investigation is needed to determine whether this is due to the GCSE changes or to factors outside the school, such as reductions in family income or local service provision described elsewhere in this volume.

Wider outcomes for children and young people are much harder to measure consistently, and no conclusive overall picture can be given. In our more extended work on the coalition's record (see Lupton and Thomson, 2015a), we attempted to review progress on the 41 indicators introduced by Labour to monitor progress on its five *Every Child Matters* objectives – that children should 'be healthy', 'stay safe', 'enjoy and achieve', 'achieve economic well-being' and 'make a positive contribution'. Many of these are hard to monitor before 2010 because the data sources were new and no trend could be established. Of those that could be monitored, most improved – for example, the

Table 4.2: Performance against key attainment measures by FSM status, 2002-14, England

Year	Key Stage 2 maths expected level			GCSE 5+ A*-C			GCSE 5 A*-C including English and maths		
	FSM eligible	Non-FSM eligible	Attainment gap	FSM eligible	Non-FSM eligible	Attainment gap	FSM eligible	Non-FSM eligible	Attainment gap
2002	54	77	23	23	53.7	30.7			
2003	53	76	23	24.4	55.2	30.8			
2004	55	78	23	26.1	56.1	30			
2005	56	78	22	29.9	58.9	29			
2006	58	79	21	32.6	60.7	28.1	19.6	47.7	28.1
2007	60	80	20	36.5	62.8	26.3	21.4	49.4	28
2008	63	81	18	40	67	27	23.8	51.7	27.9
2009	64	82	18	48.9	72.8	23.9	26.6	54.3	27.7
2010	66	83	17	58.6	78.8	20.2	31.2	58.8	27.6
2011	67.1	83.3	16.2	64.7	83.1	18.4	34.6	62	27.4
2012	72.6	86.7	14.1	68.9	85.3	16.4	36.3	62.6	26.3
2013	73.8	87.1	13.3	69.3	85.3	16	37.9	64.6	26.7
2014 Old rules	75	88	13	61.2	81	19.8	37	64.2	27.2
New rules				41.6	69.6	28	33.5	60.5	27

Notes: Data are for all pupils in state-funded schools; in 2010, industrial action meant the state school participation rate for Key Stage 2 tests was 74%.

Sources:

Key Stage 2: Figures for 2002-06 are reproduced from previous analysis of the National Pupil Database in Lupton and Obolenskaya (2013); 2010 onwards is from 'National curriculum assessments at Key Stage 2 in England' (DfE SFR 35/2010, DfE SFR 33/2012, DfE SFR 50/2014 (DfE 2010d, DfE 2012a, DfE 2014d))

GCSE: Figures for 2002-05 are reproduced from previous analysis of the National Pupil Database in Lupton and Obolenskaya (2013); 2006 onwards is from 'GCSE and equivalent attainment by pupil characteristics' (DfE SFR 37/2010, DfE SFR 06/2015) (DfE 2010e, DfE 2015e)

falls in school absence reported earlier and the proportion of children staying in full-time education after 16. Vizard and Obolenskaya (2013) report reductions in infant mortality and the closing of socioeconomic gaps and a halt in the long-run trend towards greater child obesity after 2006-08.

Under the coalition the wider goals relating to child wellbeing, as expressed in the *Every Child Matters* framework, were largely dropped, and some data was no longer collected. There were some improvements – for example, in the proportion of young people aged 16-18 not in education, employment or training (NEET), which fell after a long period of stagnation when Labour's Raising the Participation Age (RPA) policy, announced in 2007, came into effect in 2013. Of those indicators that show decline under the coalition, many relate to vulnerable groups such as disabled children, care leavers and looked-after children. Such indicators include the percentage of children subject to child protection plans for a second (or subsequent) time, child protection cases reviewed within required timescales, special educational needs (SEN) statements issued within 26 weeks and care leavers in employment, education or training. The education attainment indicators included in the *Every Child Matters* indicator set for looked-after children have either improved or stayed stable since 2010. However, the government's own impact indicators covering this issue, which are slightly different measures, show the trend getting worse. These partial and sometimes conflicting data serve mainly to illustrate the heavy emphasis currently given in English policy to cognitive attainments rather than other aspects of children and young people's development.

Conclusion

In some of the other policy areas reported in this book, the key story of the 'cold climate' era is one of cutbacks and their effects. For schools policy, a protected spending area, differences in spending before and after 2010 are much less pronounced than differences in policy. Many commentators, the lead author of this chapter included (see Lupton, 2011), have pointed to policy continuities in some areas, or at least the ways in which the logics of a marketised system (standardisation, performance measurement, institutional autonomy, competition and choice) became embedded in the Labour years and were extended under the coalition. Nevertheless there were huge differences in policy between Gordon Brown's Labour government with Ed Balls as Education Secretary and David Cameron's coalition government with Michael Gove at the helm. For Brown and Balls, there were academy schools to raise standards in the most disadvantaged areas, a broad vision of education including wider childhood outcomes and multiagency working as well as vocational routes, and the beginnings of a withdrawal from testing, as well as a centralised approach to improving schools. For Cameron and Gove, an academised system was to become the norm, based on the principle that school autonomy works best, an overhaul of curriculum and assessment at all levels, emphasised traditional academic rigour, linear examinations and increased testing, and there was a liberalised approach to school improvement based on school autonomy, chains and federations. The coalition's reforms of the teaching profession and training were another key difference.

The scale and pace of the reforms since 2010 are exceptional in the history of education policy in England. As we write in 2015, they are still rolling out. It is far too early to produce any conclusive evaluation of their effects. Given the scale of the changes and the inevitable data time lags, learning from historical and international comparison, qualitative studies and practice will be as important as scrutinising the quantitative evidence in the UK. Early indications are that there substantial challenges in managing an autonomous schools system, and risks to quality, and that despite the emphasis given to addressing disadvantage through the Pupil Premium, outcomes for some of the most disadvantaged students may have been negatively affected by the broader curriculum and assessment changes, as well as, perhaps, by the broader austerity measures documented elsewhere in this book. Education cannot be considered in a vacuum.

The Conservative government elected in 2015 promised more of the same: compulsory e-Bacc subjects, re-sits in Year 7, more academies and free schools, more scrutiny of 'coasting schools' leading to new leadership or closures, along with a continued emphasis on narrowing inequalities through the Pupil Premium, but continued welfare reform and the abolition of child poverty targets. At the same time, it promised to protect school funding in cash terms, implying a real terms decrease, in the face of rising pupil numbers and cost pressures. Whether schools can be expected to relentlessly increase attainment and narrow inequalities in a colder funding climate and in the face of deeper austerity measures across the board remains to be seen. The challenge of so doing may well ultimately stimulate a broader debate about what schools are for and their contributions to the fairer, more social mobile society to which both the current government and its mainstream political opponents are committed.

Notes

[1] Tests were taken in English, maths and science, and the results vary slightly according to subject. Parsimoniously, the figure given here reflects the average of the maths and English scores.

[2] Sibieta (2015) points out that one reason that individual school income has increased more than the overall schools budget is that more of the schools budget is now devolved to schools. However, they have had to take on greater responsibilities correspondingly. The change in the overall schools budget, per pupil, is therefore a better guide to the real change in school resources.

[3] Prior to 2010, teacher and teaching assistant numbers were sourced from the School Census or local authority data returns (Form 618g), and were collated to produce figures for overall numbers in January of each year. From 2010, the data started to be collected in the School Workforce Census, but only 83 local authorities had completed this to a satisfactory standard by January 2010, and so the figures for January 2010 contain data from the School Workforce Census and the other sources used previously. From November 2010, all data derives from the School Workforce Census, but figures for teaching assistants in November 2010 are estimates due to large amounts of missing data. We therefore use January figures for years to and including 2010, and November data for years thereafter.

[4] A-level and vocational equivalents are covered in Chapter Five, on further and higher education and skills.

[5] Due to post-2010 changes in measures and assessments, we cannot consistently report on Key Stage 2 English over this whole period, only reading.

FIVE

Further and higher education and skills

Ruth Lupton, Lorna Unwin and Stephanie Thomson

The situation on the eve of the crisis

In December 2006, six months prior to Gordon Brown's new ministerial team taking office, the Leitch Review of Skills (2006) set out an analysis of the challenges the government faced. Using qualifications as a proxy for skills, Leitch argued that the UK's skills base had improved significantly. Between 1994 and 2005, the proportion of people with a qualification at Level 4 (sub-degree level) or above had risen from 21% to 29%, and the proportion with no qualifications had fallen from 22% to 13%, while 42% of those aged 18-30 were participating in higher education (HE), more than ever before. The number of apprentices had more than trebled since Labour took office in 1997. However, other countries had also been improving their skills, often from a higher base, so the UK's skills base was mediocre by comparison with international competitors. The proportion of people with no or low qualifications was more than double that in Sweden, Japan and Canada. Youth unemployment was already rising, even during the boom years of the 2000s, and the proportion of 16- to 18-year-olds not in education, employment or training (NEET) hovered steadily around the 9 to 10% mark, despite rising school attainment. Post-16 participation in education and training was below the OECD average. Fewer than 40% of people were qualified to intermediate level, compared with more than 50% in countries such as Germany and New Zealand. The situation for high skills was better, around the international average, but the UK was investing substantially less in higher education than leading competitors, and being overtaken by countries that were improving their participation rates faster (OECD, 2010).

Thus, although the UK was in a strong economic position, with a comparatively high employment rate and sustained economic growth, its competitiveness was increasingly at risk, with productivity lagging well behind countries such as France, Germany and the US. Leitch argued that improving skills was central to achieving a fairer and less unequal society: unequal access to skills had contributed to high rates of child poverty and income inequality, and there were clear links between skills and wider outcomes such as health, crime and social cohesion. Importantly, Leitch pointed out that the task of improving skills could not be left to schools, since 70% of the 2020 workforce had already completed their compulsory education.

The Leitch Review was criticised at the time for assuming that the level and volume of skills in the UK could be raised by setting targets (expressed as qualifications), and that employers would respond to the call to raise their demand for skills (see, among others, Wolf, 2007; Keep, 2008) – both problems that have plagued subsequent policy efforts. Nevertheless, its positioning of the UK as 'behind the game' in the late 2000s has been reiterated in a number of other reviews. Partly the problem was demand-led – the UK as a whole had (and has) too few businesses in high-skill, high-value-added industries (UKCES, 2009; Mayhew and Keep, 2014). However, many commentators also agreed that the education and skills system was partly to blame. The landscape of provision was exceptionally complex, with no state-led system for awarding qualifications, and a plethora of awarding bodies, training providers and intermediary bodies such as Sector Skills Councils (SSCs) (Unwin et al, 2004). The system was also prone to frequent re-organisation, a point noted in a critical OECD review (Hoeckel et al, 2009), which also cited problems of weak employer engagement and a weaker apprenticeship system. Although concentrating primarily on adult skills, Leitch asserted that the structure of the UK education system was a major barrier to developing post-16 participation. He argued that the government must deliver a fully integrated 14-19 phase with parity of esteem for vocational routes, a recommendation also made by the Tomlinson Working Group on 14-19 reform (DfES, 2004), whose proposals had largely been rejected by the Labour government (for a discussion, see Pring et al, 2009).

In relation to HE, although the need to expand participation and equalise access was recognised, successive governments had struggled with finding a sustainable funding solution. Labour's Higher Education Act 2004 had controversially introduced variable ('top-up') fees to a maximum of £3,000 per year, and moved them from an up-front payment to the model of taxing graduates, with effect from 2006, while reinstating maintenance grants. But further reform was widely expected as leading universities complained that the fee income was insufficient while large social class gaps in participation remained.

Thus, even before the global financial crisis and ensuing recession led to rising unemployment and low labour demand, the area of post-compulsory education and training was one that represented a sizeable policy challenge – a 'mountain to climb', as the Labour government described it (HM Government, 2007, p 6).

Labour policies, 2007-10

A first swift response to the Leitch Review came in departmental reorganisation following Gordon Brown's election as Labour leader. A new Department for Innovation, Universities and Skills (DIUS) brought universities under the same remit as other adult learning, although still leaving education for 16- to 18-year-olds with the former Education Department (renamed the Department for Children, Schools and Families [DCSF] in a controversial move that removed 'education' from the title). In 2008, it was announced that the Learning and Skills Council (LSC) would be replaced in April 2010 by the Skills Funding Agency (SFA) covering 19+ and the Young People's Learning Agency (YPLA) covering 16- to 18-year-olds.[1] In 2009, the National Apprenticeship Service was established. These changes were enshrined in the Apprenticeships, Skills, Children and Learning Act 2009, which provided a statutory framework for apprenticeship including an entitlement for all 'suitably qualified young people' to the offer of an apprenticeship place from 2013.

Brown's government pledged to climb the skills mountain, committing itself to Leitch's ambition of making England[2] a world leader in skills by 2020, benchmarked against the top quartile of OECD countries. However, the new policies fell short of radical change, and importantly, accepted Leitch's emphasis on raising the volume of qualifications, taking these as a proxy for skills. For adults, a key decision was to more than double the funding for the Train to Gain programme introduced in 2006 between 2007/08 and 2010/11.

Train to Gain was the policy response to Leitch's recommendation that training should be 'demand-led'. The scheme provided funding for individuals who were already employed to train (both in and outside the workplace) and gain qualifications in line with both individual and employer needs. Employers with fewer than 50 employees received funding to compensate them for the time employees spent training away from the workplace. Training eligible for full funding included basic literacy and numeracy and training leading to NVQ Level 2 for employees who had not already achieved this. Full funding was also available for Level 3 qualifications for 19- to 25-year-old employees, with employers expected to co-fund Level 3 for other employees. Skills brokers were appointed to provide advice to employers (including those considered 'hard to reach') and help them source training. Learner Accounts were introduced to record individuals' training and how much it cost.[3] Despite the fact that by April 2009, government data showed that 1.25 million people had started training and 554,100 had gained a qualification, Train to Gain was heavily criticised for concentrating on accreditation rather than on new skills development and on the grounds of value for money. The National Audit Office (NAO) also found that 50% of employers would have funded the training provided by Train to Gain in any case, and concluded that 'over its full lifetime the programme has not provided good value for money' (NAO, 2009, p 7).

Among other policies, a new UK Commission on Employment and Skills (UKCES) was set up to advise the government on skills and employment strategy and targets, monitor progress, ensure the integration of employment and skills services and oversee reformed SSCs. A voluntary skills pledge was introduced for employers, committing them to supporting their staff to gain basic literacy and numeracy skills, and also to work to towards achieving a first full Level 2 qualification. The government continued to support the work of Union Learning representatives through the Union Learning Fund (ULF), originally set up in 1998 and from 2007 managed by UnionLearn, a branch of the Trades Union Congress (TUC). Other reforms already underway following a 2006 White Paper included the introduction of 14-19 diplomas in a range of vocational sectors, the establishment of national skills academies and more HE in further education (FE) colleges.

The Brown government retained the Educational Maintenance Allowance (EMA), a weekly cash allowance of up to £30 payable to young people aged 16-19 from low-income families remaining in full-time education. But perhaps the key decision in this later period was to announce the intention to raise the compulsory education and training participation age (Raising the Participation Age [RPA]), to 17 in 2013 and 18 in 2015, a policy that would rely on future governments to carry it through.

Finally, the last year of Labour's term in office saw a further departmental reorganisation. The financial crisis had stimulated Labour to drop some of its previous antipathy to intervening in the way businesses operated, and in 2008, Peter Mandelson was brought back by Gordon Brown from serving as a European commissioner and given a seat in the House of Lords so that he could re-enter government, as Secretary of State at the Department for Business, Enterprise and

Regulatory Reform (BERR). Two White Papers, *Innovation Nation* (DIUS, 2008) and *New Industry, New Jobs* (BERR, 2009) set out plans to identify key sectors and industries for intervention in what was called a strategy for 'industrial activism', to be funded through a Capital Fund of £750 million. In 2009 the departments were merged to form the Department for Business, Innovation and Skills (BIS), with Mandelson as Secretary of State, meaning that one department now controlled adult (19+) and HE, science and innovation, and regional policy. An early BIS White Paper, *Skills for growth* (BIS, 2009) called for greater emphasis on technician and associate professional skills, an aspiration that continued into the coalition. It also noted that government had the power to grant 'skills strategy setting powers' to sub-regional bodies. This aligned with provision in the Local Democracy, Economic Development and Construction Act 2009 to enable some cities (initially London, Leeds and Manchester) to develop combined city authorities. At the same time, the nine Regional Development Agencies (RDAs) set up in 2001 were to be strengthened. Labour took steps, therefore, towards a 'localism agenda' that would be pursued more vigorously under the coalition.

One of Mandelson's key decisions was to appoint Lord Browne to review HE funding and to make recommendations to ensure that university teaching in the future could be 'world class', sustainably financed and accessible to anyone with the talent to succeed. The outcome of the review was still unknown at the time of the election.

Coalition policies, 2010-15

As we elaborate in our earlier working paper (see Lupton et al, 2015a), substantial proposals around FE and HE and skills were developed in opposition both by the Liberal Democrats and by the Conservatives, but these were very different from each other. The Liberal Democrats' proposals included abolishing tuition fees, fully meeting the up-front costs of adult apprenticeships and bringing GCSEs, A-levels and vocational qualifications together in a general diploma. The Conservatives made no pledges on HE funding (preferring to wait for the outcome of the Browne review), but promised to divert Train to Gain funding into apprenticeships and establish an all-age careers service. The Conservative agenda largely triumphed once the coalition was elected, with an ambitious reform programme attempting to address many of the challenges Leitch had identified, although through a less centrally managed approach, and with a strong emphasis on the quality of provision. However, none of these policy areas were protected from the coalition's cuts to departmental budgets, so the reforms were made in the context of substantial financial cutbacks, as we document in the next section.

In 2010, BIS published its new skills strategy document, *Skills for sustainable growth*, citing Leitch's argument for the need to increase adult skills, but abolishing Leitch's targets and desirous of moving away from the 'machinery of central control' (BIS, 2010a, p 13). The new government's purpose was to 'return the economy to sustainable growth, extend social inclusion and social mobility and build the Big Society', saying that 'underpinning every aspect of this purpose is the improvement of skills' (BIS, 2010a, p 4). Again, echoing Leitch, the goal was a 'demand-led' system with employers and individuals rather than the state making decisions, although they would also now be expected to share more of the costs. In 2011, the government took up UKCES' plan for an Employer Ownership of Skills initiative to establish a a co-investment approach with public contributions being channelled through employers in order to ensure employer ownership (UKCES, 2011, p 22). However, a government-commissioned evaluation of the first round pilots concluded that 'sustainability is an ongoing concern due to a general view that, without the continuing stimulus of public funding, the continuation of projects is unlikely' (BIS, 2015b, p 14). Moreover, perhaps surprisingly, given the emphasis on employers driving the system and in light of the cuts, the new government continued to match the funding commitment of Labour to UnionLearn until 2013, when funding was cut back to £18.7 million, to £15.3 million in 2014, and to £14 million in 2015.

In the arena of adult skills, the coalition immediately carried through on plans to cut back on Train to Gain, and to focus on expanding apprenticeships, which were now positioned as the main vehicle for skills training for both young people and adults. Reforms of the apprenticeship system followed in 2013, after a review by Doug Richard. Pre-apprenticeship traineeships were introduced in 2013 for 16- to 23-year-olds, and Trailblazers (employer panels) were set up to develop new apprenticeship standards, with a minimum 12-month term. The funding arrangements were to be changed so that funds would go directly to employers (with a compulsory cash contribution from them), not providers, enabling them to shape provision and drive down costs. As we write, the details of the new funding arrangements are still being thrashed out, including a consultation over whether an apprenticeship levy should be introduced. While these reforms seemed to address some of the longstanding criticisms of apprenticeships in the UK (low quality and lack of employer engagement), the impact of the Trailblazers on raising standards is yet to be seen. Beyond apprenticeships, during 2013 and 2014, some adult qualifications began to be reformed. The SFA removed public funding from 2,800 qualifications and adopted new business rules for approving future funding. Cuts to funding for another 5,000 qualifications was scheduled for 2014/15. A stronger regulatory framework was promised to ensure quality. A significant change, from 2013, and in tandem with a decline in the Adult Skills Budget (ASB), was the introduction of Advanced Learning Loans for people aged 24 and upwards to study at Level 3 or above. One Conservative policy pledge not carried through was the creation of an all-age careers service. The National Careers Service was created to focus on guidance for adults but with a smaller budget for advertising than its predecessor, while responsibility for careers guidance for young people was placed with schools.

As Chapter Thirteen explores more fully later, both regional economic rebalancing and 'localism' became prominent themes under the coalition. Early moves were the abolition of the RDAs, the establishment of 39 Local Enterprise Partnerships (LEPs), the 2011 Localism Act, which included an invitation to city leaders to make the case for more devolved powers, and a series of City Deals providing funding for initiatives covering transport, labour markets and economic development. Further momentum was gathered following Lord Heseltine's report, *No stone unturned: In pursuit of growth* (BIS, 2012), commissioned by George Osborne and BIS Secretary of State, Vince Cable, which was widely welcomed across the political spectrum and noted for its echoes of Peter Mandelson's 2009 White Paper. Funds available to LEPs were boosted through the establishment of the Local Growth Fund and in November 2014, the government took the significant step of a 'devolution deal' with Greater Manchester Combined Authority (and later Sheffield, West Yorkshire and Cornwall), extending certain powers related to economic development to the city-region level. Initially, in relation to skills, the Greater Manchester Agreement states that devolution is intended to enable the local authorities 'directly to re-shape and re-structure the Further Education (FE) provision within Greater Manchester so that a new, forward looking FE system is in place by 2017' (HM Treasury and Greater Manchester Combined Authority, 2014, p 11), and some funds are delegated, including local control of the Apprenticeship Grant for Employers (worth £1,500 for each apprentice recruited), but not yet apprenticeships.

Both schools and FE were affected by a review of vocational qualifications for 14- to 19-year-olds by Professor Alison Wolf (Wolf,

2011). For 16- to 18-year-olds, the coalition kept the academic/vocational divide, while strengthening the maths and English component of vocational courses. Courses focused purely on job-related skills were replaced by study programmes thought likely to facilitate progress into further learning or skilled employment and, from 2014, all students in full-time education who had not yet achieved grades A*-C in GCSE maths or English were required to continue studying them. A new Technical Baccalaureate was introduced for 16- to 19-year-olds and a review of Level 3 vocational qualifications was promised from 2016. Work experience was made mandatory for this age group, but a requirement for young people under 16 was abolished, as was the Young Apprenticeship programme for 14- to 16-year-olds. A-levels were reformed as part of a wide-ranging review of the school curriculum, and AS-levels were made a stand-alone qualification. Content, structure and assessment were all changed, with the first new courses introduced in autumn 2015. Most assessment was to take place by end-of-course examination.

In a joint White Paper published by the DfE and BIS in April 2013, the government announced yet more intervention was needed to 'put rigour and responsiveness at the heart of our skills system' (DfE and BIS, 2013, p 3). This continued the longstanding mantra that, '[i]n today's global race we need a highly skilled workforce' (DfE and BIS, 2013, p 4). A key recommendation was the appointment of an FE commissioner with powers to take action, including closure, on failing colleges. In his first annual report in November 2014, the new commissioner reported that four colleges had been placed in 'administered college status' and that the financial pressures facing FE meant there would be a need for 'some consolidation and indeed some specialisation, as well as neighbouring colleges, institutions and providers considering joint plans for their respective communities' (BIS, 2014a, p 17). This warning was taken up in a BIS consultation paper in March 2015 (BIS, 2015a). It referred to deterioration in the financial health of some colleges, and raised the potential for mergers. It also proposed that colleges should take steps to become specialist institutions, choosing between providing basic skills and higher vocational education, and between 16- to 19-year-olds and adult students. In May 2014, the government announced that the first new institution to become an incorporated FE college since 1992 would be called the Prospects College of Advanced Technology (see Bailey and Unwin, 2014).

The previous Labour government's plan to raise the participation age to 17 took effect in 2013, placing a requirement on young people to remain in education or training for an extra year post-GCSE (and two extra years from 2015). However, alongside this, the coalition replaced the EMA available to students from lower-income families with a 16-19 Bursary Fund. The EMA had been paid to around 650,000 16- to 18-year-olds in full-time education at an annual cost of £560 million. The new bursary was significantly less generous, costing £180 million a year, with around 250,000 fewer students receiving support in 2012/13.

Controversially, given the Liberal Democrat election commitment on tuition fees, but in line with recommendations from the Browne review, which reported after the election, the government abolished teaching grants for most HE courses from 2012/13, leaving universities to raise much more income through fees. The cap on annual student tuition fees was raised from £3,290 to a maximum of £9,000 (full-time) and £6,750 (part-time). Most higher education institutions chose to charge the maximum annual tuition fee of £9,000 from 2012/13 onwards. The existing loan system was adjusted to enable students to borrow substantially larger amounts, and the earnings threshold for repayments by graduates was raised from £15,000 to £21,000 a year. Maintenance grants for the lowest income students were increased while the amounts for students whose family annual income was between £25,000 and £42,000 were restricted. As a concession to the Liberal Democrats, a national Scholarship Programme for low-income students was also introduced, but later cancelled. Aimhigher, a national scheme providing encouragement and support for school students aspiring to university, was discontinued. Important reforms to the HE sector were also made beyond the immediate question of fees, as the government pursued goals of expansion and liberalisation, changing regulations on degree-awarding powers to encourage new HE providers, and from 2015/16, removing the cap on student places, allowing HE to expand to meet demand. Box 5.1 provides a policy summary.

Spending

The effect of these policies on spending in this period was broadly speaking one of expansion of funding under Labour, who continued to extend spending after the financial crisis, and contraction under the coalition, especially in the 2013 Spending Review. Some areas were more heavily affected than others.

The real loser in spending terms up to 2014/15 was adult learning and skills. The total cost of adult skills programmes in England in 2006/07 was approximately £4.2 billion (in 2014/15 prices). Nearly three-quarters of this was made up of spending on adult

Box 5.1: Further and Higher Education and Skills policy timeline

2007	2008	2009	2010	2011	2012	2013	2014	2015

Establishment of Department for Innovation, Universities and Skills (DIUS)

Establishment of UK Commission for Employment and Skills

Establishment of Department for Business, Innovation and Skills to replace DIUS and Department for Business, Enterprise and Regulatory Reform

Wolf Review of vocational education

Bursary Fund replaces Education Maintenance Allowance

- Participation age raised to 17
- New 16-19 programmes of study
- New funding system – money following student

Cuts to funding for 18-year-olds

- Participation age raised to 18
- First teaching of new A-levels

Browne Review of higher education

New HE student finance system takes effect

Cap on HE places increased by 30,000

Cap on HE places removed

Expansion of Train to Gain

Decision to expand apprenticeships at the expense of Train to Gain

Skills for Sustainable Growth strategy

Moves to localism in skills agenda with industrial strategy and enablement of combined authorities

Employer Ownership of Skills Initiative

Richard Review of apprenticeships

- First trailblazers for new apprenticeships
- Adult learning loans
- Traineeships for 16- to 23-year-olds
- Rigour and Responsiveness in Skills White Paper

Fewer qualifications available for public funding (adult)

apprenticeships, Train to Gain, and other workplace learning – items that subsequently became incorporated into the ASB. The remaining spending was on programmes funded by the European Social Fund, learner financial support, community learning, offender learning, careers guidance and various initiatives and infrastructure projects such as a local initiatives fund, UnionLearn and Aimhigher. Under Labour from 2006/07 to 2009/10, real terms spending on subsequent ASB programmes increased by £377 million, or 13%, although overall programme spending increased by only 6%. Train to Gain was the main beneficiary of extra spending.

Under the coalition, the ASB was cut by 31% between 2009/10 and 2014/15, slightly more than programme spending overall, which fell by 27%. Worse was yet to come, with the Skills Funding Statement for 2013-16 indicating a further 11% cut to the ASB between 2014/15 and 2015/16. Comparing 2014/15 with 2009/10, £816 million had come off the annual budget for Train to Gain, and £488 million off other classroom-based learning, while an additional £372 million was being spent on adult apprenticeships. As we show in the next section, much of the fall in spending was caused by a fall in the number of funded learners, but there were also reductions in the cost per learner. BIS reports that its funding per 'learning aim', a single course or qualification, fell from £987 in 2009/10 to £678 in 2012/13 (in cash terms – a fall of about one-third in real terms).

Up until 2013/14, the coalition cut 16-19 funding rather less (falling by 10% from 2009-10 to 2013/14). Nevertheless, this is a larger cut than for the schools budget (see Chapter Four). Replacing the EMA with a less generous bursary fund saved £515 million (in 2014/15 prices), equivalent to more than a two-thirds cut in financial support to learners. There were also cuts of 6% to education in FE colleges and 4% to school sixth forms, in the context of a 2% rise in the student population in this age group in the same period. The 2013 Spending Review brought worse news. With the deficit not having been reduced as much as was hoped and the DfE determined to protect schools (and to introduce universal free school meals [FSM] for infants), 16-18 funding bore the brunt, with a 17.5% reduction in funding for 18-year-olds in FE colleges being announced with effect from August 2014.

The effect of HE reforms under both Labour and the coalition, but most markedly under the latter since 2012, was a cut in direct spending on universities through the Higher Education Funding Council for England (HEFCE), which makes up the bulk of the non-departmental public bodies (NDPBs) total shown in Figure 5.1. HE NDPB spending

Figure 5.1: Government spending on higher education, 2006/07 to 2014/15, England (real terms 2014/15 prices)

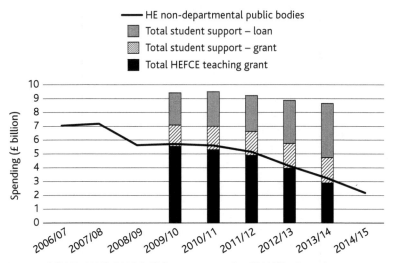

Source: BIS (2013, 2014b, 2015c). All figures converted to 2014/15 prices using HM Treasury GDP Deflators published July 2015 (HM Treasury, 2015c)

fell by 19% under Labour from 2006/07 to 2009/10 and a much larger 62% under the coalition from 2009/10 to 2014/15, with a further fall planned for 2015/16. These data do not account for the cost of student loans and grants. BIS data showing total spending on HE grant, grants and loans for the period 2009/10 and 2013/14 are shown in the bars in Figure 5.1. They show an overall real-terms drop of 8% (9% per FTE student) in that period, with a 48% fall in HE grant offset by a 69% increase in loan spending and 17% increase in maintenance grants. The real saving to the public purse of moving to a system funded by loan-financed fees is unknown, since it depends not just on the number of students taking out loans and their value, but on the rate of repayment, which, in turn, depends on graduate earnings over the life course. Another key factor is the earnings threshold at which loans become repayable, substantially raised under the coalition. According to one estimate (Crawford et al, 2014a), once unpaid debts have been written off, the new system, as currently configured, will cost taxpayers only 5% less than the system it replaced.

Inputs and outputs

As for many of the issues covered in this book, it is in many respects too early to see the effect of the coalition's policies either on the shape of the FE and skills system, or on the outcomes for learners and society. Neither the curriculum and assessment reforms for the 16-19 age group, nor the post-Richard apprenticeship reforms, have yet been fully implemented, so what we can see at this stage only reflects the coalition's early interventions and spending, prior to the major changes announced between 2011 and 2013 and now being rolled out. On the other hand, the changes to HE funding came into effect in 2012, and the immediate effects can be seen.

Looking first at educational participation after 16, the data show an increase in participation in full-time education, both under Labour and the coalition, continuing a trend beginning in the early 2000s and coinciding with a decline in youth employment (see Figure 5.2). There was a particularly sharp increase in the proportion of this group in full-time education between 2008 and 2010 (from 64.2% to 68.6%), perhaps reflecting actual or perceived difficulties with labour market entry. A further upturn in 2013 largely reflects the first year of Labour's RPA policy, which also accounts for a small upturn in the proportion training and a decline in the NEET rate. Increased competition between schools and colleges and continuing poor youth labour market prospects may also have been factors. By 2014, the proportion of 16- to 18-year-olds NEET had fallen to 7.3%, the first substantial drop in this indicator for over a decade,

Figure 5.2: Trends in participation of 16- to 18-year-olds 1997-2014, England

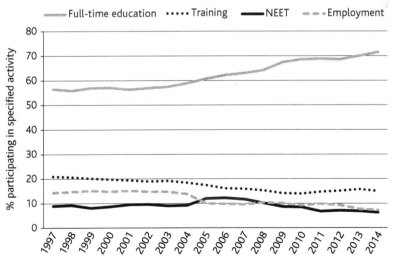

Notes: All data at end of each year. 2014 data are provisional.
Source: 'Participation in education, training and employment: age 16-18' (DfE SFR 19/2015) (DfE, 2015g)

and the proportion in full-time education was at its highest ever. However, despite the new requirement, it is clear that not all of the first RPA cohort were participating at age 17. Local authority data show that some areas had under 90% meeting the duty. The effect of the coalition's removal of the EMA seemed surprisingly small, with just 1% fewer eligible 16- to 18-year-olds (8,100) participating in education following its abolition, although the evaluation also suggested that the level of support available for some of the most disadvantaged learners under the new bursary scheme appeared inadequate (Britton et al, 2014).

By contrast, adult participation, as measured by funded adult learners, rose by 10% under Labour between 2006/07 and 2009/10, and then fell by 17% under the coalition to 2013/14. 'Funded adult learners' reflects, of course, each government's funding priorities, and does not fully reflect all the learning that may be going on. As Figure 5.3 shows (with data from the first year available, 2002/03), the number

Figure 5.3: Trends in numbers of funded adult learners at different levels, 2002/03 to 2013/14, England

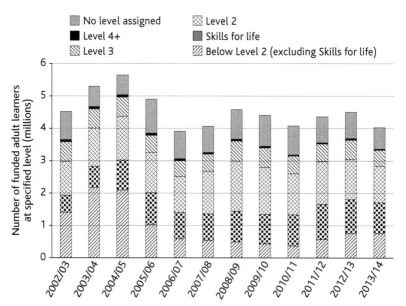

Notes: Includes all kinds of funded provision (apprenticeships, workplace learning, community learning, FE, sixth form and specialist colleges and external institutions). The number of learners funded for each qualification is shown. Learners may take more than one qualification. Figures for 2008/09 onwards are not directly comparable to earlier years as the introduction of demand-led funding changed how funding learners are defined.

Sources: SFA FE data library, www.gov.uk/government/collections/fe-data-library, for years up to 2007/08, SFA (2014, 2015)

of learners peaked in 2004/05, driven by Labour's early emphasis on funding low-level skills. In the period from 2007, there was an increase in the proportion doing Level 2 qualifications under Train to Gain. These numbers then fell again under the coalition, as might be expected given the cut in budgets, but with growth again in 2012/13 in the numbers taking qualifications below Level 2 and at Levels 3 and 4. There was then a substantial fall in 2013/14, especially in the numbers at Levels 3 and 4. This was the first year of the introduction of adult learning loans, as well as coinciding with the removal of funding for a large number of qualifications deemed to have low quality or value.

Figure 5.4 shows the effect of the different policy approaches of Labour and the coalition in relation to apprenticeships and workplace learning. The roll-out of Train to Gain in 2006 initiated a large surge in workplace learning starts, while apprenticeships gradually increased. Under the coalition, apprenticeship numbers increased (until 2013/14, when they were affected by the introduction of adult learning loans) – with 161,000 more starts in 2013 than in 2009/10 (up 57%). However, there were 672,000 fewer workplace learning starts (down 87%). In total, 511,400 fewer people started one of these two types of training in 2013/14 than in 2009/10, although the number was still greater than in 2006/07.

Some limitations of the pro-apprenticeship shift under the coalition are revealed by closer analysis. Almost all the growth in apprenticeships up until 2013/14 came from an increase in the number of adult learners aged over 25, precisely those who were targeted by Train to Gain. This

Figure 5.4: Total number of workplace learning and apprenticeship starts, 2006/07 to 2013/14, England

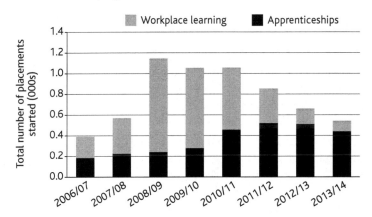

Source: SFA FE data library and SFA SFR 29 (SFA, 2015)

tends to suggest the ongoing practice (and perhaps rational response of employers) of 'converting' the skills and knowledge of existing workers into qualifications, rather than using apprenticeships to create new roles. Moreover, both under Labour and the coalition, service sector occupations (health and social care, business administration, management, hospitality and catering and customer services) have dominated the growth of apprenticeships, and these are also the sectors in which the conversion of adult employees into apprentices has been most used. Although these data predate the Richard reforms of 2013 onwards, the practice of 'conversion' continues, and some 40% of learners are aged 25 or over (Fuller et al, 2015). Despite the Richard Review's call for apprenticeship to be distinguished from forms of training that would form an expected part of any job, it has now become an umbrella 'brand' under which there is considerable variation in activity. The demise of Train to Gain has not led to the development of a specific strategy for supporting the type of shorter adult training it promoted.

In relation to HE, our interest in this chapter is principally trends in access (which we report in the next section), not the shape of provision. However, changes in the system following the coalition's reforms are notable. Trends in student recruitment have not been experienced equally across the university sector. Acceptances by research-intensive Russell Group universities remained relatively stable from 2008-12 and rose in 2013, but acceptances by newer universities or those offering more applied courses fell in 2011 and, by 2013, had not recovered to their pre-2011 levels. Over the same time period, there was a steady increase in acceptances by Guild HE universities and FE colleges.

Outcomes

Achieving the Leitch ambition that the UK should be among the top quartile of OECD countries in terms of skill levels would have demanded a rapid increase in qualifications, particularly at intermediate levels – increasing the proportion of the adult population qualified to at least Level 2 to more than 90% by 2020 (from 69% in 2005). While a focus on chasing short-term gains in quantity of qualifications is disputed (arguably giving rise to some of the 'conversion' practices previously described rather than resulting in any genuine increase in skill levels), the scale of the task set out when Gordon Brown's government took over is worth bearing in mind when considering subsequent progress.

For young people up to the age of 19, qualification levels had been on a rising trend before 2007, and this continued, although the rate of improvement slowed after 2012 (see Figure 5.5). In 2014, as shown by the combined bars in Figure 5.5, 87% of 19-year-olds had achieved Level 2 compared with 81% in 2010 and 74% in 2007. The line in Figure 5.5 shows that 60% reached Level 3 in that year, compared with 54% in 2010 and 48% in 2007. As we show in more detail in Lupton et al (2015a), the increase in Level 3 qualification was driven by a growth in the number of young people taking vocational courses. While A-levels accounted for the vast majority of qualifications at this level, there was no increase in A-level passes.

Two worrying trends underlie the slowing down of progress under the coalition government from 2012. One is that a continued increase in Level 2 qualification was entirely driven by an increase in the proportion qualifying by 16: the proportion qualifying between 16 and 19 declined in this period (Figure 5.5). The other is that socioeconomic gaps at Level 3 stopped narrowing. The gap between students eligible for FSM who reached Level 3 and others remained static after 2010 (at around 24 percentage points), having fallen since 2005.

The level of adult qualifications, overall, also continued to rise, making progress towards the Leitch ambition. By 2014, nearly 85% of

Figure 5.5: Trends in Level 2 and Level 3 qualifications at age 16 and 19, 2004-14, England

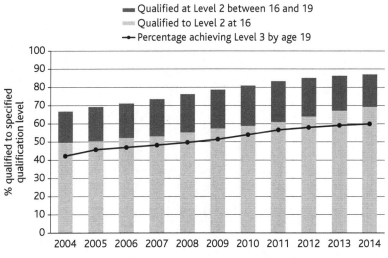

Source: Level 2 and 3 attainment by young people aged 19 in 2014' (DfE SFR 11/2015) (DfE, 2015d)

economically active adults (not all adults) were qualified at least to Level 2, again with progress slowing after 2012. The increase was driven by an increase in Level 4 qualifications, rising from 36.9% in 2007 to 43.8% in 2014, with negligible change at Levels 2 and 3. However, the government's monitoring of the achievement of qualifications year-on-year shows a less promising picture, with achievements both of full Level 2 and Level 3 qualifications being on a downward trend since 2010/11 (see Figure 5.6). The number of full Level 3 achievements fell by around 46,000, or 15%, between 2009/10 and 2013/14. These data show the numbers of qualifications achieved, not the number of adults achieving qualifications. This number also fell, from 2.57 million in 2009 to 2.27 million in 2013/14. One possible explanation that the government provides for these falling numbers is the shift to apprenticeships, where the emphasis is on progression rather than there being a clear funding incentive to achieve the qualification. It is also noticeable that as adult apprenticeship numbers increased, success rates fell, from a peak of 78.2% in 2010/11 to 72.6% in 2012/13.

The key story in relation to access to HE is that the coalition's contested reforms do not seem to have had the detrimental effect that many expected. Despite Labour's top-up fees, the number of English applicants to UK universities had continued on an upward trend after 2006. With the introduction of the new fee regime in 2012, applications fell sharply, partly because school leavers who had intended to defer places decided not to do so, in order to get in before the new fees (Universities UK, 2014), but they subsequently bounced

Figure 5.6: Achievement of adult qualifications 2005/06 to 2013/14

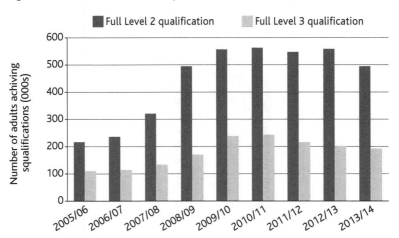

Source: SFA FE data library

back. This is despite a drop in the overall number of school leavers, who make up the majority of applicants. Application rates for 18-year-olds in England actually rose, from 31.3% in 2010 to 33.2% in 2014 (ICOF, 2015). Table 5.1 shows, however, that the recovery in numbers was convincing in England than in the rest of the UK where the same fee regime has not applied.

As Table 5.2 shows, despite particular concerns about the impact of higher fees on lower-income families, the application rate for young people eligible for FSM continued to increase after 2012, reaching 17.9% in 2014 (up from 11.4% in 2007). However, application rates from other students also increased, leaving no real change in the percentage point gap between 2007 and 2014. Pupils not eligible for FSM remained over twice as likely to apply to university. As the Independent Commission on Fees (ICOF) (2015) has noted, the gap remains much larger at the most selective universities – it being still 8.5 times more likely that a student will gain a place at one of the most selective 13 universities if they come from the top quintile of

Table 5.1: Trends in the number of applicants to UK universities (by March deadline), by country of domicile, 2010-15

	2010	2011	2012	2013	2014	2015	2012 vs 2010 (%)	2015 vs 2010 (%)
England	444,610	449,590	405,110	413,810	428,260	431,700	−8.9	−2.9
Scotland	40,980	41,790	40,980	41,310	42,460	42,910	0.0	4.7
Wales	22,200	22,670	22,140	21,450	22,060	22,070	−3.4	−0.6
Northern Ireland	18,940	19,640	18,800	19,960	19,930	22,040	5.4	7.9
Total	526,730	533,690	487,030	496,530	512,710	520,880	−5.7	−1.1

Source: UCAS applicant figures, reproduced from (ICOF 2015)

Table 5.2: Application rates (%) for English 18-year-olds (by March deadline) by FSM status, England

	2006	2007	2008	2009	2010	2011	2012	2013	2014
Non-FSM	30.3	30.8	31.9	33.1	35.2	36.4	34.7	35.9	37.1
FSM	10.5	11.4	12.4	13.4	14.8	16.2	16	16.6	17.9
Percentage point gap	19.8	19.4	19.5	19.7	20.4	20.2	18.7	19.3	19.2
FSM:non FSM ratio	2.89	2.70	2.57	2.47	2.38	2.25	2.17	2.16	2.07

Source: UCAS (2014)

areas than from the bottom (although this is slightly better than the 9.8 times gap in 2010).

Where the increase in fees really does seem to have had a marked effect is on participation in HE by mature and part-time students, which has suffered a 'precipitous fall' (ICOF, 2015, p 3). From 2012/13, part-time students have not been eligible for maintenance grants or loans, and are only eligible for loans if they are studying for a qualification at a higher level than the one they already hold. The recession and the government's cuts to public sector spending have also restricted the extent to which employers have been willing to fund university courses (HEFCE, 2014). The number of first-year part-time undergraduate students enrolled at UK universities fell by 48% between 2009/10 and 2013/14, and the total number of mature undergraduates (aged 25+) by 36%, with most of this trend being driven by trends in England (HEFCE, 2014). As the ICOF says, this is a matter of particular concern because the part-time market has traditionally been a 'second chance' route for learners from circumstances where automatic progression from school to university was either not expected or not possible.

Conclusion

The acknowledged deficiencies of the UK FE and skills system, the challenges of funding both in FE and HE, and the desire to keep pace with international competitors presented some formidable hurdles for both the Labour and coalition governments, regardless of the crisis and its implications for public spending.

Taking FE and adult skills training first, the reforms initiated by the coalition in the second half of its term in office from 2012 represented a more systematic attempt to transform the quality and responsiveness of the system than Labour's changes between 2007 and 2010. However, it remains to be seen whether the post-Richard apprenticeship reforms will be successful in securing greater employer engagement and financial contribution, whether they will really result in substantial increases to the length and quality of apprenticeship training, and whether they will provide significant new opportunities for skills acquisition and upgrading rather than simply the accreditation of existing skills. For the younger age group, the period from 2013 onwards was notable for an increase in 16-18 participation, with declining NEET figures as a result of the implementation of Labour's RPA policy. However, the majority of the growth in apprenticeships was for adults, not for young people, while the complex funding system and the fragmentation of the careers advice and guidance service for young people meant that for those not going to university, treading a clear path from school to skilled work remains an uncertain business – perhaps an increasingly uncertain one. There has been little progress in closing socioeconomic attainment gaps at 19, over and above the progress made at GCSE level up to age 16.

Alongside its reform programme, the coalition's term in office has primarily been notable for the substantial cuts it has made to funding for FE and skills, and the resulting falls in the number of funded places and achievements of qualifications. Improvements to quality notwithstanding, it is hard to argue that the strategy of heavy cuts to post-compulsory education, while maintaining funding on schools, matches the government's ambition for a world-class system and an internationally competitive labour force, or that it will contribute to greater equity or social mobility.

In terms of access to HE, a sigh of relief might be breathed that the trebling of tuition fees did not have a more significant negative effect on applications to HE, especially among students from less advantaged households. The graduate tax model and increases in maintenance grants for the poorest students seem to have been effective in this sense. However, there has been a huge and worrying drop in part-time and mature student participation, and only very modest reductions in the gap in participation between young people from poorer and richer households, especially to the top ranking universities, while the potential longer-term savings to the public purse, of the system as currently configured, are projected to be very modest. The announcement by the new Conservative government that student grants will be abolished and replaced by further loans, and that some universities will be allowed to increase fees in line with inflation, prompted the ICOF to call for an investigation into whether the current system represents value for money and for stronger coordination of work to widen participation.

Overall, then, this period must be regarded as one in which only modest progress has been made, with significant concerns remaining in major areas. The current Conservative government still faces a 'mountain to climb' while funding cuts continue to fall hard on this area of social policy.

Notes

[1] The intention was that the YPLA would oversee the devolving of 16-18 funding to local authorities. In April 2012, the coalition government replaced the YPLA with the Education Funding Agency.

[2] FE, HE and skills are all devolved responsibilities, so the government's policies discussed here applied to England only. However, the UKCES, like its predecessor, the Skills Sector Development Agency, and the Sector Skills Council, was established as a UK-wide body.

[3] In 2001, Labour had closed down Individual Learning Accounts after only a year due to government concerns about fraudulent practice on the part of providers (NAO, 2002). Variations of Individual Learning Accounts are still in use in Scotland and Wales.

SIX

Employment policy since the crisis

Abigail McKnight

The situation on the eve of the crisis

On the eve of the financial crisis, the labour market, from an historical perspective, was in good shape. Employment rates were high and had been increasing for some time; largely due to increases in employment rates among women. The labour market had not been hit by a major economic recession since the early 1990s.

New Labour had pursued supply-side policies to meet their ambition of achieving 'employment opportunity for all' (their 'modern definition of full employment'). These were centred round extensive active labour market programmes (ALMPs) (New Deals) designed to increase activation among unemployment benefit recipients and increasingly for groups claiming other out-of-work benefits (lone parents and people with limiting longstanding illnesses or disabilities) who had previously not been required to search for work as a condition of benefit receipt nor given access to ALMPs. Activation programmes were complemented by a number of policies designed to 'make work pay' and to increase financial incentives to take up low-paid job opportunities (the National Minimum Wage, in-work cash benefits, lower taxes for low-paid workers).

The working-age population had historically high levels of educational attainment, and despite a large expansion in higher education, the graduate wage premium had held up well. This had continued to provide incentives for young people to gain a degree, even though the costs of doing so rose with the introduction of annual top-up tuition fees.[1] The introduction of a National Minimum Wage in 1999 led to the (legal) eradication of extreme low pay, but low wage jobs on the eve of the financial crisis accounted for a larger share of employment than in most OECD countries. Real average wages had been growing for some time, but overall earnings inequality remained high in the UK.

Despite reasons to be optimistic about the labour market, some fault lines were evident. Youth unemployment and unemployment among young adults more generally started increasing in the early to mid-2000s (McKnight, 2009). The Labour government's reforms to ALMPs (greater activation alongside increased conditionality) contributed to increasing employment rates among lone parents (Gregg and Harkness, 2003), although targets had been missed, but unemployment and inactivity rates remained high among long-term sick and disabled people.

Out-of-work benefits for those claiming on the basis of long-term illness or disability were in the process of being reformed at the time of the 2010 General Election. The Employment and Support Allowance (ESA) was introduced in October 2008 for which new applicants have to undergo a Work Capability Assessment (WCA) (contracted out to the private sector), the outcome determines whether an individual qualifies for ESA, and if they should be assigned to the 'work-related activity group' (those expected to find work) or the 'support group' (those with little prospect of working) with a higher level of benefit.

Spending on ALMPs had increased under the Labour government with expansion in the number and range of activities made available to jobseekers – on a voluntary basis for some, and compulsory for others.

A review of ALMPs and welfare policy had been conducted, on behalf of the Labour government, by David Freud (now Lord Freud, a Conservative Party Peer) in 2007. Some of the recommendations made by this review (Freud, 2007), new ALMPs, the new Jobseeker's regime and Flexible New Deal, were in the process of replacing the separate New Deal programmes and Employment Zones when Labour lost the 2010 General Election and the Liberal Democrats formed a coalition government with the Conservative Party.

Policies, 2008-15

Labour policies up to 2010 in response to the financial crisis

The Labour government continued its planned programme of reforms to ALMPs with the introduction of the Flexible New Deal in phases from April 2009 and reforms to the out-of-work benefit system with the introduction of ESA in October 2008. Initially ESA was restricted to individuals making a new claim for out-of-work benefits on the basis of limited or no capacity for work due to illness or disability. There were also plans to reassess the stock of existing Incapacity Benefit claims and relevant Income Support claims.

In response to increasing unemployment, the Labour government acted swiftly, increasing the budget for the Department for Work and Pensions (DWP) to fund Jobcentre Plus activities: initially by £1.3 billion in autumn 2008 (HM Treasury, 2008a), and then by a further £1.7 billion in spring 2009 (HM Treasury, 2009a). Additional policies and funding were also announced to help those facing redundancy (through Train to Gain and the Rapid Response Service). Various guarantees were introduced to help young unemployed people. Initially, JSA claimants aged 18-24 and unemployed for 12 months were offered the chance of a subsidised job, a work placement, work-related skills training or a volunteer opportunity for at least six months (HM Treasury, 2009a). This was later brought forward to the sixth-month point of an unemployment benefit claim from January 2010, and take-up of one of the options became mandatory after 10 months of unemployment. A September Guarantee for 16-/17-year-olds guaranteed these young people a place in education or training (HM Treasury, 2009a) and was supported by an Education Maintenance Allowance (EMA). A Future Jobs Fund was set up to support the creation of subsidised community-focused jobs for unemployed young people (October 2009, to be made available until March 2011; later extended to March 2012, and was projected to cost up to £1.3 billion in total).

Unemployment increased sharply, but was lower than anticipated. This allowed the government to divert some of the £1.7 billion initially set aside to fund Jobcentre Plus expenses (for handling unemployment benefit claims and ALMPs) to boost ALMP provision. This was used to provide extra help for young people and help for those facing redundancy (an eight-week package of personalised support and a Rapid Response Service).

An Employment Summit, led by former Prime Minister Gordon Brown, was held in London in January 2009, at which extra support for people who remained unemployed for over six months was announced (subsidies for employers, training places, volunteering opportunities and help for those wanting to start up their own business).

Coalition policies, 2010-15

The coalition government continued the evolution of ALMPs that had begun in the mid-1990s (increased conditionality and greater activation) for an increasingly wide set of benefit claimants. Their first major reform to employment services was the replacement of the Flexible New Deal with the Work Programme. This effectively took on more of the recommendations made by the Freud Review, and David Freud was appointed Minister for Welfare Reform. The Conservative manifesto for the 2010 General Election largely determined what was included in the coalition agreement as the Liberal Democrats had very few welfare reform or employment policies in their 2010 General Election manifesto. Service delivery was contracted out to private providers who were mainly paid according to the results they achieved (job outcomes and their sustainability). Unemployed people were referred earlier (at the start of their claim, for some), and could remain on the programme for longer (up to two years). A wider set of people claiming out-of-work benefits due to illness or disability were referred to the Work Programme (including a group who were not considered to be work-ready for 12 months).

The coalition government also continued the reform of disability-related benefits that had begun under the Labour government. Existing Incapacity Benefit claimants were gradually reassessed on the basis of the WCA and moved on to Jobseeker's Allowance, an ESA work-related activity group or ESA support group. Other welfare changes included greater use of benefit sanctions for those not meeting conditions of benefit receipt, a cap on the maximum amount of welfare a family could claim in cash benefits, and lone parents with dependent children as young as five were no longer entitled to claim Income Support.[2] Entitlement to Working Tax Credits was limited to those on the lowest incomes (lowering the income threshold and increasing the withdrawal rate).

Other employment policies introduced or reinforced under the coalition government included more support for unemployed people wanting to start up their own business (New Enterprise Allowance and assistance), and a series of programmes to help the short-term unemployed prior to entering the Work Programme (job clubs, mandatory basic skills training for some, sector-based academies, mandatory work activity, work experience and enterprise clubs). In addition, a joint departmental programme, the Youth Contract, was introduced to tackle high unemployment among young adults and disengagement from education and training among some 16-/17-year-olds. This programme largely replaced the various guarantees introduced by the Labour government and the Future Jobs Fund.[3]

Under the coalition government one of the main changes was the policy shift to almost exclusive provision of labour market services by private providers for the long-term unemployed and for those considered to have the most challenges to finding and maintaining employment. These providers were given greater freedom in terms of what jobseekers could be offered. A timeline of key employment policies since 2008 can be found in Box 6.1.

Box 6.1: Employment policy timeline

2007	2008	2009	2010	2011	2012	2013	2014	2015

Additional £1.3 billion to DWP to fund Jobcentre Plus and ALMPS in response to recession

Flexible New Deal (Phase 1 pilot areas)

Further £1.7 billion to fund Jobcentre Plus

Jobseeker's Regime and Flexible New Deal (Phase 2 national roll-out)

Young Persons Guarantee and Future Jobs Fund for 18- to 24-year-old Jobseeker's Allowance claimants

Introduction of Employment and Support Allowance and Work Capacity Assessment for new claims

Launch of New Enterprise Allowance

Introduction of the Work Programme (delivered through private providers)

Launch of Youth Contract aimed at helping 18- to 24-year-olds in sustained employment and 16/17 in education or training. Wage incentives for employers. (DfE component ended March 2015)

Reassessment of Incapacity Benefit claims through a Work Capacity Assessment

Guarantee all 16-/17-year-olds offered a place in education or training by local authorities

Apprenticeship grants for employers taking on young apprentices

Six-month offer for claimants out of work for over 6 months

Graduate Guarantee, graduate internship if unemployed for 6 months

Benefit cap announced

Roll-out of benefit cap begins in four London boroughs

Work Choice replaced WORKSTEP in supporting people with a disability move into work

Introduction of Work Experience programme (2-8 week placements for 18- to 24-year-olds unemployed for 3-6 months)

National roll-out of Universal Credit for some new claimants

Introduction of Help to Work scheme for some new claimants

Introduction of Help to Work scheme (Jobseeker's Allowance claimants after 2 years on Work Programme)

Announced introduction of the National Living Wage from April 2016

Youth Obligation from day 1 of Universal Credit claim

Election

Election

Spending

Expenditure on employment policy, either in real terms or as a percentage of GDP, cannot be interpreted simply as an increase or decrease in provision, at least in terms of the quantity and quality of provision participants receive. The reason for this is that spending on employment policy tends to increase when unemployment increases and decline when unemployment declines, as most expenditure on employment policy is allocated to ALMPs. This makes meaningful interpretation of expenditure figures in this policy area more challenging because falling expenditure can be due to falling need (unemployment) rather than falling provision for those in need.

Ideally we would compute a measure that expresses expenditure on employment policy in terms of demand, such as dividing expenditure by the total number of weeks unemployed people claim out-of-work benefits within a financial year. This information is not readily available, and the alternative of dividing expenditure by the stock of unemployed people at a point in time is not particularly informative, especially when unemployment is rising or falling within a year.

A second issue that needs to be considered is that, starting under the Labour government and increasing under the coalition government, there has been a shift to using contracted providers for the delivery of employment services (activation programmes) to unemployed people, and paying these providers according to the results they achieve. Payments reward providers in terms of their success in getting people back into work and the sustainability of any job secured. The consequence is that there is a lag between the time when the provider incurs the expenditure and the time that the DWP pays the provider. For example, in the Work Programme a participant claiming Jobseeker's Allowance must be in work for six months before the provider can claim a job outcome payment. When such a system is well established there is simply a time lag, and high levels of unemployment in one year can lead to higher levels of expenditure in the following. However, when this payment model is first introduced or expanded it can give the impression that expenditure is initially reduced. The Work Programme was introduced in June 2011, and we would therefore expect to see a fall in expenditure in 2011/12.[4]

The final issue that needs to be borne in mind is that the groups of out-of-work claimants who are entitled to receive back-to-work support through employment programmes has expanded over time (in particular to lone parents and people with disabilities); this means that simply looking at the unemployment rate to assess expenditure on employment policy can be misleading.

Spending on employment policy is only a very small fraction of GDP despite the central role employment takes in the welfare of individuals, families, and the economy as a whole. The OECD and the European Commission have for some time been urging governments to switch funding from passive to active forms of employment policy. Expenditure on employment policy in the UK was boosted between 1997/98 and 2001/02 through funds from a one-off £5 billion windfall tax on privatised utility companies, which was used to fund the New Deal programmes (see Figure 6.1). As employment continued to rise and unemployment fell throughout much of Labour's time in government, expenditure on employment policy as a share of GDP fell back to 0.22% in 2007/08. The 2008/09 economic recession led to an increase in expenditure from 2008/09 as unemployment increased, reaching a peak of £5 billion in 2010/11. The increase in unemployment led to an increase in the share of GDP being spent on employment policy to 0.27% in 2009/10 and 0.30% in 2010/11. The sharp fall in expenditure

Figure 6.1: Spending on employment policy, 1997-98 to 2014-15, UK

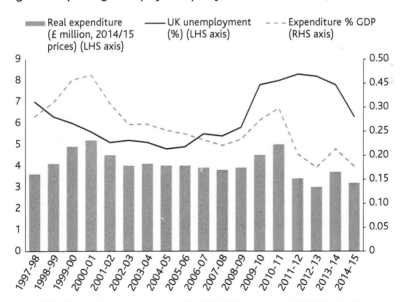

Notes: (1) Real terms figures are expressed in 2014/15 prices using GDP deflators from ONS release 30 June 2015 (ONS, 2015g); (2) On advice from HMT the figure for 2007/08 is taken from PESA 2011 series (HM Treasury, 2015c; HM Treasury, 2011).

Source: Public Expenditure Statistical Analyses (PESA) (2015 and 2011) Table 4.3 and Table 4.4; ILO unemployment data series LF2Q Labour Market Statistics September 2015 release (age 16-64) (ONS, 2015g)

in 2011/12 to £3.4 billion is associated with the shift to a deferred payment scheme under the Work Programme. This also explains the increase to £3.7 billion in 2013/14 (0.17% GDP) as providers were paid in arrears for the outcomes they achieved. Falling unemployment has contributed to the decline in expenditure in 2014/15.

In Chapter Two figures for cash transfers to unemployed people were included in the totals, but here we look in a bit more detail at caseloads and expenditure on working-age benefits, focusing in particular on those that are paid to people out of work. Figures 6.2a and 6.2b show the working-age out-of-work benefit (income replacement) caseloads and expenditure on associated benefits. They show how caseloads increased following the recession but have since declined, as has expenditure on these benefits as unemployment has fallen. However, the fall in expenditure is not as steep, suggesting that the value of means-tested cash transfers have had to increase, most likely due to recipients being in greater need (lower household income from other sources relative to need). They also show the shift from Incapacity Benefit to ESA. Universal Credit take-up is still very low and it is not included in these figures.

Outcomes

We assess outcomes by examining the performance of individual ALMPs, where evaluation evidence is available, and follow with a general assessment of the labour market.

Performance of active labour market programmes

ALMPs were in the process of reform when the crisis hit. The Labour government pressed ahead with its plans to introduce the Flexible New Deal, and this was supplemented with a number of interventions designed to respond to increasing unemployment, particularly high rates of youth unemployment. There is no specific evaluation evidence on how well the New Deals coped with the crisis, but the fact that unemployment didn't increase by as much as anticipated, and levelled off in the autumn of 2009, suggests that the programmes were coping fairly well. As we will see below, unemployment among young adults (aged 18-24) also levelled off well below what was forecast given the severity of the economic recession. This suggests that the extra assistance for young people, through the September Guarantee, the Young Persons Guarantee and the Future Jobs Fund, was helping to keep unemployment rates down. However, without good evaluation

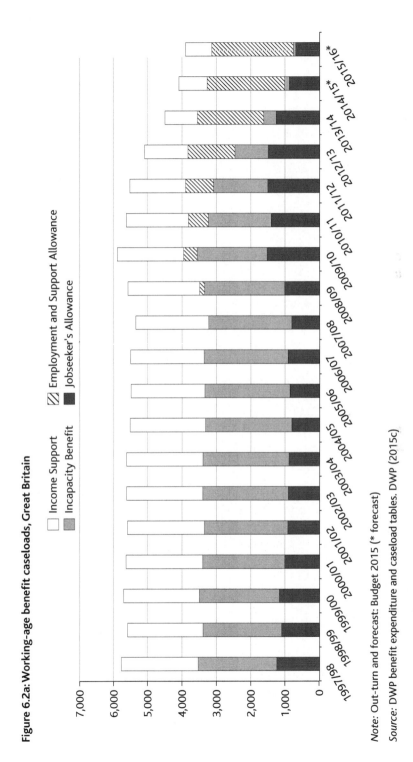

Figure 6.2a: Working-age benefit caseloads, Great Britain

Legend:
☐ Income Support
▨ Employment and Support Allowance
▨ Incapacity Benefit
■ Jobseeker's Allowance

Note: Out-turn and forecast: Budget 2015 (* forecast)

Source: DWP benefit expenditure and caseload tables. DWP (2015c)

Figure 6.2b: Expenditure on working-age benefits by type, Great Britain

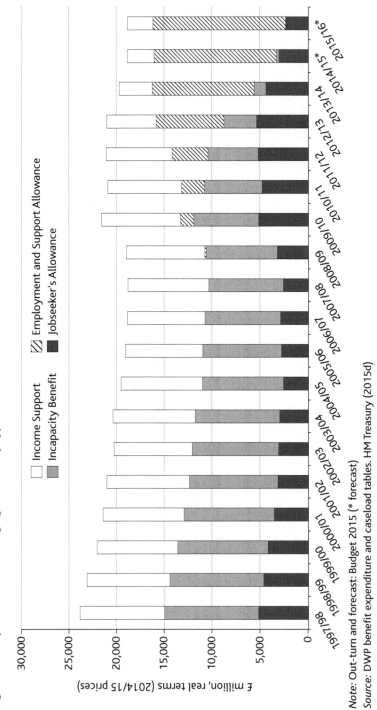

Note: Out-turn and forecast: Budget 2015 (* forecast)

Source: DWP benefit expenditure and caseload tables. HM Treasury (2015d)

evidence it is not possible to say with any certainty what impact ALMPs had. The Flexible New Deal was in the early stages of being rolled out, and although the DWP commissioned evaluations, there is no definitive net impact assessment, and given that the coalition government abolished it before it was established, it is not possible to make a fair performance assessment. One piece of evaluation evidence that looked specifically at the Future Jobs Fund found positive net impacts on employment and time-off benefits (DWP, 2012c), but this evaluation evidence was published after the coalition government abolished the initiative.

There have been assessments made of the Work Programme that was introduced by the coalition government in June 2011, and the DWP regularly publishes descriptive statistics on participants and their outcomes. Figure 6.3 shows the share of entry cohorts

Figure 6.3: The share of entry cohorts achieving at least three/six months in work after a year on the Work Programme (all claimants and selected payment groups)

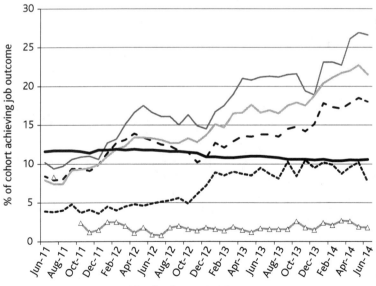

Source: DWP (2015b)

participating in the Work Programme who achieve a job outcome (three or six months in work, depending on the claimant group[5]) after being on the programme for a year. Work Programme performance was considerably below minimum expected levels (defined by the DWP based on what they expect would occur in the absence of the programme) for cohorts entering the programme during the first six months. Minimum expected levels of outcomes vary across groups (not shown), and with the exception of ESA, ex-Incapacity Benefit claimants are all now achieving these levels. Given the recovery in the labour market, this should not be surprising, although statistics for the most recent cohorts show that outcome rates have fallen once again (particularly for new ESA claimants).

Higher rates of job outcomes are achieved for Jobseeker's Allowance claimants than for ESA claimants, despite the fact that ESA claimants are only required to work for at least three months in total to meet this measure of performance, and payment incentives to providers delivering the programme are higher (see McKnight, 2015). ESA claimants who had previously been claiming Incapacity Benefit have very low success rates, and a recent National Audit Office (NAO) evaluation (NAO, 2014d) raised concerns that providers are 'parking' some of the hardest to help participants due to low expected outcomes while focusing resources on easier to help individuals ('creaming'). The first component of the DWP's official evaluation of the Work Programme (Newton et al, 2012), while stating that it was too early to draw firm conclusions on the issue of 'parking', did record evidence that some providers were engaging in this practice. The second DWP-commissioned evaluation report (Lane et al, 2013) found that the differential pricing model was not sufficiently encouraging providers to support the most disadvantaged customers. Providers acknowledged that they were spending considerably less (an estimated 54% less) on this harder to help group than they initially intended (NAO, 2014d) and less than they spent on Jobseeker's Allowance claimants. This could be seen as evidence that the financial incentives are considered to be too low for providers to spend resources on this group. For example, only 6.6% of new ESA claimants with a 12-month prognosis (assessed to be work-ready in 12 months at the point that they are referred) who complete the Work Programme are expected to achieve a job outcome,[6] and therefore providers could well consider that the expected return on investments for this group is simply not high enough. More recent cohorts of new ESA claimants with a short prognosis in terms of the time in which they are expected to be work-ready (three or six months) had achieving higher levels of job outcomes after a year than previously, but recent figures show a fall, despite the DWP's expectation that higher rates would be sustained. The most recent cohort for which outcome information is available started the Work Programme in June 2014, and after a year, 7.7% had achieved a job outcome, down from 9.5% for those who started the Work Programme a year earlier. This is above the minimum expected level of 7.2% for this group. The gap in outcomes between Jobseeker's Allowance claimants and new ESA claimants (excluding the 12-month prognosis group) has widened considerably since the start of the programme.

If we look at outcomes after two years, we find that many more participants go on to achieve job outcomes (DWP, 2015b). These rates have also improved for later cohorts, but for early cohorts were well below minimum expected levels. The recent NAO evaluation concluded that up to March 2014 the Work Programme, after a poor start, helped Jobseeker's Allowance claimants get into work and stay in work at about the same rate as previous welfare-to-work schemes, but this was well below the Department and contractors' initial expectations when the programme was designed and when contractors submitted their bids (NAO, 2014d). This should be evaluated in the context that the coalition government introduced the Work Programme because it believed that existing welfare-to-work schemes performed poorly (described as 'failing' in the 2010 Conservative manifesto), and therefore the Work Programme needs to deliver results that are much better than minimum expected levels for it to be deemed a success against its objective.

There is some evaluation evidence for the Youth Contract. This programme was made up of a Work Experience Scheme, a Wage Subsidy Scheme and an Apprenticeship Incentive Scheme, and a Department for Education [DfE] component designed to re-engage 16-/17-year-olds not in education, employment or training [NEET]. In particular, an evaluation of the DfE component found that the NEET rate was directly reduced by 1.8 percentage points, and cost-benefit analysis estimated that the intervention was cost effective with a net benefit of £12,900 for each sustained re-engagement (Newton et al, 2014).

In general, there is a shortage of robust evaluation evidence from which activation programme development can be judged. There are disappointing results from Mandatory Work Activity (DWP, 2012a) and Skills Conditionality (Dorsett et al, 2011), but these relate to early impact assessments or pilots, and it is not known if performance has improved.

General labour market assessment

Employment among the working-age population increased under Labour, reaching a peak of 29 million (73%) in April-June 2008 (ONS, 2015g). Despite falling over the recession, employment recovered fairly quickly; in fact, the main concern has been poor productivity levels and falling real wage rates alongside growth in precarious forms of employment, such as zero hours contracts and some forms of self-employment.

On the eve of the financial crisis, unemployment stood at 5.3% (August-October 2007), and increased rapidly, by 3 percentage points, as the 2008/09 recession hit the real economy from spring 2008. Unemployment remained at around 8% from June 2009 through the May 2010 General Election, but started rising again under the coalition government from spring 2011 (see Figure 6.4). After peaking at 8.6% in September-November 2011, unemployment started falling gradually, and then fell fairly rapidly from autumn 2013, but since October 2014, unemployment has largely plateaued at around 5.7% (the most recent figures show some improvement).

Figure 6.4 also shows the unemployment rates for 16- to 17-year-olds and for 18- to 24-year-olds. Unemployment rates among these age groups are in general higher than among older age groups,

Figure 6.4: Unemployment rates (%) by age group, March-May 1997 to May-July 2015

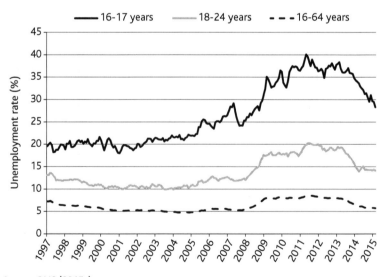

Source: ONS (2015g)

even during periods of buoyant growth. This is mainly due to frictional unemployment as labour market entrants search for suitable employment opportunities. In addition, it has become increasingly likely that young people stay on at school until age 18, with many going on to pursue higher education and then entering the labour market at age 21. Those not staying on at school tend to pursue further education opportunities or apprenticeships, with only a minority of school leavers seeking work. Those that do tend to be the least advantaged, and this largely accounts for the high rates of unemployment among 16-/17-year-olds. As new job opportunities dry up in recessions it is typically the case that young, new entrants to the labour market experience the highest unemployment rates, and the 2008/09 recession was no exception. Unemployment rates among young adults had started increasing prior to the recession – from as early as 2005 (McKnight, 2009) – starting to rise in earnest from the beginning of 2008. Among 16-/17-year-olds, unemployment increased from around 24% to a peak of 40% in the summer of 2011, and unemployment among 18- to 24-year-olds increased from around 12% to a peak of 20% in September–November 2011, with rates not falling until the autumn of 2013. Rates stopped falling at the end of 2014/beginning of 2015, considerably above their pre-recession levels.

The evaluation of the Youth Contract provides evidence that some of this fall can be attributed to the success of the DfE component re-engaging young people into education and thereby reducing the NEET rate by 1.8 percentage points. Raising the education leaving age to 17 from September 2013 coincides with the steep fall in unemployment rates for 16-/17-year-olds. A further increase to age 18 in 2015 should also have helped keep rates down, but this does not appear to have led to a further decline. However, despite these improvements, Chapter Twelve later highlights how young people have been hit especially hard in the recent recession and its aftermath.

Unlike in previous recessions, older workers did not experience particularly high rates of unemployment during the crisis (McKnight, 2015), and inactivity rates increased by only a little for men; the downward trend in female inactivity rates was unperturbed by the recession.

The reasons why unemployment didn't rise as high as anticipated, given the severity of the recession and on the basis of previous recessions (peak of early 1990s recession 10.8%; peak of early 1980s recession 12%; see McKnight, 2009) and started falling earlier than expected, is thought to be due to a number of factors. It is noteworthy that the recession was not accompanied by large-scale industrial restructuring.

This tends to be associated with increased rates of unemployment and inactivity among older workers who find their skills redundant and struggle to find work as the economy recovers. In addition, the labour market was in good shape in the run-up to the financial crisis, and this helped its resilience in the face of recession: the labour force was better qualified, arguably more flexible and adaptable, and there were opportunities for self-employment.

A second factor was the move, starting in the mid-1990s, from a largely passive welfare system to a highly active system with a range of ALMPs accompanied by conditional receipt of out-of-work benefits and incentives to take up low-paid work through tax credits and a minimum wage. Changes in the benefit regime for those claiming out-of-work assistance on the basis of limiting longstanding illness or disability, limited the possibility (and incentive) for people to move on to inactive benefits, and gave those claimants access to ALMPs (although activation for this group of claimants has produced disappointing results). The Labour government moved swiftly at the start of the recession to ensure that Jobcentre Plus had sufficient funds to provide necessary employment services in the face of rising unemployment, and new policies were introduced to help individuals facing redundancy and for young unemployed people. The coalition government continued with ALMP reform through the introduction of the Work Programme for the long-term unemployed and 'those requiring early assistance. Changes were also made to activation programmes for the short-term unemployed, but there is very little evaluation evidence on their effectiveness. Unfortunately the initial poor performance of the Work Programme led to lower outcomes for early cohorts entering the programme between June 2011 and December 2011, coinciding with (and possibly the reason behind) a rise in unemployment. As highlighted earlier, Work Programme outcomes have improved for later cohorts, but recent figures have shown a decline.

Self-employment also played a key role in the labour market recovery, accounting for all of the net employment growth prior to July–September 2013 (see Figure 6.5). The latest Office for National Statistics (ONS) analysis shows that the number of self-employed people (4.6 million) and the share of total employment made up of self-employment (15%) was higher than at any point over the past 40 years (ONS, 2014b). Since then the number of self-employed has fallen back to 4.5 million (14.5% of employment) (ONS, 2015g).

Perhaps the most remarkable difference between the recent recession and previous recessions in the second half of the 20th century was the fall in real wages (Bovill, 2014; Gregg et al, 2014; see also Chapter

Figure 6.5: The number of individuals working as employees or in self-employment relative to Jan-Mar 2008 levels (000s)

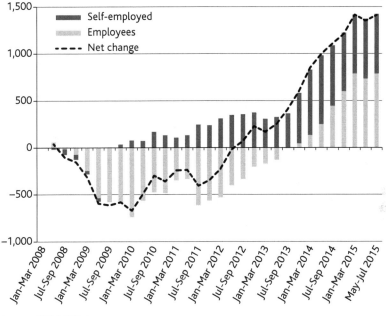

Source: ONS (2015g)

Eleven, this volume). This occurred not just on average or at the median, but across the wage distribution, with significant proportions of workers, including those continuously employed, receiving real and nominal pay cuts (McKnight, 2015; McKnight and Gardiner, 2015). Young age groups have seen average earnings fall behind levels achieved by earlier cohorts at the same age (ONS, 2014b). Employers have been able to keep labour costs down without making large-scale redundancies. This makes even more sense in a recession where there isn't large-scale industrial restructuring as workers' skills don't become redundant. Employers effectively hoard labour, waiting for the upturn. This is likely to have contributed to the low levels of productivity that have caused considerable concern and hampered the return to strong and sustained growth.

The self-employed were not immune from falling earnings, and the ONS estimates that average weekly income from self-employment fell by 22% since 2008/09 (ONS, 2014b), some of which is due to a reduction in hours of work and some due to changes in the composition of the self-employed population and the work they do (D'Arcy and Gardiner, 2015).

A system of in-work benefits in the form of tax credits and Housing Benefit has helped to support household income among low-earning households, but changes introduced under both the Conservative-Liberal Democrat coalition and under the new Conservative governments will remove this protection for many families. Unless Income Tax changes and increases in the Minimum Wage are enough to compensate, this potentially threatens a consumption-led recovery. Anticipated interest rate rises will put further pressure on household income through higher private household mortgage and financial debt repayment.

Analysing change: relationships between policies and outcomes

Many employment policies and ALMPs introduced under the coalition government have not undergone robust evaluation, and it is therefore difficult to assess how effective they have been in meeting their aims. Some have been shown to be largely ineffective, such as Mandatory Work Activity, but may have improved since then. The NAO, in a recent assessment (NAO, 2014d), concluded that the Work Programme is producing job outcomes and employment sustainment at rates that are comparable with previous welfare-to-work schemes. More recent cohorts appear to be faring better than early cohorts of jobseekers, and there is a potential for improvements to continue (NAO, 2014d). They also highlight the hardest to help groups where the Work Programme was judged to be doing less well than the employment programmes that it replaced, programmes described as 'failing' in the Conservative 2010 manifesto. The government was arguably too hasty in its decision to scrap the Future Jobs Fund, which evaluation evidence has demonstrated produced good results and value for money.

While the majority of unemployment benefit claimants are out of work for short periods of time – around 90% of Jobseeker's Allowance claimants are no longer claiming after 12 months (McKnight, 2015) – those that do go on to experience long-term unemployment, despite all of the innovation we have seen, are still struggling to move back into employment. Even for the most recent cohorts, the majority of those who have received two years on the Work Programme are returned to Jobcentre Plus without securing a job: 70% of all those who had completed the programme up to June 2015 returned to Jobcentre Plus. These two years are in addition to interventions claimants joined the Work Programme, that could be for a period of 12 months. It is hard to believe that the coalition government's policy response (continued by the Conservative government) – Help to Work (introduced in April 2014 with compulsory participation) – is likely to succeed for this group.

Financial incentives to providers to increase efforts for the 'hardest to help' don't appear to have succeeded. There remains evidence of 'creaming' and 'parking' and disappointing results.

There are a number of positive features in the way employment policy evolved under the coalition government, such as extending the length of time assistance is provided for the long-term unemployed and those facing the greatest challenges to securing work to two years (up from 12 months). The stronger focus on longer-term outcomes and employment retention with incentive payments to private providers to back this up is a welcome development. And a system that provides greater incentives to help those hardest to reach and hardest to help may produce positive results but it is too early to judge. Whether the 'black box' model is really producing innovation remains to be seen, and may remain unknown as this information has become commercially sensitive.

Conclusion

As the recession hit the labour market in 2008, unemployment rose steeply, but flows into unemployment slowed sooner than many had anticipated. The rate at which unemployed people found jobs also fell, but again, the fall was not as severe as in earlier recessions nor as sustained. Given the severity of the financial and economic recession. The consequence was that unemployment did not rise by as much as anticipated, and began to fall earlier and faster than expected.

A major reason was the fact that real wage rates fell – not just on average or at the median, but right across the wage distribution. This meant that employers were able to cut labour costs and hold on to workers.

The fact that the recession was not associated with large-scale industrial restructuring meant that it made sense for employers to hang on to employees, particularly skilled employees. This contrasts with the 1980s and 1990s recessions that were characterised by demand shifts and restructuring, leaving large numbers of employees with redundant skills. This provides an explanation for why unemployment and inactivity rates among older workers were much lower than in the 1980s and 1990s recessions.

An increase in self-employment also provides a key to understanding the recovery in the labour market forming a high degree of flexibility, but also great income volatility for this group of workers. The growth in self-employment accounted for all of the recovery in employment rates up to the summer of 2013.

The Labour government acted swiftly as the recession hit the labour market, increasing funding for Jobcentre Plus and employment programmes. Over 2009 a number of guarantees were put in place to help protect younger people from long-term unemployment, with subsidised employment opportunities, through the Young Person's Guarantee and the Future Jobs Fund, training opportunities and extra assistance with finding work. Labour also pressed ahead with reform of disability-related benefits with the introduction of ESA and reform of ALMPs through the phased introduction of the Flexible New Deal.

The coalition government replaced the Flexible New Deal with the Work Programme in June 2011 to provide employment services to the long-term unemployed and those deemed to need extra assistance. Participants can stay on the programme for longer (up to two years), and services are delivered through private providers who are largely paid according to the sustainability of any job outcomes. A harder regime of benefit sanctions is ready to punish those who don't comply with the conditions of benefit receipt. The coalition government also continued the reform of disability-related out-of-work benefits, beginning the process of transferring the stock of Incapacity Benefit claimants to ESA through WCA. The way in which these assessments have been managed and conducted has attracted considerable criticism.

The Work Programme initially failed to meet expectations, but as the economy picked up, outcomes have improved for more recent cohorts joining the programme. However, results are still disappointing for many disabled people referred to the programme, and concerns remain that providers are 'cherry picking'. The government expects that only 6.7% of ESA claimants with a 12-month prognosis and 8.6% of claimants moving from Incapacity Benefit to ESA will secure a job outcome (12 weeks in work) by the time they complete the programme. This raises serious questions about the reliability of the assessments that deem these claimants work-ready, whether the Work Programme is the right intervention for this group, and whether the incentive payments are sufficient to motivate rational profit-making providers to invest in these groups with such a low expected rate of return. The coalition government over-estimated the share of Incapacity Benefit claimants that would be found to be capable of work in a limited capacity (based on WCA). It also overestimated the extent to which those who were assessed to be capable of work would secure employment with the assistance of the Work Programme. These findings call into question what the WCA outcomes mean in practice, given that only 6-7% of some ESA claimants are expected to have found 12 weeks of work at the end of two years of participating in a welfare-to-work programme.

Even though outcomes have improved, it remains the case that the majority of those who join the programme return to Jobcentre Plus after two years (around two-thirds) without securing a job. Work Programme contracts have been extended but come to an end in March 2017, and there is currently no indication of what will replace it.

Falling real wages, underemployment both among employees and the self-employed, mean that living standards have fallen. A strong recovery in real wages seems unlikely without significant increases in productivity. The first budget of the Conservative government in summer 2015 made it clear that a tougher welfare regime was being put into place. The benefit cap was lowered, working-age benefit rates were frozen and in future, ESA claimants will receive the same benefit rate as Jobseeker's Allowance claimants. However, in a surprise move, it was announced that a National Living Wage would replace the National Minimum Wage from April 2016, increasing to reach 60% of median income by 2020. This fundamental change now means that the target has been set by the government rather than the previous model where the independent Low Pay Commission recommending rates to the government. The move reflects a desire to shift the financial 'burden' of low-wage employment from tax credits to employers. However, a recent evaluation of the reforms announced in the Summer Budget 2015 (Elming et al, 2015) highlights the fact that even with the announced increases to the legal minimum wage, many low-earnings households are set to lose out due to the changes in the generosity of in-work cash transfers. While the labour market appears to have weathered the recession well, with a strong legacy left by the Labour government and a sound policy platform to build on, there remains uncertainty on how employment will fare in the recovery phase with changes to ALMPs on the horizon and large changes to wages and household incomes for low-paid workers and low-earning households soon to take effect.

Notes

[1] Initially introduced in 1998, with the cap increasing from £1,000 to £3,000 in 2004.

[2] Prior to November 2008, lone parents with a youngest child up to the age of 16 could claim Income Support. Since then, the threshold age has been

reduced, first to 12, and then 10. The age reduced to 7 in October 2010, and then to age 5 in October 2011.

[3] The Future Jobs Fund supported the creation of subsidised community-focused jobs for unemployed young people. These opportunities were mainly made available through the Young Persons Guarantee.

[4] When the Work Programme contracts began in June 2011, providers were paid an attachment fee to help fund start-up costs. These were phased out and eliminated altogether from July 2014.

[5] Typically Jobseeker's Allowance claimants have to accumulate six months of employment before providers can claim a job outcome payment, and ESA claimants only need to accumulate three months.

[6] Work Programme: DWP provider guidance, see www.gov.uk/government/publications/work-programme-dwp-provider-guidance

SEVEN

Housing

Rebecca Tunstall

The situation on the eve of the crisis

Despite its importance, successive governments have always had an ambiguous and changing approach to addressing housing need and the housing market. Home ownership is the dominant and promoted tenure, and the voluntary sector plays a substantial role in all aspects of social housing provision. Furthermore, devolution and the privatisation of state housing activities have played a substantial role in moves to 'roll back' the state (see, for example, Harloe, 1995; Kemeny, 2001; Hodkinson and Robbins, 2013). Housing is also capital-intensive, which means that it is at particular risk of cuts in times of fiscal withdrawal.

Housing policy is devolved to the Scottish, Welsh and Northern Irish governments, although macroeconomic policy and benefits policy have, up to this point, been retained at UK level (Wong et al, 2011). This chapter focuses on the radical changes to English housing policy and expenditure since 2007.

The coalition's inheritance from the 1997-2010 Labour government

An assessment of English housing policy during 1975-2000, commissioned by the Department for Communities and Local Government (DCLG) (Stephens, 2005), noted that although housing quality improved and people had more choice, nevertheless, demand outstripped supply in many places, making private sector housing unaffordable for many. The rented and owner-occupied housing sectors were often separately concentrated in their own enclaves, and the market was unstable, with potential knock-on effects for the economy (Stephens et al, 2005). Under Labour, the government view was that 'the housing market has structural problems' (DETR, 2000, p 7).

For the 1997-2010 Labour governments, the position of housing within social policy was ambiguous at best. On the one hand, social housing was a key area for efforts to 'roll back' the state (continuing the Thatcher/Major governments' policies of the Right to Buy for council housing and the transfer of council housing to housing associations). In addition, there was active government support for growth of home ownership, and latterly support for the private rented sector too (Hodkinson and Robbins, 2013). On the other hand, state intervention also enjoyed something of a revival under Labour. As in other policy areas, there was a dramatic growth in government expenditure on housing from 2001, peaking in 2009/10. From 1999, the Decent Homes programme set a new housing quality standard, and funding aimed to ensure all social housing reached the standard by 2010. There was also an ambitious and fairly successful programme of neighbourhood renewal (Lupton et al, 2013a). By the early 2000s, concerns about low rates of new building had gained a relatively high profile. The government planned 150,000 new homes per year from 2005 to 2016 (ODPM, 2005) using Regional Spatial Strategies with local targets for building, and continuing capital subsidies for the development of social housing. In reaction to the growing cost of Housing Benefit, the amount that low-income tenants in the *private* rented sector could claim was capped at a Local Housing Allowance (LHA) pegged to local median private rents. Meanwhile, the average price of a home rose from £75,000 to £189,000 during 1997-2007. Social housing waiting lists grew. There was a substantial effort to reduce rough sleeping (DGLG, 2010),[1][2] but the number of homeless households in temporary accommodation almost doubled during 1997-2007.[3]

Housing and the global financial crisis

Housing was blamed – rightly – as one of the triggers of the global financial crisis, due to the meltdown of the infamous 'subprime' mortgage market in the US. From 2008, UK lenders began to be increasingly cautious and demanded higher deposits. This worsened the affordability problems created by big house price increases over the 2000s. From 2009, homeowners with mortgages, concerned about house prices and job security, switched from withdrawing equity from their homes to paying down their mortgages, which meant less spending in the economy (Pawson and Wilcox, 2013). In reaction to the overall problems, government and Bank of England intervention was 'substantial and unprecedented' (Hall, 2011, p 74). The Bank reduced bank base rates from 4.7% to 0.6% in 2009, and then to 0.5% in 2010, significantly reducing the cost of mortgages (Wilcox et al, 2015). The government introduced a Special Liquidity Scheme and a Credit Guarantee Scheme that lent lenders £312 billion, to be repaid by 2014 (Hall, 2011). The government temporarily raised the threshold for stamp duty (house purchase tax) from £125,000 to £250,000 for first-time buyers and those in disadvantaged areas, and funded stalled development schemes. However, in 2010, a new coalition government was elected.

The coalition's housing policy goals

Coalition ministers agreed with the outgoing Labour government and other commentators (Stephens et al, 2005; Hall, 2011; Wong et al, 2011; HM Government, 2012) that the housing system was 'dysfunctional' and suffered from 'persistent market failure' (see, for example, HM Government, 2011a; Prisk, 2012, 2013b). Failure was demonstrated not only in the building slowdown since 2007, but in at least 15 years' undersupply of new homes, growing social housing waiting lists, rising private rents and problems for younger people getting into home ownership (HM Government, 2011a; Shapps, 2011; Boles, 2013). Despite this analysis, there was considerable continuity between the broad goals of the Labour and coalition governments (see, for example, Crisp et al, 2009; Hodkinson and Robbins, 2013; Archer and Cole, 2014). The coalition promoted home ownership, despite acknowledging that it had declined, and that rising prices were at least implicated in the overall downturn. It also promoted private renting for frustrated would-be buyers, rather than social housing. The coalition wanted to increase supply, but without additional expenditure. Housing policy was subordinate to deficit reduction: as the new housing minister Grant Shapps said, 'Housing must take its share of the burden. If we don't there is a real threat to the economic future' (Shapps, 2010).

The coalition's broad housing policy goals for England, among its 224 policy aims stated by 2014, were:

- Increasing the number of available homes;
- Helping people to buy a home;
- Improving the rented sector;
- Providing housing support for older and vulnerable people;
- Simplifying the welfare system and making sure work pays.[4]

The government adopted a set of key indicators to monitor DCLG's performance in policy delivery in England, which cover some of these aims: (1) new home starts and (2) completions; (3) affordable housing starts and (4) completions; (5) households in temporary accommodation; (6) average energy efficiency of new homes; and (7) percentage of planning applications granted permission (DCLG, 2012a).

Increasing the number of available homes

The Localism Act 2011 introduced significant changes to the planning system. A number of these aimed to make getting planning permission easier or more predictable, such as the general presumption in favour of development, the modification of Planning Policy Guidance note 3 (planning advice to local authorities on housing), allowing developers to renegotiate existing contributions to affordable housing and infrastructure, and replacing the previous system of negotiated agreements with fixed Community Infrastructure Levy payments. However, others appeared unpredictable or likely to make getting permission more difficult. These included the abolition of Regional Spatial Strategies and local building targets, and the introduction of neighbourhood planning (Wong et al, 2011). The New Homes Bonus gave an incentive to local authorities to grant permission for development by providing them with funds matching the Council Tax to be charged on new homes for the first six years of their life (and also when empty homes were brought back into use) (Wilson, 2015b). Various schemes were established to encourage building – to pay for infrastructure, to restart stalled schemes, and to delay payment for public land. There were also schemes to bring empty homes into use.

Helping people to buy a home

Ninety-five per cent mortgages, which had made up the majority of products available before 2008, become rare and more costly after the global financial crisis. After the growth in prices in the 2000s, a 10% deposit was on average a prohibitive £20,000. The coalition introduced a major new policy, Help to Buy, to bridge the gap between what lenders were demanding and what aspirant buyers could afford. This built on previous policies but on a much larger scale (NAO, 2014b). Help to Buy had two forms: first, government equity loans to buyers of up to 20% of the price, and second, near-full government mortgage guarantees to lenders of up to 30% of the price. Both enabled 95% mortgages for buyers of homes priced up to £600,000. The other NewBuy scheme enabled 95% mortgages for first-time buyers to buy newly built homes priced up to £500,000. This scheme was the only element linked to the building of new homes rather than buying existing ones. The equity loans involved a total of £3.5 billion in loans and the mortgage guarantee involved a total of £12 billion in guarantees over the life of the schemes (Chandler and Disney, 2014; HM Treasury, 2015a). These large sums were not grants or simple government spending, but in effect, forms of loans, which the government expects will be paid back. However, they carry a risk: payback to the government depends on predictions of house prices, interest rates, inflation and the extent of default.

The Right to Buy, introduced by Margaret Thatcher in 1980, and giving council tenants the right to buy the council property they live in, is probably the best known of recent British housing policies, and is an emblem of welfare state restructuring (Hodkinson et al, 2013). Annual sales peaked at 167,000 in 1982/83, by 2010 they had fallen to 6,000 per year (Wilcox et al, 2015). By then, the most attractive homes were no longer available, discounts had not kept pace with prices, and the recession had affected all types of sales. However, the coalition wanted to 'reinvigorate' the policy (DCLG, 2012b). In April 2012, the maximum discount was extended to £75,000 in England and to £100,000 in London. This would cost the government £45 million a year at the rate of sales seen in 2010, or more if rates increased. Meanwhile, in Scotland the Scottish government went in the opposite direction, effectively ending the Right to Buy in order to protect the stock of affordable housing (Wilcox et al, 2015), while the coalition ended the Labour government's temporary increase in the stamp duty threshold (HM Government, 2010).

Improving the rented sector

As planned in the coalition agreement, changes were made to how council housing was funded (through the Housing Revenue Account). English councils were required to refinance their housing, in a once-off settlement involving write-offs for some authorities, after which central government ceased involvement. This ended the previous longstanding and central role of national government in providing money for council housing building and improvement, and funding historic housing debt. It was of net benefit to most local authority housing departments (Wilcox et al, 2015), but meant that henceforth, central government saw the finance of council housing improvement as a 'local responsibility' devolved to local authorities alone, under the new Localism Act 2011 provision.

This Act also introduced 'a radical programme of reform' for social housing (HM Government, 2011a, p ix). Local authorities were allowed to give greater priority to working households, and other groups such as ex-service personnel in deciding whom to let available homes to, with lesser priority for 'housing need'. The automatic long-term security of tenure for new social housing tenants was abolished. The idea was to introduce different types of tenancies targeted on the periods of life when people were in of greatest need (particularly when on low incomes). Under Labour there had been what, in hindsight, appeared a relatively modest reform, allowing landlords to offer an initial temporary 'probationary' tenancy to new tenants for the first year, to be extended based on 'good behaviour'. The vast majority of landlords were using this power by 2010, although the vast majority of tenancies were also successfully converted into secure ones after the first year. Under the coalition, social landlords were allowed to offer fixed-term tenancies of only five years as standard, with extension dependent not only on good behaviour, but also on evidence of continuing housing need. A large minority of landlords began to experiment with the new power, and in 2012/13, 9% of new lettings were fixed-term tenancies (CIH, 2014). The 2015 Autumn Statement introduced firm plans to abolish lifetime social housing tenancies entirely, and make a five year review of continuing housing need compulsory for new tenancies after April 2015 – paving the way to evict tenants no longer deemed to be in sufficient need. The Act also allowed local authorities to 'discharge' (fulfil) their duty to homeless households by helping to organise tenancies in the private rented sector, rather than by providing them with tenancies in the social housing sector itself. Again, this built on, but markedly extended, a Labour change. The previous Labour government had allowed local authorities to discharge their duty in the private rented sector, but only if the homeless household agreed to it.

Policies also included the promotion of private renting. Since the 1980s, commentators on the UK housing system had raised concerns about private rented housing supply (see, for example, Rugg and Rhodes, 2008). These were at least partially superseded from 1988 when the sector began to increase as a proportion of the whole system. By 2010 there were more households renting privately than in social housing. In addition, the purchase of new build homes by those intending to rent them out (often termed 'buy to rent') had become widespread, and was causing concern in some markets from the mid-2000s. However, one minister said 'we need a bigger and better private rented sector' (quoted by Prisk, 2013a), and attempts to encourage institutional investment and new build specifically for private renting persisted. Some saw the move to minimal capital subsidy and higher rents in social housing as the end of social housing. In addition, the 2011 Budget announced funding for pilots to encourage private landlords and investors to invest in new build for private renting at full market rents (HM Government, 2011a), and reduced stamp duty tax for businesses that bought multiple new homes. The Finance Act 2012 altered the existing Real Estate Investment Trusts that provide tax breaks for institutional investment in the housing market, particularly the private rented sector.

Simplifying the welfare system and making sure work pays

Spending on Housing Benefit (HB) constitutes a major element of total government expenditure on housing policy across the UK (Hills, 2007), although central government does not directly build, maintain or improve any actual housing stock, it may, in effect, act as a subsidy for investors or employers paying low wages. Both the Labour governments and coalition government sought to reduce expenditure, as well as to avoid work disincentives. From 2011, the cap – introduced by Labour – on Housing Benefit subsidising private rents or LHA was reduced from the median to the 30th percentile of local rents (so only rents for the cheapest third of homes would be fully funded). Weekly LHA was capped at £400, regardless of household size or actual rent paid. From 2013, LHA caps increased in line with a different, generally less generous, measure of inflation (the consumer price index [CPI] rather than the retail price index [RPI]), so the proportion of properties where Housing Benefit would cover all the rent for those on low incomes was progressively reduced.

The Welfare Reform Act 2012 contained important additional changes to Housing Benefit for social tenants, each of which aimed to reduce the overall cost to the Treasury. It was also presented as creating particular forms of 'fairness' between claimants and others, alongside other policy goals. The idea was that if households not eligible for benefit could not afford homes in high-cost areas, neither should tenants get public subsidies through Housing Benefit to live in these more desirable areas. In addition, a social rented sector size criterion (widely known as the 'bedroom tax' and applying to social tenants of working age) mirrored the 'bedroom standard' that already applied to private rented tenants – not subsidising 'extra' bedrooms. Unlike the policy for private renters, it was introduced for all tenancies, not just new ones, in a tenure that much higher proportions of tenants had made their lifelong home, and of whom much higher proportions had disabilities or other special needs requiring 'extra' rooms. Either people moved (often difficult due to lack of smaller properties), 'freeing up' larger homes (DWP, 2012b), or their benefits were cut, leading to savings for the government. In practice, by far the biggest effect has been savings for the government, although the policy contributed just 2% of all cuts by 2014/15 (Wilcox S, 2014), and did not prevent an overall increase in overall Housing Benefit expenditure.

The main means to 'simplify' the welfare system was Universal Credit, intended to provide a combined replacement for Housing Benefit, Jobseeker's Allowance, Employment Support Allowance (ESA) and some tax credits. It was intended that the single benefit would be easier to understand and would mean that claimants were not subject to varied and multiple clawbacks as their incomes rose. Payment of Housing Benefit to tenants rather than to landlords (previously the norm) was intended to make tenants take responsibility for budgeting. It was also presented as creating a level playing field between social and private landlords, who generally already had to get rent from tenants and manage the risk of arrears.

To help manage the impact of these various changes, local authorities were given additional money in a discretionary fund to support residents facing short-term problems meeting housing costs (Discretionary Housing Payments, or DHPs). This budget rose from to £60 million in 2012/13, to £180 million in 2013/14 and £165 million in 2014/15, although this was still only a small fraction of the savings expected from the policy changes.

The welfare system had been almost entirely run at UK level. The greater use of DHPs, alongside the devolution of Council Tax Benefit, was a marked development of the nations' and English local authorities' roles in the welfare system, and substantially increased local variation and discretion in the welfare system The Scottish government successfully requested permission to make its own contributions to DHP budgets, sufficient to compensate all those affected by the 'bedroom tax' in 2014/15 (Wilson, 2014). This constituted an important step into the development of Scotland's own benefits system.

The new Conservative government, 2015

During the 2015 General Election, the Conservative Party campaigned to extend the coalition's radical policies on the social housing and Housing Benefit elements of the housing safety net, and to continue its policies on housebuilding and home ownership, which had been at most only modestly successful. It promised a review of lifetime social housing tenancies. Social tenants with incomes over £30,000 a year (or £40,000 in London) would be charged market or 'near market' rents or encouraged to leave. It promised to extend the Right to Buy to all housing association tenants on similar terms to those for council tenants, even where housing associations were charities. This would be achieved without net costs to central government, but with a multiplied impact on total social housing stocks, because local authorities would be required to sell higher value council homes and provide the revenue to the Treasury. Most people aged 18-21 who were not in work would no longer be eligible for Housing Benefit, and would thus have to be accommodated by their families or friends. The Party promised to enable the building of 200,000 new homes to be sold to first-time buyers under 40 for 20% less than market prices, although details were limited. Further schemes to stimulate new building on public sector and other brownfield land were proposed. The Party promised to extend Help to Buy to 2020, and a tax-free savings account to help those saving for a deposit. It also promised but did not fully specify £12 billion in welfare cuts (The Conservative Party, 2015).

After the May 2015 General Election, the Conservative Party was able to form a single-party government and put its housing pledges into action. In July 2015, a summer budget provided details of welfare changes and other spending (HM Treasury, 2015b), and further proposals were announced in the Chancellor's Autumn Statement (AS) in November 2015. Social landlords were required to reduce rents by 1% a year until 2020, a substantial real terms cut, so that social landlords could 'play their part in reducing the welfare bill' (HM Treasury, 2015b, p 37). This replaced the previous regime agreed in the 2000s and confirmed as recently as 2013, by which social housing rents rose annually by inflation plus 1% (Wilson, 2015a). Over the 1990s and 2000s, social landlords had collectively borrowed billions to build new homes on the assumption of steady growth in rent income. There was no direct policy on rents in the private rented sector. However, the amount of money all Housing Benefit claimants could earn before affecting their benefit was to be reduced, and the rate of clawback was to be increased. The LHA (maximum Housing Benefit for private tenants) would be frozen until 2020, a substantial real terms cut, and the benefits cap was reduced further, to £20,000 and £23,000 in London, meaning an increase in the number of households facing shortfalls between actual rent and Housing Benefit. The AS also announced plans to restrict social housing rents to the relevant Local Housing Allowance rate levels, for new tenancies from April 2016. In addition, contributions to the public sector by private developers (s106) would no longer be used to subsidise rental housing but solely for lower-cost home ownership. Discretionary Housing Payments would continue until 2020, at a similar nominal rate.

A few spending reductions affected those who were not tenants. Private landlords would no longer be able to claim higher rate mortgage tax relief for their homes. Support for Mortgage Interest payments for homeowners who were out of work would be converted from a grant into a loan to be repaid. In a rare planned increase in spending on housing, estates of up to £1 million (likely to be dominated by residential property) were excluded from inheritance tax (HM Treasury, 2015b).

Spending on housing

As long ago as the mid-1990s, it was recognised that the benefits to homeowners of tax concessions on property ownership significantly outweighed wider government social policy expenditure on housing and community amenities (Hills, 2007). Given a government deficit, housing is a potential area where additional taxation on owners might have been introduced. However, rather than doing this, the vast majority of the government's economic policies for housing took the form of cutting spending. The following sections report Public Expenditure Statistical Analysis (PESA) for the DCLG, the main department with responsibility for housing in England.[5,6] Similar patterns were seen for housing expenditure across UK central government (Tunstall, 2015).

Department for Communities and Local Government budgets for England

The DCLG is responsible for the main elements of government spend on housing, as well as for providing the majority of funding for local government. Under Labour, DCLG day-to-day (revenue) and capital investment budgets grew before and after the recession, to a peak in 2009/10. Spending fell sharply under the coalition government.

Figure 7.1 reports DCLG's revenue budgets,[7,8] which include housing and all other types of spending by the department in England. There was a dramatic downward trend from a peak at £41 billion (in 2014/15 prices) in the last full Labour government year 2009/10, to £16 billion

Box 7.1: Housing policy timeline

Timeline years: 2007 | 2008 | 2009 | 2010 | 2011 | 2012 | 2013 | 2014 | 2015

2007

No direct policy on rents in the private sector

Regional Spatial Strategies aim for 150,000 new homes per year

Social housing 'Decent Homes' programme continues

Capital subsidies to developers building new social housing

Local Housing Allowance (LHA) maximum Housing Benefit for private tenants, linked to median local rents

2009

Government creates Special Liquidity Scheme and Credit Guarantee Scheme, lending mortgage lenders £312 billion

Stamp duty threshold raised from £125,000 to £250,000 for first-time buyers

2010

Regional Spatial Strategies abolished, replaced by 'New Home Bonus' incentive for local authorities to permit building

2011

Localism Act 2011. Local authorities given more autonomy over the allocation of social housing. English councils required to refinance their housing, devolved from central government. Lifetime tenancies abolished. New social tenancies 'probationary' for first year, convertible to 5-year fixed tenancy dependent on evidence of need and good behaviour

LHA reduced from the median to the 30th percentile of market rents (lowest third only fully funded by Housing Benefit). LHA capped at £400 per week regardless of household size or actual rent paid

2012

Welfare Reform Act 2012, the 'bedroom tax' removes the 'spare room subsidy' for all social tenancies (aims but fails to reduce Housing Benefit expenditure)

2013

LHA cap increases by CPI instead of RPI, lower measure of inflation

Help to Buy for first-time buyers; equity loans for up to 20% purchase price and mortgage guarantees to lenders of up to 30% of the price. Reintroduces some 95% loan-to-value mortgages

2014

Mortgage lending criteria for borrowers reformed

2015

LHA frozen until 2020

Unemployed 18- to 21-year-olds no longer entitled to Housing Benefit

Social tenants earning over £30,000 (£40,000 in London) charged market rents

Mortgage interest payments. unemployed home-owners, converted from grant to repayable loan

Figure 7.1: DCLG's revenue expenditure, 2007/08-2015/16 (in real terms at 2014/15 prices, £ billion)

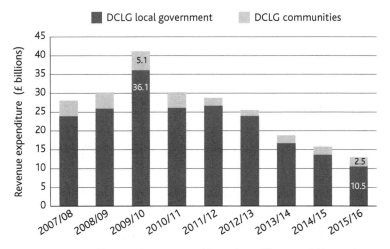

Source: PESA 2012, Table 1.4 and PESA 2015, Table 1.4, https://data.gov.uk/dataset/public_expenditure_statistical_analyses

under the coalition in 2014/15, and with further reductions planned by the Conservative government to £13 billion in 2015/16.

Taking into account the fact that the DCLG had some responsibilities added and some taken away,[9] the cut to continuing 'local government' and 'communities' responsibilities under the coalition was at least 41% during 2009/10-2014/15. These cuts were equivalent in scale to the budgetary transitions immediately after 1945, when the UK government was withdrawing at speed from its war effort (Taylor-Gooby, 2012). The Conservative government planned further cuts for 2015/16 at least (HM Treasury, 2015b).

In relation to local authority funding, Hastings et al (2013) calculated that the overall cuts in core local authority budgets in England 2008/09 to 2014/15 totalled 29% in real terms. Reductions in spending on housing by councils during 2010/11-2014/15 averaged 34% for unitary authorities and 17% for districts (NAO, 2014a).[10] Expenditure on homelessness, housing advice, private sector regulation and renewal, housing-linked support and new building were reduced (Wilcox et al, 2015). These changes meant that the local government had fewer means to ensure that housing policy goals were delivered.

DCLG capital spend mainly consists of funding for the Homes and Communities Agency to support new building for social housing and low-cost home ownership by housing associations. Under Labour, DCLG capital expenditure grew to a peak of £10.3 billion in 2009/10. Under the coalition, capital expenditure fell even more dramatically than revenue expenditure, to a low of £2.7 billion in 2012/13 (at 2014/15 prices). This represents an overall decline of 54% during 2009/10-2014/15, the largest fall among departments with significant capital budgets. The Affordable Housing Programme, 2010/11-2013/14, announced in the 2011 Budget, provided one-sixth of the total public subsidy for new social housing and low-cost home ownership housing development seen in the previous programme (Pawson and Wilcox, 2013).

The government intended that the gap in finances would be filled by charging higher rents, to be paid by tenants (or for those on low incomes, by Housing Benefit), at up to 80% of market rents, well above standard social rents for most homes in most parts of the country. But this could be also described as the end of the direct support for the development of new social housing.

New policies to support home ownership were treated quite differently, however. In the 2012 Autumn Statement, DCLG home ownership received among the largest absolute increases in capital budgets[11] of any departments, of £0.8 billion in 2013/14 and £0.9 billion in 2014/15 (in 2014/15 prices) (HM Treasury, 2013a, p 47). This was continued in the Budget 2013 which saw £1.3 billion in 2013-14 and £1.9 billion in 2014-15 to underwrite Help to Buy and the smaller Build to Rent scheme (HM Treasury, 2013a, p 47). The National Audit Office (NAO) commented on Help to Buy: 'The scheme's size and design matches the Department's intention to make a substantial impact on the housing market' (NAO, 2014b, p 7). The Conservative government continued this policy. However, this still left capital expenditure in 2015/16 at just £5.3 billion, about half the peak level (see Figure 7.2).

UK government spending on Housing Benefit, 2007/08-2014/15

Unlike all previous forms of housing spending, spending on tenants and landlords via Housing Benefit rose under the Labour government, then continued to rise under the coalition government. Total spending in real terms rose during 2009/10-2012/13 by 9%.[12] However, the rate of growth of Housing Benefit expenditure slowed under the coalition.

The £2 billion increase in spending on Housing Benefit under the coalition was considerably less than, and no compensation for, the total £10.5 billion coalition cuts in other housing budgets over the same period.[13] As a rent subsidy it also was paid to landlords, rather than being a capital investment into housing assets.

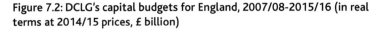

Figure 7.2: DCLG's capital budgets for England, 2007/08-2015/16 (in real terms at 2014/15 prices, £ billion)

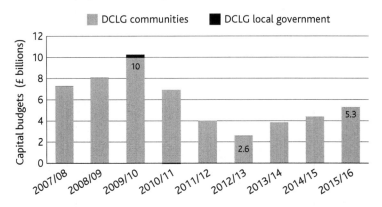

Source: PESA 2012, Table 1.7 and PESA 2015, Table 1.9, https://data.gov.uk/dataset/public_expenditure_statistical_analyses

Nevertheless the cost of Housing Benefit did not change significantly as a percentage of all welfare benefits and tax credits for most of the period. It made up 14.4% of the Great Britain total in 2009/10 and 14.9% in 2012/13. A drop was projected for 2013/14, due to effects of welfare reform and employment growth (Wilson, 2014).

But, and this is a crucial point, Housing Benefit expenditure made up an increasing proportion of all expenditure on housing. In 2009/10, UK Housing Benefit expenditure was 58% of the total, but by 2012/13, it had grown to 71%. Housing development had fallen from 28% of the total to 17%. It was a marked development in an ongoing trend away from spending on the housing stock to effectively using housing funding to provide short-term wage subsidies.

Outputs and outcomes

This section reports policy implementation and impacts judged against the main goals of policy and key DCLG business plan indicators.

Impacts on 'Increasing the number of available homes'

Since the recession began in 2007, there has been a modest net increase in the total number of homes in the UK, from 27.0 million in 2008 to 27.9 million in 2013. However, the rate of new development dropped markedly (Figure 7.3).[14]

Figure 7.3: UK housebuilding completions, 2007-08 to 2014-15

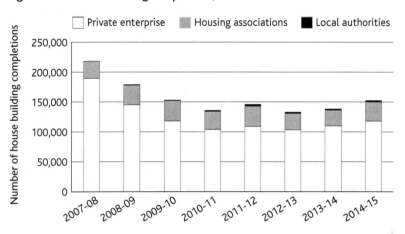

Source: DCLG Live table 211 https://www.gov.uk/government/statistical-data-sets/live-tables-on-house-building (last accessed January 2016)

The number of new home completions continued to fall slightly during 2009/10-2013/14 (by 8%). In contrast, the number of new home starts increased by 40%, probably linked to Help to Buy and improving economic conditions generally. Despite reduced government support for DCLG capital budgets, the number of affordable home starts also increased. This change should feed through to completions figures in 2014/15. Overall, however, supply remained well below both the 2006/07 peak and the level necessary to satisfy the needs of the estimated 180,000-240,000 new households formed per year (Whitehead and Williams, 2011).[15]

Impact on 'Helping people to buy a home'

By 2013, mortgages were becoming more affordable in relation to incomes, making things slightly easier for buyers. Mortgages were becoming more readily available after the most severe parts of the credit crunch. However, in 2014 the Financial Conduct Authority required lenders to add to tests on applicants to ensure loans would be repayable. In addition, prices were rising in most parts of the UK (Chandler and Disney, 2014).

By 2015, 47,000 homes had been bought through the Help to Buy mortgage, and in addition a further 47,000 had been bought through Help to Buy equity loans (HM Government, 2015; HM Treasury, 2015a). The majority of buyers were first-timers, and the homes involved were of around average cost. However, the NAO commented that it was difficult to assess whether the scheme had led to more or different purchases than would have occurred without it (NAO, 2014b). A large proportion of academic and practitioner commentators, including the International Monetary Fund (IMF) and NAO, thought Help to Buy had the potential to cause self-defeating price inflation (see, for example, IMF, 2013; Chandler and Disney, 2014; NAO, 2014b; Wilcox et al, 2015). Right to Buy sales fell from 15,000 per year in England in 2007/08 to 3,000 in 2009/10, probably in response to market conditions, but then increased to 16,000 in 2013/14, probably in response both to the increase in discounts and to the improvement in the overall market.[16]

The marked reductions in interest rates, introduced before the coalition government by the Bank of England in response to the financial crisis, favoured existing homeowners with tracker mortgages. These households would personally save an estimated total £20 billion (FSA, 2010), close to an entire annual Housing Benefit budget. In contrast, social housing rents continued to increase above inflation, and the Affordable Rents in social housing were closer to market rates, while the coverage of Housing Benefit was reduced.

Overall, the proportion of households spending more than a third of their income on housing costs rose from 8% at the start of the 2000s to 18% in 2008/09, and then fell, largely due to the falls in mortgage costs. Under the coalition it was stable, at about 14%. On a median income, and using 35% of income as a measure of affordability, a couple with one child could not afford to buy a two-bedroom home in 22% of local authorities in 2010/11, including most London boroughs, and could not afford to rent privately in 18% of local authorities (Alakeson and Cory, 2013).

Impact on 'Improving the rented sector'

After increased spending under Labour, coalition policy reduced expenditure on existing rented housing. The Decent Homes programme was much reduced (Pawson and Wilcox, 2013), and following Housing Revenue Account reform there will be no further support from central government of this kind. Just 6,000 private rented homes received improvements via local authority funding in 2012/13. The abolition of the Tenant Services Authority and reductions in local authority budgets have reduced the regulation of rented housing. Changes to social renters' tenancy and Housing Benefit eligibility were partly intended to improve 'fairness' between tenures, by levelling down.

Impact on 'Simplifying the welfare system and making sure work pays'

Reductions in the numbers of households eligible and amount of rent eligible for Housing Benefit support reduced out-of-work income after housing costs but did not increase in-work income. These changes (making non-working households poorer and not rewarding working households) were intended to incentivise work, and there is some evidence that employment rates for people affected by Housing Benefit changes increased, but it is hard to determine whether benefit changes were responsible (Clarke et al, 2014; Hickman et al, 2014).

The number of claimants increased each year from 2002/03 to 2014, but then fell slightly to 4.8 million in 2015, probably as reforms began to have an impact. The average weekly payments per household increased every year to 2015.[17] Thus, the overall cost of Housing Benefit continued to grow to 2015.

Impact on 'Providing housing support for older and vulnerable people'

People over pension age have been exempted from many reforms that restrict housing and other benefits. However, cuts in local authority budgets have meant a concentration on child protection at the expense of adult services. Local authorities reported 45% reductions in Supporting People budgets (funding hostels and housing-related support for homeless and vulnerable people) and 43% reductions in housing welfare budgets during 2010/11-2014/15 (NAO, 2014a). Under the coalition, the DCLG stopped collecting data on local authority grants for facilities for disabled people, but it seems likely that expenditure reduced. Chapter Nine also considers changes in the provision of personal care to older and vulnerable people.

Homelessness

Action on homelessness was not among the coalition's key policy goals, but it is a good indicator of housing system problems of supply, affordability and distribution.[18] Fewer people became homeless as a result of mortgage repossessions than in previous recessions, due to lower unemployment, lower interest rates and different lender behaviour. However, counts of rough sleepers in England had increased from 1,768 in 2010[19] to 2,744 in 2014 (DCLG, 2015a). The number of households accepted as unintentionally homeless and in priority need by local authorities in England fell by 33% from 65,000 in 2007 to 42,000 in 2009, but then rose by 26% to 53,000 in 2014.[20,21] The number of households in temporary accommodation after being accepted as homeless, a DCLG performance indicator (DCLG, 2012a), fell by 43% from 87,000 in 2007 to 50,000 in 2010, but then grew again, by 30%, to 65,000 in 2015.[22] Budgets for managing homelessness received a much smaller cut than other housing funds, although demand for services was higher (NAO 2014a).

The effect of policy on different social groups

The coalition pledged that when it acted to reduce the deficit, the rich would 'pay more than the poorest, not just in terms of cash, but as a proportion of income as well' (HM Government, 2010). However, most of the effects of coalition housing policy appear to be at best neutral between income groups and at worst markedly unfavourable to poorer or more disadvantaged people. The same appears likely to be true of Conservative policies true of initially announced Conservative policies. The marked reductions in budgets available to councils and welfare reforms are likely to have a regressive effect. Some groups have gained, such as those with flexible rate mortgages already in place who have not needed to move, those in areas where housing prices have recovered and grown (especially London and the South East), some of those taking up Help to Buy, and larger developers.

Conclusion

Over the period 2007/08-2015, the UK housing system has been widely diagnosed as structurally unsound, and it played some role in the transmission of the global financial crisis into the UK economy. Nonetheless, Labour, coalition and Conservative policies have all shown broad continuity with pre-crisis policies, and have focused on stimulating the market. Since 2010, this has been accompanied by dramatic major funding cuts through more lending and less planning. Coalition and Conservative policies to date have all further reduced government involvement in housing, the 'wobbly pillar' of the welfare state. Coalition changes weakened each of the three main housing elements of the UK's welfare state 'safety net' – protection for priority homeless households, social housing and Housing Benefit – transferring risk to individual households and to some extent, to social landlords.

The coalition set important precedents, including housing association rents rising above traditional 'social rent' levels; social housing development by social landlords without public subsidy; the end of the assumption of security of tenure for council tenants which was introduced by Margaret Thatcher in 1980; and Housing Benefit at sub-cost levels leaving tenants with shortfalls. The Conservative government has challenged the property of charities and the assets of local authorities, presenting a potential end game for the 125-year-old national, local and charitable project of social housing in the UK. Conservative policies have already extended these changes for social housing and Housing Benefit.

Housing has contributed more than 'its share' to deficit reduction that the coalition's first housing minister required. The one major exception to the spending cuts on housing was the boost given to housing purchase, development and lending from 2012 through Help to Buy, although this still left spending below historic levels. Helping tenants in existing homes and their landlords via Housing Benefit, rather than supporting new housebuilding, already dominated total government expenditure on housing when the coalition took power (unless tax concessions to owners and landlords are taken into account). The coalition continued the trend of shifting government expenditure from new development to Housing Benefit. The Conservative government will make a further substantial effort to reduce spending, at the likely potential cost of reduced social and affordable housing development, as well as tenant hardship and increased homelessness.

In summary, the coalition did not have significant or unambiguous successes against its housing policy goals (increasing the number of available homes; helping people to buy a home; improving the rented sector; providing housing support for older and vulnerable people; simplifying the welfare system; and making sure work pays).[23]

The Conservative government's housing policy goals are yet to be fully set out, but it still faces all the problems identified by Stephens et al (2005) 10 years earlier and acknowledged by the coalition, and some of these problems have actually worsened. In 2014, the Governor of the Bank of England said that the housing market still had 'deep, deep structural problems'.[24] In 2015, demand ran even further ahead of supply than it had done in 2005. There were still affordability problems, and tenure and spatial polarisation. The fragmentation of the governance of new housing development and the fraying of the welfare safety net had been intentionally increased by the coalition and the Conservative government in the name of localism, economic goals and restructuring. The individual and systemic risk relating to home ownership remained, and additional risk had been transferred to households and social landlords.

Notes

[1] For previous published figures on the street count of people sleeping rough in England, by local authority, 1998-2009, see DCLG (2010a).

[2] Voluntary sector counts produced estimates 10 times higher; see www.londonspovertyprofile.org.uk/indicators/topics/housing-and-homelessness/rough-sleeping-in-london/

[3] See DCLG (2012a), live table 782, 'Household types in temporary accommodation, 2006-15'.

[4] See www.gov.uk/government/policies

[5] PESA data provide a good guide to budgets and expenditure, but do not fully separate out housing budgets or expenditure.

[6] PESA data distinguish between planned budgets and 'out-turn expenditure' (actual expenditure), which may be different to planned budgets.

[7] Officially termed 'resource departmental expenditure limits' (DELs).

[8] These cover both the 'local government' sub-department, including funds local authorities spend on housing, and a small contribution to the 'communities' sub-department, including some spending on housing-linked activities provided by central government programmes such as projects for rough sleepers and neighbourhood regeneration. For more details, see HM Government (2013, pp 154-6).

[9] For details of changes, see HM Treasury (2013a, p 15). The coalition also changed the name of the department, from 'CLG' to 'DCLG'.

[10] Reductions would have been greater for the period 2009/10-2014/15.

[11] Officially, 'resource DELs'.

[12] The relevant United Nations (UN) expenditure category is 'Social protection: Housing'. These data are used in preference to the very similar Department for Work and Pensions (DWP) data for comparability with other PESA government data.

[13] A total of £6.3 billion from 'housing and community amenities' and £5.3 billion from 'housing development', at 2014/15 prices.

[14] DCLG live table 17c, 'Dwellings by tenure in Great Britain, Northern Ireland and the United Kingdom', www.gov.uk/government/organisations/department-for-communities-and-local-government/about/statistics

[15] DCLG live table, 'Household interim projections, 2011-2021, England', www.gov.uk/government/statistics/household-interim-projections-2011-to-2021-in-england

[16] DCLG live table 678, 'Social housing sales: Annual sales by scheme for England: 1980-81 to 2013-14', www.gov.uk/government/statistical-data-sets/live-tables-on-dwelling-stock-including-vacants

[17] DCLG live table 113, 'Housing Benefit caseload statistics'; see www.gov.uk/government/collections/housing-benefit-and-council-tax-benefit-caseload-statistics--2

[18] Other potential policy outcomes that are not looked at here include housing quality, environmental sustainability and the contribution of the housing system to sustainable economic growth.

[19] This figure was based on a new method introduced in 2010.

[20] See DCLG (2012a), DCLG live table 770, 'Statutory homelessness'; see www.gov.uk/government/statistical-data-sets/live-tables-on-homelessness

[21] These changes followed a long rise in the number of homeless households, from 105,000 in 1998 to 136,000 in 2003, followed by a fall during the late 2000s and into the recession.

[22] The number of households in temporary accommodation rose from under 50,000 in 1998 to over 100,000 in 2006, followed by a fall during the late 2000s.

[23] See www.gov.uk/government/policies

[24] Governor of the Bank of England, Mark Carney, in an interview with Sky News, 18 May 2014, http://news.sky.com/story/1263732/carney-house-prices-biggest-risk-to-economy

EIGHT

Health

Polly Vizard, Polina Obolenskaya and Emily Jones

The situation on the eve of the crisis

On the eve of the financial crisis, in the summer of 2007, the UK was experiencing a period of substantial and sustained increases in real public expenditure on health. Looking back to 1997, Labour had made the transition into power with health at the top of the political agenda, with Blair urging voters to support Labour in order to 'save the NHS'. Successive Labour Party manifestos, in 1997, 2001 and 2005, had put emphasis on an overall commitment to the NHS, free at the point of delivery and based on need, not the ability to pay, while highlighting the need to finance a major programme of healthcare investment, modernisation and reform. Real public expenditure on health in the UK had almost doubled during Blair's decade in power, with a real increase from £64.4 billion in 1997/98 to £116.9 billion in 2007/08 (HM Treasury, 2015c).

The results of Labour's large-scale cash investment in healthcare are discussed in detail in our companion paper (see Vizard and Obolenskaya, 2013). The substantial growth in resources during Labour's first two terms in office financed a major supply-side expansion in healthcare, with a considerable expansion of NHS inputs and outputs including staffing, services and healthcare activities. Substantial returns to Labour's investment in health over this period were also reflected in overall indicators of healthcare quality and satisfaction. In 1997, the public had been highly dissatisfied with the NHS, with long waiting lists, pressure for more expenditure on healthcare and demand for private medical insurance going up. By 2007/08, waiting list length and waiting times were down, growth in spending on private medical insurance cover was down, and satisfaction with the NHS had increased substantially.

On healthcare modernisation and reform, a new framework for inspection and regulation had been put into place after 1997 and further evolved during Labour's first two terms. The purchaser–

provider split that had been introduced under previous Conservative administrations was retained under Blair, and further reforms emphasised commissioning, organisational decentralisation, competition and patient choice, and information on outcomes. By 2007/08, Labour's healthcare delivery model included autonomous NHS foundation trusts, practice-based GP commissioning and a new system of payment by results, based on the principle that resources should 'follow' the patient to the service they choose. These policy arrangements continued to be combined with the extensive use of targets, Public Service Agreements and centralised forms of management (so-called 'command and control').

An increasing trend towards health services that are publicly financed but that are provided by non-NHS (private and third sector) providers was also apparent at the beginning of Labour's third term in office. However, it is important to note that the growth in health services that are publicly financed but provided by non-NHS (private and third sector) bodies was from a very low base, and that the share of public expenditure on such services in total public expenditure on healthcare remained relatively low in 2007/08.

There can be no doubt that, as a result of Labour's programme of investment, modernisation and reform, the coalition that came to power in 2010 inherited an NHS that had been radically improved compared with the NHS of 1997. Independent assessments and research study evidence are reviewed in our companion paper (Vizard and Obolenskaya, 2013); important limitations relating to policy development, implementation, performance management, impacts and outcomes are also highlighted in these analyses. Debate also continues regarding the contribution of organisational decentralisation and commissioning, and competition and patient choice, vis-à-vis other policy instruments – such as resource and capacity expansion; more specialised service delivery; improvements in primary care provision; and inspection, regulation and information – as drivers of quality improvement. Overall, however, key assessments identify a 'step-change' in NHS performance during Labour's early years (The King's Fund, 2005) with 'considerable progress in moving the NHS towards becoming a high-performing health system' by 2010 (Thorlby and Maybin, 2010, p 113).

Nevertheless, by summer 2007, it was becoming clear that the task that Labour had set itself of improving overall health outcomes and tackling health inequalities was yielding only limited results against the targets that had been set. Despite substantial and important reductions in premature death rates for heart and other circulatory diseases and lung cancer, and in smoking prevalence, progress in addressing obesity had been disappointing. Health inequalities, a major priority for Labour, remained deeply embedded. Health inequalities targets aimed, among other things, to reduce absolute and relative inequalities in life expectancy and mortality from the 'major killers' between the so-called 'spearhead' areas and England a whole, and to reduce inequalities in the infant mortality rate among different occupational groups. Disappointing progress against these targets was already apparent at the end of the Blair years – although, as we note in the 'Outcomes' section of this chapter later, progress in relation to the infant mortality inequalities target picked up during Labour's third term.

The UK's position on international health outcomes league tables also remained problematic in 2007. The UK was still lagging behind the best performers and comparator countries in relation to a range of outcomes based on OECD comparative data.

On healthcare quality, the full scale and implications of the Mid Staffordshire NHS Trust scandal had yet to emerge in the summer of 2007. However, an expanding body of evidence on variations in hospital performance and sub-standard healthcare posed a major challenge.

Political debates around the sustainability of real increases in public expenditure on healthcare, as well as 'value for money' and productivity, had begun to intensify by the summer of 2007. A planned easing off of the rate of increase in public expenditure on healthcare after 2007/08 had been foreseen in the Wanless Review (Wanless, 2002). This reflected a shift from a 'catch up' towards a 'keep up' trajectory – with the growth of public expenditure on healthcare falling back following a substantial hike in the five years following the 2002 Budget. By autumn 2007, the new Chancellor, Alistair Darling, was warning of the gravity and depth of the crisis, and that purse strings would need to tighten further. However, the 2007 Comprehensive Spending Review assumed that GDP would continue its steady growth, and expenditure plans were set on this basis (Hills, 2011).

Policies under Labour, 2007-10

Labour's overarching goals on health and its healthcare delivery model stayed broadly unchanged with the transition of the premiership from Brown to Blair in June 2007. However, there were changes of policy emphasis and direction. While the pace and scope of healthcare reform had accelerated during Blair's second term, the transfer of the premiership to Brown from Blair in the summer of 2007 was associated with less emphasis on further structural reform and on the 'competition and choice' policy agenda. Nevertheless, a 'free choice' of hospital providers that conformed to NHS quality and price standards (including Independent Sector Treatment Centres), piloted after 2006, was expanded in April 2008. The policy of financing long-term infrastructural investment in healthcare through public–private partnerships (private finance initiatives, or PFIs) also continued.

The publication of the Darzi Review (DH, 2008b) was followed by a consultation and the establishment of the NHS Constitution in 2009. This represented a key new accountability measure, reaffirming the right to NHS services free of charge (with equal access for all); setting out waiting time commitments, including commitments to 18-week waiting times for referral to non-urgent treatment; confirming patient choice; and imposing a legal duty on all NHS organisations to take account of the Constitution.

On public health, a ban on smoking in public places had been included in the Health Act 2006, and came into effect in England in July 2007. This was perhaps Labour's most significant public health measure during its three terms in office. The legal age for tobacco sales was increased from 16 to 18 in October 2007, and further provisions to protect children and young people from the harm caused by tobacco were introduced in the Health Act 2009. Emphasis on early intervention continued with the publication of a new children and young people's health strategy.

A review of progress during Labour's period in power concluded that health inequalities are 'persistent, stubborn and difficult to change' (DH, 2009a, p 12). While ambitious health inequalities targets had been set out in Labour's Public Service Agreements and in departmental objectives, there was more emphasis on local accountability after 2006/07, with Joint Strategic Needs Assessments and Local Area Agreements becoming statutory requirements in 2008. This emphasis on local accountability reflected, among other things, concerns that health inequalities targets had been insufficiently embedded; that national and local performance management systems had been insufficiently aligned; and that levers and delivery systems for implementation had been insufficiently coordinated and too weak (DH, 2008a, 2009a; NAO, 2010). In a bid to speed up progress on reducing health inequalities, a Health Inequalities Intervention Tool was introduced. This identified three key interventions (increasing the prescribing of drugs to control blood pressure and to reduce cholesterol, together with an increase in smoking prevention activities) as the most cost-effective ways of reducing the gap in life expectancy (NAO, 2010).

Three major reviews published findings during this period. First, the Darzi Review (DH, 2008b) made recommendations on the development of a patient-focused NHS and on 'outcome-orientated' monitoring. Second, following the publication of a Healthcare Commission report in 2008, the Independent Inquiry into the Mid Staffordshire NHS Foundation Trust, chaired by Robert Francis, was announced. This set out findings on the full extent of the Mid Staffordshire scandal in February 2010 (Francis, 2010). Third, the Marmot Review (Marmot, 2010) was published in the months running up to the 2010 General Election. Building on the World Health Organization (WHO) Commission on the Social Determinants of Health as well as earlier reviews including the Black Review (Townsend et al, 1992) and the Acheson Inquiry (Acheson, 1998), this recognised the need for a new health inequalities strategy and set out proposals for moving forward. The Review proposed a new indicator-based framework for monitoring health inequalities using a social determinants approach. Existing health inequalities targets based on Labour's 'spearhead' approach were criticised for being too insensitive to 'within-area' inequalities, and new indicators capturing inequalities *within* as well as *between* areas were proposed.

Policies under the coalition, 2010-15

The pause in further structural reform, from 2007 to 2010, ended abruptly following the 2010 General Election. Reforms emphasising decentralisation, competition and outcomes were rapidly, simultaneously and controversially implemented under the coalition government, and resulted in new arrangements for health services commissioning, management and provision.

The coalition's health reforms were implemented in the context of a broader vision of a reforming government emphasising the de-centralisation of power, the creation of a 'smaller'/'smarter' state, and the restructuring of public services. The coalition argued in its *Programme for government* that Conservative thinking on markets, competition and choice, combined with the Liberal Democrats' emphasis on advancing democracy, had resulted in shared plans 'more radical and comprehensive than our individual manifestos' (HM Government, 2010, p 8). An *Open public services* White Paper set out the coalition's public service model based on decentralisation, competition and provider diversification – with an expanded role for the private and third sector as providers of public services – and outcomes (HM Government, 2011b).

Policy development under the coalition (2010-15) is examined in detail in Vizard and Obolenskaya (2015); see also Glennerster (2015a) for further analysis. An overview of the coalition's health reforms is provided in Box 8.1. The Health and Social Care Act 2012 transformed the policy landscape for the commissioning, management and provision of health services in England, with many of the changes introduced on 1 April 2013. The new decentralised organisational structure established by the Act included an independent NHS Board, the abolition of strategic health authorities and existing primary care trusts (PCTs), with all trusts expected to become foundation trusts, and the creation of GP-led clinical commissioning groups (CCGs). On competition, the Act applied an 'any qualified provider' rule to commissioning, intended to promote competitive tendering between public, private and third sector providers. Monitor was given new responsibilities as an economic regulator and to combat anti-competitive behaviour. The Act also lifted the cap on private patient revenue, empowered hospitals to generate 49% of their income from private patient revenue, and established a new trust failure regime for 'financially unsustainable' bodies.

The White Paper, *Equity and excellence: Liberating the NHS*, stated that 'the primary purpose of the NHS is to improve the outcomes of healthcare for all' (DH, 2010, p 21). This emphasis on outcomes was reflected in the Health and Social Care Act 2012, which introduced new statutory duties to improve the quality of healthcare, as well as in the introduction of the new outcomes-orientated frameworks for evaluating progress in healthcare (such as the new NHS outcomes and public health outcomes frameworks). The Health and Social Care Act 2012 also established new statutory duties on the part of the Secretary of State, the NHS Commissioning Board (NHS England) and local commissioning groups to reduce health inequalities. The Secretary of State is required under the Act to 'have regard to the need to reduce inequalities between the people of England with respect to the benefits that they can obtain from the health service' (Section 4).

The quality regulator, the Care Quality Commission (CQC), was retained under the Health and Social Care Act 2012. Minimum care standards, inspection and quality regulation were revised and strengthened following the Mid Staffordshire NHS Foundation Trust Public Inquiry (Francis, 2013). This concluded that there had been a widespread failure of the healthcare system, including regulatory as well as management failure, and put forward 290 recommendations with the aim of ensuring the effective enforcement of fundamental standards of care in the future, including minimum standards of care

Box 8.1: The coalition's healthcare reform programme

Overall framework of political responsibility and accountability for health services in England

- Secretary of State retains ministerial responsibility to Parliament for health services in England and holds the commissioning board to account
- Services provided as part of the health service in England must be free of charge except in so far as the making and recovery of charges expressly provided under any enactment, whenever passed
- Duties of the Secretary of State include to promote a comprehensive NHS; to uphold the NHS Constitution; to improve quality of services 'securing continuous improvement' in outcomes; to improve public health; to reduce health inequalities; to promote autonomy

Increased focus on outcomes

- Creation of outcome-orientated duties on the part of the Secretary of State, NHS Commissioning Board and commissioning bodies (see above)
- New indicator-based frameworks for monitoring outcomes intended to function as accountability tools (e.g., NHS outcomes framework, public health outcomes framework, CCG framework)

Patient involvement

- NHS England and CCGs given duties to promote patient involvement in Care
- Creation of Healthwatch England and network of local Healthwatch bodies

Creation of Public Health England

- New autonomous national executive agency for promoting public health (Public Health England)

Economic regulation and financial sustainability

- Commissioners empowered to purchase services from any willing provider (includes private and third sector organisations)
- Monitor developed as an economic regulator, with duties to promote provision which is economic, efficient and effective and to promote anti-competitive practices
- Establishment of a new failure regime for providers that are financially unsustainable

Quality inspection and regulation

- Monitor given duties to regulate quality
- Care Quality Commission (CQC) retained and strengthened
- Chief inspector of Hospitals, new fundamental standards and new inspection regime established following recommendations of Mid Staffordshire NHS Foundation Trust Public Inquiry (2013)

New role for local government in public health

- Public health budget transferred to local government (commissioning role)
- Local authorities given general duties in relation to public health
- Establishment of new Health and Wellbeing Boards, as part of local authorities, with responsibilities to promote public health/assess and plan for local needs/promote integrate services / and tackle health inequalities (bringing together local authorities, adult social services, children's services, public health, elected representatives, Local Healthwatch, and CCGs)
- Introduction of public health premium

Commissioning bodies, providers and other new bodies

Creation of NHS Commissioning Board (NHS England)

- Key functions include:
  - Commissioning primary and specialist health services
  - Allocating resources to local budget holders (CCGs)
  - Overseeing local commissioning
- Duties of the NHS Commissioning Board (NHS England) include improving the quality of health services and reducing health inequalities

Creation of local budget holding/ commissioning bodies (CCGs)

- Creation of 211 CCGs which purchase services on behalf of local populations (GPs have a major role, but multidisciplinary teams)
- CCGs have duties to reduce inequalities in access to healthcare

Emphasis on autonomous providers with new revenue-raising powers

- All NHS hospitals to become autonomous foundation trusts (compulsory/time bound)
- Abolition of primary care trusts (previous commissioning bodies) and strategic health authorities (which previously provided oversight)
- Lifting of cap on private patient revenue, with hospitals allowed to generate 49% of their income from private patient revenue

and quality standards. Accepting the majority of these findings, the coalition moved to strengthen inspection and minimum standards following the Inquiry, introducing new minimum standards of care in 2015. Other measures included a new 'duty of candour', the 'friends and family' test, strategies to promote safety, dignity and respect, and revisions to the NHS Constitution. A Chief Inspector of Hospitals was appointed and the CQC introduced a new inspection model. The National Institute for Health and Care Excellence (NICE) issued guidelines on 'safe' nursing levels in hospitals. A review of hospitals with higher than expected mortality ratios, led by Sir Bruce Keogh, subsequently led to 11 trusts being put into special measures by Monitor/the NHS Trust Development Authority.

A strategy paper, *Achieving better access to mental health services by 2020*, signalled an important new policy development. The stated aim was to 'start' to ensure that mental and physical health services are given equal priority by 2020, with the first mental health waiting time standards being introduced in April 2015 (DH and NHS England, 2014).

The coalition's health reform programme also brought about a major new role for local government in public health. Building on the coalition's decentralisation and localisation agenda, as well as the objective of increasing democratic participation and accountability, new Health and Wellbeing Boards were established. These were intended as multidisciplinary bodies bringing together local authorities, adult social services, children's services, public health, elected representatives, Local Healthwatch, and CCGs, with duties to assess and plan for local needs, to promote integrated services, and to tackle health inequalities. Local government assumed a new commissioning role, while the public health budget was devolved to local government in April 2013 in the form of a ring-fenced grant. A new public health premium was announced and a new body, Public Health England, was created.

Broader measures on public health included Prime Minister David Cameron's announcement that the coalition would bring in minimum unit pricing for alcohol in March 2012, which was followed by a U-turn in July 2012 when the plans were dropped. However, in 2014, the government signalled its intention to ban 'deep discounting' of alcohol prices (a measure intended to prevent supermarkets cutting the prices of alcohol to below cost price). The government also moved ahead with plain, standardised cigarette packaging, and a free vote to allow a ban on smoking in private spaces was passed in February 2014. Regulations to ban smoking in vehicles where children are present were put before Parliament in December 2014, and became law in October 2015.

On finances, the coalition committed to protecting health expenditure within an overall framework of fiscal consolidation and deficit reduction. The coalition agreement (The Conservative Party, 2010) and *Programme for government* (HM Government, 2010) pledged to increase real spending on health each year of the Parliament. In 2012, the coalition launched PF2, with the stated aim of improving value for money in public–private partnerships including investment projects involving public sector equity. The Quality, Innovation, Productivity and Prevention Initiative (QIPP) was developed in response to estimates that the NHS needed to make £20 billion in efficiency savings between 2011 and 2014/15. The measures adopted included wage restraint policies, cuts to administration budgets and cost savings on drugs and procurement.

Comprehensive Spending Reviews announced transfers of the NHS budget to local authorities and pooled budgeting for integrated health and local authority social care services. The principle of allocating resources based on need was retained, with NHS England introducing a new health inequalities component to the resource allocation formula.

Spending

There was a general tightening of purse strings against a backdrop of contracting GDP following the financial crisis and downturn that began in autumn 2007. However, public expenditure on healthcare continued to grow during 2008/09-2009/10 in real terms. In contrast, the May 2010 General Election and policies of fiscal consolidation and austerity that followed resulted in a seismic break in the previous trend.

The expansion of resources under Labour

Looking back over Labour's period in power (1997-2010), real public sector expenditure on health in the UK increased between 1997/98 and 2009/10 from £64.4 billion to £128.6 billion in 2014/15 prices, a real terms increase of 99.6% over Labour's period in government as a whole. The average annual growth rate of real public expenditure on health in the UK over this period was 5.6%. This figure breaks down into an average annual growth rate of 4.3% under Blair's first term (1997/98-2000/01), rising to 8.7% under Blair's second term (2001/02-2004/05), with an easing back to 4.3% during Labour's third term (2005/06-2009/10) (see Table 8.1).

Table 8.1: Public expenditure on health: historical trends and by political administration (UK, unless otherwise stated)

	Average annual growth rate (%, real terms)
Historical trends	
Historical trend (1950/51-1996/97)	3.6
Historical trend (1950/51-2009/10)	4.0
Conservative (1979/80-1996/97)	3.3
Thatcher (1979/80-1982/3)	3.2
Thatcher (1983/84-1986/87)	2.4
Thatcher/Major (1987/88-1991/92)	3.3
Major (1992/93-1996/97)	3.8
Labour (1997/8-2009/10)	5.6
1st term (Blair: 1997/98-2000/01)	4.3
2nd term (Blair: 2001/02-2004/05)	8.7
3rd term (Blair/Brown: 2005/06-2009/10)	4.3
– Blair (2005/06-2006/07)	4.0
– Brown (2007/08-2009/10)	4.5
Coalition (2010/11-2014/15)	0.8
Coalition (2010/11-2013/14) England[a]	0.7
Coalition (2011/12-2014/15), England, DEL[b]	1.3

Notes:

[a] Based on HM Treasury expenditure framework where the figures refer to total (current and capital) identifiable expenditure on health in England for each year.

[b] Based on HM Treasury budgeting framework and refers to the total resource DEL (current and capital) excluding depreciation.

Average annual growth rates are calculated using a geometric mean of the real annual growth rates within each time period.

Sources: Authors' calculations using data in HM Treasury (2014a, 2015c), Harker (2011, p 20) and GDP deflators (HM Treasury, 2015f).

The scale of the resources squeeze under the coalition

Under the coalition government, growth in real public expenditure on health was exceptionally low by the standards of previous governments. Spending on health across the UK as a whole grew from £128.6 billion in 2009/10 to £134.1 billion in 2014/15 (in 2014/15 prices), a real terms increase of 4.3%.[1] Cuts of 0.3% and 0.6% in the first two years were followed by real increases of 0.9%, 1.8% and 2.4% in the subsequent three years.

Looking at trends in England separately, total NHS health expenditure within departmental expenditure limits (DELs) increased by 5.4% with an average annual growth of 1.3% over the period 2010/11 to 2014/15 (HM Treasury, 2015c). With inflation below the levels anticipated at the time of the 2010 Comprehensive Spending Review, growth in health expenditure outpaced the rates set out in the initial budget plans. Year-on-year growth was positive for each year during 2011/12-2014/15 (which is important, given the pledge in the coalition *Programme for government* for real year-on-year increases in each year of the Parliament). The growth of real average annual expenditure on health during 2010/11 to 2014/15 was therefore positive but exceptionally low. Average annual growth rates of public expenditure also lagged behind the rates that are widely deemed necessary to maintain and extend NHS care in response to increasing need and demand. An estimated 1.2-1.5% per annum increases in real funding is required just to keep pace with demographic pressures.[2]

Spending, need and demand

While health was protected relative to other expenditure areas, this commitment was made in (real) cash terms, not relative to need. A real resources squeeze in health occurred over the period 2010-15, with average annual growth rates in expenditure lagging behind simple indicators of need and demand.

Between 1997/98 and 2007/08, growth in real expenditure on health (adjusted for inflation) and volume expenditure on health (adjusted for NHS-specific inflation) outstripped growth in real GDP and real household disposable income by a considerable margin, both in terms of real growth and real growth per capita. This trend broadly continued over the period 2007/08-2009/10, in the wake of the crisis (see Figure 8.1a and b). Growth in volume public expenditure on health also outstripped other common indicators of need, such as growth in the population aged 65 and over, and 85 and over (Figure 8.1a). However, growth in real and volume expenditure on health between 2009/10 and 2014/15 was less than the modest increase in GDP. It also lagged behind 13.3% and 12.3% increases in the population aged 65 and over, and 85 and over, respectively. There was virtually no growth in real expenditure per capita over this period (adjusted for general inflation) and volume growth per capita (adjusted for NHS specific inflation), with growth of 0.5% and 0.6% respectively (Figure 8.1b).

Figure 8.1: Growth of real expenditure on health and demographic pressure, UK

a) Growth of public expenditure on health vs growth in older populations, GDP and household disposable income (indexed:1997/98=100 and 2009/10=100)

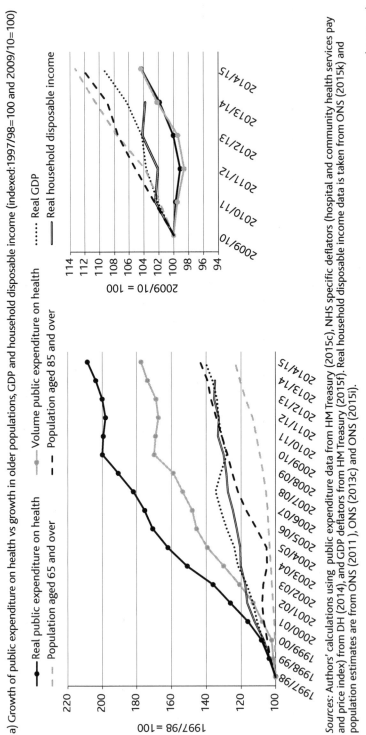

Sources: Authors' calculations using public expenditure data from HM Treasury (2015c), NHS specific deflators (hospital and community health services pay and price index) from DH (2014), and GDP deflators from HM Treasury (2015f). Real household disposable income data is taken from ONS (2015k) and population estimates are from ONS (2011), ONS (2013c) and ONS (2015i).

(continued)

b) Growth of public expenditure on health vs growth in GDP and household disposable income per capita (indexed: 1997/98= 100 and 2009/10=100)

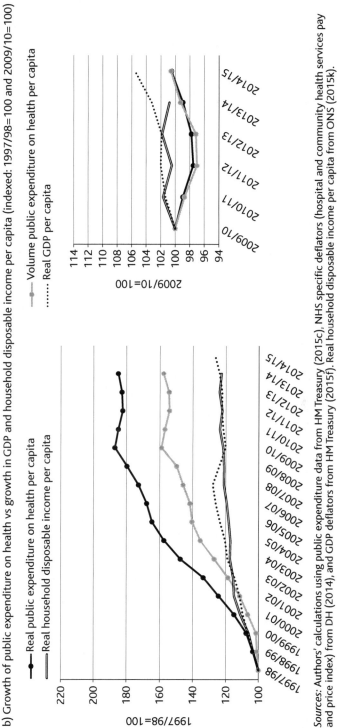

Sources: Authors' calculations using public expenditure data from HM Treasury (2015c), NHS specific deflators (hospital and community health services pay and price index) from DH (2014), and GDP deflators from HM Treasury (2015f). Real household disposable income per capita from ONS (2015k).

Resource allocation

The 'weighted capitation' formula used to allocate resources to PCTs under Labour is discussed in Vizard and Obolenskaya (2013). This aimed to allocate resources in a way that eventually secures 'equal access to healthcare for people of equal need' (DH, 2011, p 45). The formula took account of a range of variables including the size of a local population, gender, age, need and cost.

A health inequalities component of the formula was recommended by ACRA in 2008 and was subsequently introduced for the 2009/10 and 2010/11 allocations. This aimed to meet the additional objective of contributing to the reduction in avoidable health inequalities. For the 2009/10 and 2010/11 allocations, disability free life expectancy (DFLE) was used as the measure of health inequalities, and the health inequalities adjustment was given a weight of 15% (DH, 2011, p 23; ACRA, 2010).

Allocations to each PCT continued to move incrementally towards the targets determined by the resource allocation funding formula at a rate determined by a further formula – the so-called 'pace of change' formula. Prior to the 2010 General Election, the rate of progress towards resource allocation targets was criticised for being too slow – resulting in a gap between officially recognised 'need' on the one hand, and resources allocated via the funding formula on the other (Glennerster, 2015b; Vizard and Obolenskaya, 2013).

Under the coalition, the organisational changes brought about by the Health and Social Care Act 2012, including the creation of CCGs and the devolution of public health responsibilities to local authorities, required changes to resource allocation arrangements. The geographic boundaries and characteristics of the new CCGs are different to those of the previous PCTs. The new public health arrangements required a new formula as a basis for allocating resources to local authorities.

The development of the new formula for allocating funds to CCGs proved controversial. Nuffield Trust was asked to develop a new formula for allocating funds to CCGs. However, while there was agreement that the formula proposed ('person based resource allocation') captured existing service usage in an appropriate way, an immediate debate arose regarding the extent to which resource allocation to CCGs should make an adjustment for health inequalities and unmet need.

As Glennerster (2015b) notes, in developing and applying the healthcare funding formula, a balance must be drawn between the weight to be given in allocations to patterns of need identified through existing utilisation of services on the one hand - taking account of the age and health profile of existing service users - and addressing unmet need and tackling health inequalities on the other. The Advisory Committee on Resource Allocation (ACRA) had advised in 2010 that the health inequalities adjustment introduced under Labour be retained (ACRA, 2010). However, in 2011/12 ACRA set out proposals to allocate funds to CCGs based on the 'Nuffield formula'. It noted that 'due to the lack of quantified evidence, ACRA does not at this time recommend the inclusion of a correction for unmet need in the formula for allocations to CCGs' (ACRA, 2011, p 20). Further research regarding the desirability and size of an adjustment for unmet need was proposed (ACRA, 2011, 2012; Wood and Heath, 2014). NHS England subsequently raised concerns that ACRA's recommendations did not sufficiently account for unmet need and would shift funding away from the North of England and London towards the South, East of England and Midlands (Wood and Heath, 2014; NHS England, 2013b). The ACRA proposal was rejected and the old (PCT) formula (with an up-rating) was used to allocate funds for the year 2013/14 pending a review of funding formula.

In December 2013, NHS England adopted a new funding formula reflecting age, population and deprivation as a basis for allocating resources for 2014/15 and 2015/16. The Board agreed that adjustments for unmet need should be made in the context of CCG allocations as well as in the primary health context. A 10% unmet need adjustment for CCG allocations, and 15% in the context of primary care, were proposed. In line with new ACRA recommendations, it was agreed that the best measure to be used as a basis for the unmet need adjustment is the under 75s standardised mortality ratio, applied at the Middle layer Super Output Area (MSOA) level, to take account of inequalities *within* as well as *between* areas (NHS England, 2013a, 2013b).

While the new arrangements for allocating funds to CCGs incorporate an unmet need component, the slow pace of change towards target allocations remains an important critique. Under the new arrangements, the pace of change towards target allocations is even slower than under the system under Labour – partly because resource allocation in general has slowed (Glennerster, 2015b).

In the context of public health, the development of a new resource allocation formula was less protracted. A new public health formula was developed with funds explicitly targeted at areas with the poorest health outcomes. In line with the original ACRA recommendations, the new public health resource allocation formula adopted the standardised mortality ratio for those aged under 75 years of age (SMR<75), applied at the small area level, as a measure of health status and need for public health (ACRA, 2011; DH, 2013c).

International comparisons

Internationally, health budgets were cut in many countries following the economic crisis and downturn. OECD analysis suggests that while health budgets were maintained in many European countries at the beginning of the crisis, growth in health spending per capita ground to a halt in OECD countries and become negative in 2010 among European Union (EU) members of the OECD, reversing pre-crisis trends in many countries. While growth rates had begun to increase again in 2012 and 2013 in a number of countries, rates in Europe lagged behind those elsewhere in the OECD, climbing to just above zero in 2013 (Morgan and Astolfi, 2013, 2014; Eurofound, 2014; OECD, 2015a).

OECD data (2015a) suggests that the decline in average growth rate in per capita total (public and private) health expenditure in the UK between 2009 and 2013 was relatively sharp. When measured in purchasing power parity terms, annual average growth of −0.1% over this period was considerably less severe than the −7.2% annual average growth rate for Greece, but was nevertheless below the OECD average, and contrasting with positive growth in France, Germany and the US.

The share of health expenditure within GDP, which increased under Labour (1997-2010) by a substantial margin, was also under pressure during this period. Total (public and private) expenditure on healthcare as a percentage of GDP increased in the UK from 6.2% in 1997 to a peak of 9.4% in 2009, falling back to 8.8% in 2013. The percentage point gap in this indicator between the UK and the EU-14[3] average decreased from 1.6 percentage points in 1997 to 0.7 in 2009 before widening again to 1.1 in 2013 (see Figure 8.2).

Inputs, outputs and productivity[4]

The volume of healthcare inputs (nurses, GPs, prescribed drugs, clinical supplies, capital consumption etc) and outputs (hospital treatment, GP consultations etc) continued to grow after 2007. However, based on the latest available data (to 2012), their pace of growth slowed markedly after 2010, as the effects of the resource squeeze took hold (see Figure 8.3).

Inputs

The annual average growth rate of healthcare inputs fell from 4.8% under Labour (1997-2009) to 1.4% under the coalition (2010-12).

Figure 8.2: International comparisons of total (public and private/current and capital) expenditure on health as a percentage of GDP, 1997-2013

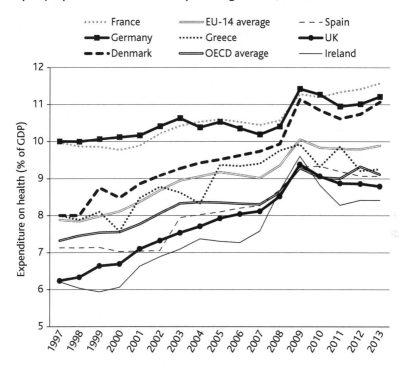

Notes:

EU-14 average is an arithmetic average for the EU-15 countries excluding UK, based on non-missing data. No data was available for total expenditure for Belgium and Italy.[3] Data for the EU-14 countries therefore covers Austria, Denmark, Finland, France, Germany, Greece, Ireland, Luxembourg, the Netherlands, Portugal, Spain, and Sweden. The 2013 figure is based on non-missing figures for OECD counties in 2013. However, 2013 figures were not yet available for Australia, Ireland, Luxemburg and Spain, and 2012 figures were therefore used instead.

OECD average is an arithmetic average for the OECD countries excluding UK, based on non-missing data. No data was available for total expenditure for Belgium and Italy. Figures for 2013 for Australia, Ireland, Luxemburg and Spain are based on 2012 figures.

Source: OECD.Stat (online)

The slow-down was driven by a fall in the growth rate for goods and services procurement (prescribed drugs, clinical supplies etc) from an average of over 8.0% per year between 1997 and 2009, to 3.1% between 2010 and 2012. Labour inputs (numbers of nurses, GPs, consultants, managers etc) were broadly flat between 2010 and 2012, compared to 2.8% per year average growth between 1997 and 2009 (ONS, 2015b).

Increasing the ratio of nurses was a key recommendation in the Mid Staffordshire NHS Foundation Trust Public Inquiry (Francis,

Figure 8.3: Growth of public services healthcare inputs, outputs and productivity, 1995-2012 (indexed: 1995=100), UK

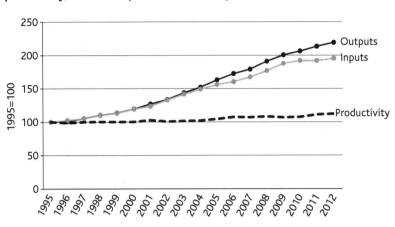

Source: ONS (2015b, reference table 1)

2013). While the number of full-time equivalent qualified nursing, midwifery and health visiting staff dipped in 2011 and 2012, there were annual upturns in 2013 and 2014 (HSCIC, 2015a), and monthly data suggests that this trend of increase was sustained up to June 2015 (HSCIC, 2015c). The number of full-time equivalent GPs dipped in 2010 but has subsequently risen to above the 2009 peak, totalling just under 37,000 in 2014 (HSCIC, 2015a). Meanwhile, the number of full-time equivalent managers declined by a fifth, from over 40,000 in 2010 to under 35,000 in 2013, although from 2013, numbers have since started to rise (HSCIC, 2015a, 2015c).

Outputs

Annual average growth rates in the volume of (quality-adjusted) healthcare outputs (hospital inpatient services, A&E attendances, GP consultations etc) fell from 5.4% under Labour (1997-2009) to 3.0% under the coalition (2010-12). The supply-side expansion of the 'catch-up' years under Labour were apparent in high growth rates during the period 2000-08. Office for National Statistics output growth figures include a quality adjustment which has a small impact on the overall output estimates. In 2012/13, the quality adjustment (of 0.01 percentage points) was the smallest positive adjustment since the series began (ONS, 2015b).

The growth rate of outputs that were publicly financed by the taxpayer, but which were provided by non-NHS providers (for example, clinical services sub-contracted by trusts to the private and independent sector, services commissioned by CCGs [formerly PCTs] and NHS-financed community services) was higher than for other components of output growth (not quality-adjusted), at 13.3% per year between 1994/95 and 2012/13. This breaks down to an average annual growth rate of 16.3% during Labour's period in power (1997/98 to 2009/10), and 6.6% under the coalition (2010/11 to 2012/13).[5] The share of public expenditure on non-NHS provision within total public expenditure on healthcare increased from around 4% in 1994/95 to over 10% in 2011/12 (ONS, 2015b).

Productivity

Latest ONS estimates suggest that despite annual fluctuations there was positive growth in public services healthcare productivity (the ratio of inputs to outputs) over the period 1997-2009, including three years of consecutive productivity growth during 2003-06, with an average annual growth rate of 0.6% (1997-2009). Under the coalition, public service healthcare productivity growth was positive year on year, averaging at 1.7% per year (2010-12), with a notable increase of 3.5% in 2012. Positive productivity growth under the coalition may reflect policy measures aimed at increasing efficiency (discussed previously). It might also be anticipated that there would be a more rapid slowdown in input growth compared to output growth during the initial phases of a fiscal adjustment programme.

Outcomes

There were few early signs of an immediate 'crisis and recession effect' on healthcare access and quality in 2007/08. However, signs of pressure on the healthcare system were mounting by the May 2015 General Election, with pressure on hospital waiting times, A&E departments and cancer waiting lists.

Healthcare access and quality

Comparing trends in hospital waiting times with the standards set out in *The Handbook to the NHS Constitution* (NHS, 2009), the proportion of admitted and non-admitted patients receiving non-emergency consultant-led treatment within 18 weeks of referral improved between 2007 and summer 2010. In contrast, the proportion of non-admitted patients treated within 18 weeks fell between June 2010 and June 2015 (although still just meeting the operational standard set in England for waiting times between GP referrals and treatment). The proportion of admitted patients treated within 18 weeks declined from June 2009,[6] to the extent that the 90% operating standard was regularly breached after February 2014 (see Figure 8.4). The 18 week standards for admitted and non-admitted patients were dropped in July 2015, following a review by Sir Bruce Keogh (Keogh, 2015). This proposed focusing on an alternative operational standard that was introduced in 2012, which measures waiting times for patients waiting to start treatment at the end of the month (so-called 'incomplete pathways'). There was substantial improvement against this measure between 2007 and 2009, as the proportion of patients referred to start treatment within 18 weeks increased from 57.2% in August 2007 to 90.2% in August 2009. Performance remained fairly stable between 2009 and 2011, before improving during 2011-12, and remained above the 92% operational standard after that date (although looking at the level of individual trusts rather than aggregate performance, Monitor (2015) reports an increase in the number of foundation trusts failing to meet this target in the first quarter of 2015/16). Following moves to address very long waiting times and a policy of 'managed breach', improvement was seen in the number of patients with very long (over 52 weeks) waits. After falling between 2007 and 2010, this improvement continued between 2010 and 2014 for patients on all pathways, although the first quarter of 2015/16 has seen some deterioration against this measure for patients on incomplete pathways (NHS England, 2015a).

In July 2015, the total number of patients waiting to begin treatment was at the highest level since 2008. Median and 95th percentile wait times for admitted, non-admitted and incomplete pathways were all rising after 2013/14 (NHS England, 2015a). Pressure on cancer waiting lists has also been evident in the most recent period. While some of the cancer waiting time standards continued to be met, provider-based figures show a drop in the proportion of patients receiving first definitive treatment within 62 days of an urgent GP referral, since the first quarter of 2013/14, with the operational standard of 85% being breached for the sixth consecutive time in the first quarter of 2015/16 (NHS England, 2015e). Monitor (2015) suggests more general pressure on diagnostic tests in the first quarter of 2015/16.

The percentage of individuals for whom the revised A&E target was met fell from 98.4% in the first quarter of 2010/11 to 94.1% in the first quarter of 2015/16, with particular pressure evident in the last quarter of 2012/13, the last two quarters of 2014/15 and the first quarter of 2015/16, when the target has been breached (see Figure 8.5).

Figure 8.4: Percentage of patients referred for hospital treatment within 18 weeks, various operational standards, 2007-15, England

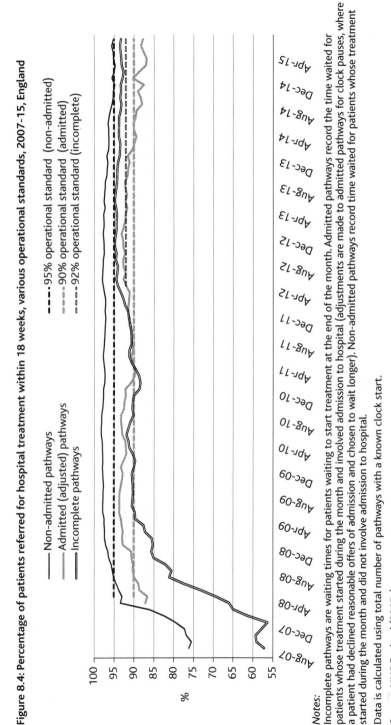

Notes:

Incomplete pathways are waiting times for patients waiting to start treatment at the end of the month. Admitted pathways record the time waited for patients whose treatment started during the month and involved admission to hospital (adjustments are made to admitted pathways for clock pauses, where a patient had declined reasonable offers of admission and chosen to wait longer). Non-admitted pathways record time waited for patients whose treatment started during the month and did not involve admission to hospital.

Data is calculated using total number of pathways with a known clock start.

Source: NHS England (2015a)

Figure 8.5: Percentage of patients waiting four hours or less in A&E, 2003/4-2014/15, England

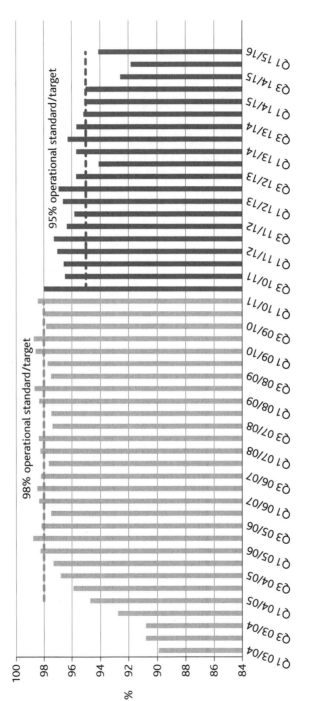

Notes: Quarterly monitoring of A&E services data is used from 2004/05 to Q4 2010/11; A&E weekly situation reports data is used from 2011/12 onwards. Figures for years 2003/04 are based on data points in a chart by The King's Fund (see Appleby et al, 2013, p 27); figures for 2004/05 onwards are from NHS England (2015d)

Major A&E departments (as a group) have failed to meet this target consistently since the third quarter of 2011/12 (with the exception of Q2 2012/13), and data for the first quarter of 2015/16 shows the lowest quarter one performance in over 10 years (NHS England, 2015d). Media reports of worsening access focused on GP waiting times of more than one week, and the GP Patient Survey shows an increase in the number of patients waiting a week or longer to see or speak to someone, from 12.8% in 2011-12 to 17.9% in 2014-15 (NHS England, 2015b).

Public satisfaction with the NHS, measured by the annual British Social Attitudes Survey, fell from a high of 70% in 2010 to 58% in 2011, before rising back to 65% in 2014 (NatCen, 2015). The overall adult inpatient experience score increased from 2011-12 to 2013-14, but fell significantly in 2014-15 (NHS England, 2015c). Adverse movements in relation to patient experiences of mental health and GP services have also been evident in recent years. The overall patient experience score for NHS community mental health services fell significantly from 2012-13 to 2013-14 (NHS England, 2015c). Satisfaction with both GP surgeries and out-of-hours GPs both fell between 2011-2012 and 2014-2015 (NHS England, 2015b).

Obesity, alcohol consumption, smoking and diet

In England, adult obesity continued to increase over the period despite fluctuations, while signs of improvement among the youngest children evident from 2009-12 started to drop off in 2013. The proportion of adults meeting physical activity recommendations has been improving since 1997. While the proportion of adults meeting revised physical activity recommendations increased by 1 percentage point between 2008 and 2012, there was little sign of a 'jump' in the rate of improvement around the Olympics (HSCIC, 2014b). There was a substantial decline in the proportion of children meeting physical activity recommendations, from 24% in 2008 to 18% in 2012, with the greatest fall among 13- to 15-year-old boys (HSCIC, 2014b).

Improvements were seen in the reduction of heavy drinking among both men and women from 2009 to 2013 (HSCIC, 2014b). In England, there was a 1 percentage point decline in smoking prevalence between 2007 and 2013. The socioeconomic gap in smoking prevalence in Great Britain peaked in 2012, when the difference in smoking rates of managerial and professional occupations, and those in routine and manual occupations, stood at 19 percentage points. The widening of the gap in 2012 was largely driven by female trends, with a 7 percentage point increase in the gap for females between 2009 and 2012. In 2013, the overall gap returned to its 2008-11 figure (15 percentage points) (ONS, 2010b, 2013a, 2014d).

The Marmot Review (2010) focused attention on the underlying social determinants of health such as poverty, unemployment, long-term receipt of benefits, early years education and housing conditions. The 2014 update of the Marmot Indicators identified deterioration in relevant social indicators since the downturn and crisis. It also pointed towards poor children's development and insufficient income to live a healthy lifestyle as likely causes of health inequalities in the future. There is evidence that the downturn and crisis may have put downward pressure on the consumption of fruit and vegetables, halting the prior trend of overall increased consumption over the 2001-06 period. The steepest deterioration in fruit and vegetable consumption is found among children (see Table 8.2).

Table 8.2: Percentage of adults and children consuming five or more portions of fruit and vegetables a day, 2001-13, England

	2001	2002	2003	2004	2005	2006	2007	2008	2009	2010	2011	2013
Men	22.2	22.3	21.9	23.1	26.0	27.8	27.5	25.1	24.6	25.3	24.5	25.1
Women	24.7	25.3	25.9	26.8	29.5	31.5	30.7	29.0	27.7	26.8	28.6	27.7
All adults	23.6	23.9	23.9	25.0	27.8	29.7	29.1	27.1	26.2	26.0	26.6	26.4
Girls	12.7	11.9	11.8	12.1	17.0	22.1	21.4	20.3	21.8	20.2	19.8	17.2
Boys	13.6	11.5	9.8	13.2	17.6	19.2	20.7	18.7	20.9	19.3	15.9	15.7
All children	13.2	11.7	10.8	12.7	17.3	20.6	21.0	19.5	21.4	19.7	17.8	16.4

Notes:
Data from 2003 onwards has been weighted for non-response.
Fruit and vegetable consumption was not measured in 2012.
Source: HSCIC (2014b)

Suicide and mental health

Suicide rates have shown a medium-term decline going back many years in many OECD countries. However, in the period coinciding with the economic crisis and downturn, there appeared to be a turning point in a number of countries including in countries hard hit by the crisis, such as Greece (see Figure 8.6). In the UK as a whole, there was a statistically significant increase in the suicide rate, from 10.6 deaths per 100,000 population in 2007 to 11.9 in 2013 (ONS, 2015e). In England, following an improvement in age-standardised suicide rates going back to 1981, there was a similar, statistically significant rise

Figure 8.6: Standardised suicide rate per 100,000 population, 1994-2012, selected countries

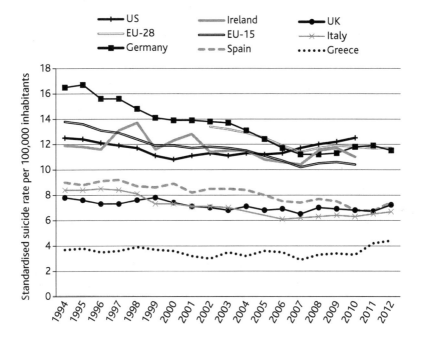

Notes:

Figures are for deaths where the cause is reported as 'intentional self-harm'.

Data for Ireland and the US, taken from OECD.Stat (online) is age-standardised to the 2010 OECD population. All other data is taken from Eurostat and is standardised according to the 2013 revised European Standardised Population (ESP). Suicide rates for Ireland and the US are therefore not directly comparable to other countries in the graph.

Data from 1994-2010 and 2011 onwards are not always comparable, due to the fact that 2011 data is the first data collection with a legal basis (and in part due to the different groupings of causes of deaths).

See ONS (2015j, pp 19-20) for a note on the comparability of international suicide data.

Sources: Eurostat (online) and OECD.Stat (online)

between 2007 and 2013. The increase was particularly notable among men, with the rate for men aged 45-59 rising from 16.2 to 23.4 deaths per 100,000 population (ONS, 2015e). Age-standardised suicide rates increased across all English regions except London, where there was a small, non-statistically significant decline. Statistically significant increases occurred in the North East, the West Midlands, the South East and the South West (for both males and all persons); the greatest increase occurred for males in the North East, where the suicide rate increased from 16.6 in 2007 to 22.1 in 2013 (ONS, 2015e).

Annual data available for the UK as a whole shows an overall reduction in the percentage of the population identified as at risk of poor mental health from 2007-12 (ONS, 2015f). However, there is evidence that the percentage at risk of poor mental health in England increased over the period coinciding with the crisis and downturn. Based on Health Survey for England data, the overall percentage identified as at risk of poor mental health increased by 1.6 percentage points over the period 2008-12, with a particularly striking increase among women. Notable increases are observed among middle-aged men and women in the 40-44 and 45-49 age bands, with overall increases in the prevalence of those at risk of poor mental health of 4.4 and 3.6 percentage points. For women, the biggest rises were among those aged 16-24, 40-44 and 55-59 (Table 8.3; for further data, see Vizard and Obolenskaya, 2015, pp 102-3). Individuals from the poorest households may also have been most affected, with a 4.1 percentage point increase among individuals living in households from the lowest quintile of equalised household income, compared with a

Table 8.3: GHQ-12 score of 4 or more by age group, England

	All		Males		Females	
	2012 (%)	Change 2008-12 (% point)	2012 (%)	Change 2008-12 (% point)	2012 (%)	Change 2008-12 (% point)
Overall	15.0	1.6**	11.9	0.7	18.0	2.5**
16-24	13.7	3.3	7.8	0.6	21.0	7.2*
20-24	16.7	2.2	10.7	−1.8	21.5	5.1
25-29	15.7	1.0	11.1	−1.1	20.1	2.7
30-34	12.3	1.2	7.6	−1.0	16.6	3.3
35-39	15.8	2.7	13.4	2.4	18.2	3.1
40-44	17.2	4.4*	15.5*	3.2	18.9	5.5*
45-49	16.5	3.6*	12.2	3.5	20.2	3.8
50-54	16.7	−1.1	13.4	−1.5	20.2	−0.8
55-59	16.1	1.7	10.9	−2.3	21.1	5.8*
60-64	15.2	3.1	17.4**	7.1	13.1*	−0.7
65-69	9.5	−1.5	7.2	−1.5**	11.8*	−1.5
70-74	12.2	0.4	14.8*	5.1	10.1**	−3.5
75-79	12.3	−2.6	10.7	−1.8	13.8	−2.9
80 or over	16.1	−1.2	13.2	−3.3	17.7	−0.1

Note: * denotes a statistically significant difference at the 95% level; ** denotes a statistically significant difference at the 99% level. For the cross-sectional 2012 analysis, significant differences relate to subgroup differences compared to a reference group marked in bold. For the change over time analysis, significant differences relate to the change in the subgroup proportion over time. Significance testing has been performed using a logistic regression test

Source: Centre for Analysis of Social Exclusion (CASE) calculations using Health Survey for England (2008) and (2012) data sets; for the full table and additional breakdowns, see Vizard and Obolenskaya (2015, pp 102-3)

2.5 percentage point increase among the least deprived (see Vizard and Obolenskaya, 2015).

Mortality and life expectancy

As noted earlier in the chapter, disappointing progress against Labour's health inequalities targets for life expectancy and mortality from circulatory disease and cancer was already apparent in the summer of 2007. Subsequent data confirmed that despite overall improvements in life expectancy during Labour's period in power, targets to reduce both absolute and relative inequalities in life expectancy between the 'spearhead' areas and England were ultimately missed for both men and women in the period to 2010. Similarly, while there were important reductions in age-standardised mortality rates from circulatory disease and cancer over the period, inequalities in mortality from the major killers remained a major challenge at the end of Labour's period in power (Vizard and Obolenskaya, 2013).

Nevertheless, progress in meeting the target to reduce the relative infant mortality gap between routine/manual occupational groups and the all England average was a 'good news' story of Labour's third term – with considerably better progress after 2007 (Vizard and Obolenskaya, 2013). Furthermore, notwithstanding the disappointing progress in terms of the health inequalities targets that Labour actually set, other indicators may provide a more positive picture of the progress that was made on health inequalities over the period 1997-2010. For example, Buck and Maguire found that 'the Marmot curve improved significantly between 1999-2003 and 2006-10' (2015, p 31). Their analysis is based on an examination of the relationship between life expectancy and income deprivation measured at the MSOA level in each of the two periods. The authors identify both an *upward shift* and a *shallowing* of the Marmot curve over the period. This implies that there was an improvement in the *social gradient* in life expectancy – as well as an improvement in *levels* of life expectancy – comparing the data for 1999-2003 and 2006-2010. They conclude that 'income inequalities in health seem to have improved overall over time' and that 'Marmot's goal – 'to shift the gradient' – happened' (Buck and Maguire, 2015, pp 19-20, 4).

Labour's health inequalities targets were dropped under the coalition. Data from the NHS outcomes framework shows a strong social gradient in under-75 mortality rates per 100,000 population from cardiovascular disease, cancer, respiratory and liver diseases by Index of Multiple Deprivation (IMD) decile in 2013 (see Figure 8.7).

Figure 8.7: Inequality in under-75s mortality from cardiovascular disease, cancer, respiratory disease and liver disease by IMD decile, 2013, England

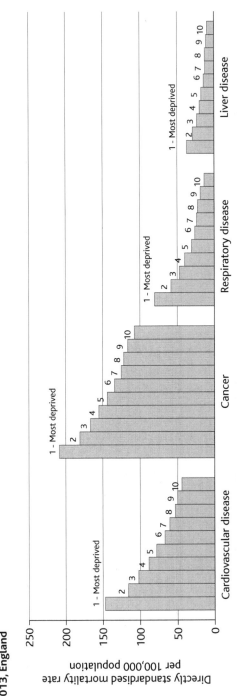

Note: Confidence intervals are provided in the original source.

Source: HSCIC indicator portal (HSCIC, online), NHS outcomes framework indicators

The public health outcomes framework for England includes two overarching indicators to monitor progress in preventing premature deaths: a comparison of life expectancy between different groups, and an assessment of 'healthy' life expectancy. Averaged over three-year periods, figures available show a gap of 9 years in average life expectancy between men living in the poorest and most prosperous areas and 6.9 years for women. The gap for 'healthy' life expectancy was wider still – at 18.3 years for men and 18.9 years for women in 2011-13 (ONS, 2015a) (see Figure 8.8).

The UK's international position

Efforts to rank countries based on OECD international comparative health data have been criticised on a number of grounds. Data limitations and lags can make comparisons problematic, and the differences in country rankings are often not statistically significant. Nevertheless, as reported in our companion papers (Vizard and Obolenskaya, 2013, 2015), it seems important to note that the UK remains below the best performers and comparator countries in relation to a number of international health outcome indicators.

While declines in mortality from circulatory disease in the UK have been notable compared to other OECD and European countries, the latest OECD data suggests that the UK's 30-day mortality rates following heart attack and stroke lagged behind the best performers in 2011 (OECD.Stat).[7] While there has been a considerable decline in the overall cancer mortality rate with notable reductions for some specific cancers (for example, male lung cancer), UK mortality rates for all cancers remain high by international standards, with female cancer mortality particularly poorly ranked, relative to other OECD countries (OECD.Stat). The UK's relative five-year survival rates for breast, cervical and colorectal cancers (for the period 2007-12 or nearest period), and the UK's mortality rates for breast, ovarian and prostate cancer, also remained disappointing in 2013 (OECD.Stat). The UK's international rankings for female life expectancy, infant mortality and obesity remain an important challenge. While male life expectancy remained fairly stable at 14th place, the UK's ranking for female life expectancy dropped from 20th in 1997 to 24th out of 34 OECD countries in 2013[8] (see Figure 8.9). Of 30 OECD countries with available comparative data for infant mortality rates in 2013, the UK was ranked 23rd (OECD, 2015b) and in 2012, the UK ranked as the second worst performer on obesity among EU-26 countries, after only Hungary (OECD, 2014).[9]

Figure 8.8: Inequality in life expectancy and healthy life expectancy at birth by IMD decile, 2011-13, UK

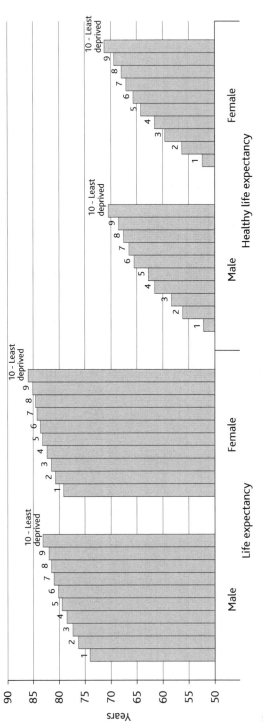

Notes:
Life expectancy data is for period life expectancy, based on current death rates in the specified period.
Healthy life expectancy is an extension of period life expectancy that combines morbidity and mortality data to produce estimates of the span of life that a person can expect to live in good health.
Excludes residents of communal establishments except NHS housing and students in halls of residence where inclusion takes place at their parents' address.
Data is aggregated over a three-year period to achieve sufficiently large sample sizes to enable meaningful statistical comparison.
Confidence intervals are provided in the original source.
Source: ONS (2015a)

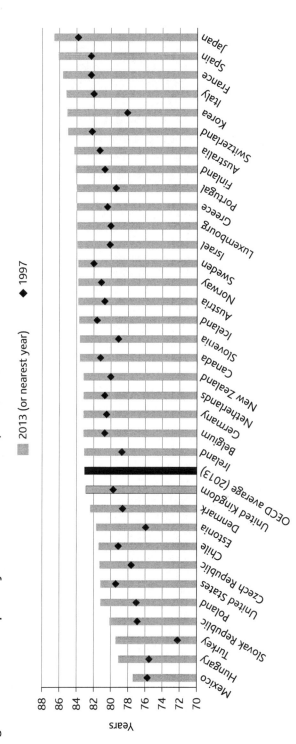

Figure 8.9: Female life expectancy at birth in OECD countries, 1997 and 2013

■ 2013 (or nearest year) ◆ 1997

Note: Data is for period life expectancy, based on current death rates in the specified year.
Source: OECD (2015b)

Conclusion

The NHS *Five year forward view* (NHS England, 2014c) highlighted the relative resilience of the NHS in terms of weathering the financial crisis and downturn compared to other health systems internationally. It suggested that the NHS has improved substantially over the last 15 years, and that progress continued even in the wake of the financial crisis and austerity, with protected funding and efficiency measures both playing a role. Whereas '[n]o health system anywhere in the world in recent times has managed five years of little or no real growth without either increasing charges, cutting services or cutting staff ... [t]he NHS has been a remarkable exception' (NHS England, 2014c, p 6). The *Five year forward view* also cites a recent international comparative assessment of health systems by the Commonwealth Fund (Davis et al, 2014b) which ranked the UK in first overall place for healthcare performance, above 10 other countries (Australia, Canada, France, Germany, the Netherlands, New Zealand, Norway, Sweden, Switzerland and the US).

Continuity or change?

It is certainly important to note that as of May 2015, the NHS remained free at the point of delivery, based on need, not ability to pay. No major changes were made by the coalition to its financing model, and the NHS continued to be funded through general taxation and National Insurance Contributions. Challenges elsewhere to the 'right to health' – such as high out-of-pocket payments and healthcare depending on ability to afford private insurance and gaps in health insurance coverage and health protection – continue to be avoided in the UK. The private healthcare sector – beyond services commissioned by the public sector – remains extremely limited. Private spending on healthcare remained low as a proportion of GDP and expenditure on private medical insurance remained stable. Under the new healthcare arrangements, resource allocation continued to be via a needs-based formula with a health inequalities component.

There are, moreover, a number of important continuities between the coalition's health reforms (2010-15) and those undertaken by Labour during its three terms in office (1997-2010). While the pace and scope of reform slowed under Brown in the final years of the Labour government, health reforms over Labour's three terms included a raft of radical policies to promote organisational decentralisation, commissioning based on a purchaser–provider split, competition and patient choice.

Nevertheless, a number of factors suggest a radical break with the past and a significant and deeply entrenched new fiscal and policy landscape for health services in England under the coalition after the May 2010 General Election. On the eve of the crisis, the UK was experiencing a period of sustained and substantial increases in real public expenditure on health. While there was a general tightening of purse strings against a backdrop of contracting GDP following the economic crisis and downturn that began in autumn 2007, public expenditure on healthcare continued to grow during 2008/09–2009/10 in real terms. But the May 2010 General Election and policies of fiscal consolidation and austerity that followed resulted in a seismic break in the previous trend. A real resources squeeze in health ensued, with growth in expenditure and supply lagging behind demand and need over the period 2010-15.

In addition to the fiscal climate, factors that point to a discontinuity with previous arrangements that have been cited in the literature include the extent of the shift towards a decentralised organisational structure; the likely magnitude of the shift towards private provision of publicly financed healthcare services in the future; the possibility of hospital trusts retaining 49% of private patient revenue; the introduction of a trust failure regime; the central role of competition brought about by the 'any qualified provider' rule; emphasis on anti-competitive behaviour; and the potential application of international competition rules.

Furthermore, whereas reforms under Labour were introduced incrementally against the backdrop of unprecedented growth in resources, major health reforms were implemented by the coalition in an extremely short time period against a backdrop of a real resources squeeze (Mays and Dixon, 2011). The speed and scale of the reforms as well as their compulsory (rather than opt in) nature has resulted in considerable controversy, costs and organisational upheaval, as well as creating a myriad of new and untested bodies and systems. Multiple reforms have been implemented simultaneously.

Impact

It is early days to evaluate the impact of the coalition's health reforms. Some early evidence is reviewed in Vizard and Obolenskaya (2015), and presents a mixed picture. In the medium term an evidence base will be required to evaluate the impact of organisational decentralisation; increased competition; emphasis on outcomes; new inspection regimes; duties to address health inequalities; and the new arrangements for public health, on outcomes and inequalities.

The analysis in this chapter suggests that by the time of the May 2015 General Election, the resources squeeze was having an important impact. Real average annual growth rates of public expenditure were lagging behind the rates that are widely deemed necessary to maintain and extend NHS care in response to increasing need and demand. Input and output growth slowed markedly after 2010 as the effects of the resources squeeze took hold, and signs of pressure on healthcare access and quality were increasing.

Current financial pressures on NHS bodies

Concerns relating to the fiscal sustainability of NHS foundation trusts and NHS trusts were also mounting by the 2015 General Election. The House of Commons Committee of Public Accounts (2015a), National Audit Office (2014b) and The King's Fund (Appleby et al, 2015) warned of a worsening of the finances of NHS bodies, with a reduction in the net surplus run by NHS commissioners, foundation trusts and NHS trusts in 2012/13 and 2013/14; an increase in the percentage of NHS trusts and foundation trusts in deficit; and deteriorating expectations for the upcoming period. Monitor (2015) and the NHS Trust Development Authority (2015) highlighted a substantial deterioration of NHS foundation trust and NHS trust finances in the first quarter of 2015.

Pressures on financial sustainability identified in these analyses include tight budget settlements, demand pressures (with increases in expenditure outpacing increases in income), payment systems (the payment system for emergency admissions and NHS tariffs), increasing staff needs following the Francis Reviews, staff shortages and consequent agency costs and bed availability affecting patient flow. Underlying concerns regarding 'bed blocking', delayed discharges and lack of integration between health and social care have all been highlighted in this context, as has the scale of the financial squeeze in social care, discussed in this volume next, in Chapter Nine. The NAO also noted that CCGs with the widest gap between their target funding allocation and the income they receive have the largest deficits. It further noted that among bodies with PFI commitments, those with the highest ratio of capital charges to income were more likely to report weak financial results in 2013/14 (NAO, 2014b).

Forecast of the funding gap by 2020/21

In the run-up to the May 2015 General Election, a range of authoritative forecasts painted a bleak picture in terms of the extent of the medium-term funding gap that will have an impact on the NHS in the period up to 2020 (Appleby et al, 2009; OBR, 2011, 2012, 2013; Crawford and Emmerson, 2012; Roberts et al, 2012; Appleby, 2013; Buck and Dixon, 2013; Monitor, 2013; Barker and The King's Fund, 2014). Exercises of this type apply a range of different projections for demographic change, morbidity, income, growth, technological change, costs including pay and the management of chronic conditions, inflation, and productivity gains (see Vizard and Obolenskaya, 2015). Some (see, for example, Wanless, 2002) also include a range of different assumptions about health-related behaviours.

Among the major forecasts that were published in the run up to the 2015 General Election, Nuffield Trust analysis (Roberts et al, 2012) suggested that demand and need pressures on the NHS would grow at a rate of 4% per annum in the period to 2020/21. Based on this assumption this analysis suggested that if the growth in NHS real spending were to be held flat beyond the 2010-15 Parliament, the NHS in England could experience a funding gap of £28 to £34 billion by 2020/21 in the absence of offsetting productivity gains. In late 2013, Monitor published 'Closing the NHS funding gap: how to get better value health care for patients'. The regulator warned that for the decade ahead 'the NHS budget is likely to remain flat in real terms or, at most, to increase in line with growth in the rest of the economy', while demand would increase (Monitor, 2013, p 1). The gap between need and resources could potentially amount to £30 billion a year by 2021 in the absence of off-setting productivity and funding increases (Monitor, 2013).

The projected health funding gap in 2020/21 is narrowed and even eliminated under alternative scenarios that assume a combination of offsetting productivity gains, demand-side control and real funding increases. Three alternative scenarios were set out in the NHS *Five year forward view* (NHS England, 2014c) as a basis for discussions about the minimum funding requirements of the NHS during the 2015-20 Parliament. The most optimistic scenario was that efficiency and demand gains of 2-3% net each year could potentially be made over the next Parliament. These potential gains assumed the implementation of supply-side transformational change and service reconfiguration (for example, integrated health and social care, and new primary care models). They further assumed increasing control of the demand side, with a major shift towards a more activist prevention and public health agenda, intensified efforts to address obesity, smoking and alcohol consumption and changes to health behaviours in the medium term. Achieving these efficiency and demand gains in turn assumed 'staged funding increases' close to 'flat real per person'. This would fund the investment needed for transformational change (NHS England, 2014c, p 36). This model is presented as scenario three, under which 'the NHS gets the needed infrastructure and operating investment to rapidly move to the new care models and ways of working described in this Forward View, which in turn enables demand and efficiency gains worth 2%-3% net each year. Combined with staged funding increases close to 'flat real per person' the £30 billion gap is closed by 2020/21' (NHS England, 2014c, p 36).

The *Five year forward view* became a critical reference point for negotiations between NHS England and the main political parties in the run up to the 2015 General Election. Given the extent of the projected gap between need and resources by 2020/21, identified in major forecasts as around £30 billion, even with NHS England committing to massive savings of £22 billion to be achieved through implementing new care models and preventative health measures, funding would need to increase by at least £8 billion a year in real terms by the end of the decade in order to bridge the gap (NHS England, 2014c; Triggle, 2014; DH and Treasury, 2015; Stevens, 2015; Dowler and Culkin, 2014).

Outlook

The 2015 Conservative Party manifesto highlighted the importance of the NHS as a 'profound expression of our values as a nation' and pledged 'continue to increase spending on the NHS ... so the NHS stays free for you to use' (The Conservative Party, 2015, p 37). The manifesto commitment to real term year-on-year increases in public expenditure on health, resulting in a minimum increase in spending in England of £8 billion by 2020, was characterised by the new government as implementing the *Five year forward view* model and 'backing the NHS'. The pledge followed the announcement of additional funds for 2015/16 in the 2014 Autumn Statement, which aimed to address financial pressures and the need for service reconfiguration.

Organisational reforms such as those proposed in the 2010 Conservative Party manifesto were absent from the Conservative Party manifesto in 2015, although commitments to a '24/7' NHS and integrated health and social care were included. Organisational changes in the upcoming period are also likely to result from the implementation of the *Five year forward view* by NHS England.

The *Five year forward view* concluded that given the overall fiscal outlook and the size of the potential funding gap in health by 2020, service reconfiguration and demand side control are necessary conditions for sustaining a comprehensive NHS, free at the point of delivery and funded through tax, over the next five years. It suggested that with measures of this type in place, there was nothing that suggested that 'continuing with a comprehensive tax-funded NHS is intrinsically undoable' (NHS England, 2014c, p 37).

Yet while there is a general consensus that new care models and a shift towards a more activist and preventative public health agenda are essential, the assumption of a further £22 billion efficiency and demand gains in the next Parliament (on top of the assumed £20 billion efficiency gains under the coalition) is highly optimistic in the light of previous productivity trends. In the absence of the assumed efficiency savings from new integrated health and care models being delivered – or of changing health behaviours in the medium term resulting in more emphasis on preventative health – the apparent consensus reached between NHS England and the government on the way forward for the NHS in the upcoming period could unravel.

Furthermore, the question of whether the new government was fulfilling its commitment to meet even the minimum funding requirements for the NHS set out in the *Five year forward view* received close scrutiny in November 2015. The negotiations over the 2015 Spending Review resulted in Simon Stevens, Chief Executive of NHS England, issuing five tests as to whether government proposals were in line with the requirements and 'maths' of the *Five year forward view* plan, including front loaded increases in expenditure and demands on the NHS (such as 24/7 working) being phased in with funding increases. Stevens also highlighted that further cuts in public and social care would impose extra costs on NHS over and above the minimum funding requirement (Dunhill, 2015).

Ultimately, the November 2015 Spending Review announced a £10 billion increase in real NHS funding between 2014/15 and 2020/21, with an element of front-loading for 2016/17. This figure included the extra £2 billion for 2015/16 which had already been announced prior to the General Election, and was presented by the government as delivering the resources required by the *Five year forward view*. The figures imply real average annual growth rates of NHS expenditure of 1.55% per annum between 2015/16 and 2020/21. The

Spending Review documents also put emphasis on policy measures and expectations including 7 day services, integrated health and social care by 2020 and the delivery of £22 billion of savings as 'set out in the NHS's own plan, the Five Year Forward View' (DH and Treasury, 2015, p 183).

Analysis by Nuffield Trust, The Health Foundation and The King's Fund suggests that the November 2015 Spending Review expenditure increases are substantially less than initially thought. This analysis notes that the government figures are based on a significant change in the meaning of 'NHS spending' and involve cuts in 'other health spending' of 20% - including reductions in public health. Based on the 'old' definition (the totality of the Department of Health budget), spending on the NHS in England over the current parliament is projected to increase at a lower rate – at an average of 0.9% a year. The authors note that this figure is similar to that over the last parliament and will result in a substantial fall in health spending as a share of GDP by the end of the current parliament. With social care funding also projected to be lower than need in the upcoming period, the authors conclude that the health settlement is not sustainable (Nuffield Trust et al, 2015).

Meanwhile, at the time of writing in late 2015, a range of other evaluations by regulators and independent bodies provide further evidence that the climate for health policy is becoming even colder. Monitor (2015) is warning of 'unprecedented' financial and operational challenges, with the current level of deficit 'not affordable' and underperformance against key operational standards. A summary of findings by the CQC under the new inspection regimes stated that England's health and social care system is 'under increasing pressure, driven by changing care needs and financial demands on all public services' (CQC, 2015a, p 5). Latest King's Fund assessments point towards 2015/16 as 'the most challenging year in recent NHS history', taking account of the overall fiscal climate, the scale and magnitude of the financial deficits of NHS trusts, waiting lists and staff shortages (Appleby et al, 2015).

The projected growth of real expenditure on the NHS set out in the November 2015 Spending Review confirms that growth rates will continue to be low by historic standards and that austerity in health will continue over the five years to 2020/21. The figures serve as a timely reminder of the scale of the ongoing resources squeeze in health; the minimal nature of the funding requirements set out in the NHS *Five year forward view*; the highly optimistic nature of the savings assumptions built into this model; the fragility of the apparent consensus between NHS England and the government on how the

NHS should move forward; and the gravity of the public policy and political challenges in the period to come.

Notes

[1] HM Treasury (2015c) spending figures under 'Expenditure on services' framework.

[2] Crawford et al (2014b, p 44) suggest that an average growth rate of real expenditure on health of 1.2% per annum is required by population growth and demographic change between 2010/11 and 2018/19 (with the level of spending for each person of a given age held constant in real terms). Planning assumptions by NHS England (NHS England, 2014a, Appendix A) are based on demographic pressures of 1.5%-1.7% in 2013/14 in different expenditure areas. Non-demographic pressures are cited as ranging from 0.9% to 3.4% in different expenditure areas. Similar pressures are assumed for 2014/15. For CCG programme costs (the biggest allocation), demographic pressures are assumed at 1.5% and non-demographic pressures at 0.9% for both years.

[3] Data for total expenditure on health was not available for Italy and Belgium in the OECD 2015 database. Italy revised their time series back to 1995 and included only current health spending in their figures. Belgium has historically provided only current health spending since 1995. In previous OECD health spending publications the aggregate of reference was 'total health spending' in the OECD database, and so figures for current health spending were used as total health spending, marking it with 'D' for deviation. From 2015, the main aggregate is current health spending, and it was decided against displaying a value for total health spending for Belgium.

[4] The figures for input, output and productivity growth in this section are either taken directly from ONS (2015b) or have been calculated using the data from this source; there may be small differences with the data in the original source due to rounding.

[5] Non-NHS provision is measured indirectly using the assumption inputs = outputs. See ONS (2015b).

[6] Based on year-to-year comparisons, taken at the same month each year.

[7] Statistics measure case-fatality within 30 days after admission for heart attack/stroke in adults aged 45 and over (age-sex standardised rates per 100 admissions). The OECD publishes both admissions and patient-based 30-day mortality rates. Patient-based data is regarded as the more robust data, and the UK's ranking improves slightly when patient-based rather than admission-based data is used. See OECD (2014, pp 90, 92) for a note on the limitations and comparability of this data.

[8] Data is for 2013, or the nearest available year.

[9] Note taken from OECD (2014, p 56): 'For most countries, overweight and obesity rates are self-reported through estimates of height and weight from population-based health interview surveys. The exceptions are the Czech and Slovak Republics, Hungary, Ireland, Luxembourg and the United Kingdom, where estimates are derived from health examinations. Estimates from health examinations are generally higher and more reliable than from health interviews.'

NINE

Adult social care

Tania Burchardt, Polina Obolenskaya and Polly Vizard

The situation on the eve of the crisis

In 2007/08, just before the financial crash unfolded, spending on adult social care in England[1] had reached £20 billion (in 2014/15 prices) after a period of sustained budget increases under Labour in response to the expanding ageing and working-age disabled populations, and in recognition of the historic under-investment in social care. This was providing services to 1.8 million adults, including some of the most vulnerable people in our society: the oldest of the old, younger physically disabled people, people with mental illness or cognitive impairments, and people with drug and/ or alcohol problems.

Complexity in the financing and provision of social care, especially long-term care, was a widely acknowledged problem. Boundaries between the NHS and local authority services, between residential and community care (including domiciliary or home care), between universal and means-tested entitlements and privately paid care, and between formal services and unpaid care provided by family and friends, combined to produce considerable uncertainty among people in need of care and their families about what services they might receive and how much they would be required to pay. Major commissions and inquiries at a rate of one per decade (Griffiths, 1988; Sutherland, 1999; The King's Fund, 2006) had produced recommendations for reform, but none had been fully implemented, as a result of lack of cross-party support or due to concerns about the cost to the public purse. However, in Scotland, the Sutherland Commission's recommendation to fund personal care costs from direct taxation while retaining means-testing for housing and living costs was adopted in 2002 for people aged 65 or over.

Meanwhile, the trend away from direct provision by local authorities and increasing use of private and not-for-profit providers was continuing (HSCIC, 2014a, Figures 4.5 and 5.1), as was the increase in the number of people receiving payments from local authorities with which to arrange their own care ('direct payments'). Between 2000/01 and 2008/09, there had been more than a 10-fold increase in the number of working-age people using direct payments, and an even faster increase among the over-65s (from a much lower base), so that by the end of this period there were more than 86,000 recipients of direct payments in England (HSCIC, 2014a, Annex M).

Policies, 2008-15

The final years of the Labour administration saw a renewed focus on social care with the publication of a raft of statements of principle setting out core standards and the intended direction for future policy and service delivery, including for carers (2008, as well as the launch of a new dedicated survey of carers), for people with dementia (2009) and for people with learning difficulties (2009). There was also work to develop a national outcomes framework for adult social care. These were widely welcomed within the sector and in voluntary organisations, although specific policies were slower to develop as funding began to be squeezed. Also in 2008, a vision for the future of social care was produced under the banner of 'Putting People First', with a strong emphasis on increased personalisation through direct payments and individual budgets. It sought to establish 'a collaborative approach between central and local government, the sector's professional leadership, providers and the regulator. It seeks to be the first public service reform programme which is co-produced, co-developed, co-evaluated and recognises that real change will only be achieved through the participation of users and carers at every stage' (HM Government, 2008, p 1).

The Wanless Review in 2006 recommended a minimum guarantee of free care, topped up by matched funding between individuals and central government. Cross-party talks on the funding of long-term care followed, but they fell apart in the run-up to the general election, amidst accusations and counter-accusations, with the result that the three main parties put forward three different approaches in their manifesto. Labour argued for the gradual introduction of a tax-financed national care service with free personal care, the Liberal Democrats promised to establish (another) commission, and the Conservatives proposed to rely on voluntary private insurance.

In the event, the coalition agreement went with the Liberal Democrat proposal of a commission on funding long-term care, which became the Dilnot Commission. The recommendations were subsequently implemented, in modified form, in the Care Act 2014, and became the flagship social care policy of the coalition government. The Act established a lifetime cap on the care costs an individual can be required to make (not including costs of daily living or housing), initially set at £72,000 for people of pension age (DH, 2013d). The Act also made allowance for the cap to vary by age, and the government indicated its intention that the cap would be set at zero for those who have eligible care and support needs when they turn 18 (in line with Dilnot).

The government also accepted the Dilnot Commission's recommendation that the capital means test threshold for residential care should be raised. Presently, people must spend down their assets (including the value of their house, unless a close relative continues to live there) to £23,250 before qualifying for any state funding. The March 2013 Budget announced that this upper threshold would be increased to £118,000 for residential care – more than a fourfold increase. Together with the lifetime care cap, Hancock et al (2013) estimated that there would be an additional 115,000 people receiving some public funding for social care by 2030, around a 9% increase.

The lifetime cap and a more relaxed capital means test can be seen as going some way towards pooling the risk of high care needs, shifting responsibility from individuals to the state for those with high needs and modest wealth. This reduction in uncertainty would be welcome, but since low-income and asset-poor individuals are already entitled to free care, the reforms are strictly regressive in terms of income and wealth distribution (Hancock et al, 2013). This would be offset to some extent by the government's original intention to pay for these reforms through a freeze on inheritance tax thresholds and changes to National Insurance Contributions (Humphries, 2013), both of which could have been progressive.

The cap and revised capital means test were to be implemented from April 2016 (and applied to costs accrued from then on). However, in July 2015, following representations from local government that the reforms were under-funded and too complex to implement at a time of significant strain in the social care system, the new Conservative government announced that implementation would be postponed until 2020, raising questions about whether the policy will, in fact, be shelved altogether.

The coalition government did, however, press ahead with other reforms to adult social care, giving new emphasis to the role of preventative and rehabilitative services, while introducing from April

2015 new national minimum eligibility criteria which, in effect, raise the threshold for receiving care to 'substantial needs'. A handful of local authorities (2%) will have to widen their provision as a result, while a much larger proportion (12%) will be given the 'green light' to further restrict their eligibility (DH, 2013a, para 3.3). Together these reforms promote a somewhat bizarre situation in which an individual may be offered services to delay the need for care (perhaps the installation of some assistive equipment), but when they actually need care (for example, someone to help with a weekly bath), they will not be entitled to assistance until there is deemed to be a significant risk to their wellbeing.[2] Even in the context of significant funding constraints, it is hard to see the logic of this hollowing out of the middle range of care and support, concentrating resources on prevention at one end and on high-intensity needs at the other, when in reality, care needs are on a continuum, with appropriate support at each stage being likely to reduce, delay or prevent further needs developing. The assumption, presumably, is that unpaid carers will step in to meet the shortfall.

Other areas of policy development under the coalition are summarised in the policy timeline in Box 9.1, including reforms to the monitoring and inspection framework for assessing the quality of care in residential and community settings.

Spending, 2008-14

Local government funding from central government fell by 40% over the course of the coalition period in office (LGA, 2015), and since social care spending is not ring-fenced, it has been among the services exposed to cuts. However, many authorities have sought to protect frontline services in general and social services in particular (ADASS, 2014; LGA, 2014b). In any case, some adult and children's social care provision is statutory, which reduces the room for manoeuvre in implementing cuts. Indeed, adult social care is second only to children's social care in the degree of protection that has been afforded to its budget within non-ring-fenced local authority spending (DfE, 2014c). The reductions in spending reported in this section are therefore not as great as the overall fall in local authority spending, although, as we shall see, once increasing need is taken into account, the real reductions are substantial.

Box 9.1: Adult Social Care policy timeline

2008	2009	2010	2011	2012	2013	2014	2015	2016

'Putting People First' vision for future of social care

National Carers' Strategy

National Dementia Strategy for England

Valuing People Now (strategy for people with learning disabilities)

Adult social care outcomes framework

Commission on Funding of Care and Support (Dilnot Commission)

Health and Well-Being Boards (Health and Social Care Act 2012)

Changes to the right to request flexible working

CARE ACT 2014

New inspection regime by Care Quality Commission

New national criteria for social care eligibility based on level of need

Extension of statutory rights of carers to social services support

Stronger statutory basis for Adult Safeguarding Boards

Local authorities responsible for continuity of care when providers cease to function

More pooling of existing NHS and social care resources (Better Care Fund – delayed implementation)

Lifetime cap on care costs paid by an individual (not implemented)

Significant relaxation of capital means test for residential care (not implemented)

Table 9.1: Expenditure by councils with adult social services responsibilities by accounting category, 2007/08 to 2014/15, England (£ billion, in 2014/15 prices)

	2007/08	2008/09	2009/10	2010/11	2011/12	2012/13	2013/14	2014/15 (provisional)	% change 2009/10 to 2014/15
A: Gross total cost	19.83	20.43	21.09	21.04	20.30	19.96	19.66	19.53	−7.4
minus									
B. Income from client contributions	2.48	2.51	2.58	2.61	2.61	2.62	2.64	2.64	+2.5
C. Income from NHS and joint arrangements	1.54	1.60	1.81	2.01	1.53	1.66	1.63	1.73	−4.1
D: Total income (including other income)	4.40	4.49	4.84	5.10	4.49	4.60	4.56	4.95	+2.3
equals									
E: Net total cost	15.43	15.94	16.26	15.94	15.81	15.36	15.10	14.59	−10.3
minus									
F: Capital charges	0.24	0.31	0.35	0.31	0.30	0.22	0.25	0.18	−49.1
equals									
G: Net current expenditure	15.19	15.63	15.91	15.63	15.51	15.14	14.85	14.41	−9.4

(continued)

Table 9.1: Expenditure by councils with adult social services responsibilities by accounting category, 2007/08 to 2014/15, England (£ billion, in 2014/15 prices) (continued)

Notes:

1. Definitions of accounting categories:

   A. Gross total cost = net current expenditure + capital charges + total income (ie, the most comprehensive definition, including spending funded by non-CASSR (Councils with Adult Social Services Responsibilities) sources).

   B. Income from client contributions (ie, user charges).

   C. Income from NHS and joint arrangements (ie, funding from these sources for CASSR activity).

   D. Total income = income from client contributions (B), NHS and joint arrangements (C), and other income.

   E. Net total cost = A – D = net current expenditure + capital charges – total income (ie, spending by CASSRs themselves).

   F. Capital charges.

   G. Net current expenditure = E – F = expenditure *excluding* capital charges – total income (ie, spending by CASSRs themselves excluding capital).

   For a detailed explanation of accounting categories and changes in recording practices, see HSCIC (2014c).

2. Data for 2014-15 has been sourced from a new collection, the Adult Social Care Finance Return (ASC-FR), and is provisional. It has replaced the previous finance return (PSS-EX1). It includes data from all 152 councils but some of these data are not complete and therefore the figures for expenditure in 2014-15 may be understated.

3. Percentage changes are calculated from figures expressed with 3 decimal places, ie, with greater precision than those shown in the table.

Source: Authors' calculations using 2007/08-2013/14 data from HSCIC (nd). Original data source: PSS-EX1, and 2014/15 data from HSCIC (2015e) and GDP deflators from HM Treasury (2015f)

193

Local authorities finance most social care activity, but some activities are financed by client contributions or by joint arrangements with other public bodies, including the NHS. These distinctions are reflected in the accounting categories used in Table 9.1. *Gross total cost* (see Table 9.1, row A) reflects all expenditure relating to local authority social care activity, however financed. It includes capital charges (row F) and spending funded through client contributions, the NHS and joint arrangements with the NHS (rows B and C) (see below for further discussion of these joint arrangements). 'Gross total cost' is therefore the total resources going into adult social care via local authorities.

But we might also be interested in what social services are themselves financing; this is reflected in *Net total cost* (row E), which excludes client contributions and funding via joint arrangements and the NHS. Finally, *Net current expenditure* (row G) is the most minimal definition of expenditure, excluding capital charges[3] as well as client contributions and any other funding from the NHS and joint arrangements.

Whichever definition one adopts, Table 9.1 shows that the peak in adult social care spending was in 2009/10 (in real terms), the final year of the Labour government. Since then, there has been a consistent drop in real annual spending. By 2014/15, there had been a 7.4% fall in gross total cost (row A), a 10.3% fall in net total cost (row E, what local authorities themselves are financing), and a 9.4% fall in net current expenditure (row G, the most minimal definition of expenditure).[4]

Figures for net current expenditure reported by the Health and Social Care Information Centre (HSCIC) (nd) go back consistently[5] to 1994-95. These show that the rate of increase in spending began to slow before the change in government, and indeed, before the financial crash, but that the 1.7% fall in real terms in net current expenditure between 2009/10 and 2010/11 was the first year-on-year real terms fall since 1994-95 (see also Figure 9.1).[6]

Despite cuts in social care spending, the costs were not mainly passed on to the users in the form of charges. Income from client contributions (which include sales, fees and charges) rose only slightly (in real terms) over the period when social care expenditure declined (2009/10 to2014/15). However, it is worth noting that since the number of users also declined over this period (see the next section), user charges per head have, in fact, increased.

Table 9.1 shows that total income was increasing up to 2010/11 and then decreased by 12% in 2011/12 with a slight increase the following year, and again in 2014/15. The large fall in total income between

2010/11 and 2011/12 is mainly accounted for by changes in the way the Valuing People Now initiative, which focuses primarily on adults with learning difficulties, was recorded.[7]

Separately, there is new NHS funding for social care from 2011-12. This includes a non-recurrent primary care trust (PCT) allocation to local authorities that is for the provision of social care that would also benefit NHS, for the years 2011-12 and 2012-13 (DH, 2010a), and subsequently the Better Care Fund. Examples of such allocations are telecare, maintaining eligibility criteria for social care, early supported hospital discharge schemes, re-ablement services and bed-based intermediate care services. In 2010-11 to 2012-13, additional funding was transferred from the NHS to local authorities under the Winter Pressures transfer, which is also part of the income to local authorities. These sums are included in gross total cost but not in net current expenditure in Table 9.1.

Capital charges have halved over the period as the number of local authority-owned residential homes has continued to decline, but capital charges were a very small proportion (1.6%) of gross total cost to start with, so the fall has not had a major impact on total spending.

Longer-run trends in expenditure and demand

Pressure on publicly funded social care predates the budget reductions that we have shown that began in 2009/10.

Figure 9.1 shows the growth in net current expenditure on adult social care for the over-65s and overall,[8] alongside an indication of demographic pressure from the ageing population expressed as a growth in the population aged 65 and older and in the population aged 85 and older, taking 1997/98 as the base year. Three periods can be discerned. Until 2005/06, spending was increasing faster than demographic demand, contributing to a reduction in unmet need. Between 2005/06 and 2009/10, overall spending began to flatten off while the growth in the ageing population continued, especially the over-85s. Finally, from 2010/11 onwards, spending began to fall, with an especially sharp drop in spending on the over-65s, despite strong growth in the number of people in this population group.

The shortfall between spending and need is also shown by Fernandez et al (2013) in their calculations of demand-adjusted expenditure. These need-adjusted, or standardised, figures were derived by applying multivariate regression techniques to control for changes across the time period in the council-level sociodemographic factors, such as population age and gender profiles, standardised mortality ratios,

Figure 9.1: Growth in real net current spending and population estimates by age group, 1997/98-2013/14, England

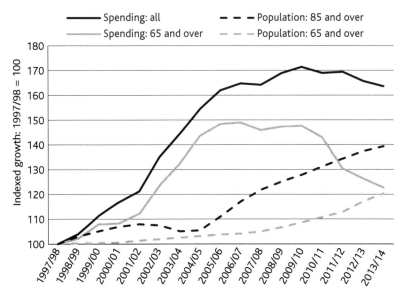

Note: Spending figures for over-65s include spending on older adults and older mentally ill. Spending figures for 'all' adults include expenditure on both under-65s and over-65s as well as additional spending such as on asylum-seekers and on 'other adult services' (eg, assessment and care management, HIV/AIDS). For consistency overtime, all expenditure figures exclude the Supporting People grant, which was introduced in 2003/04.

Sources: Authors' calculations using expenditure on adult social care figures (HSCIC, 2014d) and population estimates (ONS, 2011, 2013c, 2013d, 2015i). GDP deflators from HM Treasury (2015f).

rates of limiting longstanding illness and population density. Their findings suggest that the need-standardised gap in levels of net social care expenditure in 2012/13, relative to the levels of expenditure in 2005/06, was approximately £1.5 billion. The reduction in the level of local authority investment per unit of need (demand-adjusted expenditure) accelerated significantly from 2010/11 (Fernandez et al, 2013).

The over-65s have been particularly hard-hit, relative to demand.

Figure 9.2 compares the real growth in net current spending plus non-client income by local authorities with the demand-adjusted (or 'standardised') estimates, for the population as a whole and for the over-65s (authors' calculations using figures from Fernandez et al, 2013). It covers the period from 2005/06, when spending on over-65s began to decline, up to 2012/13. Between 2005/06 and 2012/13 the fall in observed spending on older adults was 10.6% while demand-

Figure 9.2: Real terms growth in observed and standardised net current spending plus non-client contributions for the whole population and aged 65 plus, 2005/06-2012/13, England

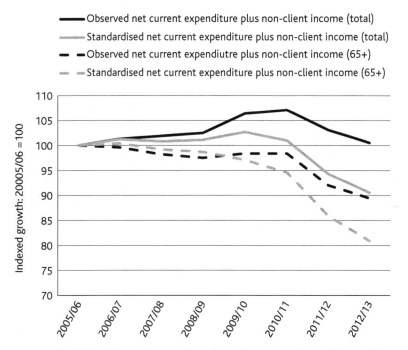

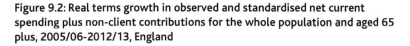

Source: Authors' calculations using expenditure figures from Fernandez et al (2013, Tables 4 and 5)

adjusted net current spending on this age group was estimated to be 19.1%. The gap between observed and demand-adjusted spending on older people has widened significantly since 2009/10: in that year it stood at 1.3 percentage points (using an index based on 2005/06=100), while by 2012/13, it was 8.5 percentage points.

Inputs and outputs, 2008-14

Services

The total number of adults receiving services, whether in their own home or in residential or nursing care, or direct payments, rose to a peak of 1.78 million in 2008/09 before falling in each consecutive year to 1.27 million in 2013/14 (see Figure 9.3, black line). This is a fall of 29%, or nearly one-third of the total caseload. For the period 2006/07 to 2009/10 – the longest run of data we have on a consistent basis

Figure 9.3: Number of clients receiving residential or community care provided or commissioned by local authorities, by age group, 2007/08-2013/14, England (millions)

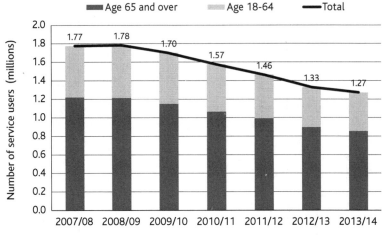

Source: HSCIC (nd). Original source: Referrals, Assessments and Packages of Care (RAP) proforma P1

for the Labour administration – the average annual change since the previous year was –0.7%, whereas for the period 2009/10 to 2013/14, the average change was –6.9%, nearly 10 times as fast.

The decline in residential care has been continuous since this data series began in 2005/06, and has fallen by a total of 17% since that time. Annual rates of change actually slowed under the coalition government, from an average of –3.1% up to 2009/10 and –1.4% thereafter. The number of community care recipients has fallen much faster (see Figure 9.4), and this is consistent with the policy of 'service intensification', that is, withdrawing services from people with moderate needs and concentrating resources on those with more severe or complex needs (Humphries, 2013). The fall in community-based services since the peak in 2008/09 has been 32% (34% for the 65 and over age group and 27% for those aged 18-64).[9] Average annual rates of change were –0.4% over the period of data we have for the Labour administration, and –7.9% for the period since 2009/10: a very substantial shift, albeit in a direction that had already begun under Labour. The cut in one year alone (2011/12 to 2012/13) was 10.5%.

These falls in the number of service users are all the more striking when put in the context of increasing need over this period as a result of growth in the older population and especially the very old, as described in the previous section.

Figure 9.4: Number of adults receiving community-based services each year, by age group, 2005/06-2013/14, England (millions)

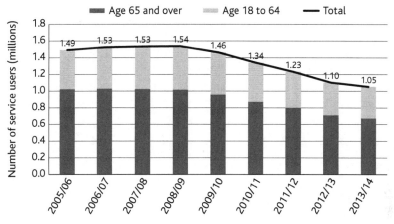

Source: HSCIC (nd). Original source: RAP proforma P2f

Community-based service users are classified by primary client group, that is, whether the main reason they are in need of support is because of physical disability, mental health, learning disability, substance misuse or another vulnerability. Table 9.2 shows that the only client group for whom services have increased over the period is people with a learning disability (whether working-age or older), although this has to be set against an increase in the numbers of people in this group in the population (Emerson and Hatton, 2008). All the other large client groups have seen significant decreases in services since 2008/09, continuing and in some cases accelerating under the coalition government. The percentage changes in numbers of service users in the last four years of the Labour period and the first four of the coalition are shown in columns 3 and 5 of Table 9.2. Community-based services for working-age people with mental health problems have been cut by 37% since 2009/10, more than reversing the widening of the service in the preceding period. Physically disabled older people have experienced a cut of one-third, and their working-age counterparts have seen a cut of more than a quarter. Some of the smaller client groups, while contributing less to the overall retrenchment in absolute terms, have experienced even larger proportional cuts in services: for example, the number of 18- to 64-year-olds receiving services for substance misuse has almost halved – a trend that presumably increases pressure elsewhere, such as in the health service and/or the voluntary sector.

Table 9.2: Percentage changes in the number of community service users, by client type, in Labour and coalition periods

Age 18-64	No of clients In 2005/06	% change 2005/06 to 2009/10	No of clients In 2009/10	% change 2009/10 to 2013/14
Physical disability	200,295	−1.1	198,160	−27.7
Mental health	157,650	+19.0	187,600	−36.7
Learning disability	96,280	+7.0	102,985	+4.0
Substance misuse	9,825	−0.9	9,740	−46.4
Other vulnerable people	7,765	+3.8	8,060	−35.6
Age 65 plus	In 2005/06	2005/06 to 2009/10	In 2009/10	2009/10 to 2013/14
Physical disability	903,840	−8.0	831,770	−31.3
Mental health	75,645	+26.7	95,870	−18.7
Learning disability	6,870	+18.3	8,130	+22.6
Substance misuse	705	−1.4	695	−20.1
Other vulnerable people	34,885	−39.5	21,120	−40.4

Source: HSCIC (nd). Original source: Referrals, Assessments and Packages of Care (RAP) proforma P2f

The distribution of hours of community-based services provided per client has also been changing. In 2008/09 (when this series began), 39% of clients were receiving care packages of up to and including 5 hours per week, but by 2013/14, this had fallen to 27% of clients (see Figure 9.5). Conversely, the percentage of clients receiving care packages of more than 10 hours per week, including overnight care and/or live-in care, has risen from 34% to 46% – another aspect of 'intensification'.

For those receiving a small number of hours, concerns have been expressed about the brevity of some home care visits. A total of 110 out of 149 local authorities commissioned care visits as short as 15 minutes (for example, to provide a meal, or get someone up, washed and dressed) in autumn 2014, an increase of 5% on the previous year (based on a UNISON Freedom of Information request). Commentators have argued that visits as short as these are unlikely to be compatible with treating the client with dignity and consideration (Cheshire, 2013), and also place considerable strain on the care workers.

Unpaid care

Many people receive unpaid care from family and friends in addition to, or in lieu of, formal services. One might expect, therefore, that a

Figure 9.5: Distribution of community-based services clients by planned contact hours per week at 31 March each year, England

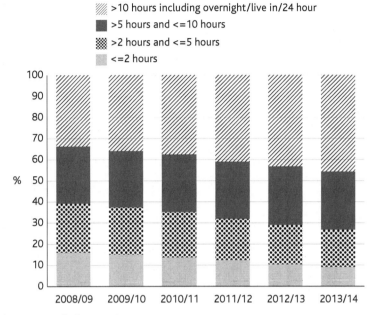

Source: HSCIC (nd). Original source: RAP H1

reduction in formal services would produce an increase in informal care. This is given some support by data from the Family Resources Survey, which has collected data on unpaid care of people who are disabled, ill or elderly since 2002/03. The number of people providing unpaid care increased in recent years (see Figure 9.6): 4.8 million individuals were providing care at least weekly in 2009/10; this rose to 5.6 million by 2012/13, before falling back in the latest figures to 5.1 million. Most of the additional carers are people of working age.[10]

There also appears to be a long-term trend towards receipt of more intensive care: in 2002/03, 29% of all individuals receiving unpaid care received continuous care; by 2007/08 this figure had risen to 35%, and in 2013/14 it was 39% (Family Resources Survey 2013/14, Table 5.6, and unpublished data for previous years).

Even before the recent increase, the UK already depended heavily on unpaid care, by international standards. According to OECD figures, only around 8 or 9% of people aged 50 or over were providing unpaid care in Sweden and Denmark in the mid-2000s, compared to 15% in the UK. Moreover, while in Sweden and Denmark only 13 and 15% respectively of these carers were providing 20 hours per week of care or more, in the UK the corresponding figure was 27% (OECD, 2011).

Figure 9.6: Number of unpaid carers, by age group, 2002/03-2013/14, UK

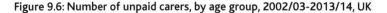

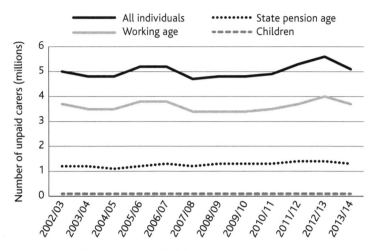

Note: Prior to 6 April 2010, women reached the State Pension age at 60. From 6 April 2010, the qualifying age for women has been gradually increasing. The changes do not impact on the State Pension age of men, currently 65

Source: Family Resources Survey 2012/13, Annex figure 5.1 and Family Resources Survey 2013/14, Figure 5.1

Outcomes, 2008-14

Social care users

At the most fundamental level, the aim of social care is to enable people with additional needs to lead full and fulfilling lives, and in this sense, a wide range of outcomes are relevant for assessing the effectiveness of social care. This is reflected in the adult social care outcomes framework (ASCOF), developed under the previous administration and published for the first time in 2010/11 (see Table 9.3). Some changes in definition were introduced for the 2014/15 data collection period, but nevertheless some trends can be discerned. Of the 24 indicators or sub-indicators, the trends since 2010/11 are positive for 9 (shaded dark grey), negative for 5 (shaded black), and are unavailable or show no clear direction for the remaining 10 (shaded light grey).

The first group of indicators, or 'domains', relates to quality of life, and are mostly drawn from the Social Care Users Survey or the Carers Survey, as are the third group of indicators on the experience of care and support. These suggest that for those in receipt of services, quality of life and satisfaction with services have generally been improving.

Table 9.3: Summary of Adult Social Care Outcomes Framework (ASCOF) measures, by year, England

	Units	2010/11	2011/12	2012/13	2013/14	2014/15
1A	Social care-related quality of life[1]	/24	18.7	18.7*	18.8*	19.0*	19.1
1B	Proportion of people who use services who have control over their daily life[1]	%	75.0	75.1	76.1*	76.8	77.3
1Ci	Proportion of people using social care who receive self-directed support	%	29.2	43.0	56.2	61.9	:
1Cii	Proportion of people using social care who receive direct payments	%	11.7	13.7	16.8	19.1	
1D	Carer-reported quality of life[2]	/12	..	..	8.1	..	7.9 ▼
1E	Proportion of adults with learning disabilities in paid employment[3]	%	6.6	7.1	7.0	6.7 b	6.0
1F	Proportion of adults in contact with secondary mental health services in paid employment[4]	%	9.5	8.9	8.8	7.0	6.8
1G	Proportion of adults with learning disabilities who live in their own home or with their family[3]	%	59	70	73.5	74.9	73.3
1H	Proportion of adults in contact with secondary mental health services who live independently, with or without support[4]	%	66.8	54.6	58.5	60.8	59.7
1I(1)	Proportion of people who use services who reported that they have as much social contact as they would like[1,9]	%	41.9	42.3	43.2	44.5*	44.8
1I(2)	Proportion of carers who reported that they have as much social contact as they would like[2,9]	%	..	..	41.4	..	38.5 ▼
2Ai	Permanent admissions to residential and nursing care homes for younger adults, per 100,000 population[5,6]		15	19.1 (14)	15	14.4	:
2Aii	Permanent admissions to residential and nursing care homes for older adults, per 100,000 population[5,6]		686.6	695.9 (694.2)	697.2	650.6	:
2Bi	Proportion of older people (65 and over) who were still at home 91 days after discharge from hospital into reablement/rehabilitation services (effectiveness of the service)[7]	%	82.0	82.7	81.4	82.5	82.1

(continued)

Table 9.3: Summary of Adult Social Care Outcomes Framework (ASCOF) measures, by year, England (continued)

		Units	2010/11	2011/12	2012/13	2013/14	2014/15
2Bii	Proportion of older people (65 and over) who were offered reablement services following discharge from hospital[7]	%	3.0	3.2	3.2	3.3	3.1
2Ci	Delayed transfers of care from hospital per 100,000 population[6]		10.6	9.7	9.4	9.6	11.1
2Cii	Delayed transfers of care from hospital, attributable to adult social care per 100,000 population[6]		4.1	3.7	3.2	3.1	3.7
3A	Overall satisfaction of people who use services with their care and support[1]	%	62.1	62.8	64.1*	64.8 b	64.7
3B	Overall satisfaction of carers with social services[2]	%	..	..	43.1	..	41.2 ▼
3C	Proportion of carers who report that they have been included or consulted in discussion about the person they care for[2]	%	..	..	73.3	--	72.3
3D	Proportion of people who use services and carers who find it easy to find information about services [1,8]						
	Adult Social Care Survey component only[1]	%	74.2	73.8	74.1	74.5	74.5
	Carers' Survey component only[2]	%	..	..	68.9	--	65.5 ▼
	Total	%	74.2	73.8	71.4	--	--
4A	Proportion of people who use services who feel safe[1]	%	62.4	63.8*	65.1*	66.0*	b 68.5
4B	Proportion of people who use services who say that those services have made them feel safe and secure[1]	%	..	75.5	78.1*	79.1*	b 84.5

Notes:

b Denotes break in series; .. These data are not available.

* The Adult Social Care Survey and Carers' Survey use sampling and therefore differences in outcomes for the measures based on these data (1A, 1B, 1D, 1I, 3A, 3B, 3C, 3D, 4A and 4B) may not be statistically significant (changes in survey outcomes are considered statistically significant when there are no overlapping confidence intervals between years). Where data are comparable between years, a statistically significant increase in the outcome score as compared to the previous year is denoted by * and a statistically significant decrease by ▼. For measure 1A, the figure for 2011-12 is marked as being a statistically significant increase from 2010-11. The two figures appear to be the same because they are rounded to one decimal place. In 2014-15, a new weighting methodology was implemented for the Carers' Survey at regional and national level; the 2012-13 scores have been reweighted accordingly.

(continued)

Table 9.3: Summary of adult social care outcomes framework measures, by year, England (continued)

1. Measures 1A, 1B, 1I(1), 3A, 3D(1), 4A and 4B are based on the Adult Social Care Survey. When making comparisons over time it should be kept in mind that stratified sampling was introduced for 2011-12 and there was also a change to the way in which councils checked if a service user had the capacity to consent to take part in the survey. Therefore, care should be taken when comparing 2011-12, 2012-13 and 2013-14 data with data from 2010-11.

2. Measures 1D, 1I(2), 3B, 3C and 3D(2) are based solely on the Carers' Survey. This is a biennial survey that took place for the first time in 2012-13. Therefore no data are available for these measures for 2013-14, 2011-12 and 2010-11.

3. When making comparisons over time for measures 1E and 1G, it should be borne in mind that there have been changes to the definitions. The restriction to capture employment and accommodation status at assessment or review was removed for 2011-12 onwards. Instead, service users could be included irrespective of whether they had a review during the year, but these data did need to have been captured or confirmed within the yearly reporting period 1 April to 31 March. This change should be borne in mind when comparing 2011-12, 2012-13 and 2013-14 data with data from 2010-11.

4. Measures 1F and 1H are based on the Mental Health Minimum Dataset (MHMDS). In April 2011 a new version of the dataset (MHMDS V 4.0) was implemented and associated changes to the way these data are processed have had an impact on overall record volumes. For 2013-14 there has been a change to the calculation of these measures that are now derived from an average of the monthly outcomes using the latest dataset (MHMDS V 4.1). These changes affect the comparability of data over time.

5. Where 'adjusted' figures are shown in brackets: when making comparisons over time for outcome measures 2A(1) and 2A(2) it should be kept in mind that in 2011-12 there was a transfer of funding of service users with a learning disability from the NHS to councils. These service users were classed as new admissions in 2011-12 as the source of funding had changed even though they had been receiving a service previously. Had no such transfer taken place, it is estimated that the national outcome values in 2011-12 for 2A(1) and 2A(2) would have been the figures shown in brackets.

6. The mid-year population estimates used to calculate the final ASCOF figures for 2013-14 are for the midpoint of 2013 from the ONS.

7. In 2011-12 there was a small change to the data collection behind measures 2B(1) and 2B(2). Service users who were discharged from hospital and provided with a rehabilitation service following an assessment from social care services only, resulting in an individual support plan that involved active therapy, treatment or opportunity for recovery, could be included. Previously, only those where a joint health and social care assessment had taken place could be included. Comparisons over time should be made with this in mind.

8. Measure 3D was based only on Adult Social Care Survey data for 2010-11 and 2011-12. For 2012-13 it was based on a combination of Adult Social Care Survey data and Carers' Survey data. For 2013-14 this measure has been replaced by 3D(1) and 3D(2) which provide separate measures for users and carers. Comparisons over time should be made with this in mind.

9. Measure 1I has been included for the first time in 2013-14. Time series data have been based on historical releases of the Adult Social Care Survey and Carers' Survey.

Source: HSCIC (2015d, Tables 2.1-2.4)

(The exception is the employment rate among mental health service users, which shows a negative trend.) These results may at first sight seem hard to square with evidence presented in the previous two sections – the 10% cut in social care expenditure in real terms since 2010/11 and the 19% fall in the number of clients, in a context of rising demographic demand – until we note that the Social Care *Users* Survey does not, of course, include ex-users, non-users or would-be users. A smaller group are getting more help.

For carers, on the other hand, the picture is much less positive. Four out of the five 'black' indicators relate to the experience of carers, who are less likely in 2014/15 than in 2012/13 to report a good quality of life, to have as much social contact as they would like, to be satisfied with social services, or to find it easy to find information about services. This is consistent with the possibility that some of the strain created by reductions in formal social services is being felt by carers, including, of course, those caring for people no longer receiving services and hence not represented in the Social Care Users Survey.

The second domain relates to delaying and reducing the need for care. These show no clear trend, although for the pair of indicators on delayed transfers (2Ci and 2Cii), there is evidence of an initial improvement, followed by a worsening in the most recent year. There is also some concern that the indicator on the *number of people* subject to delayed transfers from hospital attributable to social care may be open to manipulation. The aggregate *number of days* delayed for any reason has been rising (NHS England, 2014b).

The final domain relates to safeguarding vulnerable adults. A higher proportion of service recipients reported feeling safe in 2013/14 than was the case in 2010/11, and although the data are not directly comparable, the trend appears to have continued in 2014/15. This is very important, especially in the context of the emerging evidence on the scale and seriousness of abuse and poor standards of care. Trends in the Abuse of Vulnerable Adults series (see Table 9.4) – compiled from statutory returns made by local authorities – show that there were referrals for abuse of over 100,000 individuals in 2013/14, and given the multiple barriers to abuse being reported, these cases must be considered to represent the tip of the iceberg. This actually represents a slight rise over time. The HSCIC caution that this trend in the number of alerts and referrals could reflect changes in local authority recording and reporting practices, as well as more widespread awareness of safeguarding procedures, but the fact that the proportion of completed cases that have been substantiated or partially substantiated has been

Table 9.4: Abuse of vulnerable adults, 2010/11 to 2013/14, England

Year	Alerts[1]	Referrals[2]	Substantiated or partially substantiated (as % of completed investigations)
2010/11	92,865	95,065	30,365 (41%)
2011/12	133,395	106,165	34,670 (41%)
2012/13	172,130	107,650	37,410 (43%)
2013/14[3]	n/a	104,050 individuals	43%

Notes:

[1] Alerts are usually the first contact about a concern that a vulnerable adult has been, is, or might be the victim of abuse. Not all councils record information on alerts and referrals separately and some councils do not include alerts as part of the safeguarding process. Councils who do not collect alert data were instructed to submit blanks for this section of the table.

[2] An alert/concern is progressed to referral status when it is assessed to meet the local safeguarding threshold and an investigation is opened. Referrals for which age, gender and client type are known are reported here.

[3] Data for 2013/14 are calculated on a different basis and are not directly comparable. Data on alerts are no longer centrally collected. 'Referrals' is the number of unique individuals for whom safeguarding referrals were opened, while in previous years one individual with multiple referrals could have been counted multiple times.

Source: Authors' calculations based on HSCIC (2012, 2013b, 2014,e,f)

sustained at a high level suggests that the increases are not due to an increase in frivolous complaints or to purely administrative changes.

A summary of the Care Quality Commission's (CQC) inspections in adult social care in 2012/13 revealed that there had been concerns about staffing and quality monitoring in 1 in 10 home care services inspected, as well as safety concerns (such as failure to give out medicines safely) in 1 in 5 nursing homes inspected, and serious concerns about the quality of care, staffing or safeguarding in 1 in 10 residential homes inspected (CQC, 2013). A separate investigation indicated a link between high staff turnover and the number of deaths in residential care homes (CQC, 2013). The following year, the CQC (2014, p 14) highlighted a lack of trained nurses, failure to have a registered manager in place, and the size as risk factors for poor standards, with large, corporate institutions in general and nursing homes in particular performing worse than other smaller settings and residential care.

Unmet need

Given the (understandable) reliance of much of the official outcomes framework on the experiences of recipients of services, it is important to complement this perspective with indicators of unmet need. Unmet need is difficult to define, and there have been a number of different estimates. Forder and Fernandez (2010) used the Personal Social Services Research Unit (PSSRU) dynamic micro-simulation model to predict levels of unmet need from 2008/09 to 2012/13, given expected budget cuts to adult social care. The results indicated that unmet need could rise to just over one-quarter of a million people with high dependency by 2012/13, equivalent to a shortfall of 119 million hours per year overall. This scenario was based on the assumption that informal care would meet some needs not met by state-funded care; without informal care the gap was predicted to be even greater, at 231 million hours.

Vlachantoni et al (2011) used the 2001/02 General Household Survey (GHS) and 2008 English Longitudinal Survey of Ageing (ELSA) to estimate unmet need among people aged 65 or over. They found that 39% to 61% of those needing help with bathing, dressing and/or getting in or out bed received no help in 2001/02, and that 32% to 62% of those needing help with bathing and/or dressing received no help in 2008. ('Help' here is defined as state support, privately paid care or informal care.) In more recent work, they have also analysed the characteristics of those most likely to receive care, and find that socioeconomic factors are significant alongside those more directly related to the person's physical and mental needs (Vlachantoni et al, 2015).

Whalley (2012), using the Health Survey for England, found that 22% of men and 30% of women who needed help with at least one 'activity of daily living' (ADL) received none in the last month, while 14% of men and 15% of women who needed help with at least one 'instrumental activity of daily living' (IADL) received none.[11] There is also a suggestion that rates of unmet need may be higher amongst low-income households and those living in areas with a high Index of Multiple Deprivation (IMD), although the published findings are not conclusive on this point.[12]

Finally, our own analysis of trends in unmet need over time using the Family Resources Survey – based on a broad definition of need but assuming that *any* help received (state, privately paid-for, or unpaid family and friends, and of whatever duration) is sufficient to meet a person's need – suggests very high and increasing levels of unmet need for those with moderate difficulties, and lower and falling levels of unmet need among those with four or more areas of difficulty (see Figure 9.7). This is consistent with the concentration of resources on those with the most severe needs and the withdrawal of services from those with moderate needs, and suggests that the increase in unpaid care has not been sufficient to fill the gap.

Figure 9.7: Unmet need for care, by number of difficulties, age group and year, UK

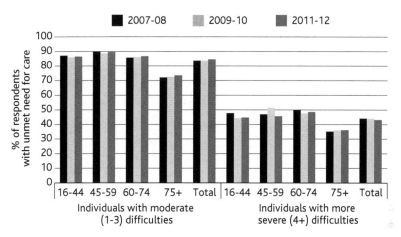

Source: Authors' calculations using Family Resources Survey 2007-08, 2009-10 and 2011-12

Conclusion

On the eve of the financial crash in 2008, adult social care was better placed than it had been for some time after a sustained period of investment, increasing faster than demographic pressure. Spending continued to increase until 2009/10, but was no longer keeping pace with the growth in the older population. The coalition government therefore inherited a system already under pressure, but far from addressing the funding shortfall, the coalition introduced cuts of around 40% to local authority core funding (LGA, 2015). Local authorities sought to shield social care budgets (down by 'only' around 10%), but in the context of a 9% increase in the population aged 85 and over, the consequences for the numbers of people social services can support have been serious: down by between 30 and 40% for many client groups (see Table 9.3).

The central challenge for the new government elected in 2015 is therefore how to meet the gap in social care funding. The Conservatives have already signalled their intention to instigate yet further cuts in local government funding, so the solution is apparently not going to come from there. This is despite warnings that councils cannot make significant further cuts without putting basic services for vulnerable people at risk (LGA, 2014b), and despite continued growth in the older population (see Figure 9.8).

Some see integration between health and social care as a silver bullet that will resolve the tension between increasing needs and decreasing

Figure 9.8: Projections of total local authority funding and population aged 75 or over, 2010-19, England

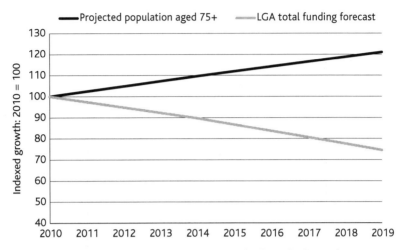

Note: Population is for mid-year 2010, 2014 and 2019, funding is for financial years 2010/11, 2014/15 and 2019/20. Local Government Association (LGA) forecast is based on their model for total funding including grants, Council Tax, business rates and other sources of income, in real terms.

Sources: ONS (2013c, 2013d, 2013e) for population projections, and LGA (2014b) for local government funding

funds. The desirability of integration is increasingly widely recognised, for example, in Barker and The King's Fund (2014), in the Labour Party manifesto for the 2015 General Election, and, latterly, by the Conservative government's endorsement of the devolution to Greater Manchester of £6 billion of NHS spending as part of an experiment in integrating health and social care. However, the evidence to date is that establishing effective integration is time-consuming, dependent on high levels of trust between organisations (in short supply at times of job losses and funding scarcity), and is by no means guaranteed to produce cost savings, at least in the short run – although it may well improve quality of care (Bennett and Humphries, 2014).

Perhaps, then, the solution is to be found in reducing costs. But there are two problems with this strategy. First, there are concerns over the quality of care in both residential and community settings, and over the financial viability of some major private sector care providers. This means that attempts to drive costs down even further could backfire. Second, costs in social care are principally wage costs, and the care sector is already heavily reliant on low-paid, often migrant workers. A total of 2.5% of domiciliary workers are actually paid below the National Minimum Wage, and a further large proportion at the minimum wage (Bessa et al, 2013). As many as 6 in 10 are estimated to be on zero hour contracts (Skills for Care, 2012). In fact, the Conservative government's first budget in July 2015 announced substantial increases to the Minimum Wage, and social care workers will be a significant group of beneficiaries. However, it is unclear where the estimated £1.4 billion cost to local authorities will come from (Gardiner and Hussein, 2015).[13]

An alternative way to plug the social care funding gap would be to hope that families' own expenditure will rise. There is some evidence that both the number and proportion of older and physically disabled people self-funding residential care is increasing (Laing and Buisson, 2014) – but this is, of course, only possible for those who can afford it. The lifetime care cap and relaxation of the capital means test that were to have been implemented in 2016 would have resulted in an increase of around 9% in the number of people receiving at least some state funding for their care by the year 2030 (Hancock et al, 2013). The principal beneficiaries would have been those with modest wealth. This represented a move *away* from individual responsibility towards collective responsibility for bearing the financial risk of needing highly intensive and/or very long-term care, a move that Dilnot and many other commentators argued was long overdue, but also, of course, increasing demands on social care budgets. Local authorities appealed to central government to delay the implementation, and the new government announced in July 2015 that it would be postponed 'until 2020'. The flagship of the coalition government's social care policy is not being implemented, and cannot be without new funding.

Finally, if both public and private funds look set to continue to be inadequate, one might look to unpaid care by families and friends to fill the gap. The new government has announced that they will produce (another) strategy to support carers (Jeremy Hunt's speech to the Local Government Association, 1 July 2015), although modest Liberal Democrat proposals to guarantee respite breaks for carers did not even make it into the coalition agreement in the last administration. The number of unpaid carers and intensity of care appears to have increased in response to rising levels of need and reductions in services, as detailed above, but the strain is beginning to show up in worsening outcome indictors for carers (see Table 9.3), and in the longer term, the availability of unpaid care is forecast to fall (Pickard, 2015).

The gap between needs and provision of adult social care has widened under the coalition. What will the new government's strategy be to close the gap? At the time of writing, there are no indications that a coherent, well-evidenced plan will emerge. On the contrary, early announcements on further cuts to local government grants, accompanied by substantial increases in the social care wage bill, look set to turn the screws several more turns. The concession in the 2015 Autumn Statement, permitting local authorities to add 2% to Council Tax in order to fund social care, will be likely to exacerbate inequalities, since authorities with the highest need are least likely to be in a position to raise funding in this way. Pressures on unpaid care, and levels of unmet need, already high, therefore look set to rise.

Notes

[1] Social care is a devolved policy area, and there are significant differences of approach between the jurisdictions. For reasons of space and resources, this chapter focuses mainly on England, but where relevant, highlights important differences in policies between the devolved countries.

[2] There was some evidence of this tension already in the London boroughs studied as part of the Social Policy in a Cold Climate programme (Fitzgerald et al, 2014). In Redbridge, an adult social care officer reported that they were being less restrictive about giving out small pieces of equipment to help people help themselves (for example, a handrail or microwave), following the preventative logic, while in Brent, an officer reported that eligibility criteria for assistive equipment were being applied more strictly, as a means of making savings.

[3] Capital charges include an allowance for depreciation of assets and write-offs of deferred charges. Capital charges fell significantly between 2009/10 and 2013/14, but have always been a very small component of gross total cost (1.6% at the beginning of the period and 1.3% at the end).

[4] Figures for expenditure in 2014/15 are sourced from a new collection and are provisional. See note 2 to Table 9.1. However, using 2013/14 figures (which are consistent with previous years and based on a final release) as the end point indicates a similar trend for all rows except row D, total income, which was lower in 2013/14 than in 2009/10, but higher in 2014/15.

[5] This is ensured by removing funding for Supporting People. Prior to 2003/04, councils classified Supporting People funding as housing expenditure and not social services expenditure. The longer time series therefore exclude this grant.

[6] Authors' calculations using nominal expenditure figures for net current adult social care expenditure (HSCIC, 2013a) and GDP deflators (HM Treasury, 2015f).

[7] Prior to 2011/12, Valuing People Now was recorded as income from the NHS, but funding for the programme has since been allocated directly to local authorities, and hence appears as expenditure rather than income in these accounts.

[8] Both growth in net current expenditure on adult social care and net current expenditure on older people excludes the Supporting People grant for consistency over time. Figures for total cost, that is, including spending funded by NHS and joint arrangements, are not available consistently over this longer time period.

[9] Direct payments were expanded to existing/new direct payments and personal budgets in 2009-10. Therefore the 2009-10 data is not directly comparable to previous years. However, the downwards trend continues after 2009/10.

[10] The number of carers who are children may also be increasing: a comparison of the 2001 and 2011 Census data for England suggested a 20% increase in the number of carers aged 5-17, up to 166,363 (ONS, 2013b).

[11] ADLs: stairs, bath/shower, dressing/undressing, in/out bed, getting around indoors, taking medicine, using toilet, eating, including cutting up food, washing face and hands. IADLs: shopping for food, routine housework/ laundry, getting out of the house, paperwork/paying bills. Need is defined as the respondent being able to manage the activity on their own with difficulty, only being able to do the activity with help, or not being able to do it at all. 'Help' is either formal (state or paid) or informal care.

[12] Whalley (2012, Tables 8.11 and 8.12) reports on the percentages that needed help with ADLs and IADLs, and the percentages that received help in the last month, by household income quintiles and IMD quintiles respectively. But Whalley notes that those who received help in the last month may not be the same as the people who need help, so rates of unmet need cannot be directly inferred from these data.

[13] Gardiner and Hussein's estimate is based on the difference in cost between actual wages and paying the Living Wage in 2013-14. They also estimate that around half this cost would be returned to the Exchequer through increased tax receipts and lower benefit payments, but there is no direct mechanism for these gains to be returned to local authorities.

In this chapter, data from the Family Resources Survey were accessed via the UK Data Service. In particular:

Department for Work and Pensions, National Centre for Social Research, Office for National Statistics. Social and Vital Statistics Division. (2014).

Family Resources Survey, 2011-2012. [data collection]. 2nd Edition. UK Data Service. SN: 7368, http://dx.doi.org/10.5255/UKDA-SN-7368-2.

Department for Work and Pensions, National Centre for Social Research, Office for National Statistics. Social and Vital Statistics Division. (2014). Family Resources Survey, 2009-2010. [data collection]. 3rd Edition. UK Data Service. SN: 6886, http://dx.doi.org/10.5255/UKDA-SN-6886-3.

Department for Work and Pensions, National Centre for Social Research, Office for National Statistics. Social and Vital Statistics Division. (2014). Family Resources Survey, 2007-2008. [data collection]. 2nd Edition. UK Data Service. SN: 6252, http://dx.doi.org/10.5255/UKDA-SN-6252-2.

Part Two

TEN

Public and private welfare

Tania Burchardt and Polina Obolenskaya

Welfare provision, finance and choice

The changing role of the state in relation to what may be broadly considered 'welfare' is a theme that threads through all of the policy areas considered in this book. In some domains, such as early childhood, involvement of the state has increased significantly over the past two decades, while in others, such as housing, it has shrunk. Moreover, change has taken place along several dimensions – not just in terms of expenditure, but also in relation to forms of provision, the degree of regulatory control and user choice. This complexity means that a straightforward diagnosis of 'privatisation' is not helpful or perhaps even meaningful. As Powell and Miller (2013, p 1058) note: 'The term *privatization* is multidimensional, and definitions and operationalisations of the term are often implicit, unclear, and conflicting.' Instead, what we offer in this chapter is an account of some of the changes in policy in relation to the role of the state and their consequences for the distribution of spending – public and private – on welfare activities in the period from the eve of the financial crash to the present day.

To provide a structure for this task, we build on a framework developed by Burchardt, Hills and Propper (1999) and subsequently applied by Smithies (2005), Edmiston (2011) and Hills (2011). The framework comprises three dimensions – provision, finance and decision – each of which may be public or private, and which may occur in any combination (see Figure 10.1). The 'pure public' segment is what we might consider to be the archetypal post-war British welfare state – tax-financed, provided by a publicly owned and run organisation, and with little or no choice on the part of the beneficiary about how much or from whom to receive the service. Emergency treatment in an NHS hospital is an example. At the opposite corner, the 'pure private' sector is activity undertaken by individuals at their own initiative and purchased in the free market, such as private medical insurance. Other segments of the figure represent different combinations, for example, public finance of private provision (such as adult social care contracted out to an independent provider), with the classification of the decision dimension varying according to whether the user has a care package arranged for them (public decision), or whether they have a direct payment or personal budget and make the choice over what and who to commission themselves (private decision).

The framework uses total spending (that is, collectively financed spending and individual consumer spending) as a unifying metric in order to examine the distribution of overall welfare activity across the different segments. Powell and Miller (2014) argue that this choice of metric tends to obscure the role of regulation: the extent to which the activity is subject to requirements imposed by legislation or other regulatory state controls. Other frameworks foreground regulation as a dimension in its own right, such as the mixed economy of welfare model that classifies activities into high or low regulation, cutting across state, market, third sector and informal provision, or the 'publicness' model, which uses 'control' by political or market forces as a separate criterion (Powell and Miller, 2014; drawing on Bozeman, 1987 and Pesch, 2005).

The degree of regulation does, however, feature in both the 'provision' and 'decision' dimensions of the framework applied in this chapter. The classification of providers as public or non-public is governed by the European System of Accounts 1995 (ESA95), and the key consideration is whether the body is controlled by central or local government, or by a public corporation (HM Treasury, 2013b). Control is the ability to determine general corporate policy, through ownership, specific legislation or regulation. This suggests that there are degrees of publicness, although in practice, the Office for National Statistics (ONS) (2012) provides a binary classification, and we follow that here. In any case, the degree of regulation to which *organisations* are subject helps to determine whether a provider is classified as public or independent.

The degree of regulation to which a particular *activity* is subject is reflected in the decision dimension of our framework. The decision dimension applies three tests (for a fuller discussion, see Burchardt, 2013): to what extent can the end user choose *how much* to have, to what extent can they choose *who provides* the service, and to what extent are there *viable alternatives*? These tests are intended to capture the degree of agency enjoyed by the user, including their chance of exit. A highly regulated activity is likely to restrict one or more aspects

Figure 10.1: Wheels of welfare

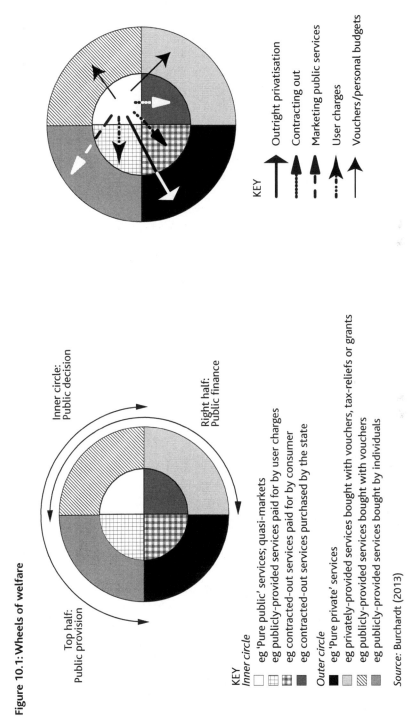

Inner circle:
Public decision

Top half:
Public provision

Right half:
Public finance

KEY
Outright privatisation
Contracting out
Marketing public services
User charges
Vouchers/personal budgets

KEY
Inner circle
eg 'Pure public' services; quasi-markets
eg publicly-provided services paid for by user charges
eg contracted-out services paid for by consumer
eg contracted-out services purchased by the state

Outer circle
eg 'Pure private' services
eg privately-provided services bought with vouchers, tax-reliefs or grants
eg publicly-provided services bought with vouchers
eg publicly-provided services bought by individuals

Source: Burchardt (2013)

of agency as defined here, and increase the likelihood that it will be classified as a 'public decision'.

Finally, although the original framework distinguished only between public and 'private' (that is, non-public) providers, in a number of areas, the involvement of not-for-profit providers has grown considerably since the late 1990s. It would therefore be desirable in principle to provide estimates of the split between for-profit and not-for-profit provision, and we provide a commentary on this below.

The following section describes the shape of welfare activity in 2007/08, on the eve of the financial crisis, in the fields of health, personal social care (including both adult and children's social care), education, income maintenance (including social security and pensions), and housing. This is followed by a discussion of some of the policies pursued in the last years of the Labour administration and by the coalition government that bore on changing boundaries of public and private welfare, including, of course, the Conservatives' avowed aim to shrink the state, as discussed in more detail in earlier chapters. Evidence of the outcomes of these policies is then presented in the form of new estimates of the distribution of total welfare spending (public and private) across different types of public and private welfare activity in England in 2013/14, compared to previous years. The chapter concludes with a discussion of continuity and change.

The devolved administrations in Scotland and Wales have increasingly pursued rather different agendas from Westminster in relation to public and private health, education, social care and housing. The Welsh Assembly described their approach as one of encouraging collaboration rather than competition and choice between providers (National Assembly for Wales, 2013), and engaging employees in a social partnership, rather than developing alternative ownership models such as mutuals and community enterprises. The Scottish government differentiated its model from that of Westminster, emphasising simplification of organisational structures and cooperation between different services rather than quasi-markets (Salmond, 2008). However, it also committed itself to promoting 'partnership' between public services, private and voluntary organisations and the communities they serve as part of public service reform. Alongside policy divergence has come divergence in data sources and definitions, making it increasingly difficult to draw meaningful comparisons, or to produce UK-wide statistics on public and private welfare activity. Accordingly, the figures presented below concentrate on England. This contrasts with earlier versions of this analysis (including Hills, 2011), which have been UK-wide. In the comparisons across time below, we have recalculated figures for the years up to and including 2007/08 on an England-only basis.

The areas of welfare activity included in the figures together comprise a significant proportion of overall welfare activity, but we do not claim to have comprehensive coverage of the policy areas discussed elsewhere in this book: we are not including area regeneration or employment policy, for example. More detailed, sector-specific, analyses of the changing role of the state in England are available elsewhere, including on schools (Hicks, 2015), adult social care in the home (Glendinning, 2012), foster care (Sellick, 2011), healthcare (Powell and Miller, 2014), housing (Hodkinson, 2011; Blessing, 2015), and pensions (De Deken, 2013). Other aspects of the relationship between the public and private sectors, including the use of outsourcing and joint ventures by local authorities, particularly for 'back room' functions such as information and communication technology (ICT), human resources and estates, are discussed in Smith and Jones (2015). Moreover, the estimates presented here are inevitably somewhat rough around the edges, drawn as they are from scores of different statistical sources, each using their own definitions and accounting practices, and requiring numerous judgements to be made about what to include and exclude (see Obolenskaya and Burchardt, 2016). In some cases we have prioritised consistency with previous years over more comprehensive figures for the most recent year, and this may, in turn, produce inconsistency with other data sources. Despite these caveats, the broad pattern of changes in public and private welfare emerges quite clearly.

The situation on the eve of the crisis

Overall social spending in the UK in 2007/08, on the eve of the financial crisis, stood at 26.8% of GDP (Hills, 2011, Figure 1).[1] This was higher than in the early 2000s, but little different from the levels of the mid and early 1990s, and was certainly nothing exceptional by historic standards. There had been some changes in the proportions spent on different areas of welfare activity since Labour came to power in 1997 – health and education had gained, and, on a much smaller scale, social services, while spending on pensions and other social security had fallen as a proportion of overall social spending.

But public spending is, of course, only one part of how welfare activities are paid for: individuals and families also pay directly or through their employers for some alternative or top-up services and benefits. In 2007/08, public spending in England accounted for £396 billion (in 2014/15 prices) but an additional £221 billion, or one-third of total welfare spending, was by individuals (Obolenskaya and Burchardt, 2016). Moreover, not all of the £396 billion of public spending was on services provided by the public sector; around a quarter (£99 billion) was on private or voluntary sector provision.

So already by 2007/08 there was a 'mixed economy' of welfare. The 'traditional' welfare state, publicly financed, publicly provided and with key decisions determined by the state, made up less than half of total welfare activity. The scale of welfare activity overall had grown significantly in real terms over the preceding decades – from 26.1% of GDP in 1979/80 to 35.6% in 2007/08 (Table 10.1) – but the share of public spending within that had fallen steadily, from 73% in 1979/80 to 64% in 2007/8 (based on figures in Table 10.2). In other words, our increasing demand for welfare services as living standards and the economy grew had outstripped the growth in publicly financed services, and the shortfall had been made up by an increasing volume of out-of-pocket and private insurance expenditure.

Independent sector *provision* had also grown, some of it financed by public spending. In many cases this was as an explicit policy intent, as, for example, with the transfer of social housing into owner-occupation with significant subsidies under the Right to Buy, initiated by the Thatcher government, the expansion of personal pensions in the 1980s, fuelled in part by generous tax treatment and National Insurance rebates, and the increasing use of contracting out adult social care to private and voluntary sector care homes and agencies, especially after the Community Care Act 1992. Public sector provision in many areas continued to decline as a proportion of overall provision under Labour after 1997, although the pace of change was slower than under the preceding Conservative administrations. One area of significant change was housing, where large-scale stock transfers from local authorities to independent (not-for-profit) housing associations produced a contraction in public provision (although not in public finance).

In aggregate, however, changes to the boundaries of the welfare state under Labour up to the eve of the crash were gradual and represented more of a continuity than a break with the past.

Goals and policies, 2008-15

The final years of the Labour administration were marked by the unfolding global financial crash and the subsequent recession and fall in GDP. The decision to implement planned spending increases in health and education at the levels planned prior to the crash was taken in part to counter the effects of the recession. It came together with unplanned increases in social security spending that occurred as a direct effect of the recession. This combination meant that social spending increased sharply as a proportion of GDP (see Chapter Fourteen, this volume). It is worth remembering that around a quarter of public spending in health and over a quarter in education was on non-state provision, so these increases were directly contributing to sustaining the private sector, as well as providing welfare services to the population.

The coalition government announced a significant change of direction, both in relation to overall public spending and in relation to the shape of the welfare state. First, public spending was to be curtailed. Second, the private and voluntary sectors – including mutuals – were to be given a much greater role in delivering public welfare services. And third, more was to be done on a local, self-organised basis, particularly in order to fill gaps left by the shrinking state. This was the 'Big Society', not 'big government'. As Prime Minister David Cameron said:

> I believe this coalition has an once-in-a-lifetime opportunity to transform our public services. From schools to the NHS, policing and prisons, we have developed a clear plan for modernisation based on a common approach. A Big Society approach, which empowers not only services users but professionals, that strengthens not only existing providers, but new ones in the private and voluntary sectors too. (Cameron, 2011b)

and

> ... isn't it better if we are having to make cuts in public spending, to try and encourage a bigger and stronger society at the same time? If there are facilities that the state can't afford to keep open, shouldn't we be trying to encourage communities who want to come forward and help them and run them? (Cameron, 2011a)

A White Paper on public service delivery was produced in 2011, developing the idea of employee-led public sector mutuals (HM Government, 2011b), and by March 2014, 85 had been established, delivering over £1 billion of services. Le Grand (2013) argues they could and should be an enduring innovation, but it is perhaps too early to tell whether they will be given the necessary support to live up to their potential (Smith and Jones, 2015).

During the period of the coalition government, there were a number of developments within specific policy areas (especially for England where devolved, and UK otherwise) that affected the boundaries between public and private finance and provision, and also the extent to which individuals had decision-making control over the services they received. In health, the major reforms instituted by the Health and Social Care Act 2012 (for a full discussion, see Vizard and Obolenskaya, 2015) retained the principle of the health service being free at the point of use (that is, public rather than private finance), but opened the way to private provision of publicly financed healthcare to a much larger extent (that is, commissioning services from 'any qualified provider' including private and voluntary sector organisations), and also to private finance for publicly provided services (such as private patients in NHS hospitals). NHS foundation trusts remain public sector bodies according to the ONS classification, but they have a higher degree of financial and managerial autonomy than non-foundation trusts, for example, in raising income from private patients (capped at 49% of total income).

In social care, the flagship coalition policy was to legislate for a version of the Dilnot recommendations for financing long-term care, specifically, relaxing the capital means test and introducing a cap on the cumulative contribution a person can be asked to make towards the cost of their personal care (for a fuller discussion, see Burchardt et al, 2015). Hancock et al (2013) estimated that there could be an additional 115,000 people receiving some public funding for social care by 2030, around a 9% increase, if the measures were fully implemented; however, the policy was quietly put on hold by the incoming 2015 Conservative government. More immediately, the coalition cut funding to local government by around 30%, and although local authorities afforded relative protection to adult social care within their constrained budgets, spending was nevertheless reduced by around 12% (see Chapter Nine, this volume).

In relation to schooling, the most significant structural reforms were the rapid expansion of the academies programme and the creation of free schools (see Chapter Four, this volume). Academies and free schools are not under local education authority budgetary control, and have the freedom to set their own curriculum, to vary school hours and term dates, and to negotiate staff pay and conditions (free schools can even employ non-qualified teachers as teachers). They remain, however, publicly funded, non-fee-paying, and bound by the admissions code, and as a last resort, the Secretary of State may intervene directly (as, for example, following concerns raised about promotion of Islamic extremism in some Birmingham academies in 2014). For these reasons, the ONS classifies them as public sector bodies – under central government rather than local government.

Changes in higher education related more to financing than provision. Following the Browne review (BIS, 2010b), direct funding to universities for undergraduate teaching was substantially cut, to be replaced by higher tuition fees (up to a cap of £9,000) funded by student loans, and accompanied by an expansion of bursaries provided at the discretion of the institution. This was a clear shift from public to private financing – although the outcome for the figures on public spending depend on how the expected non-repayment of student loans is accounted for.

Within income maintenance, an innovation instigated under Labour and implemented by the coalition was the creation of automatic enrolment of employees into an occupational pension scheme, or the new low-cost National Employment Savings Trust (NEST), with at least minimal contributions from both employee and employer. This is interesting from the point of view of classifying welfare activity in so far as it shifts this part of occupational pension provision – privately provided, privately financed – towards being a public decision: an unusual combination. However, given that employees can opt out, and also that the amount contributed above the minimum is at the discretion of the employee, we have retained here the 'private decision' classification.

Policies in relation to income maintenance other than pensions under the coalition have been dominated by cuts in benefit levels in real terms and restrictions on benefit eligibility, accompanied by the rhetoric of austerity – although, as Figure 2.5 in Chapter Two shows (this volume), the net effects of direct tax and benefit changes (not including VAT) have been essentially neutral for the public finances.

Housing has traditionally been much less dominated by state activity than the other areas of welfare considered in this chapter. In housing, transfer of local authority stock to housing associations (classified as non-public sector by the ONS) continued during the coalition years, although at a slower rate than in the previous decade, reducing the extent of public provision. Public financing has increasingly been switched away from 'bricks and mortar' to individuals and landlords, through Housing Benefit (see Chapter Seven, this volume), the majority of which goes towards private or housing association rents. Public finance for private provision was also extended during the coalition years by a revitalised Right to Buy scheme, and a new Help to Buy policy, designed to assist first-time buyers (see Chapter Seven, this volume).

We can see, then, that the boundaries between public and private have developed very differently across welfare policy areas under the coalition. In schooling, the most significant developments have produced shifts *within* what is still categorised as public provision – from community schools to more autonomous academies and free schools. A parallel development in health, from trusts to the more autonomous but still public sector foundation trusts, was, however, accompanied by much greater encouragement of commissioning services from the private and voluntary sector, while in housing, stock transfer from local authorities to housing associations and renewed Right to Buy policies have resulted in a cross-over from public to private (profit or non-profit) provision. All of the above remains publicly financed, however. By contrast, in social care, higher education and income maintenance, significant contractions in public expenditure have de facto produced a shift in the balance between what the state pays for and what individuals must pay for – or go without. The combined result of these changes for the allocation of total welfare activity to different segments of the 'wheel of welfare' (see Figure 10.1) is analysed in the next section.

Spending in 2013/14[2]

Total spending

Before discussing the breakdown between public and private finance, provision and decision, it may be helpful to give an indication of the trends in the total volume of welfare spending, and how the shares of each policy area have changed over time. Table 10.1 shows that total welfare spending (public and private) has trebled in real terms since 1979/80. It has also grown substantially as a percentage of GDP. This reflects both increased needs, including from an ageing population, and increased volume and quality of services – more higher education, more healthcare, more expensive housing, and so on.

Within that, however, the proportions spent on different policy areas have varied. The biggest change has been in income maintenance (social security, including pensions), which has more than doubled in real terms, but fallen as a proportion of total welfare spending from nearly half the total in 1979/80 to only just over one-third in 2013/14. Spending on education (including schools and higher education) has

Table 10.1: Total (public and private) spending on welfare by policy area, 1979/80 to 2013/14, England (£ billion in real terms, GDP deflated and as a percentage of total spending)

	1979/80		1995/96		1999/2000		2007/08		2013/14	
	£bn	%	£bn	%	£bn	%	£bn	%	£bn	%
Health	33.3	14.8	63.6	17.1	77.3	18.4	115.2	18.7	120.6	17.4
Personal Social Care	6.7	3.0	21.9	5.9	25.4	6.1	35.7	5.8	37.3	5.4
Education	29.8	13.3	45.0	12.1	46.0	11.0	73.1	11.9	79.5	11.4
Income maintenance	106.9	47.5	155.2	41.8	162.8	38.8	234.3	38.0	250.2	36.0
Housing	48.2	21.4	85.4	23.0	108.4	25.8	158.4	25.7	206.9	29.8
Total	225.0	100.0	371.1	100.0	419.9	100.0	616.7	100.0	694.5	100.0
Total as % of GDP	26.1%		30.4%		30.4%		35.6%		39.6%	

Source: Obolenskaya and Burchardt (2016)

fluctuated at around 11 to 13% of total welfare spending. Health and personal social care have increased in real terms *and* as a share of total welfare spending. Peak shares of expenditure came in 1999/2000 for social care at 6.1%, and in 2007/08 for health at 18.7%. Expenditure on housing has more than quadrupled over the period in real terms, and it has steadily increased its share of overall spending, such that it now stands at 29.8%, second only in magnitude to income maintenance.

Health

In health (see Figure 10.2), despite the radical shake-up of the structure of healthcare provision brought about by the Health and Social Care Act 2012, the 'pure public' segment remains dominant, at just under three-fifths of total health spending (59%). This is partly because, in accordance with National Accounts definitions, we continue to classify NHS foundation trusts as public sector organisations. Between 2007/08 and 2013/14, public spending on the public provision of healthcare remained more or less constant in real terms, but its *share* of overall public and private spending has fallen, as other forms of provision have grown.

Figure 10.2: The changing profile of total health expenditure categorised by public/private finance, provision and decision, 1979/80 to 2013/14, England

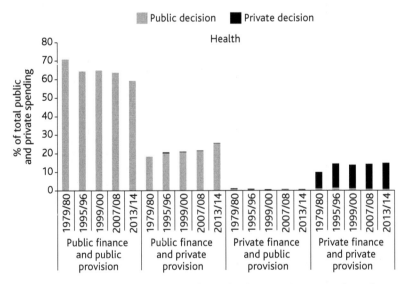

Note: The recording of expenditure on NHS hospital and community services changed between 2007-8 and 2013-14, creating a potential inconsistency in the time series on public finance and public provision.

Source: Obolenskaya and Burchardt (2016)

In absolute terms, the big expansion of contracting out of healthcare – that is, the NHS purchase of independently provided healthcare – occurred in the first half of the 2000s under New Labour, but it continued to grow in real terms between 2007/08 and 2013/14 (see Table 10.2). This is included in the 'Public finance and private provision' bars, although the magnitude of the change is masked by the much larger, and more constant, expenditure on GPs and NHS dentists, who are also treated as private providers. Overall, publicly funded, independently provided healthcare (including GPs and dentists) now accounts for 25% of total health spending, compared to 22% in 2007/08. Within this, however, NHS purchase of non-NHS-provided healthcare grew by 65% in real terms between 2007/08 and 2013/14. Lafond et al (2014) give a more detailed breakdown by type of service and type of provider.

Private finance initiative (PFI) contracts are treated as capital expenditure and are thus not included in these figures. They are, of course, a very significant form of public finance (and public decision) for private provision. The total outstanding 'unitary charge' on Department of Health (DH) PFI contracts – that is, repayment of, and interest on, debt used to finance the capital costs as well as payments for ongoing services – stood at £69 billion in 2013 (NAO, 2013).

'Pure private' spending on healthcare has also continued to increase in real terms (by 9% between 2007/08 and 2013/14), although more slowly since the financial crash than in the first part of the 2000s. This includes private medical insurance (which has remained broadly constant), out-of-pocket expenditure on medical services and over-the-counter medicines and healthcare products. However, as a proportion of overall health spending, 'pure private' spending has remained more or less constant, at 13%.

Other segments in the health 'wheel of welfare' representing more exotic combinations of public and private provision, finance and decision each account for 1% or less of total spending: 0.8% on prescription charges, 0.3% on NHS hospital charges and 0.2% on optical vouchers. NHS income from private patients has grown by 30% since 2007/08, but remains a tiny fraction (0.4%) of total health spending.

Social care

Public spending on social care (see Figure 10.3) is split between the 'pure public' segment (services provided by the local authority and NHS), contracted-out care (that is, independently provided services

Figure 10.3: The changing profile of total social care expenditure categorised by public/private finance, provision and decision, 1979/80 to 2013/14, England

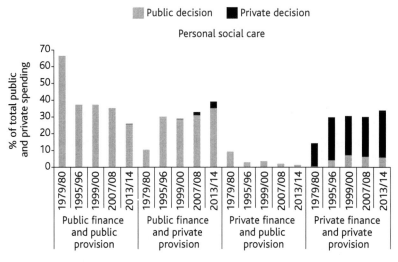

Note: Figures for private spending on private provision (private decision) for years up to and including 2007/8 are based on spending on older people, plus an estimate for the amount spent on working age adults. The figure for 2013/14 is based on spending on all adults

Source: Obolenskaya and Burchardt (2016)

commissioned and paid for by the local authority), and direct payments (public finance and private decision, mostly used to purchase private provision).[3] Public spending began to fall in the late 2000s (for more details, see Chapter Nine, this volume), despite increasing demand from the growth in the older and disabled population. A significant part of this was spending in the 'pure public' segment, which fell by nearly a quarter in real terms between 2007/08 and 2013/14. At the end of the period it accounted for just 26% of overall (public and private) expenditure. (This is a stark contrast with health, where 'pure public' still accounts for 59% of overall spending, as we have seen.)

Meanwhile, contracted-out care grew in real value, and increased its share of overall spending, and at 35% is now the largest segment in this figure. Spending via direct payments and individual budgets – that is, payments made to individuals with which to arrange their own care – increased nearly three-fold in real terms since 2007/08 (public finance, private provision, private decision – see Table 10.2), but still accounted for only 4% of total spending by 2013/14.

The gap left by reductions in public spending have not mainly been filled by increases in user charges, for either public or private provision. There does, however, appear to have been an increase in spending by individuals and families on privately arranged and provided care, as represented by the 'pure private' segment. Although the sources are not entirely consistent over time,[4] there appears to have been an increase of around one-quarter in pure private spending in real terms between 2007/08 and 2013/14, with the result that by the end of the period, and for the first time in this series, the 'pure private' segment accounted for a larger share of all spending (28%) than the 'pure public' (26%).

One other possible response to the cuts in publicly financed social care that is not reflected in these figures is an increase in unpaid (or 'informal') care. Evidence discussed in Chapter Nine of this volume suggests this may, indeed, have occurred.

Education

In education (see Figure 10.4), there are judgements to be made about how to classify schools expenditure. Following National Accounts definitions, we treat academies and free schools (and their predecessors, grant-maintained schools and city technology colleges) as public sector organisations, but they enjoy considerably more independence, for example, in terms of admissions policies, teacher recruitment and curriculum, than local authority community schools.[5] They are

Figure 10.4: The changing profile of total education expenditure categorised by public/private finance, provision and decision, 1979/80 to 2013/14, England

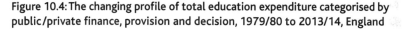

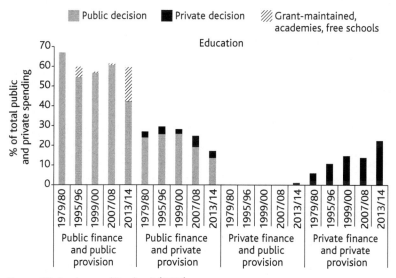

Source: Obolenskaya and Burchardt (2016)

'less public' in Powell and Miller's (2014) terms. This decision has significant implications for the description of both the outcomes in 2013/14 and the change since 2007/08. With academies and free schools treated as public (the striped bars in the figure), the share of total education spending that is public finance and public provision has fallen only slightly, from 61% to 60%.[6] But if they are excluded from public provision, the share of public finance and public provision is seen to have fallen by nearly one-third, from 61% to 43% – and the striped section of the bars would move across to make a corresponding increase in the public finance, private provision segment.

Moreover, there is increasingly a question about whether primary and secondary schooling should be classified as a public or private decision. The three tests for the decision dimension described in the opening section of this chapter give an ambivalent answer: the state decides 'how much', parents and children in principle choose 'who provides', but the existence of 'viable alternatives' is often extremely limited. 'Choice' over popular schools is limited by catchment areas and priority access rules administered by local authorities. Certainly the choice between a state school (of whatever form) and a fee-paying school remains stark, and the latter is not viable for most families. Unlike pre-school education, entitlement to primary and secondary schooling is not administered as a voucher that can be used in any setting, public or private. Accordingly, we retain the classification used in previous versions of this exercise and treat schooling as, on balance, a public decision. However, if all mainstream primary and secondary schooling, whether in community schools or academies/free schools is reclassified as a 'private decision', the 'pure public' segment (public finance, provision and decision) falls to just 12% of total spending.

A significant change since 2007/08 has been the increasing withdrawal of grant funding for higher and further education, with the burden shifted to tuition fees and student loans. This is reflected in Figure 10.4 in the fall in the 'public finance and private provision' segment. However, while public spending on further and higher education has already fallen, much of the loan repayment has yet to occur, so we can expect to see further increases in the 'pure private' segment in years to come. There are ambiguities here though. Student loan repayments are income-contingent, and in some ways more closely resemble a graduate tax than the US system of purely private loans. A proportion of student loans will never be repaid, and the value of expected future non-repayment should arguably be included as public expenditure.

A further component in the increase in the 'pure private' segment is the strategy that middle-class families increasingly use to top up state schooling with the use of private tuition. There has been a 76% increase in out-of-pocket spending on education – including on further and higher education – in real terms between 2007/08 and 2013/14. This segment now accounts for one-fifth (22%) of all education spending.

Income maintenance

Most aspects of income maintenance ('social security') can be divided simply into the 'pure public' segment (benefits and tax credits) and the 'pure private' segment (for example, private insurance against earnings loss due to unemployment or ill health, and private pension contributions net of tax relief). These two segments make up 55% and 20% of total spending respectively (see Figure 10.5). We might also wish to add an estimate for the direct support given by the voluntary

Figure 10.5: The changing profile of total expenditure on income maintenance categorised by public/private finance, provision and decision, 1979/80 to 2013/14, England

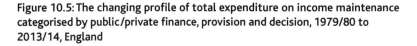

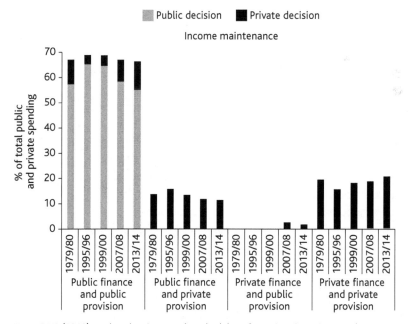

Note: ONS (2012) produced an improved methodology for estimating private and occupational pension contributions, incorporated here in the figures for 2007-08 and 2013-14. This implies a significant inconsistency with previous years, so the longer time series should be interpreted with caution.

Source: Obolenskaya and Burchardt (2016)

sector to people on very low incomes, for example, through food banks. In 2013/14, food banks provided an estimated 20 million meals in the UK, a total value of perhaps £40 million. This is small fraction of total spending on income maintenance (1/100th of a percentage), but nevertheless significant in its impact on recipients and on public debate.

Note that in this area of welfare activity we allocate payments made to, or payments made by, individuals, but we do not include the costs of administration. As a result, these figures do not include the shift towards greater use of independent contractors to carry out benefit assessments and provide welfare-to-work services. This is an interesting area to which we return in the discussion of the role of the voluntary sector below, but in practice, the costs are low compared to total spending (for example, £636 million on the Work Programme in 2013/14; see DWP, 2014).

Two areas, child maintenance arrangements and pensions, have more complex profiles across the public/private spectrum. Child maintenance has gone from being a purely private affair, arranged between individuals and occasionally enforced through the courts, to an area in which the state was heavily involved after the Child Support Agency (CSA) was created in the early 1990s, with payments from non-resident parents offset against recipients' Income Support. In the current regime, the state has once again withdrawn almost entirely. The CSA closed to new cases in 2012, and its successor, the Child Maintenance Service, is on a much more limited scale and will charge families arrangement fees and levy enforcement charges. However, even at the height of the CSA's activities, child maintenance payments were a small fraction of total income maintenance spending and we have not been able to find a reliable estimate of the value of financial transfers between non-coresident parents arranged privately, so these are not included here.

Pensions are a vastly larger component (see Figure 10.6).[7] Spending on the basic State Pension (pure public) makes up just over one-third of total pensions spending (34%). Contributions to the State Second Pension (S2P) and employer contributions to unfunded occupational pension schemes (for the civil service, NHS, teachers and so forth) (public finance and provision, but private decision[8]) add a further 17% of overall spending. In both cases the figures for 2013/14 represent an increase in real value since 2007/08, and in the latter case, also an increase in the proportion of overall spending. Spending on personal and funded occupational pensions are made up of tax reliefs (17% of overall spending) and contributions net of

Figure 10.6: Detail on pensions expenditure categorised by public/private finance, provision and decision, 2007/08 and 2013/14, England

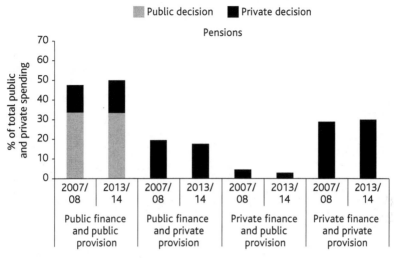

Note: Methodology to calculate pensions contributions not comparable for previous years. See Obolenskaya and Burchardt for details.

Source: Obolenskaya and Burchardt (2016)

reliefs (30% of overall spending). The degree of choice in second-tier pensions and the portability of public funding in the form of tax reliefs across schemes means that the public finance and private *decision* segments are unusually large compared to their size in other areas of welfare activity, whether in relation to public provision (S2P and public sector pensions) or private provision (personal pensions and funded occupational pensions).

Housing

In housing (see Figure 10.7), despite boom and bust and slow recovery in the economy (and house prices) the distribution of overall spending in 2013/14 continued the trends over previous periods.[9] It is worth bearing in mind that the total value of housing expenditure has grown substantially between each of our time points since 1979/80 (as shown in Table 10.1), so that the percentages shown in Figure 10.7 for 2013/14 are percentages of a much larger real amount than was the case at the beginning of the period. The 'pure private' segment is much the largest, reflecting the high share of home ownership as a tenure, and has continued to grow in real terms, though flattening off as a share of total spending. Recent declines in rates of home

Figure 10.7: Changing profile of total housing expenditure categorised by public/private finance, provision and decision, 1979/80 to 2013/14, England

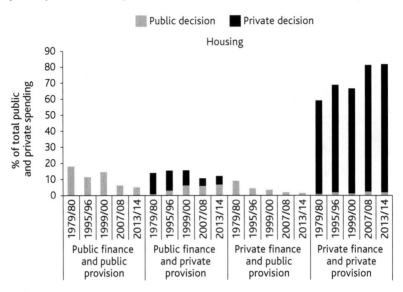

Note: Results sensitive to method for calculating economic subsidy enjoyed by social housing tenants and Right to Buy beneficiaries. For 2007/08 and 2013/14 these are based on calculations in Hills (2007).

Source: Obolenskaya and Burchardt (2016)

ownership are balanced by an increase in private renting (DCLG, 2015b). The proportion of total current spending on housing (using imputed rents to value home ownership and taking account of public subsidies to all tenures as well as direct spending) in the 'pure private' segment was 82% in 2013/14, similar to the proportion (81%) in 2007/08.

'Pure public' spending on housing fell slightly over the recent period, from 6% in 2007/08 to 5% in 2013/14, continuing the previous trend of the residualisation of council housing. Private finance for public provision – that is, aggregate rent paid directly by council tenants – continued to fall in real terms and as a share of total spending, and now makes up just 1.4% of the total, compared to 9.1% back in 1979/80.

Housing associations are classified as non-public organisations, and tenants in this sector also receive significant public subsidy through subsidised rents and Housing Benefit. These forms of public finance for private provision (classified as a public decision since social housing tenants face very restricted housing choices) grew in real terms and as a proportion of overall spending from 6% to 7% between 2007/08 and 2013/14. Other components of public finance for private provision, classified as a private decision, include Housing Benefit for private rents, and the estimated costs of Right to Buy discounts (for the methodology, see Obolenskaya and Burchardt, 2016). These also grew in real terms, keeping up with increases in other segments and maintaining their share of around 5% of overall spending.

Overall welfare activity

As this overview has indicated, trends pulled in different directions in different areas of welfare activity. Putting them all together, Figure 10.8 summarises the overall shifts in the shape of welfare spending (public and private) since 1979/80. This is, of course, affected not only by changes within each policy area, but also by the changing shares of each policy area within overall welfare spending, as given in Table 10.1.

In proportional terms, public spending on publicly provided services has declined, while private spending on privately provided services has increased – the two ends of Figure 10.8 mirror one another. Ignoring for a moment the distinction between public and private decision (that is, looking at the total height of the bars), public spending on publicly provided services now accounts for 44% of total welfare activity, down from 48% in 2007/08, while private spending on private provision

Figure 10.8: Changing profile of total welfare expenditure categorised by public/private finance, provision and decision, 1979/80 to 2013/14, England

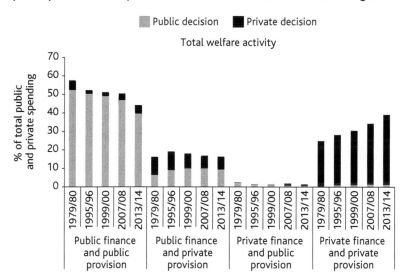

Source: Obolenskaya and Burchardt (2016)

now accounts for 39%, up from 34% in 2007/08. This is very much in line with the longer-run trend over time, although taking into account the uneven spacing of the years for which the figures have been calculated, the most recent period looks to be a faster pace of change than previously.[10] This is the case even while retaining the classification of academies and free schools as public provision; if they were to be reclassified as private provision, the decrease in public spending on public provision in 2013/14 would be even sharper (from 48% to 42%), with a corresponding increase in public spending on private provision from 16% in 2007/08 to 18% in 2013/14.

Shifts in housing expenditure are a significant part of the overall story, both because of the large and steadily increasing share of housing in total spending (Table 10.1), and because private finance is strongly dominant in this area (Figure 10.7). Excluding housing from the calculation of overall welfare activity produces a gentler reduction in the public finance/public provision sector over time, falling only to 60% of total spending in 2013/14, and a correspondingly less dramatic rise in the private finance/private provision sector, increasing only to 20.5% by the end of the period. However, the direction of change and continuity of the trends are similar, with or without housing.

Perhaps surprisingly, public finance of private provision (such as contracting out) as a proportion of overall spending remained at 16% between 2007/08 and 2013/14, although as we shall see below, it has increased in real terms.

Proportions of overall welfare tell only part of the story. The absolute changes in levels of real spending are also informative, as shown in Table 10.2. Public spending on public provision (left-hand two columns of figures) increased by 2.3% between 2007/8 and 2013/14 – in contrast to what the rhetoric of austerity and public services reform would lead one to believe. Public spending overall – whether on public or private provision – grew in real terms over this period, by 5.0%. Within this, 'contracting out' (public finance, private provision, public decision) grew by 15.7%. Public provision (some of it privately financed) also grew slightly (1.8%), although not nearly as fast as private provision (23.4%).

For-profit and not for-profit

Thus far we have treated all providers that are non-public as private. But there is increasing interest in the distinction between for-profit and not-for-profit independent providers. Many new or growing actors in welfare provision fall into the latter category: for example,

Table 10.2: Welfare activity by category and policy area, 1979/80 to 2013/14, England (£ billion in 2014/15 prices, GDP deflated)

| | Public finance | | | | Private finance | | | | |
| | Public provision | | Private provision | | Public provision | | Private provision | | |
	Public decision	Private decision	Public decision	Private decision	Public decision	Private decision	Public decision	Private decision	All
1979/80									
Education	20.0	0.0	7.2	0.9	0.0	0.0	0.0	1.8	29.8
Health	23.5	0.0	6.1	0.0	0.3	0.1	0.4	2.9	33.3
Housing	8.7	0.0	0.4	6.3	4.4	0.0	0.4	28.0	48.2
Social security	61.2	10.4	0.0	14.6	0.0	0.0	0.0	20.8	106.9
Personal social services	4.4	0.0	0.7	0.0	0.6	0.0	0.0	0.9	6.7
Total	117.7	10.4	14.4	21.8	5.3	0.1	0.9	54.4	225.0
1995/96									
Education	26.9	0.0	11.6	1.7	0.0	0.0	0.0	4.8	45.0
Health	40.7	0.0	12.7	0.3	0.3	0.3	1.1	8.2	63.6
Housing	9.8	0.0	2.6	10.5	3.8	0.0	1.7	57.0	85.4
Social security	101.0	5.6	0.0	24.3	0.0	0.0	0.0	24.2	155.2
Personal social services	8.1	0.0	6.6	0.0	0.7	0.0	0.9	5.6	21.9
Total	186.5	5.6	33.5	36.9	4.8	0.3	3.7	99.8	371.1
1999/00									
Education	26.3	0.0	11.9	1.1	0.0	0.0	0.0	6.7	46.0
Health	49.9	0.0	16.0	0.2	0.1	0.4	1.0	9.8	77.3
Housing	15.7	0.0	6.8	10.1	3.8	0.0	1.4	70.5	108.4
Social security	104.8	6.8	0.0	21.7	0.0	0.0	0.4	29.1	162.8
Personal social services	9.4	0.0	7.3	0.0	0.9	0.0	1.9	5.9	25.4
Total	206.1	6.8	41.9	33.1	4.9	0.4	4.7	122.1	419.9
2007/08									
Education	44.8	0.0	14.0	4.2	0.0	0.0	0.0	10.1	73.1
Health	73.1	0.0	24.6	0.2	0.5	0.4	1.1	15.3	115.2
Housing	10.0	0.0	9.5	7.4	3.3	0.0	3.9	124.4	158.4
Social security	136.4	20.1	0.0	27.7	0.0	6.2	1.0	43.0	234.3
Personal social services	12.6	0.0	11.1	0.6	0.8	0.0	2.3	8.4	35.7
Total	276.9	20.1	59.2	40.0	4.6	6.5	8.2	201.2	616.7
2013/14									
Education	47.3	0.0	10.8	2.8	0.0	0.8	0.0	17.8	79.5
Health	71.2	0.0	30.5	0.2	0.4	0.5	1.0	16.8	120.6
Housing	10.3	0.0	14.0	10.9	3.0	0.0	4.1	164.7	206.9
Social security	137.4	28.1	0.0	28.5	0.0	4.4	1.1	50.8	250.2
Personal social services	9.5	0.1	13.1	1.5	0.6	0.0	2.2	10.4	37.3
Total	275.7	28.2	68.4	43.8	3.9	5.8	8.4	260.3	694.5

Source: Obolenskaya and Burchardt (2016)

voluntary sector providers in early years care, mutuals in healthcare, housing associations, and, some would argue, academies and free schools in education. On the other hand, a number of the controversial developments in welfare policy have concerned the use of for-profit providers: A4E and Atos in social security and welfare-to-work assessments, Circle taking over Hinchingbrooke hospital in Cambridge and then giving up again following a highly critical Care Quality Commission (CQC) report (CQC, 2015b), the crisis in social care brought about by the collapse of the largest independent provider Southern Cross, and the mis-selling of mortgage protection insurance by high street banks.

According to the Big Society Audit (Slocock, 2015), although there have been a number of initiatives to improve the chances of voluntary sector organisations securing government contracts, the market for government contracts remains dominated by a small number of multinational for-profit firms such as Atos, Capita, G4S and Serco. A similar observation is made by Raco (2013) in relation to capital spending and PFI projects.

Unfortunately, little systematic information is available on the value of welfare services provided by the not-for-profit sector. Central and local government accounts sometimes record whether spending is on 'own provision' or contracted-out services, but rarely distinguish between for-profit and not-for-profit providers. The National Council of Voluntary Organisations (NCVO) almanac charts trends in the volume of funding from central and local government for the UK voluntary sector as a whole (NVCO, 2015). It shows that voluntary sector income from government contracts fell from £12.1 billion in 2009/10 to £11.1 billion in 2012/13 (in 2012/13 prices) – a fall of 8.3% in just three years. Since we know that contracting out (public finance of non-public provision, under public decision) for welfare services increased in real terms over this period, this would seem to imply that the voluntary sector has been losing out relative to the for-profit sector during this time. NCVO's analysis of the 'whole of government accounts' (HM Treasury, 2015e) suggests that the voluntary sector secured just 4% of central government contracts by value and 10% of local government contracts, although some of these will be outside the areas of welfare activity considered in this chapter.

Provision of services by the voluntary sector outside of government contracts has also been affected by cuts to grant income from central and local government – down from £3.1 billion in 2009/10 to £2.2 billion in 2012/13 (NCVO, 2015). But only around one-third of the total income of voluntary sector organisations comes from government sources; just under half comes from individuals. Unfortunately this source of income has not expanded to fill the gap left by falling government income, but has, instead, been fairly constant over this period. Similarly, rates and mean hours of volunteering have been steady. Thus, in combination with cuts in government contracts and grants, the capacity of the voluntary sector to provide services has been increasingly restricted over this period.

Conclusion

Historians of the welfare state have argued about the most appropriate theoretical lens through which to view its development and subsequent retrenchment. Various forms of path dependency have been proposed, suggesting that welfare institutions are slow to change, although an established equilibrium may be 'punctuated' by a dramatic event, especially one external to the institution itself. Taylor-Gooby (2013) argues that the period of the coalition government following the financial crash provided a moment when such radical change could be instituted – a potential 'puncture' – and Prime Minister David Cameron appeared to agree when he called it a 'once in a lifetime opportunity' to transform public services, as we saw in the speech quoted earlier in this chapter.

The policies that followed in some areas were certainly radical in intent. The health service has been restructured, opening the door to much greater involvement of for-profit and, in principle, not-for-profit independent providers, and to a higher volume of private patients in the NHS. School education has been reshaped with the rapid conversion of primary and secondary schools to academy status and the creation of free schools (although they still account for fewer than one in five mainstream schools; DfE, 2014a). Less explicit than these programmes of restructuring, but no less substantial in their impact, has been the selective reduction of public spending, especially in social care, some parts of social security, and higher education, leaving individuals and families in the position of having to pay for equivalent services themselves – or to go without.

Yet overall, the picture of public/private activity in most of the policy areas considered in this chapter is one of continuity with previous trends – albeit in some cases an accelerated trend – rather than abrupt change. Health remains dominated by the 'pure public' segment, although it makes up a falling share, with a significant increase in the share of public finance for private provision. Income maintenance also remains strongly rooted in public finance for public provision, but here the shift has been – through pensions policy – towards a greater role for private *decision*. At the opposite extreme, housing has always been predominantly in the 'pure private' segment, and this has become even more pronounced in the most recent period, while public finance of public provision (council housing) has become increasingly residual. Education and social care each present a more mixed picture. School education has been, and remains, very largely publicly *financed*, but academies and free schools reduce the 'degree of publicness' of provision, while in higher education, the shift from grant to tuition fee loan funding has tilted the balance of funding towards private finance. Finally, in social care, sharp reductions in local authority funding mean that for the first time in this series, the 'pure private' segment accounts for a larger proportion of total spending than the 'pure public' segment, while contracted-out services continue to grow.

In the perspective of the period since 1979/80, the recent changes look less like a 'puncture' in an 'equilibrium', and more like the latest step in a gradual process of shrinking the "pure public" share of welfare activity, in the context of an overall growth in volume. Steady, long-term change in one direction can of course amount to a transformation (Thalen and Streeck, 2005). It is far from clear that the pattern of public and private finance, provision and decision that we have now arrived at is intentional or reflects a coherent rationale about the role of the state as funder, provider or regulator in relation to the characteristics of each area of welfare activity. Looking at welfare activity across the board suggests two significant trends: first, that demand for welfare (however financed) has for many decades grown faster than GDP – as we get richer, and as the population gets older, we want and need proportionately more of it; and second, that despite the distinctive starting points, policy mechanisms, trends and outcomes in each of the policy areas, there is an accelerating trend away from collectively financed activity towards individually financed activity. Whatever view we may take of the merits of public, private or indeed voluntary sector provision, and whatever view we may take of the merits of 'user choice', our increasing dependence on non-redistributive, individually financed welfare, against the background of increasing inequalities in income and wealth, must be a cause of concern.

Notes
[1] That is, public spending on health, education, personal social services, housing, pensions and other transfers.

[2] For further details of the data sources and methodology for the figures in this section, please see Obolenskaya and Burchardt (2016). All spending figures relate to current, not capital, expenditure.

[3] Figures include adult and children's social care, using Health and Social Care Information Service (HSCIC) statistics for public spending and user charges, and other sources for pure private spending – for details, see Obolenskaya and Burchardt (2016). They do not include any estimate of the value of unpaid care.

[4] The 2013/14 figure is for private spending on all privately arranged adult social care. Data sources for the earlier years were for spending of this kind on older people only; we have used the percentage of all adult social care spending that is on older people to adjust the figures for earlier years proportionately. For details, see Obolenskaya and Burchardt (2016).

[5] Note that West and Nikolai (2013) classify academies as government-dependent private schools because they have state funding but are independent in terms of admission policies.

[6] Changes in funding arrangements in 1999/2000 effectively abolished Grant-Maintained status. The figure for this year is spending on GM schools in transition to the new framework, and City Technology Colleges. Subsequently, Labour created (City) Academies. Spending on these initially increased slowly and became much more rapid under the coalition.

[7] The analysis is based on pension contributions, not pensions in payment, with the exception of the basic State Pension where it is assumed that the relevant 'contributions' are the tax and National Insurance Contributions funding the current basic State Pension.

[8] Pension arrangements are negotiated between trade unions and public sector employers, so this is a private decision only at one remove.

[9] Housing expenditure is based on the concept of the flow of services in the current year: actual rents paid, imputed rents for owner-occupiers, current Housing Benefit spending, and current value of public subsidies to social housing tenants and Right to Buy beneficiaries, as well as tax reliefs.

[10] There are unavoidable inconsistencies in definitions for some components over time – for details, see Obolenskaya and Burchardt (2016) – so interpretations of the longer-term time trend must be treated with caution.

ELEVEN

Socioeconomic inequalities

John Hills and Kitty Stewart

The chapters in the first part of this book each concentrated on a different area of social policy. They examined policy, spending and outcomes since the crash in relation to a particular pillar of the welfare state (cash transfers, education, health, housing, employment), or to a given demographic group (young children). In this chapter we consider overall trends in socioeconomic differentials, including both economic inequality and the distribution of benefits in kind. These differentials reflect the combined effects of a range of social and economic policies, although they are also affected by wider factors over which the government has limited control, including demographic change and the operation of global economic forces.

One recurrent issue is that data on socioeconomic outcomes become available with a lag. For instance, the final picture of how the 1997 Labour government left the income distribution in 2010 only became available in 2012. The coalition left office in May 2015, by which time it had set in place the main rules governing the tax-benefit system – one of the major influences on the income distribution – up to 2015/16. But the data available to us at the time of writing and used here largely relate to periods up to 2013/14 or earlier. It will be 2017 before we are able to see a more definitive picture of the coalition's legacy. The lag is particularly important because many of the coalition's key policies – including cuts to some benefits – started having their main effects from 2013 onwards, while its initial policies protected the real value of benefits and tax credits up to that point (see Chapter Two, this volume).

This chapter begins by examining labour market outcomes – employment trends and wage disparities. The second section looks at household income overall, presenting data on income inequality and poverty. We then consider the distribution of benefits in kind, and how this has changed since the crisis. A final section focuses on changes in wealth and wealth inequality.

While we present some of the labour market trends by gender in this chapter, the following chapter looks in more detail at how the overall trends presented here vary between different groups, such as by age, housing tenure and region, as well as by gender.[1] Depending on the data source available, we generally break the period from 2007 to 2013 into two, the first covering the end of the period of Labour government, and the second, the start of the coalition's period in office.

The labour market[2]

Employment

Policies towards employment and overall trends in employment and unemployment were discussed in Chapter Six, earlier. Figure 11.1 shows that employment patterns differed between men and women as they deteriorated sharply between 2006-08[3] and 2010, with a limited recovery by 2013. Men were worse affected than women. Figure 11.1(a) shows unemployment and the breakdown of employment status for those of working age who were economically active, and Figure 11.1(b) shows changes in the composition of economic inactivity.

Overall employment of any form dropped by 2.3 percentage points from 2006-08 to 2010, recovering half of the loss by 2013. However, within that, male full-time employment fell by 4 percentage points in the first period, only recovering by 0.7 points by 2013. For women, the initial drop in full-time employment was smaller. Self-employment

Figure 11.1(a): Proportion of working-age men and women employed and unemployed, 2006-08 to 2013 (%)

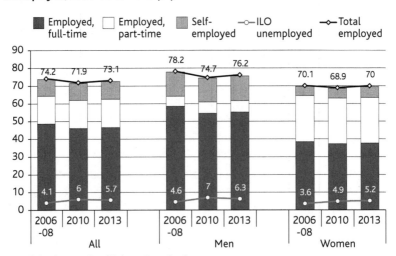

Note: ILO = International Labour Organization.

Figure 11.1(b): Proportion of working-age men and women who are economically inactive, 2006-08 to 2013 (%)

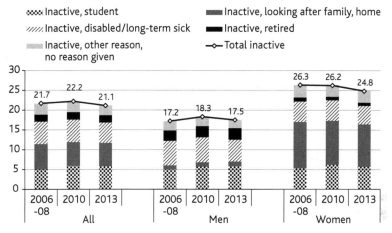

Note: Total employed also includes those who are 'employed – time not known'. The proportion of these varies between 0.3 and 0.5% of the total sample.
Source: Labour Force Survey

and part-time work grew for men, and self-employment for women. Strikingly, by the end of the period, virtually the same proportion of women were employed (70%) as at the start, but for men, employment had fallen by 2 percentage points to 76%. Male unemployment was up from 4.6 to 6.3% by 2013 and for women by the same amount from 3.6 to 5.2%. However, the time patterns differed: while male unemployment fell after 2010, female unemployment rose. Over the period as a whole, female economic inactivity dropped from 26.3 to 24.8%, with the majority of this accounted for by the fall in the proportion of women who were 'inactive looking after family or home'.

Hourly wages

The dominant feature of the labour market response to the crisis (see Chapter Six earlier) was that while employment was hit less severely than in other recent recessions, and showed some recovery after 2010, the same was not true of real wages.[4] Table 11.1 shows the changes in hourly wages for all full-time and part-time employees together, and then for male and female employees separately. Overall, mean wages fell by 1.8% in the first period and a further 3.9% from 2010 to 2013, taking the overall fall to 5.6%. The fall was faster for men than for women, particularly in the first period, although the median

Table 11.1: Percentage changes in hourly wages for all employees, and for men and women, 2006-08 to 2013, UK (2013 prices, CPI-adjusted)

	Mean	P10	P30	Median	P70	P90	90:10 ratio
2006-08 to 2010							
All	−1.8	−2.4	−3.6	−2.8	−1.5	−1.7	+0.03
Men	−2.3	−3.9	−4.5	−2.8	−2.1	−1.7	+0.10
Women	−1.4	−2.1	−2.3	−1.7	−0.5	−0.9	+0.04
2010 to 2013							
All	−3.9	−4.5	−3.9	−3.1	−3.5	−2.4	+0.08
Men	−3.9	−4.7	−3.2	−3.4	−3.5	−2.6	+0.09
Women	−3.7	−5.1	−4.4	−4.8	−3.5	−4.2	+0.04
2006-08 to 2013							
All	−5.6	−6.8	−7.3	−5.9	−4.9	−4.0	+0.11
Men	−6.1	−8.4	−7.5	−6.2	−5.5	−4.2	+0.19
Women	−5.0	−7.1	−6.5	−6.4	−4.0	−5.0	+0.08

Source: Labour Force Survey. All the changes at the mean are significant at the 1% level.

(middle) wage for women fell a little faster than that for men. These were the first falls in real wages in the absence of direct government wage controls since the Great Depression (Gregg et al, 2014).

Table 11.1 shows that wage inequality as captured by the Labour Force Survey increased in both periods: across all the breakdowns shown, the falls were greater near the bottom of the distribution (the 10th percentile, P10) than near the top (90th percentile, P90).[5] Again, this was more marked for men than for women, with the male 90:10 ratio growing by 0.19 and the female ratio by 0.08. For all employees together, the 90:10 ratio grew from 3.85 to 3.97 between 2006-08 and 2013.

Within this overall picture, two points are worth highlighting. First, inequalities in part-time pay grew more quickly than in full-time pay (see Hills et al, 2015a, Figure 2.4). At the median, real pay fell by nearly 6% for both men and women working full-time and women part-time employees, and by 5% for men employed part-time. But the falls were smallest for the highest paid in each case, and were less than 2% for the best-paid women part-timers (whose pay actually grew in the period up to 2010). At the bottom, pay fell by 7% for male full-timers, and by between 8-9% for both groups of women, but by 10% for male part-timers.

Second, the falls in real wages were greater – often much greater – after 2010 than before it. Unlike the signs of improvement in employment, real wages fell faster between 2010 and 2013, and inequalities grew further.

Weekly full-time earnings

As well as hourly wages falling (and part-time employment growing, while full-time employment fell for men), hours of work reduced for full-timers. This meant that full-time weekly earnings fell even faster than hourly wages. Median full-time real earnings fell by 7.6% overall between 2006-08 and 2013, compared to the fall of 5.9% in the full-time hourly rate. For the worst paid men and women, weekly earnings fell by more than 8%, faster than the fall in the hourly rate in each case. However, at the top the fall at the 90th percentile was only 2.2% for men and 3.5% for women, in each case a *smaller* fall than in the highest hourly wages because, for instance, the best paid were increasing their hours, while hours fell for others.

These changes meant that inequalities in full-time weekly earnings also increased – for men in the last Labour years and for women under the coalition. For men the 90:10 ratio rose from 3.7 in 2006-08 to 4.0 in 2010 and 2013; for women it rose from 3.5 in 2006-08 and 2010 to 3.7 by 2013.

Household income[6]

Between 2007 and 2013 there were increases in labour market inequality – more unemployment and inactivity, more disparity in hourly pay, a drop in hours for lower earners and a rise for higher earners and (a result of the previous two developments) an increase in inequality in weekly earnings. Unemployment and inactivity were moving in a positive direction by 2010-13, but disparities in earnings were static or continuing to grow.

These trends contributed to growing inequality in earnings between households. Focusing on non-pensioners in working households, the Institute for Fiscal Studies calculates that household earnings fell by a cumulative 14.8% between 2007/08 and 2013/14 for the household at the 10th percentile of the distribution, compared with a fall of 6.7% at the median and 3.1% at the 90th (Belfield et al, 2015). The scale of the drop in lower-earning households was partly driven by large falls in self-employment income, compounding the inequality-increasing effects discussed above for employee wages.

Yet despite these trends in its largest component, inequality in disposable income (after benefits and direct taxes) was stable or declining in the years after the crash, while the poverty rate was also broadly stable, even when measured against a fixed income poverty line. As discussed in Chapter Two, until 2012/13, the tax-benefit system generally protected the poorest from falls in real income, and this countered the growth in inequality of market incomes (although in the period up to 2015/16 as a whole, policy effects tended to help those with higher, rather than those with lower, incomes). However, there are important differences across sub-periods within this six-year time frame, and also differences in what happened for different demographic groups. We turn to discuss these now.

Changes in income across the distribution

Figure 11.2 shows (at an annual rate) changes in the real incomes of those at the mid-point of each 10th of the income distribution,[7] for four time periods: the first Labour decade, under Blair (1996/97 to 2007/08); the Brown years (2007/08 to 2009/10); the year straddling the change of government (2009/10 to 2010/11); and the coalition years for which data are available (2010/11 to 2013/14).

Figure 11.2: Annualised rate of change in income by decile group (before housing costs) (%)

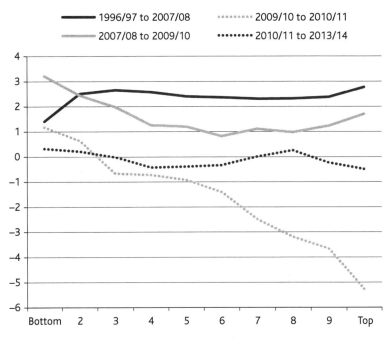

Note: Derived from the Institute for Fiscal Studies (IFS) poverty and inequality spreadsheet 2015 (using figures for Great Britain). Lines show change at mid-point of each decile group (ie 5th percentile, etc). Incomes are equivalised and are before housing costs.

Over the Labour period to 2007/08, incomes grew at an annual rate of 2-3% for all but the bottom 10th of the distribution. Between the second 10th and the ninth 10th, growth was faster for those nearer the bottom of the distribution than those nearer the top. But it was lowest for the bottom 10th (at the 5th percentile) and as high for the top 10th (95th percentile) as for any of the other groups. As shown below, this means that inequality trends that compare those near the top and bottom of the distribution (such as the '90:10 ratio') differ for this period from those affected by the very top and bottom (including the Gini coefficient).

Under Brown, the pattern of growth was very different, with the bottom half of the distribution seeing more positive growth than the top half. Within the bottom half, those worse off to begin with saw higher rates of growth; as high as 3% annually for those at the 5th percentile, making this group the only one to see incomes grow faster annually in the Brown post-crash years than during the Blair decade (see Chapter Two). Up to 2009/10, however, those in the top 10th continued to do better than average.

In the election year from 2009/10 to 2010/11, the picture is different again, with incomes falling progressively more for each successive 10th up the distribution. Average incomes for the top 10th fell more than 5% in a single year, while for the bottom two 10ths income rose in real terms, the effect of price protection in the benefit system alongside above-inflation increases in some elements of tax credits, as explained in Chapter Two (see Figure 2.4). Finally, in the three years from 2010/11 to 2013/14, real incomes remained fairly stable for all groups, but with very small falls in the middle and at the top.[8]

These results show, among other things, the sensitivity of any conclusion on inequality trends under the Labour and coalition periods to which year is seen as the final 'Labour year' and so the base for the coalition's period. The year 2009/10 was Labour's last full year in government, but the rules of taxes and benefits for 2010/11 were almost entirely set by Labour, taking effect from April 2010, before the election. If responsibility for 2010/11 is allocated to Labour under Brown, income changes under Brown appear to have been considerably more equalising than under the coalition. If, instead, 2009/10 is taken as the base and 2010/11 allocated to the coalition (as in some coalition ministerial statements), it is the coalition instead that looks more progressive, albeit with lower rates of growth for all.

Income inequality

The effect of these changes was that income inequality, whether measured by the Gini coefficient or the 90:10 ratio, was initially stable following the financial crash, but fell sharply between 2009/10 and 2010/11, as higher incomes fell fastest (see Figure 11.3). In the following three years, the Gini remained relatively flat, rising by an insignificant amount in the last year available, while the 90:10 ratio was initially flat but fell slightly between 2012/13 and 2013/14. Again, the picture highlights the sensitivity of conclusions to which is the final Labour year: if 2009/10 is taken as the base year, inequality fell at the start of the coalition government, while if 2010/11 is taken as the base year, it remained broadly flat under the coalition, and Labour's record improves. Either way, the 90:10 ratio in 2013/14 was the lowest it had been since 1986: half of the sharp rise that took place in this indicator in the second half of the 1980s had been reversed over the subsequent two-and-a-half decades. The long-term trend in the Gini coefficient is different: the Gini continued to rise slowly under the Labour government, reaching a peak in 2009/10, but then fell in

Figure 11.3: Income inequality, 1979 to 2013/14, Great Britain (before housing costs)

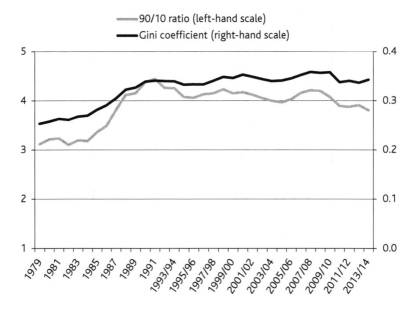

Source: IFS inequality and poverty spreadsheet, 2015. Data are from the Family Expenditure Survey until 1993/94, and from the Family Resources Survey from 1994/95.

2010/11, leaving it for the next three years back at the same level as 2005/06.[9]

That income inequality (and relative poverty, as discussed below) remained flat between 2012/13 and 2013/14 is something of a surprise, given that some of the sharpest benefit cuts started affecting particular groups in that year. Predictions taking account of this had suggested that poverty and inequality would start rising as a result. It is yet to be seen whether out-turns for later years of the coalition reflect these effects, with the single survey of 2013/14 proving in some way an aberration, or whether there are other changes going on which offset the otherwise regressive effects described in Chapter Two (see Belfield et al, 2015, pp 63-4).

The differences between the Gini coefficient and the 90:10 ratio indicate that something particular is going on at the very top or bottom of the distribution. Indeed, while the 90:10 ratio fell from 4.4 to 3.8 between 1990 and 2013/14, the share of income going to the top 1% increased from 5.7% to 8.3% (Belfield et al, 2015). From 2009/10 the share of the top 1% fell substantially, from a peak of 8.8 to 7% by 2012/13, equivalent to its share when Labour took office in 1997 (Belfield et al, 2015, Figure 3.5). Its share rose again sharply between 2012/13 and 2013/14. This explains the (insignificant) rise in the Gini coefficient in that year, although part of this seems to have been artificially driven by individuals shifting income into the 2013/14 financial year to take advantage of a cut in the top rate of Income Tax.

Poverty

Figure 11.4 shows changes in the proportion of the population living in poverty, measured against two alternative poverty lines before allowing for housing costs – 60% of the median income in 2010/11, held constant in real terms (panel a), and 60% of the contemporary median income (panel b). For children and for pensioners, poverty rates continued to fall in the initial years following the financial crisis, between 2007/08 and 2009/10. The drop was particularly sharp against the relative poverty line, as median incomes fell, and with them the poverty line, while incomes at the bottom were protected by the benefit system. Panel (a) shows that poverty also fell for pensioners against a fixed income line until 2009/10, and for children until 2010/11, reflecting real increases in benefits as the recession took hold (see Chapter Two). Since 2010/11 poverty rates have been fairly stable for both groups, including the final years for which data are available, 2012/13 to 2013/14.

Figure 11.4: Proportion of population with incomes below 60% of 2010/11 median income in real terms and below 60% of contemporary income, by population group (before and after housing costs)

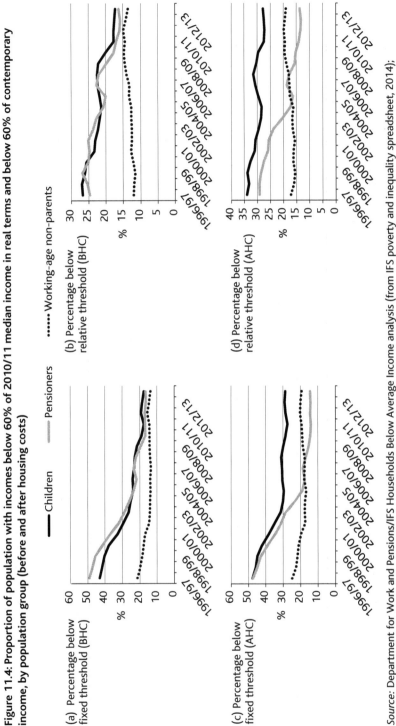

Source: Department for Work and Pensions/IFS Households Below Average Income analysis (from IFS poverty and inequality spreadsheet, 2014); Great Britain figures until 2001/02, UK from 2002/03

In light of the deepest recession since the 1930s, this picture is encouraging, and indicates that, at least up until 2013/14, the social security system was successfully fulfilling one of its key functions, to protect households against poverty during hard times. But several caveats should be highlighted. First, for working-age adults without children living with them, poverty continued to rise between 2007/08 and 2011/12 against both lines. As a result we see the near completion of the remarkable convergence in poverty rates across the three demographic groups that began in the late 1990s. Increasing poverty for this group also meant that poverty overall (for the population as a whole) rose against a fixed income threshold between 2009/10 and 2010/11, from 15.9 to 16.9%, although it dropped again to 15.6% in 2013/14.

Second, if poverty is measured after housing costs have been accounted for, the pattern is rather different, especially for children, as shown in panels (c) and (d) of Figure 11.4. On this measure, poverty did fall for children against both thresholds from 2007/08, but by very little against the fixed line, and in 2013/14 children remained far more likely to live in households below the after housing costs poverty line than other groups. On the other hand, pensioner poverty fell further compared to other households against after housing cost measures: since 2007/08, pensioner poverty rates have fallen well below those for working-age non-parents. Given the direction of tax-benefit policy since 2013 (before and after the 2015 General Election), further divergence between pensioners and the rest of the population is to be expected.

Third, *within* the groups shown there are substantial differences. As shown in Chapter Three earlier, the greatest reductions in child poverty during the Labour years were for households with children under five, but children this age (or with siblings this age) have fared worse under the coalition than older families. In particular, poverty for children in households with a child under age one has risen against a relative line since 2010/11. Differences in outcomes among working-age adults (by gender, age and ethnicity) up to 2010/11 are examined further in Chapter Twelve.

Fourth, there are questions about how effectively these two income poverty measures capture the full extent of material poverty. Some commentators have raised concerns about the counter-intuitive results that can be created by a relative poverty measure during recession, when poverty falls because median income falls faster than low incomes. This possibility makes it important to present trends in poverty against a fixed as well as a relative line, as we have done. But even taken together these income measures still have limitations as indicators of material living standards, both because of the arbitrary nature of any given poverty threshold, and because the same level of income will afford families different living standards depending on their needs. Adjustment of incomes for household size ('equivalisation') cannot fully correct for this. A further issue is differential price inflation facing different households. Adams and Levell (2014) and Davis et al (2014a) estimate that prices rose more quickly post-crash for those with low incomes than for other households (although this began to reverse, with more favourable changes in food and fuel prices, after 2013).

To address the arbitrariness of the 60% poverty threshold a poverty *depth* measure would be very useful, capturing the extent to which households fall below the poverty line, rather than just whether or not they do so. But no such information is published in the UK, largely because of concerns about the reliability of data where households report very low or zero incomes (although European Union [EU] statistics avoid this problem by looking at the median poverty gap). The absence of a poverty gap measure means that if households already below the poverty line experience further falls in their income, this will not be reflected in published data. This is particularly salient in a context of cuts to the real value of benefits, reductions in benefit entitlement as a result of the welfare cap and Housing Benefit reforms, and growing benefit conditionality, with more frequent application of sanctions. Many of these changes are unlikely to affect the headcount rate of poverty, but would affect poverty depth. In particular, increasing use of sanctions (see Chapter Two earlier) means small but growing numbers of people have no legal entitlement to the safety net. Hence genuinely zero incomes are expected to rise, but this phenomenon will not be captured by official data.

A limited solution is to examine poverty against a range of thresholds (40 or 50% of income), rather than just one, although there are also concerns here about data accuracy, particularly in relation to a 40% threshold. In practice, there is little evidence of different trends since 2007/08 in published numbers measured against a 50% threshold compared to 60%, although the picture for child poverty after housing costs between 2012/13 and 2013/14 looks slightly worse against the 50% threshold, both in relative and fixed income terms.[10]

An alternative approach, which also addresses the problem that income measures do not effectively adjust for household need, is to use direct indicators of deprivation. Official statistics on households reporting material hardship to large-scale surveys showed a small rise in the number of children affected by material hardship from 22.3% in 2010/11 to 23.5% in 2013/14 (Belfield et al, 2015). As Figure 11.5 shows, there has been little or no change since 2010/11 in the percentage of children experiencing both relative income poverty and material deprivation, or in the share experiencing severe income poverty (below 50% of median income) and material deprivation.[11] However, there is growing qualitative evidence of the hardships faced by groups most affected by more recent benefit reforms (O'Hara, 2014; Power et al, 2014; Herden et al, 2015). This is also reflected in the rapidly increasing use of voluntary food banks, with, for instance, more than 900,000 people receiving three-day food parcels from The Trussell Trust charity in 2013/14, up from 350,000 in 2012/13, 60,000 in 2010/11 and 26,000 in 2008/09 (Perry et al, 2014).

Figure 11.5: Percentage of children with incomes below relative and fixed real poverty lines, and with both low relative income and material deprivation, 1998/99 to 2013/14

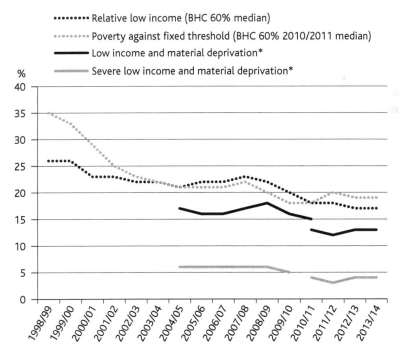

Note: *Due to a break in the series in 2010/11 it is not possible to make direct comparisons with results from earlier years for either the combined low income and material deprivation or the severe low income and material deprivation series.

Source: Shale et al (2015, Chart 4)

Income inequality and benefits in kind

Cash incomes are only part of what contributes to people's standards of living for other reasons too. Public services that are provided free (or are subsidised) also contribute. On the one hand, their existence means that people do not have to provide for them from their disposable income – because the NHS exists, people do not have to pay for private health insurance for the services that it covers.

This is important in distributional terms as well, because at any one time (but not over the life cycle), such 'benefits in kind' are more important for those on lower than on higher incomes. As Table 11.2 shows, the Office for National Statistics (ONS) (2015c) estimates that the poorest fifth of households derived a benefit from the NHS equivalent in value to 36% of their cash incomes in 2013/14. For households in the top fifth, the equivalent proportion was only 6%.

Table 11.2: Benefits in cash and kind as a percentage of disposable income, 2007/08, 2010/11 and 2013/14

	Bottom	2nd	3rd	4th	Top	All
2007/08						
Cash benefits	68	45	24	9	3	17
Disposable income	100	100	100	100	100	100
Post-tax income	69	78	80	82	87	82
NHS	41	24	15	10	5	12
Education	34	14	11	7	2	9
Final income	146	118	107	100	94	104
2010/11						
Cash benefits	66	48	28	12	3	19
Disposable income	100	100	100	100	100	100
Post-tax income	70	79	80	83	87	83
NHS	37	25	18	11	5	13
Education	28	17	12	8	3	9
Final income	138	122	111	102	96	106
2013/14						
Cash benefits	63	43	25	13	5	19
Disposable income	100	100	100	100	100	100
Post-tax income	69	78	79	81	85	81
NHS	36	22	17	11	6	13
Education	26	16	10	6	2	8
Final income	133	118	106	99	94	103

Notes: Cash benefits include tax credits; post-tax income is after indirect taxes; final income includes all benefits in kind (including housing and travel subsidies).

Source: ONS (2015c, table 14a)

The differential is not so much due to richer households deriving much less benefit from the NHS (£3,700 per household compared to £4,200 for those in the bottom fifth), but simply because their cash incomes are so much higher.

Allowing for these services in kind – which the ONS does when it adds them in to create 'final incomes' – would therefore make the income distribution look more equal. However, to reach a closer approximation to variations in living standards, one would also need to adjust for the *needs* of different groups – which would reverse at least part of this effect. This is not done in the ONS analysis, and we cannot do so here, so care is needed in interpreting the figures, but unless the needs of different groups change rapidly from year to year, *changes* in the values of what they receive may give a further guide to the relative effects of public service changes.

Given the extent of cuts in some public services described in earlier chapters, and their greater relative importance to those on low incomes, one would therefore expect 'austerity' to have had unequal effects. On the other hand, two of the most important services of this kind – healthcare and schools – had their budgets at least comparatively protected through the life of the coalition. At the same time, when implementing some of the cuts, the government attempted to protect poorer groups (for instance, through more use of means-testing) or in some cases to channel more to them (for instance, through the 'Pupil Premium' for [English] schools). Reed and Portes (2014, Figure 7.2) suggest that, taking account of spending plans up to 2013, the effect of service cuts was an overall loss equivalent to 3% of 'household living standards'.[12] But this meant a loss of 6% for the bottom tenth and less than 1% for the top tenth. By contrast, in its more recent analysis, the Treasury suggests that the effect of features such as real increases in health spending was that allowing for changes in the real value of services made the overall effect of tax and public spending changes *less* regressive, with the value of service cuts up to 2015/16 being a greater proportion of income for the top two-fifths than for other groups.[13] Again, some care is needed interpreting this kind of analysis, without adjustment for changes in the needs of different income groups, for instance, as older households, who make greater use of the NHS, have risen in the income distribution.

Some of the features covered in earlier chapters that will have had the most important effects on particular groups are hard to allow for. These include the effects of the decline in early years provision (see Chapter Three) or in social care provision at a time of rising need (see Chapter Nine) on those who do not receive care, but would have done in earlier years, or of increased university fees (see Chapter Five) on future repayments of student loans.

For the period up to 2013/14, the regular ONS analysis of the effects of taxes and benefits on household income provides some clues to the direction of change since the crisis started. This is based on a different survey from the more detailed income survey used in Figure 11.3 above, and looks at the distribution between households, rather than between individuals. It allows one to look at the effects of different stages of redistribution by the state on income defined in different ways.

In this analysis, 'disposable' income is the amount people end up with after adding cash benefits (including tax credits) to the incomes they receive from the market (such as pre-tax pay and investment income), but after deducting direct taxes (Income Tax and employee National Insurance Contributions). 'Post-tax' income also deducts ONS estimates of the effects of indirect taxes. Over the longer term (apart from a brief period in the late 1990s), it is striking that the inequality of post-tax income has been very close to that of gross income (ONS, 2015d). This implies that the combined effect of direct and indirect taxes on income distribution in the UK is neutral, together taking much the same share of income from all income groups (and indeed has been for more than thirty years). This has not changed since the crisis started. 'Final income' adds in the imputed value of services in kind (including transport and housing subsidies as well as health and education).

The ONS analysis gives information on the relative importance of public services (mainly health and education) and cash transfers, and how this has changed over time. Table 11.2 suggests that the contribution of cash benefits to disposable income rose on average between 2007/08 and 2010/11 and then remained the same in 2013/14. The value of NHS services expressed as a percentage of disposable income rose slightly in 2010/11, but that of education dipped in 2013/14. However, the changes were larger for particular income groups. For the poorest fifth of households, NHS services fell from the equivalent of 41% of disposable income in 2007/08 to 37% and then 36% in 2013/14. For education the fall was from 34% to 26%, with again the larger part of the fall coming by 2010/11.

The final line of each panel shows the ONS estimate of the value of 'final income' relative to disposable income for each fifth of the distribution (ranked by equivalised disposable income). Most notably, this fell for the poorest fifth from 146% of disposable income in 2007/08 to 138% in 2010/11 and further to 133% in 2013/14. Bearing in mind the lack of adjustment for changing needs and the incomplete coverage of public services, this implies that the combination of indirect tax changes and changes in the relative value of public services was leaving the poorest fifth in a worse position than the change in their cash income by itself would suggest.

Household wealth[14]

Finally, we can also look at changes in the distribution of household wealth, as shown by the ONS Wealth and Assets Survey. This covers Great Britain (rather than the UK), and is available for three two-year periods starting in July 2006, July 2008 and July 2010. The latest period covered here, 2010/12, therefore covers the period July 2010 to June 2012, so relating to an earlier date than the other figures discussed in this chapter, and covering only four of the years since the crisis started. Household wealth is available on three bases:

- financial and physical wealth (net financial assets plus other personal possessions, excluding housing)
- non-pension wealth (which also includes the value of housing and other property, net of mortgages)
- total wealth (which also includes an estimated value of non-state pension rights).

In this section we present results on all three bases, but in Chapter Twelve that follows, we concentrate on the second of these, changes in non-pension wealth (as there are considerable uncertainties in assessing the value of pension rights).

There is an issue with the presentation of changes in wealth over time. As shown in the figures for the level of wealth in 2010-12 in Table 11.3, wealth is much more unequally distributed than wages or incomes, and some households have very low levels of wealth by comparison with the average or median. This means that quite small changes in absolute terms can imply very large changes in percentage terms. Thus, for instance, in Table 11.3 we show the change in total wealth at the 10th percentile to have been 46% between 2006-08 and 2010-12, and 17% at the 90th percentile. But the former corresponds to a rise of £4,100 and the latter to a rise of £131,800. The percentage change shows that in technical terms the inequality of wealth became smaller – the largest amounts were not quite such large multiples of middling wealth. But the absolute change implies that wealth differences became very much larger when compared with

Table 11.3: Percentage and absolute changes in wealth, 2006-08 to 2010-12 by percentile and wealth levels in 2010-12

	10th	30th	Median	70th	90th	Mean
Financial and physical wealth						
% change	25	17	12	11	11	20
Absolute change (£000s)	1.5	3.6	5.3	8.1	19.7	16.8
Wealth 2010-12 (£000s)	7.5	2.5	48.2	84.1	197.7	99.1
Non-pension wealth						
% change	7	4	−0.3	3	8	8
Absolute change (£)	0.5	1.7	−0.4	7.8	38.2	18.1
Wealth 2010-12 (£000s)	8.0	47.8	146.2	260.0	529.9	244.7
Total wealth						
% change	46	19	11	14	17	14
Absolute change (£)	4.1	13.3	21.7	52.5	131.8	48.4
Wealth 2010-12 (£000s)	13.1	83.3	218.4	416.7	918.1	392.7

Source: ONS/Centre for Analysis of Social Exclusion (CASE) analysis of Wealth and Assets Survey

things such as income flows. For instance, mean household net income (adjusted to be equivalent to that for a couple with no children) in 2012/13 was £535 per week, or £28,000 per year. The gain in total wealth at the 10th percentile was equivalent to 15% of a year's average income; the gain at the 90th percentile was equivalent to 4.7 years of average income. To allow interpretation in both ways, Table 11.3 shows both absolute and percentage changes on all three definitions of wealth.

Concentrating on absolute changes in non-pension wealth, Table 11.3 shows the way in which higher levels of wealth recovered sharply after 2008-10, with wealth at the 90th percentile jumping by £41,000 by 2010-12, taking it to a value of £530,000. While less dramatic than the rise in total wealth at the 90th percentile, which is very sensitive to the assumptions made about valuing pension rights, this still represents approaching two years of median net incomes.

The overall conclusion from Table 11.3 is that inequalities in wealth, when considered in its own terms, generally fell between 2006-08 and 2010-12, with faster percentage growth lower down the distribution that at the top. However, differences between the parts of the wealth distribution rose considerably in absolute terms and in relation to incomes, so it would take more years of annual incomes to move across the wealth distribution. In that sense, there is no sign that the effects of the crisis and recession had been to narrow wealth differences across the bulk of the population; quite the reverse, in fact.

Right at the top, the ONS data suggest that the share of the top 1% of households in non-pension wealth fell from 12 to 11% between 2006-08 and 2010-12, and in total wealth from 13 to 12%. However, their average total wealth remained at nearly £5 million (Hills et al, 2015b, table 2.5, and p 14). This kind of survey does not capture the very greatest fortunes very well, however (Alvaredo et al, 2015). The annual *Sunday Times 'Rich List'* survey reports that the threshold to be among the richest thousand families in the UK dipped from £80 million in 2008 to £55 million in 2009 at the onset of the crisis, but had recovered to £100 million by 2015. The threshold for being in the wealthiest hundred fell from £0.7 to £0.5 billion initially, but had doubled to more than £1 billion by 2015 (*Sunday Times Magazine*, 26 April 2015).

Conclusion

Changes in overall economic inequalities during and since the economic crisis have taken a complex form. In contrast to the recessions of the early 1980s and early 1990s, for instance, the dominant feature following the economic crisis starting in 2007/08 was the subsequent fall in real wages. Employment fell, but not as fast as might have been expected. The fall in wages was greater for those at the bottom end of the wage distribution, so wage inequalities tended to increase. These features, combined with the effects of tax and benefit policy, affected household income inequality in different ways.

Men were worst hit in terms of employment falls between 2007 and 2010; they gained more in the partial recovery between 2010 and 2013 than women, but still lost overall. Pay distribution became more unequal for both men and women, with real hourly wages down by 8.4% for the worst-paid men and 7.1% for the worst-paid women, but by 4.2% for the best-paid men and 5.0% for the best-paid women. With falling hours for those in full-time work, weekly earnings for full-timers fell even faster – by 7.6% overall, and more for men than women. Inequalities in full-time weekly earnings grew as earnings fell by more than 8% for the lowest-paid men and women, but by only 2.2% for the best-paid men and only 3.5% for the best-paid women. That the bottom end experienced the greatest pay squeeze is another significant feature of the post-crash period, of particular note given the origins of the crisis in the financial services sector, and the enduring images of shell-shocked high-paid workers leaving their offices, belongings in boxes, in September 2007.

Despite these trends, however, inequality in household income did not rise, at least up to 2013/14, as through most of the period benefit and pension levels were protected in real terms. Before allowing for housing costs, real incomes grew for the bottom three-tenths between 2007/08 and 2009/10, while they fell sharply in the top half of the distribution between 2009/10 and 2010/11. They then remained roughly constant for all income groups in the three years from 2010/11 to 2013/14. The overall effect was a sharp reduction in income inequality and relative poverty in election year 2010, with little change in the first three years of the coalition government. This is testament to the effectiveness of the social security system in fulfilling one of its key functions, protecting households during an economic downturn. However, qualitative evidence indicates rising hardship among groups most sharply affected by welfare reforms or sanctions. Furthermore, there are grounds for pessimism about developments from 2013/14, with further real cuts in benefits predicted to have increased poverty rates in non-pensioner households.

It is not straightforward to allow for changes in the value and distribution of public services on top of those in cash incomes, and available analyses reach different conclusions. The fact that the NHS and schools were, relatively speaking, protected and are of greatest importance to lower-income households moderated the effects that would have been expected from across the board cuts. Nevertheless, analysis based on that of the ONS implies that the combination of indirect tax changes and changes in the relative value of public services up to 2013/14 left the poorest fifth in a worse position than the change in their disposable cash income by itself would suggest.

Inequality in wealth, when considered in its own terms, generally fell in the earlier years since the crisis, between 2006-08 and 2010-12, because wealth grew by more in percentage terms for those with less wealth to begin with. However, in absolute terms and in relation to incomes, the gain was much greater at the top: an increase of 4.7 years of annual average income for those at the 90th percentile, compared to a rise of less than two months of average income for those at the 10th percentile. Thus there is no sign that the longer-run effects of the crisis and recession narrowed wealth differences or led to a reduction in wealth holdings at the top; indeed, the reverse is the case. Like the rise in earnings inequality, this may come as a surprise. To those who placed the responsibility for the crash and the subsequent recession at the door of wealthy and irresponsible investors, and to those who saw the crash as the necessary correction of a speculative bubble, it may also appear as a sharp injustice. While ongoing austerity measures continue to squeeze benefits and public services, on which lower-income households depend most at any moment, the fortunes of wealthier households appear to have emerged intact.

Notes

[1] We therefore use data sources in both this chapter and the next, such as the Labour Force Survey, which can be broken down by characteristics of this kind.

[2] This section draws heavily on Hills et al's (2015a) background data. More detailed breakdowns of the analysis presented in this chapter and the next are available at www.casedata.org.uk

[3] We use pooled data here for the three years from 2006 to 2008, as used in the 2010 report of the National Equality Panel (Hills et al, 2010), to represent the pre-crisis position.

[4] Wages and earnings are adjusted by the consumer price index (CPI). Note that the pay for a given job or a particular worker may change differently from the population average. For further discussion, see McKnight and Gardiner (2015).

[5] But see Hills et al (2015a, Appendix 1) for a discussion of the difference between the Labour Force Survey results here and those from the Annual Survey of Hours and Earnings, which suggest that the Labour Force Survey may understate the fall for the highest earners.

[6] See Belfield et al (2015) for a detailed discussion of some of the issues discussed in this section.

[7] That is, at the 5th, 15th and 25th percentiles, etc.

[8] The picture after allowing for housing costs is similar, with the exception of the Brown years, which look less progressive after housing costs than before them: the bottom half saw income growth of between 0 and 1%, lower than growth before housing costs, while the top 10th saw growth of nearly 2%.

[9] If income is measured after housing costs, the overall pattern for the Gini coefficient is similar, peaking between 2007/08 and 2009/10, dropping sharply in 2010/11 to a level matching that when Labour came into office, remaining flat for the next two years and then turning upwards again. Changes in the 90:10 ratio since 2007/08 also tell a broadly similar story after housing costs as before, although the long-run trend looks very different. The 90:10 ratio after housing costs rose sharply from 2004/05 to a peak in 2008/09, before falling between 2009/10 and 2010/11 to a level matching that when Labour took office, and rising slightly thereafter.

[10] Data from the IFS living standards, inequality and poverty spreadsheet 2015.

[11] Using a different data source, the EU Statistics on Income and Living Conditions (EU-SILC), UNICEF's Report Card shows an increase from 5 to 12% between 2008 and 2012 in 'severe material deprivation' for children, the seventh largest out of 33 countries compared, and taking the UK to the tenth highest level among them (UNICEF Office of Research, 2014).

[12] Net incomes plus the value of allocated services in kind.

[13] HM Treasury (2015b, chart 2I). Note, however, that earlier HM Treasury (2014b, chart 2I) analysis looking up to 2014/15 had reached a different conclusion, with the poorest fifth losing the greatest share of its income.

[14] This section draws heavily on Hills et al (2015a, p 201), where some of the results are discussed in more detail. See also Hills et al (2015b), Chapter Two, for a discussion of longer-term trends.

TWELVE

The changing structure of UK inequality since the crisis

John Hills, Jack Cunliffe and Polina Obolenskaya

Introduction

Chapter Eleven looked at overall changes in inequality in the six years following the start of the financial and economic crisis in 2007. For the population as a whole, the striking features were the rapid fall in real wages, associated with growing wage inequality, but a large fall in household income inequality (allowing for benefits and direct taxes) between 2009/10 and 2010/11, followed by three years of stability. These overall patterns do not necessarily apply in the same way to all groups within the population. Indeed, the fact that recent stability in overall measures of income inequality resulted from a combination of growing inequalities in the labour market, offset by increases in the relative values of benefits and pensions, already suggests that some groups will have gained and others will have lost.

This chapter draws on detailed analysis of how the changes in the labour market, incomes and wealth affected particular population groups, and of how inequalities changed *within* those groups (Hills et al, 2015a). We present here some of the patterns this revealed when dividing the population by gender, age, ethnicity, housing tenure, region and disability status.[1] The figures are for regions across the whole of the UK, with the exception of wealth, which is for Great Britain (excluding Northern Ireland). The analysis uses the baseline of the results originally presented by the National Equality Panel (Hills et al, 2010) which was able to use data from the years around 2007. As in Chapter Eleven, we show the position up to 2013 for labour market outcomes and up to 2010-12 (the two years to June 2012) for wealth. For household incomes (both before and after housing costs) we were able to look at the position up to the financial year 2012/13, a year before the latest year available for the national statistics used in Chapter Eleven. There was little change in overall income inequality between the two years, but that stability may mask further changes between and within groups beyond those we can show here. Note that these statistics do not reflect the effects of the 'welfare' and other reforms taking place from or after 2013 discussed in Chapter Two earlier.

In the figures presented below showing changes since 2007, we generally distinguish between those occurring before and after 2010 (with a lozenge marker showing the combined net effect).

The situation on the eve of the crisis

Chapter Eleven presented information on *overall* changes in inequalities both before and since the crisis. The National Equality Panel showed in detail how inequalities in economic outcomes varied both between and within groups defined in different ways, and its results effectively describe the position as the crisis began. In summary, it highlighted five features (see Hills et al, 2010, pp 395-6):

- Some of the widest gaps in outcomes between social groups had narrowed in the decade up to 2007, particularly between the earnings of women and men, and in educational qualifications of different ethnic groups.
- Deep and systematic differences remained, however, between social groups across all of the outcomes that the Panel examined, including between women and men, different ethnic groups, social class groups, those living in disadvantaged and other areas, and between London and other parts of the country.
- Despite the elimination and even reversal of the qualification differences that often explain them, significant differences remained in employment rates and relative pay between men and women and between ethnic groups.
- Differences in outcomes between the more and less advantaged *within* each social group, however the population is classified, were much greater than differences *between* social groups. Even if all differences between groups were removed, overall inequalities would remain wide.
- Many of the inequalities the Panel examined accumulate across the life cycle, especially those related to socioeconomic background.

As the discussion below shows, these underlying broad features of inequality in the UK had not fundamentally changed by 2013, despite the intentions of, for instance, the Equality Act brought in by the Labour government in 2010. However, it was by no means the case that the crisis had equal effects on those with different backgrounds and circumstances.

Gender differences

First, because gender differences in employment patterns and pay are so important within the labour market, we already presented some of the differences in the ways men and women were affected in the last chapter. As a backdrop, qualification levels of the working-age population have continued to rise, particularly for women, who are now better qualified than men in terms of higher education and degrees.[2] The rise makes the continuing falls in real wages all the more striking.

As we saw in the last chapter (Figure 11.1), while men were worst hit in terms of employment between 2006-08 and 2010, they recovered more between 2010 and 2013 than women. At the same time, pay distribution became more unequal for both men and women, with real hourly wages down by 8% for the worst-paid men and 7% for the worst-paid women, but by 4% for the best-paid men and 5% for the best-paid women (see Table 11.1 in Chapter Eleven; see Figure 12.2 below for changes in the median by age and gender). What happened to the gender pay gap in hourly pay depends on whether we use the mean or the median level of hourly pay: using mean wages the gender gap narrowed, but the percentage gap in median pay widened slightly.

With falling hours for those in full-time work, weekly earnings for full-timers fell even faster – by 8% overall – and more for men than women. They fell fastest – by more than 10% for the lowest-paid men and by 9% for the lowest-paid women, but by only 2% for the best-paid men and only 3.5% for the best-paid women (in the survey used here) (see Hills et al, 2015a, Figure 2.5; see also Figure 12.3 below for changes in median earnings by age and gender).

Earnings are just one component of the incomes that individuals receive. Comparing the average 'individual incomes' in their own right received by men and women of different ages in the three years 2005-08 and the three years 2009-12 suggests that incomes received in their own right generally fell for men aged below 64 across the income distribution, while the individual incomes of women aged 35 or over generally rose (see Hills et al, 2015a, Table 3.3).[3] The falls were particularly marked for men aged under 35, and the gains were particularly large for women aged 55-64. While these changes refer to a slightly earlier period, they are consistent with the patterns of employment and earnings changes by age presented below, with younger men in particular losing and older women of working age increasing their employment incomes.

Looking at incomes, because the Department for Work and Pensions' (DWP) methodology used to construct the series we use assumes that households share their incomes equally, men and women within couples (and any children) are allocated the same income. Any gender differences within the distribution that it shows therefore result from differences between household types – for instance, reflecting the position of women who are single parents, or single elderly people living alone. Nonetheless, there were pronounced differences over the period in what happened to men and women, as can be seen in Figure 12.1. Whereas the median net income (before housing costs) for men fell over the whole period by 6.5%, for women the fall was only 3.2%; after housing costs the respective falls were 10.2 and 7.8%.[4] After housing costs the differentials for the poorest men and women were even greater – a fall of 12.2% at the 10th percentile for men, but only 4.3% for women. By contrast, the falls at the top of the distribution were similar for men and women. In these terms the gender income gap narrowed across most of the distribution, but not at the top.

Given the assumed equal changes for members of couples, this was driven by two main factors: incomes of non-pensioner single men fell much more rapidly than single women, while incomes of single women with children actually rose over this period, a factor also contributing to the rise in incomes at the 10th percentile of all women before housing costs shown in Figure 12.1.

Rapidly falling real wages, incomes and wealth for those in their twenties

Of all the breakdowns we examine in this chapter, the differences in fortune over time between age groups were the clearest and the most consistent, and we examine them in most detail below. As a background to this, the qualifications of those in their twenties and thirties improved rapidly by comparison with their predecessors six years earlier. By 2013, more than a third of those in their thirties had a degree or higher degree, while those then in their twenties were more likely to have them than that cohort had been at the same age, and so were heading towards an even higher level (see Hills et al, 2015a, Figure 3.2).

Despite this, full-time employment fell fastest for men and women aged 16-29, including by 10 percentage points for men and 8 points for women aged 20-24 between 2006-08 and 2013. By 2013 unemployment

Figure 12.1: Changes in household net income (before housing costs) by gender, 2007/08 to 2012/13 (adults, %)

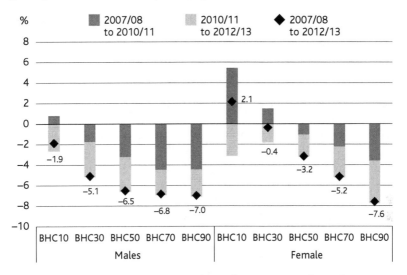

Note: Bars shows changes at 10th percentile (BHC10), 30th percentile (BHC30), etc. Price adjustments made using DWP indices. Data labels are shown for the combined net effect 2007/08 to 2012/13

Source: DWP/CASE analysis of HBAI dataset (UK)

for those aged 20-24 had reached 12%, the joint highest (with 16- to 19-year-olds) for any age group. By contrast, employment rose for those in their sixties and a fifth of those aged 65-69 were employed or self-employed by 2013 (see Hills et al, 2015a, Figure 3.5).

Wages and earnings

For those employed full-time, hourly wages fell fastest the younger workers were. Figure 12.2 shows changes in real hourly wages for men and women separately by age. The overall gradients are stark. At the median, pay for men and women aged under 30 was 10% or more below that of their predecessors six years earlier; for 16- to 19-year-olds the drop was around 20%, and was approaching 30% for the worst paid of these. But the best-paid men in their early sixties gained 10%, and the best-paid women 4%. This was not just a matter of young people at the bottom of the labour market: the *best*-paid men and women in their late twenties were paid 13% and 16% less than their predecessors, respectively (see Hills et al, 2015a, Figure 3.6). Real wages only grew for the oldest men (at the 90th percentile as well as the median) and for the best paid women aged 60-64.

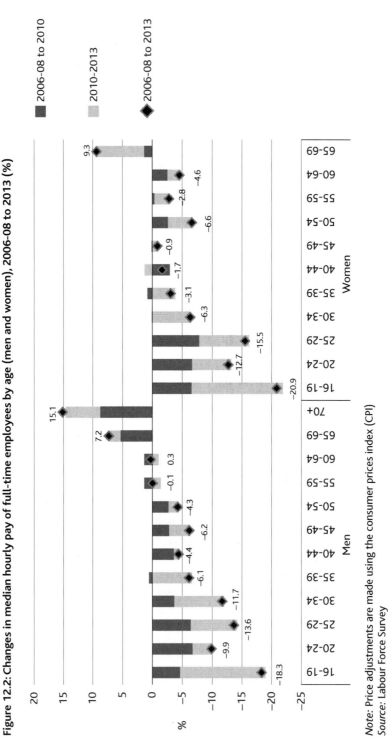

Figure 12.2: Changes in median hourly pay of full-time employees by age (men and women), 2006-08 to 2013 (%)

Note: Price adjustments are made using the consumer prices index (CPI)
Source: Labour Force Survey

A notable feature is that after 2010, those aged 30-34 did badly, as well as those in their twenties: as the cohort born in the 1980s began to reach their thirties, they still seem to be losing ground.

Figure 12.3 shows an even stronger gradient for *weekly* earnings by age, with cumulative falls of more than 15% for men and women in their late 20s (and even larger ones for those aged 16-19), but only small losses or even gains for men and women in their sixties. Similar patterns apply at the top and bottom of each age range, and again, wage inequalities grew within every age group, with higher 90:10 ratios in 2013 than in 2006-08 in all cases (see Hills et al, 2015a, Table 3.2). Earnings inequalities therefore grew sharply both within and between age groups.

Household net incomes

In the previous chapter we showed that in the period up to 2012/13, price protection of benefits meant that low household incomes did not fall in the same way as low wages and earnings. Figure 12.4 shows that this was true for some age groups, but that there were substantial losses for others.

The biggest falls between 2007/08 and 2012/13 before allowing for housing costs were for middle and higher-income people in their twenties, totalling more than 12% in real terms. While some age groups had real income increases between 2007/08 and 2010/11, those in their sixties and early seventies, net incomes fell for most age groups across the income distribution between 2010/11 and 2012/13. The main exceptions to this were some of the highest income people aged over 65 – up by as much as 13% for the richest 66- to 70-year-olds.[5]

Overall, there was some protection for the lowest-income people in their twenties. But at the median and higher up, drops in income – by about an eighth over the five years – were similar to those in gross weekly earnings shown in Figure 11.3. This was despite the way in which those in their twenties were less badly affected than some others by the combination of the coalition's direct tax and benefit reforms (De Agostini et al, 2015, Figure 5.1).

After allowing for housing costs, median incomes for those in their twenties were 18% or more below those of the same age five years before, and fell by almost as much for those with the lowest incomes, as well as for those with the highest incomes in their twenties and early thirties (Hills et al, 2015a, Figure 3.9).

As discussed in Chapter Two, overall income differences by age narrowed during the period of the Labour government (1997/98 to

Figure 12.3: Changes in median weekly pay of full-time employees by age (men and women), 2006-08 to 2013

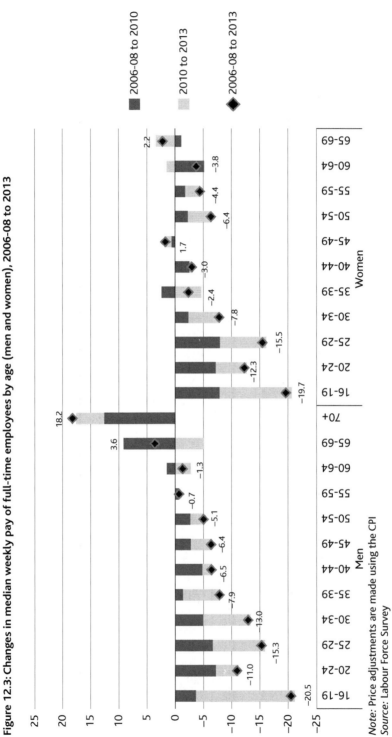

Note: Price adjustments are made using the CPI
Source: Labour Force Survey

Figure 12.4: Changes in median net incomes (adjusted for household size) by age, 2007/08 to 2012/13 (before housing costs) (%)

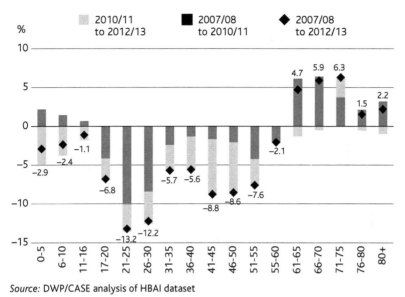

Source: DWP/CASE analysis of HBAI dataset

2010/11), reflecting that the government's focus on improving cash transfers related to children and for pensioners. In the early years of the coalition government, as Figures 2.1 and 2.2 showed in Chapter Two earlier, this trend continued for pensioners, but families with children were no longer favoured, contributing to the changes shown in Figure 12.4.

Figure 12.5 shows the results of these changes. It shows for each age group the percentage difference between the median equivalent income for that age group and the overall median in the three years 1997/98, 2010/11 and 2012/13. Variations in incomes over the life cycle, even for those with middle incomes, were much more pronounced in 1997 than in 2010. Children aged 0-10 had incomes (based on the households they lived in) more than 15% below the overall median, and older people in the age groups above 70 had incomes more than 25% below it. Those aged 46-50 by contrast had median incomes more than 25% above the overall median. As the second columns in Figure 12.5 show, these differences had narrowed (by about a third overall) by 2010/11.

The columns for 2012/13 show that for most age groups the differences from the overall median had narrowed further, especially for those in their forties and sixties. However, differences had now *widened* for children aged under 10 (falling) and people aged 56-65

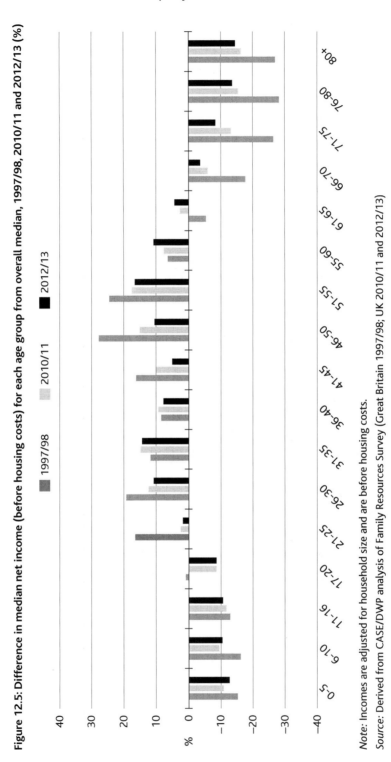

Figure 12.5: Difference in median net income (before housing costs) for each age group from overall median, 1997/98, 2010/11 and 2012/13 (%)

Note: Incomes are adjusted for household size and are before housing costs.

Source: Derived from CASE/DWP analysis of Family Resources Survey (Great Britain 1997/98; UK 2010/11 and 2012/13)

(rising). Although these two years were early in the coalition's period in office, these trends are consistent with the overall balance of policy described in Chapter Two earlier, with Labour's policies favouring pensioners being continued, but those favouring children being reversed (for instance, as tax credits for middle-income families with children were reduced). The net overall effect is very striking for those early in retirement. Back in 1997/98 median incomes for those aged 66-70 were 18% below the overall median; by 2012/13 they only fell short by 4%. For those aged 71-75 the shortfall fell from 26% to 8%. But the position of children has stopped improving, and the shortfall for children aged 0-5 is now almost as great as for those aged over 76. After housing costs the difference in the fortunes of children and older people is even more pronounced (as we saw for poverty rates in Figure 11.4 in Chapter Eleven). Those aged 66-70 had median incomes above those for the whole population by 2012/13, and those aged 71-75 median incomes matching the national figure. By contrast, the poorest age groups after housing costs are now all of the age groups of children together with those aged 17-20.

Household wealth

Changes in wealth between 2006-08 and 2010-12 were also sharply tilted against younger households, with household wealth rising for age groups aged over 55, but falling for younger ones. Table 12.1 shows that by 2010-12, median non-pension wealth for households aged 55-64 had grown to £233,000, but had fallen to £43,000 for those aged 25-34. Including pension rights, the figures were £425,000 and £60,000 respectively, a £365,000 gap between generations 30 years apart. The 90:10 ratios in Table 12.1 show that wealth inequality is not simply a matter of age-related differences of the kind that might be explained simply by life cycle savings patterns. For all the age groups from 25 to 74, the ratio exceeds 40; in working life the ratios are not that much lower than the overall 90:10 ratio of 66 across households of all ages. Wealth inequalities remain profound both between and within different age groups, and indeed, those between age groups intensified over the crisis and its aftermath.

Contrasting trends in qualifications and outcomes by ethnicity

Bearing in mind that the ethnic groupings we can analyse vary between the datasets we use (and some definitions have changed over time),

Table 12.1: Absolute changes in median non-pension household wealth, 2006-08 to 2010-12, and wealth levels in 2010-12, by age group (£000s, nominal terms)

	16-24	25-34	35-44	45-54	55-64	65-74	75-84	85+
Absolute changes								
2006-08 to 2008-10	−3.9	−3.6	−14.5	−11.8	−14.1	2.2	11.8	3.5
2008-10 to 2010-12	0.1	−1.2	−6.1	−4.5	1.9	16.8	11.3	20.5
2006-08 to 2010-12	−3.8	−4.8	−20.6	−16.3	−12.2	19.0	23.1	24.0
Level of non-pension wealth in 2010-12								
Median	8.2	42.8	101.5	169.3	232.8	233.5	207.2	180.0
90:10 ratio	n/a[1]	61	57	55	48	43	34	32

Notes:

[1] Tenth percentile wealth is *minus* £6,200 and 90th percentile is £61,400.

Age is that of 'household reference person'.

Source: ONS/CASE analysis of Wealth and Assets Survey

some broad patterns emerge that show that the experiences of different ethnic groups have varied considerably since the start of the economic crisis. Unlike the clear gradients by age, patterns of change by ethnicity have been more complex. In some cases they have led to differences between ethnic groups narrowing, but in others they have widened, not always to the advantage of the majority, White, population. These do not, however, reduce to a simple message that some groups have done uniformly better than others. We now highlight some of the main features for different groups (for more details, see Hills et al, 2015a, section 4).

More than half of *Chinese* adults of working age now have degrees. Chinese men in full-time employment in 2013 had the highest hourly wages (£16.75) and weekly earnings (£673). However, a combined group of 'Chinese and other' adults had the largest falls in net household incomes – particularly for the poorest after allowing for housing costs, where incomes fell by 28% between 2007/08 and 2012/13. At the top, the highest-income adults have greater income than any other group (before housing costs), with the result that income inequality was largest for this (possibly heterogeneous) group than for the others shown in the data. Median household non-pension wealth rose most rapidly for Chinese households, reaching £200,000 by 2010-12.

Partly as a result of age differences, *White* adults had the slowest increase in qualifications of any ethnic group, and a smaller proportion of White working-age adults now have degrees than of any other group, apart from Bangladeshis. White men had one of the smallest increases in unemployment over the whole period, with a fall after 2010, unlike several other groups. A much greater proportion of White adults were employed than other groups. Apart from Chinese adults working full time, the weekly earnings gender gap was greatest for White adults, but household income inequality was least. Net incomes remained higher for White adults than for other groups before and after housing costs and in nearly all cases across the income distribution. Household non-pension wealth, at £155,000, was lower by 2010-12 than for Indian and Chinese households.

Indian men and women had the largest increase in the proportion with degrees, reaching nearly half. The least well-paid Indian men and women had the largest falls in hourly wages (by 8% and 14%), leaving both hourly wages and weekly earnings more unequal in 2013 than for other groups where this can be calculated. Household non-pension wealth reached £195,000 for Indian households in 2010-12.

Black men had the largest (5.4 percentage points) fall in full-time employment from 2006-08 to 2013, and Black women one of the largest falls (4.1 points). Black men had the second largest increases in unemployment (3.0 percentage points), all coming after 2010. Real median hourly wages fell by 6.9% – more than for any other group of men. Apart from the mixed 'Chinese and other' group, median net household incomes of Black adults fell by more than any other – by 5.4% than before housing costs and 12.3% after housing costs, and by 22% for the poorest Black adults after housing costs. Non-pension wealth was only £34,000 for Black Caribbean and £21,000 for Black African households in 2010-12.

Pakistani men had the largest increase in unemployment over the period, and by 2013 the lowest proportion (36%) of Pakistani adults were full- or part-time employees. Median male hourly wages (£10.04) were the second lowest, and median household incomes before housing costs were also the lowest for the combined 'Asian and Asian British' group. Median non-pension wealth, however, increased by £42,000 to £129,000 for Pakistani households by 2010-12.

Bangladeshi men and women had the greatest fall in the proportions with no qualifications, but remained the most likely to have no qualifications in 2013. Bangladeshi women had the greatest increase in unemployment (5.4 percentage points) and Bangladeshi adults had the lowest full-time employment rate, just 20% in 2013, with Pakistani adults the greatest proportion who were economically inactive, 'looking after family/home'. Bangladeshi men had the lowest full-time median hourly wages (£10.00) and lowest median weekly earnings (£404). Median non-pension wealth was only £21,000 for Bangladeshi households in 2010-12.

Outcomes by housing tenure

The economic divides between housing tenures were already wide before the economic crisis, and have widened further since (for more details, see Hills et al, 2015a, section 5). Social tenants have much lower levels of qualifications than those in other tenures, and much lower levels of employment. Full-time employment fell and unemployment rose by twice as much for male social tenants as for owner-occupiers and private tenants. Figure 12.6 shows that by 2013, fewer than half of all working-age adults in social housing were in any kind of employment or self-employment. Part of the difference between tenures reflects, of course, differences in the kinds of people in each tenure, with much higher levels of lone parenthood, disability and carer responsibilities in social housing, as well as lower qualifications (Hills, 2007, chapter 5; Hills et al, 2015a, Figure 5.2).

For the social tenants who were in full-time employment, real hourly wages had fallen by 8% for men and 9% for women between 2006-08 and 2013, to only £8.48 for men and £7.77 for women, 60% or less of those of mortgagors. The falls in weekly full-time earnings were even faster – by 11% for men and 9% for women in social housing.

However, a much larger proportion of social tenants' incomes come from social security benefits than in other tenures, and the real values of many of those benefits were protected until the end of 2012/13. This meant that median net incomes before allowing for housing costs *rose* slightly for social tenants while those in the other tenures fell roughly in proportion to falling weekly earnings. But after deducting housing costs, median incomes fell as much for social tenants as for owner-occupiers, while those of private tenants fell by 13%. The best-off private tenants lost 19% between 2007/08 and 2012/13 after housing costs, but the poorest social tenants also lost nearly 10%.

Wealth differences between tenures also widened in absolute terms between 2006-08 and 2010-12, with median non-pension wealth for outright owners reaching £307,000, compared to less than £20,000 for social and private tenant households.

Figure 12.6: Employment status in 2013 by housing tenure (all) (%)

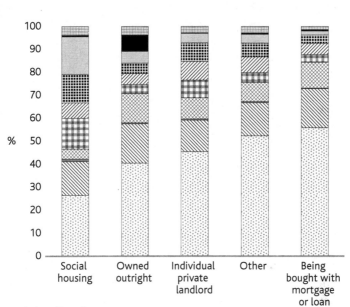

Source: Labour Force Survey

London had the smallest employment fall but became more unequal

Looking across these regional differences, two things stand out in particular – the differences *between* London and other regions, with Northern Ireland often in the least favourable position, and the differences *within* London.[6] We look at differences between London and Northern regions of England in more detail in the following chapter, but in this section we set out some of the overall differences between all of the UK regions.

Londoners had the most rapid increase in qualification levels. By 2013, nearly half of Londoners of working age had a degree or other higher education qualification, compared to fewer than 30% in Northern Ireland. London also had the smallest drop in male full-time employment and the smallest increase in unemployment between 2006-08 and 2013 – although London had the lowest employment levels to start with. Northern Ireland had the largest rise in male unemployment but one of the smallest rises for women. London started with the lowest full- and part-time employment rate, however, and still had the lowest in 2013, but now jointly with Northern Ireland.

Median hourly wages fell most for men in the South West and Eastern region, but most for women in Northern Ireland. But low wages for men fell by most (by 9%) in London according to the Labour Force Survey, and high wages by one of the least, so that wage dispersion grew rapidly in London, with the 90:10 ratio reaching 4.7 for men (and 3.9 for women) in 2013. On a weekly basis, by 2013 median weekly earnings in London were 43% higher than in Northern Ireland for men, and 56% higher for women.

Household incomes

Median net incomes (before housing costs) fell most in Northern Ireland between 2007/08 and 2012/13, by more than 8%, while incomes actually grew in Wales, the East Midlands and the North East (Hills et al, 2015a, Figure 6.8). There are greater uncertainties surrounding data on changes over time in the highest and lowest incomes in each region (because of small sample sizes), but the figures suggest that with the effects of safety net protection in real terms continuing to 2012/13 for many with low incomes, incomes grew at the tenth percentile in most regions – including by 7.5% in the East Midlands. By contrast, incomes fell at the 90th percentile by more than the median in nearly all regions, including by more than 8% for the most affluent in London and the West Midlands.

The picture after housing costs was very different (see Hills et al, 2015a, Figure 6.9).[7] Median incomes fell by 12% in London, and for the poorest Londoners – despite some recovery after 2010/11 – by 18% compared to only 10% for the highest-income Londoners. The effect of this, shown in Table 12.2, was that the 90:10 ratio for incomes in London fell before allowing for housing costs to 5.2 by 2012/13, but rose to an extraordinary 9.1 for incomes after housing costs – £1,027 per week at the 90th percentile compared to only £113 per week at the 10th percentile. Table 12.2 also shows that regional differentials in median incomes are smaller after allowing for housing costs than before them – the difference between Northern Ireland and the South East falling from 26% to 20%, once they are allowed for, for instance.

Table 12.2: Weekly net incomes by region in 2012/13 (£/week, adjusted for household size) and income inequalities by region (90:10 ratios)

	Mean	P10	Median	P90	90: 10 ratio
a) Before housing costs					
London	670	223	488	1151	5.2
South East	641	252	508	1071	4.3
Eastern	591	248	476	962	3.9
South West	529	241	456	839	3.5
East Midlands	489	232	431	795	3.4
North West	485	226	417	803	3.6
West Midlands	479	221	408	776	3.5
Yorkshire and the Humber	477	217	402	779	3.6
North East	468	229	411	753	3.3
Wales	469	217	416	759	3.5
Scotland	523	235	447	843	3.6
Northern Ireland	456	213	398	740	3.5
b) After housing costs					
South East	556	172	430	965	5.6
London	550	113	383	1027	9.1
Eastern	517	177	415	877	5.0
South West	459	170	385	775	4.6
East Midlands	433	171	377	732	4.3
North West	426	159	365	737	4.6
Yorkshire and the Humber	422	158	353	719	4.6
West Midlands	420	158	352	719	4.6
North East	414	166	358	695	4.2
Wales	414	158	360	709	4.5
Scotland	466	175	396	783	4.5
Northern Ireland	412	168	359	696	4.1

Source: CASE/DWP analysis of HBAI dataset.

Household wealth

The fastest rise in median non-pension wealth over the shorter period from 2006-08 to 2010-12 was in London – by more than a quarter, £32,000, in nominal terms (Hills et al, 2015a, Table 6.4, Figure 6.10). It also grew by more than a quarter for the wealthiest Londoners, reaching £750,000. However, net non-pension wealth at the 10th percentile, £4,500 in London in 2010-12, was the lowest in the country (the 50% increase since 2006-08 only amounted to £1,500). Inequalities in wealth remained far greater in London than elsewhere, with a 90:10 ratio of 167 (compared to 66 nationally), while median households in London had less non-pension wealth than those in the South East, South West and East of England. If ONS' estimated value of pension wealth is included, the richest tenth of London households had at least £1.1 million, but the poorest tenth less than £6,300 (after debts but including personal possessions) – a 90:10 ratio of 173 to 1 (compared to 70 to 1 nationally).

Disability status: continuing disadvantage for disabled people

Interpreting results by disability status is harder than for other characteristics, both because of definition variations between surveys and over time, and because some of the raw differences are related to age. However, regardless of the other factors associated with them, there remain stark differences between disabled groups and others in the positions shown by the most recent data (for a more detailed discussion, see Hills et al, 2015a, section 7).

People of working age classed as both 'work-limiting' disabled and Disability Discrimination Act (DDA)-disabled were less than half as likely in 2013 to have degrees as those not classed as disabled, and approaching three times as likely to have no or only low-level qualifications.

Figure 12.7 shows the employment patterns of working-age adults by 2013. Again, the much weaker labour market position of those classified as both work-limiting and DDA-disabled is clear. Only 37% of this group were in any kind of employment or self-employment, less than half the proportion of those who were not disabled. More than half were economically inactive, including, unsurprisingly, 38% reporting themselves as inactive because they were disabled or sick.

Even when they were in full-time employment, median hourly wages were 16% lower for men and 11% lower for women, if classed as disabled under both definitions, than for those who were not disabled. Weekly full-time earnings were 14% lower for men, and 10% lower for women.

Even including benefits intended to compensate for extra costs of disability, median net incomes were 16-17% lower in 2012/13 for those in households with a disabled member than those without.

At the same time, non-pension wealth was 21% lower in 2010-12 for households with a disabled member than for other households despite their age profile, which would normally mean higher wealth. Allowing for this, McKnight (2014) looks at the effects of disability on wealth accumulation, separating out the effects of disability from those

Figure 12.7: Employment status in 2013 by disability (all) (%)

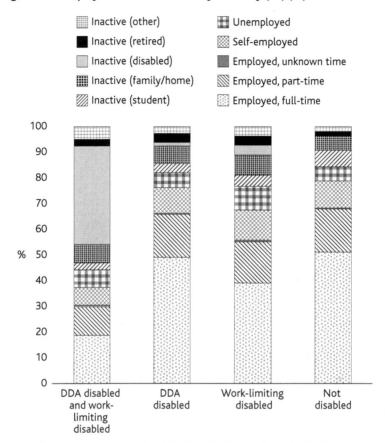

Note: Categories are exclusive, so 'work-limiting disabled' and 'DDA disabled' cases are those meeting one of the classifications only.

Source: Labour Force Survey

of ageing and other characteristics. She finds, for instance, a 'disability penalty' of £133,000 for 45- to 54-year-olds in non-pension wealth in 2005, comparing those who were disabled five and ten years earlier with their peers who were not.

Conclusion

Looking at the picture from before the financial and economic crisis up to the calendar year 2013, unemployment grew and real wages fell. But they did not do so evenly, leaving labour market inequalities wider than they were. At the same time, through the first part of the crisis and at the start of the term of the coalition government, the social security system protected many of those with the lowest incomes from real falls in income, thanks to the way in which most benefits were protected against inflation up until the financial year 2012/13. Even by 2012/13, however, increasing housing costs were affecting some households beyond the protection offered by social security, and after allowing for housing costs, incomes at the bottom had already fallen since 2010 by more than those higher up the distribution.

One way in which groups were affected unevenly by the crisis comes in the evolution of gender differences. By 2013, women of working age were more likely than men to have degrees or higher degrees, but gender gaps in pay remained despite this, widening slightly on some measures between 2006-08 and 2013, but narrowing slightly on others. Looking at net incomes based on those of the household, women as a whole were more protected than men from falling incomes up to 2012/13, partly due to some groups of women being poorer and more likely to be receiving benefits than men, and partly due to more women being pensioners, who were also protected.

There was also a contrast between the experiences of different ethnic groups in terms of qualifications and labour market position. Degree-level qualifications improved faster for all minority ethnic groups than for the White British population, who had the smallest proportion with degrees of any other group by 2013, apart from the Bangladeshi group. However, White men had the smallest increase in unemployment over the period and incomes for White adults remain higher than for other groups across the distribution (although median household wealth is now higher for some other groups).

Divides by housing tenure remained, and if anything, widened, with implications for labour market and benefit policy as well as for housing policies. Social tenants had the largest rise in unemployment and the greatest falls in wages and earnings. By 2013 fewer than half of social tenants of working age were in any kind of employment or self-employment, and even if in full-time employment had wages that were 60% or less of those of mortgagors. But it was private tenants who had the largest falls in income up to 2012/13, after allowing for their increased housing costs. In thinking about the challenges for social mobility and the next generation, wealth differences will loom large, with median non-pension wealth (including personal possessions) reaching £307,000 for outright owners by 2010-12, but less than £20,000 for social and private tenant households.

The experiences of different regions over the recession and the start of recovery also differed sharply, particularly between London and the rest of the country. These differences are not just that Londoners are on average better qualified and better paid than elsewhere, but that inequalities *within* London are far greater than in any other region. Despite some recovery after 2010/11, the incomes after housing costs of the poorest Londoners in 2012/13 were 18% lower than they had been in 2007/08. After allowing for housing costs, the 90:10 ratio (comparing incomes near the top with those near the bottom) was 9.1 in London in 2012/13, compared to 5.1 nationally. The equivalent ratio for total wealth (including pension rights) was 173 to 1 in London, compared to 70 to 1 nationally.

Limitations in the available data make it hard to compare the experiences of disabled and non-disabled people over the recession, but it is clear that differences remain wide, not just in employment rates, but also in rates of pay when employed. Even if benefits that are intended to compensate for the extra costs disabled people face are included in income, net incomes of households with a disabled member are 16-17% lower than those without a disabled member.

Many of these inequalities remained wide at the end of the period, and some widened after the onset of the economic crisis. But the clearest change was in the economic position of young adults, and in the gradients between how younger and older people have been affected. At older ages, rising employment is encouraging as a response to increased longevity, with a fifth even of those aged 65-69 in employment or self-employed in 2013. For the generation approaching retirement or recently retired, rising wealth levels are an advantage, but this is very unequally distributed. Non-pension wealth for those aged 55-64, for instance, has a ratio of 48:1 between those a tenth of the way from the top of the distribution and those a tenth of the way from the bottom.

At the other end of adulthood, those in their twenties and early thirties are better qualified than any previous generation at the same age. But they have been hardest hit by far than any other age group. They suffered the greatest drop in full-time employment, largest rises in unemployment, and greatest falls in real wages. Median hourly wages were 14-15% lower in real terms for men and women aged 25-29 working full time in 2013 than they had been six years earlier. Even the best-paid in this age group were paid 13-16% less in real terms than their predecessors. Looking at their net incomes as a whole, after allowing for housing costs, median incomes for those in their twenties were 18% or more lower in 2012/13 than five years before, and fell by almost as much for those with the lowest incomes, as well as those with the highest incomes, in their twenties and early thirties. While wealth rose for households aged over 65 between 2006-08 and 2010-12, it fell for younger ones, aged under 65.

These generational developments will have ramifications across society and for many social policies. What can be done to improve the position of even well-qualified young people in today's labour market? Is there a generation who entered the labour market in the toughest times who will now be 'scarred' by comparison with younger cohorts who may enter in better times, with a less jaded experience of the labour market? If wages are so much lower for people in their twenties and early thirties than they were for those of the same age in the late 2000s, what does that mean for the assumptions made when designing the current system of student finance, predicated on a particular level of graduate wages that we no longer have?

In the longer term the generational wealth divide is now immense in relation to annual incomes. Median total wealth (including pension rights) of those aged around 60 reached £425,000 in 2010-12. For those aged around 30 it was £60,000. For the younger generation, to bridge the gap between the two would require them to find £365,000. If this was through their own savings, it would mean saving and/ or pension contributions of £33 each and every day for the next 30 years. This is unlikely to happen as a typical experience. Instead, what will matter most will be what happens to the wealth of the older generations, and to whom it is passed on. But that is also highly unequally distributed, and with it the prospects for members of the generation that has lost most in the years described.

The legacy of the crisis did not fall equally, and the consequences of this will form the backdrop to the way society and public policies evolve over the years and decades to come.

Notes

[1] More details for particular outcomes, population groups and time periods can be found at www.casedata.org.uk or by clicking on chart links in the pdf for Hills et al (2015a). The data include further breakdowns for some outcomes by occupational social class, religious affiliation, area deprivation, whether people report they are in a same-sex couple and family composition.

[2] See Hills et al (2015a, Figure 2.1), based on Labour Force Survey data.

[3] See also Karagiannaki and Platt (2015) for a more detailed examination of changes in individual incomes by gender and ethnicity over a similar period to that covered here.

[4] See Hills et al (2015a, Figure 2.8), based on DWP/Centre for Analysis of Social Exclusion (CASE) analysis of the Households Below Average Income (HBAI) dataset.

[5] See Hills et al (2015a, Figure 3.8), which shows changes at the 10th and 90th percentiles, as well as at the median.

[6] For a more detailed discussion of the differences between regions, see Hills et al (2015a, section 6). For a detailed discussion of changes in inequalities within London during the period, see Vizard et al (2015).

[7] Changes between 2007/08 and 2012/13 in London and selected other regions are shown in Table 13.1 in the next chapter.

THIRTEEN

Spatial inequalities

Ruth Lupton, Polina Obolenskaya and Amanda Fitzgerald

Introduction

Since the economic crisis, increasing political attention has been given to spatial inequalities, perhaps more so than at any time since the late 1990s. Much of the debate and policy effort has focused on economic disparities between regions. In his first major speech as Prime Minister, David Cameron announced a determination to transform England's heavy reliance on a few industries and a few regions (London and the South East), through breathing new economic life into less well performing areas (Cameron, 2010). A number of new policies and funds ensued, largely focused on the Northern cities, as we describe later in this chapter, and by January 2015, the Minister for Cities, Greg Clark, announced that such was the revival of these cities since the coalition took power that the 'picture of a north-south divide pulling apart was certainly true in the previous decade ... in this decade it is changing. North and south are now pulling in the same direction, which is upwards' (quoted in Burton, 2015).

Much less is generally known and heard about disparities in social outcomes between regions and their trends than about economic ones. However, in the wake of the Scottish independence referendum of September 2014, political debate around the 2015 General Election revealed a new sense that the interests of 'the North' and 'the South' were increasingly diverging, to the extent that the politics and policies of London-based government might no longer adequately represent Northern interests. Proponents of a new regional federalism have argued that the issue at stake is not simply the need for a serious focus on the economic revival of areas outside London, but a degree of self-governance to reflect their different conditions, assets, issues and challenges (Mitchell, 2012). The Labour Party leadership campaign, conducted during the summer of 2015, also featured an active debate about how the Party could effectively appeal both to people in the North's working-class industrial communities, and the beneficiaries of the economic success of London and the South East, given their diverging interests and priorities. The Jeremy Corbyn campaign produced its own document on the future of the North (Corbyn, 2015). These arguments focus on the North as a region, not just the economies of its major urban centres.

An interesting feature of this new debate is its move up-scale. On the last occasion at which concerns with spatial inequalities were prominent in government policy and Prime Ministerial statements, when Tony Blair took power in 1997, the focus was on the neighbourhood scale. Pledges to have no more 'no-go' areas and that no one should be seriously disadvantaged by where they live were at the core of Blair's focus on social exclusion. They are entirely absent now, with the nature of the relationships between regional or city-regional fortunes and those of small neighbourhoods not being made explicit.

Hence both regional and neighbourhood-level spatial inequalities are the focus of this chapter. In the first part, we examine the basis for claims that different parts of England have diverged in terms of economic outcomes, and social ones, since the economic crisis, or that they have not. We give more attention to regional disparities since these are the focus of current policy interest, but we also look at inequalities between neighbourhoods and the geography of neighbourhood deprivation since the recession. Consistent with the rest of the book and with the devolution of so many relevant areas of policy and data, we do not explore differences between England, Scotland, Wales and Northern Ireland, or differences within those countries, although these would clearly be of interest in the context of parallel debates about independence and further devolution. Within England, our principal focus is on the different trajectories of London and the North (the North West, North East, and Yorkshire and the Humber regions). In other work in the Social Policy in a Cold Climate programme we show data for all regions (see Hills et al, 2015a; Obolenskaya et al, 2016).

In the second part of the chapter, we review the ways in which successive governments since the economic crisis have approached the problems of spatial disparities. In contrast to the approach taken in the first part of this book, we consider policies after considering trends in outcomes, principally to avoid the suggestion of a precise causal relationship. Explicitly spatial policies are only ever one part of the jigsaw of economic and social policies, demographic trends, population movements and economic conditions that affect the distribution of outcomes across space. The trends described here might be considered the cumulative result of all the policies described in this book, and more, not just those that have focused on regional economies or neighbourhood regeneration. Nevertheless, how governments use spatial policies in order to address spatial inequalities is an important part of the picture, and one that has been remarkably inconsistent and contested. This brings us full circle back to conclude with the policies of the current Conservative government and to look forward to the future.

Trends in economic outcomes at the regional and neighbourhood levels

It is now relatively well documented that the spatial effects of the recession were not as originally expected. Given the origins of the crisis in the banking sector, it was widely anticipated that job losses and wider impacts on the sustainability of firms would be worst in London, and in the surrounding South East economy. However, this proved to be far from the case. Figure 13.1 (see Martin et al, 2015) shows a measure of economic performance, cumulative growth of gross value added (GVA), on a regional basis back to 1971, to give a long-term perspective. Three broad trends stand out: the relatively strong performance of the South West, South East and East Midlands throughout the period; the long-run decline of the North East, North West and West Midlands; and the rapid and continued upturn in the performance of London since the mid-1990s, transforming it from being one of the lowest performing regions to one of the highest within a 20-year period. Far from the recession hitting London hardest, the capital saw virtually no dip in GVA between 2007 and 2009, and a rapid increase thereafter, outstripping every other region, while the North East, North West and Yorkshire and the Humber (the regions comprising 'the North') suffered the worst declines. The effect of the recession was not therefore to check the growing divide between London and the cities and regions of the North, but to exacerbate it. This pattern of uneven growth is also evident in house prices that continued to diverge following the recession. In London, average prices rose 25%, while in all three Northern regions, they fell between 2007 and 2013 (DCLG, 2014).

This is not to say that London was not hard hit in employment terms by the economic crisis. Figure 13.2 shows the employment rate of London and the Northern regions from 2007. As can be seen, London had a lower employment rate compared to the Northern regions at that time. In fact, it was the lowest across all regions in England. London's employment fell sharply after the summer of

Figure 13.1: GVA (2011 prices), UK regions. cumulative annual differentials, 1971-2013

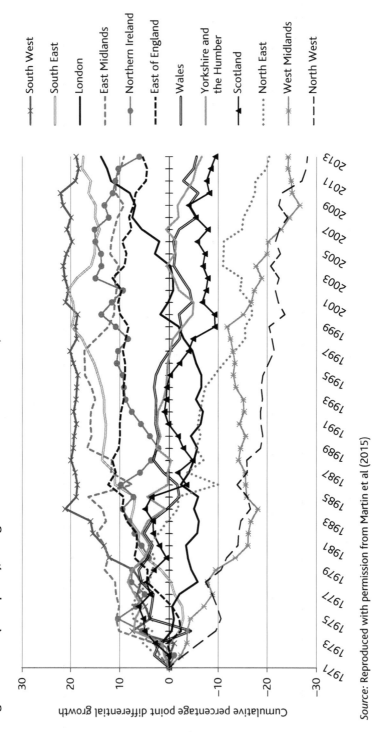

Source: Reproduced with permission from Martin et al (2015)

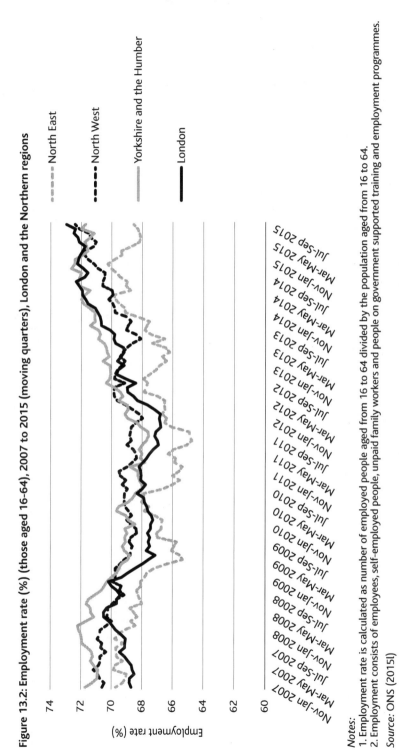

Figure 13.2: Employment rate (%) (those aged 16-64), 2007 to 2015 (moving quarters), London and the Northern regions

Notes:
1. Employment rate is calculated as number of employed people aged from 16 to 64 divided by the population aged from 16 to 64.
2. Employment consists of employees, self-employed people, unpaid family workers and people on government supported training and employment programmes.

Source: ONS (2015l)

2008, remaining lower than in the North West and Yorkshire and the Humber. But employment figures post-2012 show a rapid recovery with London's employment rate overtaking all three Northern regions for the first time (since November-January 2007) in July-September 2014. Moreover, data from the Business Register and Employment Survey (BRES), published by the Office for National Statistics (ONS), shows that growth in the total number of employees (in both private and public sector posts) between 2008 and 2013 only occurred in the Southern regions and London, the East of England and the North West. In the remaining regions, including the North East and Yorkshire and the Humber, there was a decline in the total number of employees. Growth in London was substantially greater than elsewhere: the percentage change in the total number of employees was almost 8% in London, compared to a little over 1.5% in the next closest region, the South East, and under 1% in the only Northern region with overall growth, the North West. Furthermore, the only regions where growth in the number of public sector employees occurred were London and the East of England. Public sector job growth had accounted for much of the overall growth in a number of Northern cities during the 2000s, making them particularly vulnerable to cuts in these areas (Larkin, 2009).

London's outstanding economic performance has brought its own problems, not least a growing housing affordability crisis. Affordability for first-time buyers, expressed as a gross house price to earnings ratio, had been worsening across all regions since the mid-1990s and up to the first quarter of 2008 (second quarter for London), at which point it improved briefly due to the housing market crash. Following the 2008 recession London's house prices to earnings ratio increased substantially, while remaining relatively flat across the Northern regions (see Figure 13.3).

Since the recession, real earnings fell across all region (Hills et al, 2015a), at the same time as house prices and rents increased (Valuation Office Agency, 2011; DCLG, 2012b), particularly in London. This, as we saw in Chapter Twelve, meant that the fall of real net income after housing costs was particularly sharp in London across the income distribution, especially among the least affluent Londoners. Although there are some uncertainties surrounding data on changes over time in the highest and lowest incomes in each region (because of small sample sizes), the figures suggest that between 2007/08 and 2012/13 real net income after housing costs in London fell by 11.8% at the median and 10.3% at the 90th percentile (most affluent), but by 18.3% at the 10th percentile (least affluent). A few other regions experienced

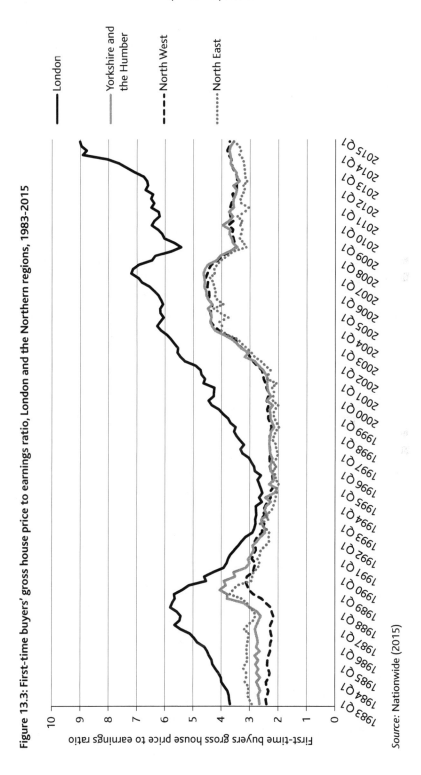

Figure 13.3: First-time buyers' gross house price to earnings ratio, London and the Northern regions, 1983-2015

London

Yorkshire and the Humber

North West

North East

First-time buyers gross house price to earnings ratio

10
9
8
7
6
5
4
3
2
1
0

1983 Q1
1984 Q1
1985 Q1
1986 Q1
1987 Q1
1988 Q1
1989 Q1
1990 Q1
1991 Q1
1992 Q1
1993 Q1
1994 Q1
1995 Q1
1996 Q1
1997 Q1
1998 Q1
1999 Q1
2000 Q1
2001 Q1
2002 Q1
2003 Q1
2004 Q1
2005 Q1
2006 Q1
2007 Q1
2008 Q1
2009 Q1
2010 Q1
2011 Q1
2012 Q1
2013 Q1
2014 Q1
2015 Q1

Source: Nationwide (2015)

comparable reductions in net income at the median and at the higher end of income distribution, but least affluent people in regions other than London appeared relatively more protected with a much lower reduction in their net income. The changes in London led to a substantial increase in income inequalities in London, as Table 13.1 shows, making London's position as by far the most unequal region even more pronounced (see also Chapter Twelve).

Turning to the neighbourhood level, it was also the case that the recession hit the poorest neighbourhoods harder than the rest – a pattern that might be expected as areas with the least secure employment and/or workers with the loosest labour market attachment are more likely to see their jobs in danger or reductions in hours or pay. Figure 13.4 shows trends in worklessness at the neighbourhood level. 'Worklessness' here is defined as the total number of people claiming Jobseeker's Allowance, Incapacity Benefit/Serious Disablement Allowance and Employment Support Allowance, and shown as a rate of the working-age population. Figure 13.4 defines the 'highest workless neighbourhoods' as the 10% with the highest worklessness rates in 2000. Neighbourhoods are defined as lower super output areas (LSOAs), areas of around 1,500 population on average. The trend to 2008 was that worklessness fell more in these neighbourhoods, closing the gap with others. The gap widened again during the recession. However, it is noticeable that the increase in worklessness rates in the recent recession did not take them back to the levels of the early 2000s, perhaps reflecting both the nature of this recession, which was characterised by reductions in hours and wages, and perhaps some sustainable economic gains made during growth

Table 13.1: Income inequalities (90:10 ratios) in 2007/08 and 2012/13 (£/week, adjusted for household size), London and the North of England

	2007/08	2012/13
a) Before housing costs		
London	5.6	5.2
North West	3.8	3.6
Yorkshire and the Humber	3.7	3.6
North East	3.6	3.3
b) After housing costs		
London	8.4	9.1
North West	4.8	4.6
Yorkshire and Humberside*	4.3	4.6
North East	4.2	4.2

Source: Hills et al. (2010, 2015a)

Figure 13.4: Worklessness rates for the highest workless neighbourhoods compared with others, 2000-13

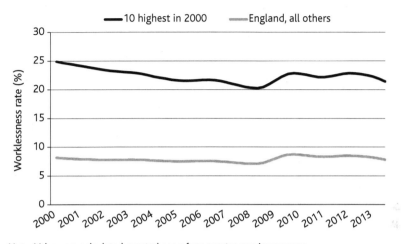

Note: Values are calculated quarterly as a four-quarter moving average.

Sources: DWP working-age client group for small areas (DWP/NOMIS). Mid-year population estimates for LSOAs, England and Wales (ONS)

in the worst-off neighbourhoods. The poorest neighbourhoods have also apparently benefited from the onset of recovery, with the gap beginning to close again from 2013. However, it is hard to be certain of this since the changes may be due in part to the tougher conditions for benefit claims. More detailed analysis, reported in Lupton and Fitzgerald (2015), also shows a more complex picture. When 'highest worklessness' neighbourhoods are defined in contemporary terms for each quarter, not in terms of a fixed set identified at the start of the period, the pattern is one of a steeper rise in worklessness during the recession and a more muted recovery. A clear trend is that worklessness rates in poor London neighbourhoods have declined more rapidly than elsewhere in the country, largely due to the rapid increase in the working-age population overall, which far exceeds the growth in the workless population.

The comparison between these two sets of figures suggests that the 'worst' areas (those most in need of targeting) are changing over time. An indication of the nature of the changes is provided by comparison between Indices of Multiple Deprivation (IMD) produced in 2010 (and using data mainly from 2007 and 2008) and those produced in 2015 (using data mainly from 2013). The IMD are heavily weighted on indicators of employment and economic deprivation. Figure 13.5 shows the distribution of the most deprived 10% of neighbourhoods by region in 2010 and 2015, ordered by the region with the highest

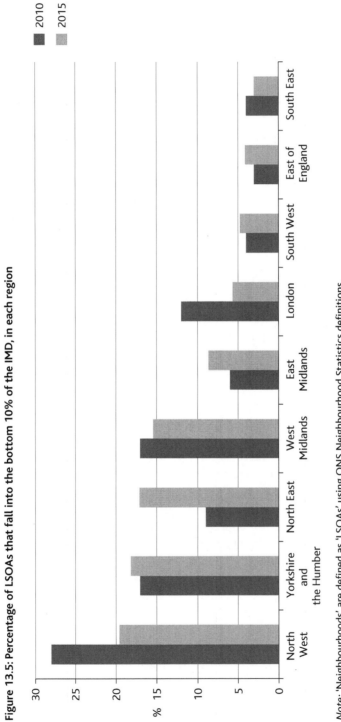

Figure 13.5: Percentage of LSOAs that fall into the bottom 10% of the IMD, in each region

Note: 'Neighbourhoods' are defined as 'LSOAs' using ONS Neighbourhood Statistics definitions.

Sources: DCLG, English Indices of Deprivation' (2010b and 2015c)

proportion in 2015. Increases in deprivation are particularly seen in the North East and East Midlands, with decreases in the North West and London. These data were released shortly before this book went to press. Further analysis is needed to reveal the types of areas that moved up and down the rankings (for example, urban, rural and coastal locations).

Trends in social outcomes

An intriguing and much less well explored question is whether the divergence of economic fortunes between different regions and areas has been mirrored by a divergence in social outcomes – for example, school attainment, levels of health or illness, or local conditions and people's satisfaction with where they live.

Our analysis at regional level suggests that the pattern of London pulling away from the rest was also seen in the early years and in education outcomes. Between 2007 and 2012 the proportion of under-fives reaching a good level of development, as assessed by the early years foundation stage profile, was increasing everywhere (Obolenskaya et al, 2016). There is a break in the series between 2013 and 2014, but the trend of improvement continued. In this period (2007-14), London moved from being among the lowest performing of the regions on this indicator to being one of the best performing. In the same period the gap between children eligible for free school meals (FSM) and those not eligible (non-FSM pupils) in London versus the rest widened on this early years' development indicator, with the difference between FSM and non-FSM performance having closed in London more than elsewhere (see Figure 13.6).

London has also maintained and in some respects increased its lead in performance at GCSE level. This is a complex picture due to changes in school performance tables and GCSE assessment in 2014 (for a fuller account, see Lupton and Thomson, 2015a). The changes to performance tables meant that vocational qualifications counted less towards school performance. As a result, some students were steered away from these qualifications. Young people eligible for FSM had tended to rely more on vocational subjects to reach GCSE expected levels (House of Commons Education Committee, 2014) so were more likely to be affected. The changes to GCSE assessment were designed to make GCSEs more challenging.

At a national level, the proportion of pupils achieving 5 or more GCSEs at grades A*-C (and including English and maths) improved between 2008 and 2013, but fell in 2014. For the lower level of

Figure 13.6: Percentage point gap in a 'good level of development' in the early years foundation stage profile between children not FSM eligible and children FSM eligible, 2007-14

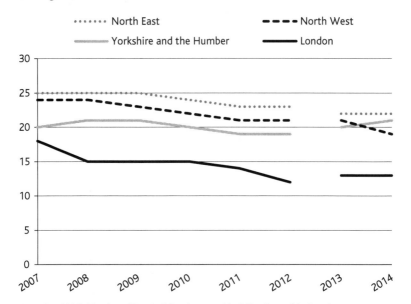

Notes: For 2007-12, a 'good level of development' is defined as achieving six or more points across the seven scales of personal, social and emotional development and communication, language and literacy and also 78 or more points across all 13 scales. For 2013 and 2014, the assessment framework was changed and a 'good level of development' was defined as reaching the expected level in the early learning goals within the three prime areas of learning and within literacy and numeracy. This means that 2013 results onwards are not comparable with earlier years. Nonetheless, the broad trend of a greater narrowing of gaps in London compared with the Northern regions persists.

Sources: DfE SFR 39/2010 (DfE, 2010f), DfE SFR 30/2012 (DfE, 2012c), DfE SFR 46/2014 (DfE, 2014e)

achievement (5 A*-C of any kind), the FSM/non-FSM gap (which had been reducing) increased in 2014, back to its level in 2006. This shows that most of the earlier improvement had been due to the uptake of vocational qualifications. At the higher level of 5 A*-C including English and maths, there was very little change in the gap, suggesting that at this level, fewer students were relying on vocational subjects (see Chapter Four for more details). Regional differences are, however, apparent. For the higher 5 A*-C with English and maths, there was little change in regional rankings between 2013 and 2014, with London remaining ahead of the Northern regions in terms of its performance throughout the years between 2007 and 2014. However, at the lower level of 5 A*-C (any subject) (shown in Figure 13.7), the pattern is different. In London, there was a smaller fall in overall

Figure 13.7: Percentage of pupils achieving 5+ GCSEs A*-C and equivalents, 2007-13 and 2014, London and the Northern regions

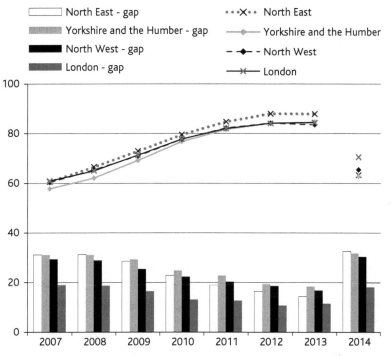

Notes: State-funded schools only. Figures for 2014 are revised; all others are final. Figures for 2014 are based on the new counting rules.

Sources: DfE SFR 03/2012 (DfE, 2012b), DfE SFR 06/2015 (DfE, 2015e)

attainment in 2014 than in the Northern regions, and the FSM/non-FSM gap increased by less. This suggests that progress made between 2007 and 2013 was more dependent on vocational qualifications in the North than in London.

While a number of health-related outcomes saw an improvement across all regions since 2007, London has been leading on these in comparison to the Northern regions. Since the recession (data for 2006-09), life expectancy at birth has seen the largest improvement in London compared to any other region for both men and women, diverging from the visibly slower improvement in the North (ONS, 2014a). Similarly, life expectancy at 75 has shown continuous improvement since before the recession in London and was maintained afterwards, but showed signs of deterioration or slowing down of progress in a number of other regions including the North in the last few years of data (2009-11 to 2011-13) (HSCIC, nd). Furthermore, improvements in premature mortality rates from major causes of death including cardiovascular disease, respiratory disease and cancer were slightly more noticeable in London compared to the Northern regions since 2007 and particularly so in the case of mortality from liver disease – which had actually increased in all regions except London (and to a certain degree the North East for women) (Obolenskaya et al, 2016). Meanwhile, risks of poor mental health and age-standardised rates of suicides in London have not seen the deterioration observed elsewhere in the country since the recession. After a long-term improvement in the age-standardised suicide rate in England up to 2007, suicides among men began to increase after the recession, rising significantly in a number of regions including both those in the North and in the South, with the only exception being London – where suicide rates continued to fall (see Figure 13.8). Furthermore, London remained unaffected by the significantly increased risk of poor mental health since 2008 observed among women in some parts of the country such as in the North East and East (Obolenskaya et al, 2016; Vizard and Obolenskaya, 2015).

However, as might be expected given widening economic inequality, falling incomes at the bottom of the distribution and rising housing costs, social outcomes relating to these issues look less favourable for London. Both child and overall poverty, defined as the proportion living in households with an income (after housing costs) below 60%

Figure 13.8: Age-standardised suicide rates among men in London and the North, 2002-13 registrations

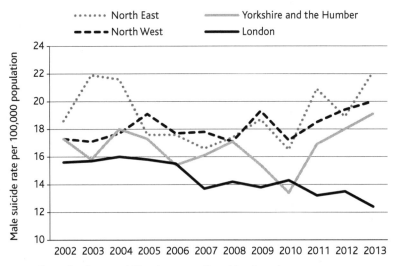

Notes: Figures for those aged 15 and over, usually resident in each area.
Source: ONS (2015e)

of the contemporary median household income, have been higher in London than in any other region since the early 2000s, with less improvement since the recession compared to many other regions, particularly compared to the North East, resulting in a divergence of London and the North. Between 2006/07-2008/09 and 2011/12-2013/14, the largest decline in child poverty was in the North East, where the rate was the highest among the Northern regions at the start of the period (35%), and fell by 9 percentage points to 26% by 2011/12-2013/14, improving the North East's relative ranking across the regions (see Figure 13.9). Child poverty in London fell only slightly over the same period, from 40% to 37%. During this time, overall poverty has also decreased, but not as much as child poverty, with overall poverty rates improving by 2-3 percentage points in both London and the Northern regions (not shown here; for more details, see Obolenskaya et al, 2016).

Indicators of housing stress also look worse for London. Although we do not have overcrowding data for the period just before the recession, census data for 2001 and 2011 clearly indicate the extent of the problem in the capital and its slow improvement. More than 17% of households in London lived in overcrowded conditions in 2001, reducing to 11% by 2011. In other regions, the proportion

Figure 13.9: Child poverty rate by region, average for 2006/07 to 2008/09 and for 2011/12 to 2013/14 (after housing costs)

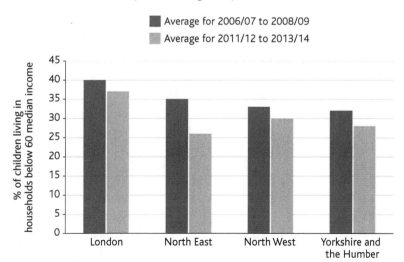

Note: Child poverty rate defined as the percentage of children living in households below 60% median income.

Source: DWP HBAI dataset 1994/95 to 2013/14

of households living in overcrowded conditions was below 6% in 2001 and down to 4.5% or lower in 2011 (The Poverty Site, nd; ONS, 2014e). Analysis by Fitzpatrick et al (2015) shows that between 2009/10 and 2013/14 homelessness increased sharply in London (an 80% increase), but fell by 14% in the North, resulting in divergence in homelessness between London and the other regions. Finally, London also falls behind across a number of indicators from the (adult) social care outcomes framework for the period between 2010/11 and 2014/15, including social care-related quality of life, feelings of control over one's daily life and the proportion of adults with learning disabilities living in their own homes (HSCIC, nd). The latter could be, at least partially, due to the capital's housing problems as a move to independence cannot be delivered by social care alone, and requires a strong partnership with specialist providers and housing authorities to deliver appropriate, affordable accommodation.

At neighbourhood level, a much more limited set of indicators can be tracked. Official poverty measures (the proportion of households below 60% of the median income) are not available at neighbourhood scale. As a proxy for poverty, we use the unadjusted means-tested benefit rate (UMBR). This is the total number of people in an area claiming Income Support or Employment and Support Allowance, Jobseeker's Allowance or the Guarantee Element of Pension Credit, divided by the number of households (for more details on this indicator, see Fenton, 2013). In both poorer and richer neighbourhoods, UMBR rates increased between 2007 and 2010 as the recession hit, and fell back slightly by 2013, partly because eligibility for some of these benefits was reduced as well as because of economic recovery. The rise and then the fall left the gap between the richest and poorest neighbourhoods higher than before the financial crisis, but lower than in 2010 (see Figure 13.10).

On social indicators, the limited evidence available suggests that progress continues to be made towards narrowing gaps in outcomes between neighbourhoods, but that gaps remain very large on key indicators. School attainment at GCSE level has been reported by decile of the Index of Deprivation Affecting Children (IDACI) of pupil residence, from 2007 to 2013 (see Table 13.2), although not yet for the first year (2014) in which gaps widened at a national level. In the period to 2013, gaps between areas reduced considerably, particularly at the level of 5 GCSEs A*-C grades, but also for the higher threshold of 5 A*-C grades including English and maths. Notably a revision to the 2013 data, applying the 2014 counting rules, suggests a slight widening of the gap, consistent with the findings reported above,

Figure 13.10: Means-tested benefit rate for the poorest and richest deciles of neighbourhoods

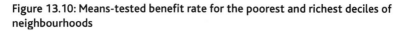

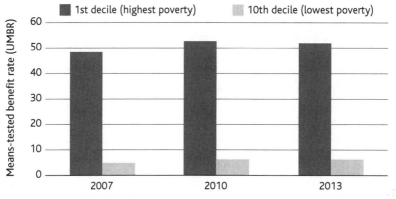

Source: Lupton and Fitzgerald (2013)

Table 13.2: Gaps in GCSE attainment between the most and least deprived deciles of IDACI, 2007-13

	2007	2008	2009	2010	2011	2012	2013
5 A*-C grades	36.3	32.6	27.2	20.6	16.2	13.4	11.8
5 A*-C including English and maths	43.1	40.5	38.9	35.6	33.7	30.6	29.6

Source: DfE SFR 06/2015 (DfE, 2015e)

that gains for poorer pupils (and areas) were largely made through vocational qualifications and are unlikely to hold up under the new assessment and accountability regime.

Following the recommendations of the Marmot Review (2010), data on life expectancy by neighbourhood deprivation is now officially monitored as part of the new public health outcomes framework. This data is only available for 2009-11 and 2010-12, thus providing no real evidence of the effect of policy change. The data, shown in full in a parallel paper by Vizard and Obolenskaya (2015), illustrates the deeply embedded health inequalities that remain in England, with a marked social gradient reflected in both the range and the slope index of inequality. The latter was as high as 20.1 for healthy life expectancy for females in 2009-2011, decreasing marginally to 19.8 in 2010-12.

Policy approaches

Since 2007, the Labour and coalition governments have responded to this unfolding issue of an increasingly dominant capital and diverging economic and social outcomes with increased effort to promote regional economic rebalancing. However, there has been little specific attention paid to addressing short-term disparities in social outcomes through spatially redistributive social policies. In fact, the coalition's reforms to the welfare system and its local authority spending cuts appear to have been 'spatially regressive' in that they have disproportionately affected areas with the greatest levels of need. Furthermore, the coalition took a more hands-off approach to the economic and social problems of the poorest neighbourhoods, discontinuing a number of central government funding streams. Arguments for reducing spatial inequalities on the grounds of social equity rather than economic efficiency have become less prominent than they were a decade ago. We review these developments in turn.

Economic development and regional economic rebalancing

The intention to narrow regional economic disparities had been a feature of Labour government policy prior to the economic crisis, with a two-part target being established to improve the economic performance of all the English regions and to reduce the gap in economic growth rates between the regions. The principal mechanism was the Regional Development Agencies (RDAs) established in 1999. RDAs were responsible for the development of regional economic strategies and aimed to create the conditions for growth through investment in physical infrastructure, business support and skills development. However, while evaluation suggested that the RDAs were successful in promoting growth (adding £4.50 of regional GVA for every £1 spent), they did not close the economic gaps between regions (Marshall, 2008; Crowley et al, 2012), perhaps not surprising in the face of broader economic trends and the lack of a more interventionist strategy that would disproportionately benefit less well performing regions. It is salient to note that the RDAs had initially been conceived as part of a broader move towards political as well as economic devolution, with elected regional assemblies also being envisaged in a 2002 White Paper, *Your region, your choice* (Cabinet Office and DETR, 2002). The overwhelming defeat of the proposal in a North East referendum in 2004 put an end to these plans, leaving London as the only region with an elected assembly and the other RDAs doing economic planning in the absence of a regional governance tier.

After 2007, Labour's policies developed in a number of ways that foreshadowed developments under the coalition. One development was a shift to a more explicit 'industrial strategy', with two White Papers, *Innovation Nation* (DIUS, 2008) and *New industries, New Jobs* (BERR, 2009) setting out plans to identify key sectors and industries for intervention, supported by a Capital Fund of £750 million. Another was an increasing focus on the 'city-region' as the engine of economic development, with the introduction of multi-area agreements between groups of neighbouring authorities and powers for some cities to develop combined city authorities. At the same time, there was a review of regeneration policy, more closely integrating economic development, housing and urban regeneration, and a refocusing of existing programmes (such as Housing Market Renewal and the Neighbourhood Renewal Fund) on economic growth and tackling worklessness (Ferrari, 2007; Lupton et al, 2013a). As we discuss later, this subsumed Blairite ambitions to correct spatial inequalities on social justice grounds under an economic regeneration umbrella.

The election of the coalition government in May 2010 brought some immediate structural changes, with the abolition of the RDAs and the establishment instead of business-led Local Enterprise Partnerships (LEPs) at the level of the functional economic area. This move signalled both a shift away from the region as the locus of activity and a move towards business leadership of economic development. Thirty-nine LEPs, of various sizes, were established covering the whole country. In an extension of Labour's 'localist' approach, LEPs could negotiate new Local Growth Deals to fund housing and infrastructure developments, while City Deal status gave 28 urban areas powers to attract private investment in return for pledges on innovation and efficiency. However, the coalition's efforts were criticised as 'piecemeal' by former minister Lord Heseltine who was brought in to review the government's growth strategy in 2012 (BIS, 2012). Heseltine made 89 wide-ranging recommendations, including re-establishing a sub-national structure (Local Growth Teams, replacing the abolished RDAs and government offices) to coordinate the activities of central government departments and build central–local partnerships. At the heart of his report, however, was 'a major reconfiguration of responsibilities for economic development' (BIS, 2012, p 7), with central government producing clear policies for each industrial sector and clear guidance on priorities, and empowering LEPs to develop and deliver local economic strategies with a single pot of unring-fenced funding created by pooling budgets for skills, infrastructure, employment support, housing, regeneration and business support.

The government took up most of Heseltine's recommendations, including Local Growth Teams, creating industrial strategies in

11 key sectors, asking LEPs to develop multi-year strategies, and encouraging the development of combined authorities. It also announced its intention to devolve some central funding for housing and infrastructure into a single pot, devolved to local level. This came to fruition in July 2014, with the announcement of a set of Local Growth Deals, negotiated with LEPs and creating local 'single pots'. Growth Deals were presented both as an opportunity to rebalance the economy, to 'end our over-reliance on the banks and the City of London and generate growth, jobs and ambition in towns and cities all across England', and as a localist move, 'we're placing power and money in the hands of the people who know how to spend it best, making a real difference to local communities' (Prime Minister's Office, 2014). In June 2014, the theme of regional rebalancing was explicitly taken up in a speech by the Chancellor, George Osborne, in which he celebrated the revitalisation of Northern cities individually but argued for the need to join them up into a 'Northern Powerhouse' capable of rivalling London – through investments in transport, science and innovation, culture and devolved power. Notably, however, the proposal for political devolution was to be at the city-region, not the regional level. In November 2014, devolution of powers over business growth and skills was extended to the combined authority of Greater Manchester, along with the announcement that the city-region would have the first elected 'metro area' mayor.

Disparities in social outcomes and the role of spatially redistributive social policies

The shift in power from Labour to the coalition arguably therefore led to a more concerted effort to address regional economic disparities. Albeit this took a cities-based approach that was perceived in some circles as a political move by the Conservative Chancellor to gain more influence over the North's Labour-led urban councils and/or to deflect any appetite for regional political devolution, statements about the need to rebalance the economy and rebuild the industrial base of the North became increasingly prominent. However, at the same time, the coalition's emphasis on 'localism' resulted in a less prominent central government focus on spatial inequalities in social outcomes.

This is a complex picture, since different approaches were being taken in different areas of social policy, and some withdrawal from the spatial policies of Labour under Tony Blair had already occurred under Gordon Brown's government from 2007.

The most prominent statement of the coalition's localist approach to reducing geographical disparities in social outcomes was in the area of area regeneration/neighbourhood renewal. Neighbourhood-level interventions to equalise living conditions and opportunities (regardless of longer-term policies on economic rebalancing) had been a hallmark of Labour policy under Blair, with the intention that 'within 10 to 20 years no one should be seriously disadvantaged by where they live' (SEU, 2001, p 3). As Lupton (2013) describes in more detail, this approach had a social justice rationale, independent of arguments about the need for economic regeneration of the poorest areas. This led to an emphasis on the quality of local public services and living conditions as well as on outcomes, because 'people on low incomes should not have to suffer conditions and services that are failing and so different from what the rest of the population receives' (SEU, 2001, p 8). It was also marked by an insistence that it was for central government to take responsibility for these disparities. Blair's government set 'floor standards' for indicators such as education and health below which no area should fall, calling these 'the social equivalent of the minimum wage' and arguing that these would make sure that the poorest areas no longer went 'unnoticed' (NRU, 2008). A new Neighbourhood Renewal Unit (NRU) and teams in the Government Offices for the Regions were responsible for coordinating and monitoring the activity of government departments in accordance with a National Strategy for Neighbourhood Renewal (NSNR). New multi-agency Local Strategic Partnerships were required to develop Neighbourhood Renewal Strategies supported by a Neighbourhood Renewal Fund (NRF).

Lupton et al (2013a) give a longer account of policies in this period, as well as documenting a substantial shift in policy under Gordon Brown. Despite evidence that neighbourhood renewal policies had been effective in their own terms (improving local conditions, services and outcomes) and represented value for money, the idea of 'neighbourhood renewal' was dropped after 2007 in favour of 'regeneration', defined in economic terms as restoring areas to market functionality and thus reducing their long-term dependence on additional subsidies. Existing programmes (Housing Market Renewal and the NRF – which became the Working Neighbourhoods Fund) were adapted to give them a stronger emphasis on tackling worklessness. Neighbourhood interventions were required to be more strongly linked to sub-regional economic strategies. The NRU was disbanded and targets for reducing neighbourhood disparities became incorporated in the emerging multi-area agreement structure for managing central/local government relations. On this basis, Houghton (2010) argues that it was Labour who 'killed' neighbourhood renewal in England. However, the coalition went several steps further, as described in Lupton and Fitzgerald (2015).

All existing neighbourhood renewal programmes were discontinued and there was no new programme of comprehensive area-based initiatives (such as Labour's New Deal for Communities or the City Challenges and Single Regeneration Budget of the Thatcher/ Major years) – although modest funds were retained for supporting community organising and specific action in coalfields and coastal communities. No aims or targets in relation to neighbourhood disadvantage or inequalities were set out in the coalition's programme for government or any subsequent policy document, and the government stopped monitoring spatial inequalities. Its policy statement, *Regeneration to enable growth: What the government is doing in support of community-led regeneration* (DCLG, 2011), instead articulated a symbiotic relationship in which local regeneration efforts would strengthen communities and stimulate economic growth, which would, in turn, help breathe economic life into areas. The document set out policies the government was already pursuing (such as reformed and decentralised public services, removing barriers to local action and targeted infrastructure investments), which would support such efforts. Crucially, the conditions of the poorest areas or spatial inequalities in general were not seen as a central government responsibility. Responding to a highly critical report from the House of Commons Communities and Local Government Committee (2011), which claimed that it had ignored the lessons of the past and had no strategy for dealing with the problems of the poorest communities, the government argued 'it is for local partners ... to work together to develop local solutions to local challenges. *If* local regeneration and growth are deemed local priorities then it is for local partners to determine the appropriate plans and strategies to deliver this' (DCLG, 2012c, p 1; emphasis added).

In other areas of social policy, the coalition also typically eschewed explicitly spatial policies, in the sense of ones targeted at specific areas or designed to narrow gaps between areas. It discontinued policies such as the City Challenges and Aimhigher in education (see Chapter Four) and the 'spearhead' areas initiative to address inequalities in health. Instead, it relied on a combination of economic growth, 'people-based' policies, for example, welfare reform (see Chapter Two), Pupil Premium funding for disadvantaged pupils (see Chapter Four) and a new public health premium to incentivise local authorities to improve health outcomes and reduce inequalities (see Chapter Eight), and 'localist measures'. The latter included the emerging policy of devolution of powers and budgets that was signalled in the Greater Manchester agreement, the extension of new rights and powers over planning, land use and community facilities to local communities in the Localism Act 2011, and reforms to local government finance such as the partial retention of business rates from 2013/14 and the New Homes Bonus that was designed to incentivise housebuilding.

The adoption, or not, of spatial policies is significant in that it signals the importance governments attach to geographical differences in opportunities and outcomes, as well as their recognition of the origins of these problems in industrial decline, and the ways in which economic and social problems combine in disadvantaged areas. Whether or not governments choose to highlight these disparities in living conditions, opportunities and outcomes in different regions, local authorities and neighbourhoods, says something about their understanding of inequality and how it might be tackled. However, such targeted policies only ever absorb a very tiny proportion of public spending. Of much greater importance is the extent to which mainstream public spending is skewed towards areas of disadvantage in response to their additional needs. The mechanisms for this distribution include the funding formulae of central government departments and spending on local government. It is beyond the scope of this chapter to conduct a spatial analysis of government spending. Nor, so far as we are aware, have other researchers carried out this exercise in the spatial disaggregation of mainstream spending. However, concerns about the spatial effects of public spending decisions have been highlighted in a number of other recent studies. Hamnett (2014) points out the marked geography of existing welfare spending towards large cities and ex-industrial areas, meaning that cuts in these 'people-based' funding streams will also fall disproportionately in these areas. He also notes that the particular characteristics of areas (for example, high rents in London and depressed labour markets in peripheral industrial areas) mean that welfare cuts implemented on the basis of overall 'fairness' will have differential effects in different places. A prominent example is the prediction that the majority of neighbourhoods in inner London will become unaffordable to people on Housing Benefit as a result of changes to Local Housing Allowance (LHA) and the overall benefit cap.

As to local government spending, our earlier analysis of local authority spending (Lupton et al, 2013a) showed that, under Labour, there was a substantial increase in funding to more deprived local authorities as a result both of specific regeneration grants and the introduction or expansion of services targeted towards reducing poverty and social exclusion (such as Sure Start). In 1998/99 the most deprived fifth of local authorities got about two-thirds more funding per head than the richest fifth of local authorities, rising to 73% more in 2008/09. For districts the percentage increase was even more pronounced. Hastings et al (2013) calculate that local authorities overall had a cut in expenditure of 29% from the peak in 2008/09, and that the effect of the cut has been to undo the 'strategy of equality' whereby more deprived authorities were better funded. They calculate that over the 2010/11 to 2014/15 period the most deprived fifth of all-purpose authorities lost £250 per capita compared with £150 per capita for the least deprived fifth. This pattern is confirmed in analysis including two-tier authorities (Berman and Keep, 2012; Keep, 2014). Berry and White (2014) show the regional effect: the North West was the biggest loser of local government spending, followed by Yorkshire and the Humber and the North East. The East and South East of England were least affected by the cuts. Although it is too early yet to see any firm evidence, it seems likely that the consequence of a local government settlement increasingly weighted towards incentives rather than need will be to further advantage local authorities in areas well placed for local economic development at the expense of others in more marginalised or peripheral situations.

Conclusion

Spatial inequalities at the regional, local authority and neighbourhood levels were pronounced in England prior to the economic crisis and had been the subject of numerous and varying policy efforts since the late 1960s (Lupton, 2003; Dorling et al, 2007; Tallon, 2010). Martin (2015, p 237) argues that one effect of the financial crisis was that it revealed that far from solving these problems, the boom of the 2000s had been 'a form of development that was highly unbalanced ... between consumption and investment, between services and production, between state revenues and spending, between rich and poor, and, spatially, between different cities and regions.' The data presented in this chapter mainly date from 2013 or 2014, thus cannot reveal the most recent trends. What they tend to show, however, is that while there is some evidence of the Northern economies picking up since 2012 (and thus 'pulling in the same direction' as London, as Greg Clark suggested), London is tending to pull further ahead, leading to a wider regional divide, not a narrower one. Moreover, there is evidence of greater improvement in London than in the North on a number of indicators of education and health, suggesting a wider social divide that could be expected to underpin further economic divergence in the future. However, inequalities within London have increased. At the neighbourhood scale, gaps in poverty rates between poorer and richer neighbourhoods increased, as might be expected, during the recession, and have not yet returned to their pre-crisis level. And while there is some evidence of continuing slow progress towards narrowing gaps in social outcomes between richer and poorer neighbourhoods, this is very modest and very large gaps remain. Thus inequality in England continues to have a marked spatial pattern.

One of the outcomes of the crisis appears to be a new political consensus around the need for regional economic rebalancing, and a new debate about how this should be done. The election of the Conservative government in May 2015 heralded further commitments to the creation of a Northern Powerhouse and further promises of further devolution of powers to enable local economic development, notably the retention of business rates by local councils. The debate leading up to the 2015 General Election and beyond also surfaced more wide-ranging proposals. For example, Martin et al (2015) propose fiscal devolution, a new governance structure based around regions or city-regions, a regionally based investment bank, and further decentralisation of public administration and employment. Jeremy Corbyn's *Northern future* policy document (Corbyn, 2015) also proposed greater access to finance as well as decentralisation of power and a regional industrial policy based on rebuilding the industrial base of the North, investing in digital infrastructure, transport and culture and policies to prevent the 'brain-drain' of graduates from Northern universities to London. These developments suggest that 'regional policy', whatever its form, is likely to take a more prominent place on the political stage than it has for several decades.

This chapter also demonstrates, however, the complexity of the problem of spatial inequalities. While in the long term disparities in social outcomes such as health and education as well as local living conditions are likely to be driven by the strength of regional economies, in the short term they reflect historical and current economic geographies and the extent to which social policies have been successful in ameliorating current problems and supporting more equal futures. Arguments for spatially redistributive social policies can therefore be made on grounds of equity and social justice as well as on grounds of economic efficiency. Since the economic crisis, and particularly since 2010, the trend in policy has been for such arguments to be neglected in favour of an emphasis on growth, and indeed, there is some evidence that spending has been increasingly disconnected from need – a move that is likely to lead to greater spatial disparities in the short term. The extent to which this happens and the extent to which an increasing public dissatisfaction with the perceived inequalities between different parts of the country stimulates a resurgence of spatial and regional policy, whether social, economic or political, will be one of the most interesting aspects of the post-2015 political environment.

Part Three

FOURTEEN

Summary and conclusion

John Hills, Ruth Lupton, Tania Burchardt, Kitty Stewart and Polly Vizard

In this book, we set out to describe how different parts of social policy in the UK have changed in the eight years from the beginning of the economic crisis in 2007 up to the end of the Liberal Democrat-Conservative coalition government in May 2015. We have also looked at what is known so far about outcomes from those policies and changes in them, although given lags in both the effects of many policies and reforms, and in data that allow one to assess them, this must inevitably remain an interim assessment.

Given the scale of the economic shock – unprecedented since the 1930s – and the effect it had on public finances, and then the change in government priorities after Labour lost office in 2010, this was, indeed, as suggested in the Introduction (see Chapter One), an era with a 'cold climate' for many areas of social policy. As the contrasts between the chapters show, however, this has been by no means a uniform history. There were some strong contrasts between the policies Labour continued to pursue until it lost office in May 2010, and those of its successors (although there were also continuities). But as we have documented, there were sharp differences *between* social policy areas under the coalition, especially in how severely each was asked to contribute to that government's plans for reducing the public budget deficit. There were some areas that were comparatively insulated, although still affected by major reform, while in others the role of the state has been redrawn or even substantially withdrawn. Writing early in the life of a new majority Conservative government, much of this conscious reshaping of Britain's welfare state is set to be continued or intensified.

Social policy in a warmer climate

In an earlier book (see Hills et al, 2009), we surveyed what had happened to a comparable range of policies in the period of Labour government ending as the economic crisis began. We concluded that the picture was neither that a government with a strong parliamentary majority, egalitarian objectives and a favourable economy had decisively reversed the gaps in society that had widened over the previous two decades, but nor was there a simple pattern of the betrayal of those egalitarian ideals. After nearly two decades of high inequality and low public spending, Labour had set out to deliver ambitious social justice goals. Its programme was expensive, with relatively fast spending increases by historic standards compared to other countries. However, the UK had remained only a moderate spender in international terms, and both the deficit and national debt were lower as a share of national income in 2007/08 than they had been in 1997. Moreover, contrary to popular belief, Labour's policies were not dominated by increased cash benefits but by reinvestment in what it saw as the 'modernisation' of public services. In health, education, early years and neighbourhood renewal, there were extra staff, more and newer and better equipped buildings, wider access, and new policy programmes and services. Spending on cash benefits increased, but was focused on children and pensioners, not on other working-age benefits, in line with its priorities of reducing child and pensioner poverty.

In many respects the UK was a more equal society by the end of Tony Blair's period as Prime Minister in 2007 than it had been at the start, in 1997. Away from the very top and very bottom, income differences had stabilised or narrowed; there had been notable reductions in child and pensioner poverty; the position of disadvantaged neighbourhoods had improved; gaps at school between children from lower- and higher-income families had declined; and increases in health and education spending had a further equalising effect. The experience, we concluded at that time, was 'far from one where nothing was tried or where nothing worked. Rather, many things were tried and most worked' (Hills et al 2009, p 358).

Nevertheless, as the chapters in this book highlight, there remained very substantial challenges for policy to address even before the crisis. Incomes at the very top had increased much faster than for others. Although employment rates and average wages had risen, so had earnings inequality, and low wage employment accounted for a larger share of employment than in many comparable countries, raising questions about the sustainability of the tax credit route for bringing down poverty. Progress on child poverty had stalled. Youth employment was rising, the UK's skills base was mediocre compared to international competitors and post-16 participation was relatively low. There were increasing regional disparities, as London pulled away from the rest of the country. And despite some progress, inequalities in health and educational attainment, particularly at higher levels, remained stubbornly high. Moreover, there were some major unresolved issues of policy delivery: how to pay for long-term adult care and for higher education; how to improve the quality of childcare provision; and how to fix what was widely regarded as a dysfunctional housing system with 15 years of undersupply, unaffordable mortgages, growing social housing waiting lists and rising rents contributing to a growing Housing Benefit bill.

Labour's response to the crisis

With the benefit of hindsight, a remarkable thing about the period of Labour government after the onset of the financial crisis in 2007 is how little its social policy programme was affected.

There were some immediate responses to the crisis. As Kitty Stewart notes earlier in Chapter Three (this volume), Labour's 2009 Budget emphasised the need to 'support vulnerable groups through the downturn' (HM Treasury, 2009a). This led to some new measures. An increase in Child Benefit was brought forward to January 2009; entitlement to childcare support became protected for four weeks if families lost qualifying hours; and a Take-Up Taskforce was established to improve the coverage of tax credits and benefits. The Department for Work and Pensions' (DWP) budget was increased to fund Jobcentre Plus activities, and there were new schemes to help those facing redundancy and to guarantee subsidised work or training for young people, as well as a Future Jobs Fund to help support the creation of subsidised community-focused jobs for unemployed young people. In an effort to kick-start the housing market and complementing reductions in interest rates, the stamp duty land tax threshold was increased from £125,000 to £250,000 for first-time buyers and those in disadvantaged areas, and the government funded a number of stalled development schemes. Similar crisis–response initiatives were also subsequently seen under the coalition.

However, the overall story of the Labour years from 2007 to 2010 was not one that some commentators might have expected, such as additional spending on specific short-term measures combined with cuts to spending plans to keep the deficit in check. Rather, it was mainly a continuation of the policies and programmes already underway. Despite the fall in GDP, but in an effort to avoid deflating the economy even more, Labour stuck to many of the plans set out in its 2007 Spending Review. These had been based on overall spending falling slightly as a share of what was assumed to be a growing economy and included, for instance, an 11% rise in real spending on the NHS in the three years from 2007/08 (Hills, 2011, Table 3). Meanwhile there were no significant tax increases until the introduction of the new 50% top rate of Income Tax and the tapering away of personal allowances for high earners in April 2010. This came after a change in Income Tax structure in April 2008 (announced a year before) that had abolished Labour's own initial '10p' band while cutting the basic rate of Income Tax, creating some lower-income losers (who were not fully protected by increased tax credits or a later rise in the tax-free allowance).

The value of benefits and tax credits continued to rise in line with inflation – a measure that protected bottom incomes through the recession and acted to reduce relative poverty and inequality, aided by some increases in tax credits for children. The Pensions Acts of 2007 and 2008 both reformed public and private pensions and increased the future value of state pension rights. Budgets held by government departments for the delivery of services also continued to increase.

One result of this is that Gordon Brown's government was able to continue with many of the social policies already initiated under the Blair administrations,[1] as well as to move in some new directions in order to tackle some of the challenges identified. This was not a period of radical structural reform: much of this work had already been done, and the Brownite wing of the Labour Party showed less appetite for additional choice and competition in public services. In some areas of policy, 2007-10 was marked by extensions of previous approaches, for example, increasing conditionality in the benefits system (including for lone parents with older children) and continuing active labour market policies (ALMPS), with the introduction of the Flexible New Deal. Other areas saw the coming into effect of policy decisions already made: some of the changes to pensions, for example, and the introduction of the smoking ban in public places. However, there were notable departures and shifts in direction as the Brown government began to establish itself. In adult social care, there was a renewed focus on improving quality and resolving the funding question. For schools, there was a shift in focus with the 2007 *Children's plan* (DCSF, 2007a) announcing a new vision of the 21st-century school going beyond academic qualifications to a broader range of children's outcomes, and the announcement of the raising of the participation age from 2013. There was an expansion of adult skills training through the roll-out of Train to Gain, as well as the beginnings of an 'industrial strategy' to regenerate regional economies. A 'localism' agenda emerged including the development of multi-area agreements and combined authorities, although commitments to regional neighbourhood renewal programmes were weakened in a shift to emphasise regional and sub-regional levels. A number of major reviews were commissioned, including on higher education funding (Browne) and health inequalities (Marmot), while the National Equality Panel was commissioned to document inequality in the UK across multiple dimensions. In the run-up to the May 2010 General Election, with the Equality Act and the Child Poverty Act, Brown's government marked new legislated commitments to a fairer and more equal society and to the 'elimination' of child poverty.

The other result of the government's decision to stick to its public spending plans while national income plummeted was that public spending as a proportion of GDP significantly increased, and contributed to an increasing deficit and national debt. By the end of 2009/10 net public sector debt had reached £1,050 billion at 2014/15 prices (62% of GDP) while the current budget deficit stood at £114.3 billion (6.9% of GDP). Both figures were very high for the UK by recent standards.

The net effect was that the coalition had, on the one hand, a better *social* inheritance in many ways than Labour had in 1997[2] – a fairer country with less poverty and expanded public services – but on the other, a much tougher *economic* climate. Strategic choices had to be made: should public spending be maintained in a Keynesian move to support economic growth, or cut in order to pay down the debt quickly? Should efforts to balance the public finances focus on tax increases or spending reductions? And who should bear the burden of these efforts?

Policies under the coalition

The incoming government declared that its most urgent task was to tackle the country's debts. But it also insisted that fairness would lie at the heart of its decisions, 'so that those most in need are most protected' (HM Government, 2010). The better-off would be expected to 'pay more than the poorest, not just in terms of cash, but as a proportion of income as well' (Chancellor's speech introducing the 2010 Emergency Budget).

Beyond deficit reduction, the coalition set a further goal of improving social mobility and creating a society where '… everyone, regardless of background, has the chance to rise as high as their talents and ambition allow them' (HM Government, 2010). Reforms to 'welfare', taxation and education were promised, with the devolution of decision-making powers from central to local government and communities. Defining its core values as 'freedom, fairness and responsibility', the coalition pledged to deliver 'radical reforming government, a stronger society, a smaller state and power and responsibility in the hands of every citizen' (HM Government, 2010).

A fundamental decision announced in the coalition's first Emergency Budget was to target deficit reduction through spending cuts (77%) much more than tax increases (23%). On the taxation side of its strategy, the coalition raised the VAT rate from 17.5% to 20%, and increased Capital Gains Tax for higher-rate taxpayers. Yet room was also made for sizeable tax cuts – including raising the Income Tax personal allowance from £6,475 to more than £10,600 by 2015/16. Corporation Tax was cut, and, from 2013/14, the Income Tax rate for people earning over £150,000 was reduced from 50% (introduced by Labour in April 2010) to 45%.

Selective austerity

The coalition chose to maintain spending in some policy areas and to implement deeper cuts elsewhere. Budgets for the NHS and schools, accounting for more than a quarter of total departmental expenditure, were relatively protected. Spending on health grew in real terms by 4.3% in total between 2009/10 and 2014/15, a real increase, although at an exceptionally low growth rate compared to previous years, and slower than the increases in need and demand (for example, as measured by the increasing elderly population). Schools expenditure was broadly stable in real terms, with figures showing a fall of 3% or a rise of 1% between 2009/10 and 2013/14, depending on the definitions used. A new Pupil Premium increased the loading of school funding towards schools in disadvantaged contexts, something that had already been happening under the Labour government (Sibieta, 2015).

Although funding for schools was protected, the budget for adult skills training was reduced by 27% between 2009/10 and 2014/15. Funding for 16- to 19-year-olds was initially relatively protected, but fell by 10% between 2009/10 and 2013/14, with further cuts announced for 2014/15 and beyond. Higher education spending was also cut in the short term by 62%, with the change from government grants for teaching to loan-funded fees, although the long-term saving to government is likely to be substantially lower.

The biggest losers among 'non-protected' services were those provided by local councils. Under the coalition local government funding in England from central government fell by 40%. Within particular service areas, spending on children aged under five fell by 13% between 2009/10 and 2013/14, including a 41% cut for Sure Start. These reductions coincided with a 6% increase in the number of under-fives between 2010 and 2014, leaving per capita spending down by one-fifth. Spending on housing and community amenities, which includes funding to build social housing, fell by 39% between 2009/10 and 2014/15. All the main central government funding streams for neighbourhood renewal were removed. Budgets for adult social care community services were cut by at least 7% between 2009/10 and 2013/14, while the population aged 65 and over grew by 10%.

Pensions were protected from coalition commitments to curtail spending on social security. A 'triple lock' was put in place, requiring them to be uprated each year by earnings growth, price inflation or 2.5%, whichever was highest. In contrast, cuts were made elsewhere by restricting eligibility for tax credits and working-age benefits and imposing new conditions on claimants. Working-age benefits were made less generous in the long term by a change to the inflation index used for annual adjustments and by what were intended to be below-inflation 1% increases for three years from 2013/14 (although, in the event, inflation fell to or below this, initially at least), accompanied by specific cuts for particular groups.

Structural reforms

Alongside the reshaping of public spending, the coalition embarked on an extensive restructuring of welfare state institutions. In education, it vastly extended Labour's programme of directly funded academies, and enabled 'free schools' to be set up by groups of parents, charities or other institutions. Higher education regulations were changed to allow new providers to offer degree qualifications. In the NHS, the government introduced major reforms emphasising decentralisation, commissioning, competition, a range of provider types (public, private and third sector) and outcomes. Delivery of a new, consolidated Work Programme, helping jobseekers to gain employment, was contracted out on a 'payment by results' basis. Social housing providers were encouraged to seek more private funding for new homes, charge rents closer to market levels, and move away from 'tenancies for life'.

'Localism' provided another key theme. Government Offices for the Regions and regeneration programmes were abolished in favour of local decision-making. Local government finance was reformed to provide more incentives for economic development. In addition, two elements of the social security system – the Social Fund and Council

Tax Benefit – were devolved to local authorities, both with reduced budgets. Local government assumed new responsibilities and powers in the context of public health and the public health budget was devolved. However, with the exception of public health, the expansion of local powers and responsibilities took place at a time when budget cuts gave local authorities less capacity to make use of them.

The coalition also shifted the boundaries of social security provision, in many cases moving away from 'progressive universalism' towards greater targeting. Eligibility was restricted for some benefits and services. Extra conditions were imposed, particularly for out-of-work benefits, along with tougher penalties for not meeting them. In some areas, financial responsibility underwent a wholesale shift from the state to the individual – for example, by trebling university student tuition fees in England and by introducing adult learning loans. In social care there were moves in both directions: on the one hand, tighter eligibility criteria for receipt of social care services shifted responsibility towards individuals and their carers; on the other hand, the Care Act 2014 introduced a lifetime cap on the total long-term care costs individuals would, in future, be required to pay.[3]

In some policy areas the coalition's reforms went deeper into the content and design of services, living up to its promise of sweeping changes. These changes are described in detail in earlier chapters. For example, the school curriculum and examination system in England were overhauled, justified on the grounds of making them more rigorous, and a new system of teacher training was introduced. In adult skills training, the coalition instituted changes to the length and quality of apprenticeships, designed to bring England closer to European systems. One of the most ambitious reforms was a complete overhaul of working-age benefits and tax credits, bringing most of them into a single system, Universal Credit, designed to incentivise work more and to get rid of complicated overlaps in means tests and taxation. While many people support the principles behind Universal Credit, it has proved challenging to implement, and there are continuing concerns about its design (Finch, 2015). Just 65,000 people were receiving it in May 2015, against an original target of 2 million by October 2014.

Overall public spending after the crisis

Looking at changes under both governments, total public spending on services rose from 37.1% of GDP in 2007/08 to 42.5% in 2009/10, partly through the maintenance of increases in spending that had been planned pre-crisis, and partly through the fall in GDP. By the final year of the coalition government, 2014/15, it had returned close to the pre-crisis level, at 37.3% (HM Treasury, 2015c).[4] This was austerity, but perhaps not quite as dramatic as some of the rhetoric on either political side would have led one to believe. However, as the preceding chapters have detailed, there was considerable variation in spending cuts across policy areas. Figure 14.1 shows the percentage change in real public spending by function, based on Public Expenditure Statistical Analysis (PESA). The black sections of the bars indicate the change during the last years of the Labour administration, and the grey sections indicate the change under the coalition. The labels give the overall percentage change from 2007/08 to 2014/15. For comparison, the real change in GDP used in the Treasury series was a fall of 5% from 2007/08 to

Figure 14.1: Percentage change in real public spending on services, by period and by function, UK, 2007/08 to 2014/15

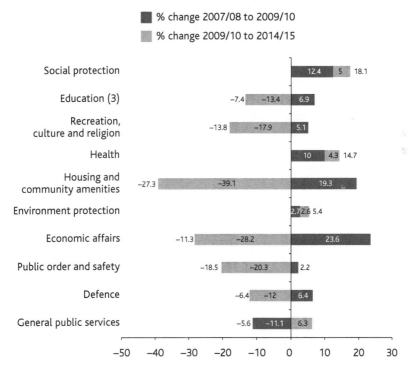

Notes:
(1) Transactions from 2008/09 onwards have been affected by financial sector interventions. Details are provided in chapter 5 Box 5.A of HM Treasury (2015c)
(3) The 2014/15 decrease in 'Education' is due to a reduction in the estimated future non-repayment of student loans, and other modelling changes.

Source: Authors' calculations based on HM Treasury (2015c)

2009/10 and a recovery of 9% from then until 2014/15, giving a rise of 4% in real terms over the period as a whole.

Changes in the earlier period were positive for all functions bar one ('general public services'), with the biggest percentage increases for economic affairs (which includes transport), housing and community amenities, and 'social protection'. Health was also a significant gainer. During the coalition period, housing and community amenities saw the largest percentage fall, followed by economic affairs, and public order and safety. The relative protection of health from cuts is apparent (and for education after allowing for the substantial effects of changes in the treatment of student loans; see the notes to Figure 14.1). Spending on 'social protection' actually increased overall, partly reflecting more generous pensions, and also the effects of recession on working-age benefits, despite tightening eligibility for tax credits and many other working-age benefits, and cuts in spending on adult social care, which is also included in this category (see Chapters Two and Nine earlier). This combination meant, for instance, that total spending on health, schools and pensioner benefits rose from 38% of total managed expenditure in 2009/10 to 41% in 2014/15.[5]

While the last years of Labour had involved comparatively little by way of new reforms, the same was not true under the coalition. Figure 14.2 summarises some of the contrasts between different sectors in terms of its spending changes and its reform programme. This is done in very broad terms – as the detail of earlier chapters has shown, there were differences in approach *within* each of these sectors. Areas where spending was cut most are in the lower half of the figure, and those where it was (relatively) protected or even increased are in the top half. Services subject to structural reform are on the right; those with organisations left largely unreformed are on the left. What is striking is that – with the exception of more generous Income Tax allowances – there is nothing in the upper left quadrant: the areas where we have looked at were either reformed or cut, and sometimes both, but little was left as it had been. As Peter Taylor-Gooby (2012) observed, the coalition was not just an austerity government, but one set on a systematic restructuring. The way this played out was, as we have shown, very different between and within sectors.

Boundaries of the welfare state

This combination of selective austerity and reform of the structure of services meant that the boundaries between public and private sectors in the areas traditionally covered by the welfare state have

Figure 14.2: Reform and austerity by sector since 2010

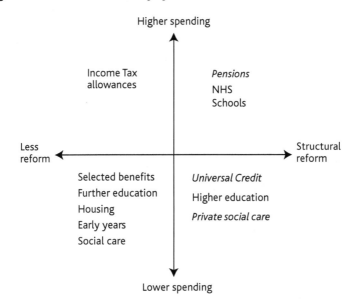

Note: Services in italics had reform planned for the longer term

shifted, and more rapidly than in previous decades. We examined what the combination of spending changes and policy reforms meant for the 'welfare mix' earlier, in Chapter Ten. This shows that healthcare remains dominated by the 'pure public' segment (with public finance, provision and decision), although it makes up a falling share, with a significant increase in the share of public finance for private provision. Income maintenance also remains strongly rooted in public finance for public provision, but here the shift has been – through pensions policy – towards a greater role for private decision. At the opposite extreme, housing has always been predominantly in the 'pure private' segment, and this has become even more pronounced in the most recent period, while public finance of public provision (council housing paid for by subsidy or Housing Benefit) has become increasingly residual. Education and social care each present a more mixed picture. School education has been, and remains, largely publicly financed, but academies and free schools reduce the 'degree of publicness' of provision, while in higher education the shift from grant to tuition fee loan funding has tilted the balance of funding towards private finance. Finally, in social care, sharp reductions in local authority funding mean that for the first time in this series (which extends back to 1979), the 'pure private' segment accounted for a larger proportion of total spending than the 'pure public' segment, while contracted-out services continue to grow.

Putting the changing patterns within the different sectors of 'welfare activity' together, the proportion that was publicly financed and provided dropped from 48% in 2007/08 to well below half for the first time, 44% in 2013/14; the proportion that was privately financed and provided rose from 34% to 39% (see Figure 10.8 in Chapter Ten). This shift reflected the combination of constraints on public spending while overall welfare activity continued to grow as a share of national income.

Results by the end of the coalition period

In earlier work, we looked in detail at the changes in social outcomes over the whole of the period of Labour government, from 1997 to 2010, and so do not repeat that here (see Lupton et al, 2013b). We drew in particular on two sets of indicators of socioeconomic outcomes – those originally produced by the Labour government itself in its *Opportunity for all* reports, and those published by the Joseph Rowntree Foundation in its Monitoring Poverty and Social Exclusion series. For the whole Labour period, both showed more indicators improving than deteriorating – 48 compared to 6 in the *Opportunity for all* series and 26 compared to 14 in the Monitoring Poverty and Social Exclusion series. But both series suggested a more mixed picture when looking at just the five years or so prior to 2010, including the start of the crisis. Twenty-five indicators improved over this period but 12 deteriorated in the *Opportunity for all* series, and only 13 improved in the Monitoring Poverty and Social Exclusion series while 20 deteriorated (Lupton et al, 2013b, table 7).

It should be remembered, of course, that there is a long lead time between government policy action and investments and their eventual outcomes, with results of, for instance, investments in early years or schools stretching long after the end of a particular administration. Nonetheless there were clearly some areas where progress against its objectives had slowed by the end of the Labour government, not least as the recession took effect.

Cuts in many services and increasing pressure on others

Turning first to indicators of the outputs from public spending under the coalition, those from 'unprotected' services were substantially reduced. In adult social care, where spending was cut despite a growing elderly population, there was a falling caseload (down 25% from 2009/10 to 2013/14) and 'intensified' focus on supporting those with the greatest needs. This has produced increasing pressure on unpaid carers – friends and family. Housing policies made little impact on the supply of new homes. Between 2010 and 2014, an average of 140,000 new homes per year were completed, compared with 190,000 under Labour. There were 17% fewer adult learners as course funding was curtailed, and loans introduced. Centrally funded neighbourhood renewal activity was drastically reduced, while economic regeneration programmes performed well below expectations in terms of business and job creation. Despite government endorsements for voluntary activity and a 'Big Society', third sector budgets also fell, with cuts estimated between 50 and 100% in some deprived neighbourhoods (Civil Exchange, 2013; Foden et al, 2014).

In early years services, the number of Sure Start children's centres fell from 3,631 in April 2010 to 3,019 in June 2014. Survey data pointed to cuts in staffing and services in many of those remaining, although other centres expected to maintain, or even expand, provision, in part by making services more targeted. There was also new early education provision for two-year-olds and the number of health visitors and Family Nurse Partnership provision for teenage parents expanded.

'Protected' areas were less hard hit. In education, the coalition kept school funding resources broadly stable. In England, the number of teachers increased, pupil-teacher ratios were maintained, and while the average class size increased in primary schools, it fell in secondary schools. Although there were more 16- to 19-year-old learners, the proportion not in education, training or employment (NEET) fell. Expenditure on health was protected relative to other areas, but average annual growth rates were exceptionally low in historical terms, and lagged behind the rates that are widely deemed necessary to maintain and extend NHS care in response to increasing need and demand. Input and output growth slowed markedly after 2010 as the effects of the resources squeeze took hold, and signs of pressure on healthcare access and quality were mounting by the May 2015 General Election. Outcomes data points towards pressure on waiting times for admitted and non-admitted patients, Accident and Emergency (A&E) departments and cancer waiting lists. Fewer hospitals met the A&E waiting times; the proportion of cancer patients seen within 62 days declined; and the number of patients waiting to begin non-emergency consultant-led treatment in July 2015 was at its highest level since 2008. At the time of writing, Monitor (2015) is warning of 'unprecedented' financial and operational challenges, while latest King's

Fund assessments point towards 2015/16 as 'the most challenging year in recent NHS history', taking account of the overall fiscal climate, the scale and magnitude of the financial deficits of NHS trusts, waiting lists and staff shortages (Appleby et al, 2015). Among employment services, the new Work Programme proved cheaper, although no more effective, than its predecessors.

Direct tax and benefit changes helped the top half of the population, but not deficit reduction

Despite the coalition's insistence that 'those with the broadest shoulders should bear the greatest burden', those in the top half of the income distribution were the biggest gainers from its changes to direct taxes, tax credits and benefits from May 2010 to May 2015. Perhaps surprisingly, overall the cost of the more generous Income Tax allowances outweighed the savings from 'welfare cuts', increasing the deficit and the need for savings in other spending and for other tax rises, rather than contributing to deficit reduction. Modelling suggests that up to 2015/16, the poorest twentieth lost nearly 2% of their incomes on average from these changes (not allowing for VAT and other indirect taxes) and people in three of the next four-twentieths of the income distribution also lost. With the notable exception of the top-most twentieth, people in income groups in the top half of the distribution were on average net gainers from the changes.

Initially, however, as a result of decisions made under Labour and continued during the coalition's first two years, benefits rose in line with inflation at a time when real earnings fell during the recession. The result was that poverty measured in relation to median incomes fell between 2009/10 and 2010/11 and then remained fairly stable until 2013/14; measured against fixed income thresholds, poverty rates have remained stable since 2009/10 (see Figure 11.4 in Chapter Eleven). Income inequality also fell during the election year 2010/11 and (depending on how measured) held steady up to 2013/14, around its lowest level for a quarter of a century.

These latest official figures pre-date many of the coalition's welfare reforms coming fully into effect. Taken as a whole, the regressive balance of direct tax and benefit changes over the whole period to 2015/16 would be expected to increase relative poverty beyond what its level would otherwise have been, while specific groups have been affected sharply by particular cuts. Qualitative evidence suggests growing hardship after 2013 among households affected by a combination of falling real wages, rising fuel and food costs, changes to benefit rules and sanctions. However, with inflation remaining lower than the government expected, the three years of most working-age benefits rising by only 1% did not result in the real cut in their value – or the spending savings – that had been expected, and so had less effect on poverty rates. For the future, with the new government extending the coalition's planned two-year freeze in the cash value of these benefits to four years, what happens to the inflation rate will be critical. The faster it is, the bigger the fall in real benefit values will be.

Pensioners were protected, children less so

As far as taxes and benefits (including pensions) are concerned, pensioners continued to be relatively favoured. As a share of national income, transfers to pensioners had increased under Labour from 5.1% of GDP in 1996/97 to 6.3% in 2009/10. This was also the proportion in 2014/15, although a peak of 6.5% was reached in 2012/13. However, pensioners with care needs were affected by cuts to adult social care.

Meanwhile, the cost of working-age benefits not related to having children fell from 3.2% in 2009/10 to 2.9% of GDP in 2014/15, and spending related to children from 2.6% to 2.2% of GDP by 2014/15. Concerns about future social mobility might be raised as young children in low-income families were affected by cuts to spending on services, as well as by reductions in benefits for the under-fives. On the other hand, poorer school-age children received additional help through the Pupil Premium. Fears that the abolition of the Education Maintenance Allowance and the rise in university tuition fees would widen socioeconomic gaps in further and higher education participation have not been borne out to date. In fact, by 2014 the proportion of young people not in employment, education or training (NEET) had declined substantially for the first time in over a decade, and increasing numbers of disadvantaged young people applied to university.

Uneven impact of the crisis

All of these changes were superimposed on changes in the labour market and in market incomes since the crisis started that were far from the same for different kinds of people, as set out earlier, in Chapter Twelve. The patterns of change between 2007 and 2013 were complex. While the employment and wages of social tenants deteriorated most, after allowing for housing costs, private tenants had the greatest falls in income. While wage inequality grew between the low and high paid, the protection of the real value of benefits while wages were falling meant that overall income inequality fell, particularly in 2010.

But one factor was pervasive across different kinds of economic outcome: young adults, especially those in their twenties, were worst hit by the recession whether one looks at employment, hourly pay, weekly earnings, net incomes or wealth. By 2012/13 median incomes for those in their early twenties were 18% lower than five years before, and had fallen sharply for better-off young people by comparison with their predecessors, as well as for those who were worse off. The wealth gap between younger and older people widened further in real terms and in relation to annual incomes, meaning that it will only be those who stand to inherit from parents and grandparents who are likely to be able to build their wealth to levels typical for the previous generation.

Another striking feature of the recent past is the way that regional fortunes have diverged, with those of London and regions in the North of England continuing to pull apart (see Chapter Thirteen). At the same time, economic inequalities within London have increased further, making it still more unequal than other regions, particularly if looking at incomes after allowing for housing costs. By contrast, the attainment gap between poorer and other children narrowed faster in London than in other regions between 2007 and 2013, and (measured in a new way) was only around half as great in 2014 as in regions in the North of England (see Blanden et al, 2015, for a discussion of this 'London effect'). Alongside these differences, it is striking that the greatest reductions in local authorities' 'spending power' between 2010 and 2015 hit Northern regions much harder than more affluent Southern ones.

Too early to tell for many social and economic outcomes

Many data indicating changes in outcomes are only available until 2013 or even only 2012, making it impossible yet to assess the full impact of the coalition government's policies. The data available to date show that progress in many areas continued in the new government's early years, but much of this could be considered the legacy of the previous government, since many policies were not fully implemented in the period it covered.

The overall picture is that there has been little significant change, as yet, in many of the key indicators of social progress and equity. Health inequalities remain deeply entrenched. There is no evidence of closing socioeconomic gaps in child development. Gaps between children on free school meals (FSM) and others continued to narrow at the end of primary school, and at GCSE level until 2013, although no immediate accelerating effect of the Pupil Premium was evident. However, in 2014 there was evidence of a widening socioeconomic gap for lower attainers (those attaining 5 GCSEs A*-C in any subject). For higher attainers (those reaching 5 GCSEs A*-C including English and maths), the coalition's changes to vocational subjects and GCSE assessment had a much smaller effect, but nevertheless gaps remained very wide at this level, falling just fractionally from 27.6 to 27.0 percentage points in 2014.

Gaps in worklessness and poverty between the poorest neighbourhoods and others reduced as the economy recovered, but not quite back to their pre-economic crisis levels. The coalition did preside over positive trends in employment rates, which rose to a new peak by summer 2014, higher than before the crisis, but wages fell, and much of the increase was in self-employment and part-time working. Some indicators were less positive. Pressure on unpaid carers increased as formal services were withdrawn. Housing became increasingly unaffordable and homelessness increased.

To try to gain an overview of trends across social policy areas, we looked at three composite sets of indicators (Lupton et al, 2015b). One was the coalition government's own 'impact indicators'. These are the measures selected by government departments and made public on their websites. We identified 55 indicators of outcomes (as opposed to the quantity or quality of delivery) relating to the policy areas covered in this book. The other indicator sets are ones discussed above, which we used to assess the previous Labour government's record on poverty and social exclusion – the *Opportunity for all* indicators and the Monitoring Poverty and Social Exclusion indicators produced by the New Policy Institute for the Joseph Rowntree Foundation.

The limitations of this exercise should be clearly understood. For the coalition, the data time lag means that these indicators can barely yet be said to reflect its policies. A bigger problem for comparability over time is what governments chose to monitor. The coalition's indicators are dominated by children and young people and by just two themes, education and health/social care. These are, of course, the areas that it prioritised in its spending/saving programme. Labour's indicator set was broader, with more indicators of poverty, differences in outcomes between areas and housing. The Monitoring Poverty and Social Exclusion set is different again, being dominated by indicators of poverty and employment, with some focus on housing and areas, but very little on health and care.

In Table 14.1 we show progress against the different indicators, looking at the coalition's indicators only for the period it was in office, and the other sets both under Labour and under the coalition. The overall trend was positive. The majority of the coalition's 'impact' indicators show progress since 2010. This is not entirely a function of the coalition's indicators being narrow in scope, as the majority of indicators in the other sets also show positive trends, although that comparison is clearly hampered by the lack of continuity of indicators through the period. Of the coalition's indicators not showing improvement, one was an education indicator – the proportion of young people attaining Level 2 by age 19 if they have not attained it by 16. The others related to housing (temporary accommodation) and health – emergency readmissions and patient experience. The *Opportunity for all* indicators which appeared worse since 2010 were absolute low income, the education and NEET rates of looked-after children, children in temporary accommodation, smoking among lower socioeconomic groups, and the percentage of the population contributing to non-state pensions. Worsening Monitoring Poverty and

Table 14.1: Progress against different sets of indicators

	Coalition impact indicators	'Opportunity for All' indicators		'Monitoring Poverty and Social Exclusion' indicators	
	Trend from 2009/10[2]	Trend from baseline to 2010[1]	Trend from 2009/10[2]	Long-term trend (10 years or so) to 2010	Trend from 2009/10[2]
Better	38	47	25	26	16
Slightly better	5				3
No change	4	4	2	5	1
Mixed		1			3
Worse	6	6	8	15	7
Not available	2	1	24	4	20
Total	55	59	59	50	50

Notes:

[1] Baseline year is usually 1997 or 1998. For some indicators based on specific Labour initiatives or data that were not collected before Labour came to power, the baseline is later.

[2] Depending on availability of data, trends are reported for years from 2009, 2009/10 or 2010 up to the last available time point.

Sources: Authors' update of coalition indicators and DWP *Opportunity for all* indicators, using data available to the end of 2014, and *Monitoring Poverty and Social Exclusion* reports from the New Policy Institute. For details, see Lupton et al (2015b) Appendix.

Social Exclusion indicators were also related to housing (homelessness and poverty risks for renters), poverty (in-work poverty and material deprivation), as well as recurring unemployment.

Overall, these results reinforce the conclusion that it is too early to assess the coalition's full impact on social and economic outcomes, and that the assessment is sensitive to which indicators one selects. Progress in many areas continued in the coalition's first years. However, the balance between positive and negative trends was somewhat less favourable after 2009/10 than in the period before then.

Social mobility

One specific focus of policy under both the Labour government up to 2010 and its coalition successor was 'equality of opportunity' or 'social mobility'. Indeed, Nick Clegg, the coalition Deputy Prime Minister, argued that, 'The over-riding priority for our social policy is improving social mobility' (speech to the Institute of Government, 9 September 2010).

Measuring success in achieving such an objective is inherently very hard, even harder than for other outcomes we have examined in this book. Ultimately what it concerns can only be measured by comparing the changing strength of links between one generation and the next, accumulating over decades. The coalition identified its own set of 'social mobility indicators' – 19 measures of factors related to differences in future life chances and the gaps in them between those from different backgrounds (some of which are also included in the 'coalition indicators' summarised in Table 14.1). It published data showing changes since 2010 in 15 of them shortly before the 2015 General Election (ODPM, 2015). As Table 14.2 shows, the patterns they show divide into six groups. Eight, more than half of them, had improved since 2010 – in four cases continuing a previous trend and in one case reversing a previous deterioration. Two of them were constant in the most recent data (in one case after a previous deterioration; there were no comparable data before 2010 in the other). But five of them deteriorated after 2010, reversing a previous improvement.[6]

Taken at face value this shows improvement in more cases than there was deterioration, which may be good news for the future. On the other hand, where there are comparable data from the period up to 2010, the balance would then have been more clearly towards improvement (nine improving and only two deteriorating). However, it is not possible to draw any strong conclusions from such indicators on whether social mobility might improve in future as a result of

Table 14.2: Coalition government social mobility indicators

Continued improvement after 2010
- Attainment at age 11 by FSM eligibility (Indicator 5)
- Attainment at age 16 by FSM eligibility (Indicator 7)
- Attainment at age 16 by deprivation area of school (Indicator 9)
- High A level attainment by age 19 by school or college type (Indicator 11)

Improved (no earlier data)
- School readiness – phonics check (Indicator 4)
- Attainment at age 11: disadvantaged pupils (Indicator 6)
- Attainment at age 16: disadvantaged pupils attainment gap (Indicator 8)

Improvement after 2010, reversing deterioration
- Higher education participation in the most selective institutions by type of school or college attended (Indicator 15)

No change after deterioration before 2010
- Higher education – graduate destinations (Indicator 16)

No change
- Proportion of lowest-earning 25- to 30-year-olds that experience wage progression 10 years later (2001-10 and 2005-14) (Indicator 18)

Deterioration reversing improvement before 2010
- Low birth weight (Indicator 1)
- School readiness (Indicator 3)
- Attainment at age 19 by FSM eligibility (Indicator 10)
- Progression to higher education by age 19, by FSM eligibility at age 15 (Indicator 14)
- 'Second chances' (age over 19 Level 2 and 3 qualifications) (Indicator 19)

Source: ODPM (2015)

recent policies, or whether any improvement has now slowed. First, the time periods involved are often very short and the changes small. Second, trends in indicators of these kinds will in any case often be the result of the accumulation of policy and other socioeconomic changes over several years and under more than one government. They provide more of a baseline for later study of long-term trends, rather than yet giving any metric with which to judge the coalition on this objective.

In fact, it is only now that data are becoming available that allow assessment of what was happening to some of the drivers of social mobility relating to what happened to children over the period of the previous Labour government, and even here the evidence is incomplete. For instance, educational attainment gaps between children with more or less affluent parents widened between those born in the late 1950s and those born in the late 1970s, but narrowed for those born since 1980 (Blanden and Macmillan, 2013). However, much of the apparent narrowing in gaps comes against thresholds that children from more affluent backgrounds were already achieving (such as the roll-out of 5 GCSEs). Allowing for this and looking at higher levels of attainment (such as A-level attainment or higher education entry) the gaps have not narrowed for those born those since 1980.[7]

For the future, two recent trends are particularly concerning: the reductions in some early years provision and falls in income and cash support for families with young children during the period since 2010 (see Chapter Three); and the growing value of wealth in relation to income, and hence in the difference in wealth between generations (see Chapter Twelve). The former suggests a reduction in some of the factors that can help compensate for differences between families. The latter suggests that, combined with the great inequalities in wealth *within* the older generation, inheritance will become increasingly important in the economic trajectories of younger ones – but a factor that will be very unequally spread.

Conclusion, and looking forward

The financial and economic crisis that hit many Western economies after 2007 has meant a much tougher environment for social policy in the UK as elsewhere – both in dealing with its aftermath in terms of unemployment and reduced incomes, and in reducing the fiscal resources available.

The Brown government's response was to continue with its spending plans, both to avoid making the recession even worse and to sustain the social programmes that had been initiated in more favourable economic times. The balance of its tax and benefit changes between 2007 and 2010 favoured those with lower incomes. In some policy areas there were new developments to tackle poverty and inequality – notably the commitments to future action embodied in the Equality and Child Poverty Acts passed just before the end of the Parliament – but also increased action on educational inequalities, and new attempts to increase skills and to improve quality in social care. As noted earlier, these developments only went some of the way to addressing some of the substantial social policy challenges facing the country, through demographic and other pressures. The immediate result of the strategy of 'business as usual' was an increase in the current budget deficit and public debt as national income plummeted.

By contrast, the incoming coalition's response was to try to reduce the resulting deficit quickly. It also decided to achieve most of its fiscal rebalancing through public spending cuts rather than increased taxes, but while protecting the NHS, schools and pensions – all very big areas of public spending – from major cuts. And it implemented some expensive commitments, notably greatly increasing the tax-free

Income Tax personal allowance and introducing a more generous system for uprating state pensions.

These decisions meant that while the overall real reduction in public expenditure was less than 3% between 2009/10 and 2014/15 (HM Treasury, 2015c), very substantial cuts were made in unprotected areas, largely in local services. In the tax and benefits system, pensions were protected and the higher tax allowances meant gains for the top half of the income distribution, but benefits and tax credits to lower-income families were cut, sharply for some of them after 2013. Despite the aim that the better-off should contribute a greater share of income than the poor, the net effect was the reverse across most of the income distribution. Meanwhile, the 'protected' NHS experienced real average annual expenditure growth rates that were positive but exceptionally low in historic terms, and adult social care services were cut, while needs continued to grow for both, so pressure on unpaid carers is increasing.

Although current public attention rests on 'the cuts', the coalition's large-scale reforms designed to reduce the size of the state, stimulate private and voluntary provision and increase personal responsibility may ultimately prove its biggest legacy. It is too soon to establish their effects on social and economic outcomes, but there is no doubt that what occurred in the wake of the crisis was not simply an effort to 'make ends meet' but to reform, in fundamental ways, the role of state and private interests in social policy.

Thus the new majority Conservative government elected in 2015 inherited a welfare state in flux, with fundamental changes to the NHS, schools, pensions and benefits already underway, but with many of the challenges of 2010 still present. These include rising demands for health and social care, increasingly unaffordable housing for those who do not already own it, a regionally unbalanced economy and continuing labour market inequalities, continuing child poverty, insufficient high-quality affordable childcare, a weak system of apprenticeships for young people and relatively ineffective mechanisms for helping workless people back into work.

Perhaps not surprisingly with a majority in place, the new government's immediate response was to intensify some of the policy directions already adopted with its coalition partners before the election. Notably, the July 2015 Budget announced plans for substantial cuts in social security benefits and tax credits for working-age people in and out of work, extending the planned freeze in benefits, removing extra support for families if they have more than two children, and making the planned Universal Credit less generous.

The 2015 Autumn Statement delayed some of those cuts, but left their intended scale by 2020 in place. Pensions will continue to be protected, however, implying a continued divergence in the treatment of different age groups which was already a feature of policy since 2010, and tax-free Income Tax allowances will continue to rise. The switch from supporting social housing towards owner-occupation has been dramatically extended.

The regressive effects of the planned reforms are offset only to a limited degree by the announced increases in the National Minimum Wage. Health spending continues to be relatively protected, but in the face of rising need and demand, while local services – including for social care – face even greater pressure. Notably, too, the protection of spending on schools has been watered down and the coalition's planned major reforms to paying for long-term care have been postponed. As we write in late 2015, the policy outlook looks like more of the same, only with greater confidence and intensity.

At the same time, however, other developments in 2014/15 signal the possibility of a new era in social policy, as the economy begins to recover. The anti-austerity mood reflected in other parts of Europe was picked up in Scotland in the run-up to the independence referendum in September 2014, and again in the Labour leadership contest of summer 2015. That resulted in the election of left-winger Jeremy Corbyn, and the opening up of new debates about future social policy directions: opposition to benefit cuts, new investments in social housing and the return of academy schools to local authority control, to cite just a few examples. While the outcomes of all these developments are still unknown, the political moment of 2016 is one in which fundamental policy and spending principles and goals are again being widely discussed. We hope that the evidence in this book will contribute to these debates.

The financial crisis and subsequent recession hit the economy hard. But in the main, Britain's welfare state did successfully protect many of the most vulnerable from its sharpest effects. However, that protection was not uniform. In the labour market, young adults were hardest hit, while those of pension age had their cash incomes protected. And the policy changes of the coalition years set in train a conscious reshaping of the welfare state, now being carried much further by the new Conservative government. Across a series of risks and life events from the early years to care needs in old age, more people will face those risks on their own. The already cold climate for much of social policy and many of those most affected by it looks likely to become colder still.

Notes

[1] Covered in more detail in Hills et al (2009) and in the series of Working Papers published online under the Social Policy in a Cold Climate programme, available at http://sticerd.lse.ac.uk/case/_new/publications/series.asp?prog=SPCCWP

[2] See the Centre for Social Justice's (2006) *Breakdown Britain* reports for a different view.

[3] An early act of the incoming Conservative government was, however, to delay the implementation of this previously 'flagship' reform.

[4] Total managed expenditure, which includes items such as debt interest payments, rose from 40.2 to 45.7% of GDP from 2007/08 to 2009/10, and fell to 40.7% by 2014/15.

[5] This combines healthcare spending from HM Treasury (2015c), pensioner benefits in Great Britain (Chapter Two, Table 2A.1, this volume), and schools spending in England (Chapter Four, this volume).

[6] Assessing somewhat earlier data on this set of indicators, the Social Mobility and Child Poverty Commission (2014, p 245) summarised trends as being for three indicators moving in 'the right direction', nine being broadly constant, and two moving in 'the wrong direction'. Longer-term trends since 2005, where available, were more clearly positive (pp 251-4).

[7] See Hills (2015c) for a summary of recent evidence on social mobility and educational achievement.

References

4Children, 2013, *Children's Centre Census 2013*, London: 4Children

4Children, 2014, *Children's Centres Census 2014*, London: 4Children

Acheson, D, 1998, *The Independent Inquiry into Inequalities in Health*, London: The Stationery Office, www.gov.uk/government/uploads/system/uploads/attachment_data/file/265503/ih.pdf

ACRA, 2010, NHS resource allocation formula, letter from ACRA to the Rt Hon Andrew Lansley MP, 27th September 2010, www.gov.uk/government/uploads/system/uploads/attachment_data/file/215878/dh_122685.pdf

ACRA, 2011, Letter from David Fillingham to the Rt Hon Andrew Lansley MP, 2nd September 2011, www.gov.uk/government/uploads/system/uploads/attachment_data/file/213327/DF-letter-to-SoS.pdf (pp 19-28)

ACRA, 2012, Letter from Andrew Lansley to the Rt Hon Jeremy Hunt MP, 17th October 2012, www.gov.uk/government/uploads/system/uploads/attachment_data/file/213327/DF-letter-to-SoS.pdf (pp 1-18)

Adam, S, Browne, J, Elming, W, 2015, The effect of the UK coalition government's tax and benefit changes on household incomes and work incentives, *Fiscal Studies*, 36, 3, 375-402

Adams, S, Levell, P, 2014, *Measuring poverty when inflation varies across households*, York: Joseph Rowntree Foundation, www.jrf.org.uk/report/measuring-poverty-when-inflation-varies-across-households

ADASS (Association of Directors of Adult Social Services), 2014, *Annual budget survey report 2014: Final*, London: ADASS, www.adass.org.uk/uploadedFiles/adass_content/policy_networks/resources/Key_documents/ADASS%20Budget%20Survey%20Report%202014%20Final.pdf

Alakeson, V, Cory, G, 2013, *Home truths: How affordable is housing for Britain's ordinary working families?*, London: The Resolution Foundation, www.resolutionfoundation.org/publications/home-truths-affordable-housing-britains-ordinary-working-families/

Alcock, P, May, M (2014) *Social policy in Britain*, London: Palgrave Macmillan

Allen, G, 2011, *Early intervention: The next steps*, London: Cabinet Office, www.gov.uk/government/uploads/system/uploads/attachment_data/file/284086/early-intervention-next-steps2.pdf

Alvaredo, F, Atkinson, AB, Morelli, S, 2015, *The challenge of measuring UK wealth inequality in the 2000s*, Working Paper 4, International Inequalities Institute. London: The London School of Economics and Political Science, www.lse.ac.uk/InternationalInequalities/pdf/III-Working-Paper-4-Alvaredo-Atkinson-Morelli.pdf

Appleby, J, 2013, *Spending on health and social care over the next 50 years: Why think long term?*, London: The King's Fund, www.kingsfund.org.uk/sites/files/kf/field/field_publication_file/Spending%20on%20health%20...%2050%20years%20low%20res%20for%20web.pdf

Appleby, J, Crawford, R, Emmerson, C, 2009, *How cold will it be? Prospects for NHS funding, 2011-2017*, London: The King's Fund and Institute for Fiscal Studies, www.kingsfund.org.uk/sites/files/kf/How-Cold-Will-It-Be-Prospects-NHS-funding-2011-2017-John-Appleby-Roweena_Crawford-Carl-Emmerson-The-Kings-Fund-July-2009.pdf

Appleby, J, Humphries, R, Thompson, J, Galea, A, 2013, *How is the health and social care system performing? June 2013'*, Quarterly monitoring report, London: The King's Fund, www.kingsfund.org.uk/sites/files/kf/field/field_publication_file/quarterly-monitoring-report-kingsfund-jun13.pdf

Appleby, J, Thompson, J, Jabbal, J, 2015, *Quarterly monitoring report, 16*, London: The King's Fund, http://qmr.kingsfund.org.uk/2015/16/

Archer, T, Cole, I, 2014, Still not plannable? Housing supply and the changing structure of the housebuilding industry in the UK in "austere" times, *People, Place and Policy Online*, 8, 2, 97-112

Bailey, B, Unwin, L, 2014, Continuity and change in English further education: A century of voluntarism and permissive adaptability, *British Journal of Education Studies*, 62, 4, 449-64

Barker, K (Chair), The King's Fund, 2014, *A new settlement for health and social care: Interim report*, London: The King's Fund, www.kingsfund.org.uk/sites/files/kf/field/field_publication_file/commission-interim-new-settlement-health-social-care-apr2014.pdf

Belfield, C, Cribb, J, Hood, A, Joyce, R, 2015, *Living standards, poverty and inequality in the UK: 2015*, London: Institute for Fiscal Studies, www.ifs.org.uk/events/1161

Bennett, L, Humphries, R, 2014, *Making best use of the Better Care Fund: Spending to save?*, London: The King's Fund, www.kingsfund.org.uk/sites/files/kf/field/field_publication_file/making-best-use-of-the-better-care-fund-kingsfund-jan14.pdf

Berman, G, Keep, M, 2012, *The Local Government Finance Settlement 2011-13 – Commons Library Research Paper*, RP11/16, London: House of Commons Library

BERR (Department for Business, Enterprise and Regulatory Reform), 2009, *New Industry New Jobs*. London. Department for Business, Enterprise and Regulatory Reform, www.researchonline.org.uk/sds/search/download.do?ref=B11956

Berry, C, White, L, 2014, *Local authority spending cuts and the 2014 English local elections*, SPERI British Political Economy Brief No 6, Sheffield: University of Sheffield, http://speri.dept.shef.ac.uk/wp-content/uploads/2014/07/Brief6-local-authority-spending-cuts.pdf

Bessa, I, Forde, C, Moore, S, Stuart, M, 2013, *National Minimum Wage: Impact on the domiciliary care sector*, London and Leeds: Low Pay Commission and University of Leeds, www.gov.uk/government/publications/national-minimum-wage-impact-on-the-domiciliary-care-sector

Bevan, G, Karanikolos, M, Exely, J, Connolly, S, Mays, N (2014) *The four health systems of the United Kingdom: how do they compare?* London: The Health Foundation and Nuffield Trust

BIS (Department for Business, Innovation & Skills) (2009) *Skills for growth: the national skills strategy*. London: BIS, www.gov.uk/government/uploads/system/uploads/attachment_data/file/228764/7641.pdf

BIS, 2010a, *Skills for sustainable growth: Strategy document*, London: BIS, www.gov.uk/government/uploads/system/uploads/attachment_data/file/32368/10-1274-skills-for-sustainable-growth-strategy.pdf

BIS, 2010b, *Securing a sustainable future for higher education: An independent review of higher education funding and student finance (Browne Report)*, London: Department for Business Innovation & Skills, www.gov.uk/government/publications/the-browne-report-higher-education-funding-and-student-finance

BIS, 2012, *No stone unturned: In pursuit of growth – Lord Heseltine review*, Independent review BIS/12/1213, London: BIS, www.gov.uk/government/publications/no-stone-unturned-in-pursuit-of-growth

BIS, 2013, *Annual report and accounts 2012-13*, www.gov.uk/government/uploads/system/uploads/attachment_data/file/329057/BIS_annual_report_and_accounts_2013_-_2014.pdf

BIS, 2014a, *Further Education Commissioner annual report 2013/14*, London: BIS

BIS, 2014b, *BIS performance indicators: funding per student in higher education*, www.gov.uk/government/uploads/system/uploads/attachment_data/file/318628/BIS_performance_indicators_Funding_per_student_in_HE.pdf

BIS, 2015a, *A dual mandate for adult vocational education: A consultation paper*, London: BIS

BIS, 2015b, *Evaluation of employer ownership pilots, Round 1: Initial findings*, BIS Research Paper No 221, London: BIS

BIS, 2015c, *Annual report and accounts 2014-15*, www.gov.uk/government/publications/bis-annual-report-and-accounts-2014-to-2015

Blanden, J, Greaves, E, Gregg, P, Macmillan, L, Sibieta, L, 2015, *Understanding the improved performance of disadvantaged children in London*, Social Policy in a Cold Climate, Working Paper 21, London: Centre for Analysis of Social Exclusion, London School of Economics and Political Science, http://sticerd.lse.ac.uk/dps/case/spcc/wp21.pdf

Blanden, J, Macmillan, L, 2013, *Education and intergenerational mobility: Help or hindrance?*, Social Policy in a Cold Climate, Working Paper 8, London: Centre for Analysis of Social Exclusion, London School of Economics and Political Science, http://sticerd.lse.ac.uk/dps/case/spcc/wp08.pdf

Blessing, A, 2015, Public, private, or in between? The legitimacy of social enterprises in the housing market, *Voluntas*, 26, 1, 198-221

Bochel, H, Powell, M (2016) *The Coalition Government and social policy: Restricting the welfare state*. Bristol: Policy Press

Boles, N, 2013, Housing the next generation, Speech presented at The Ideas Space, 10 January

Bovill, D, 2014, *Patterns of pay: Estimates from the Annual Survey of Hours and Earnings, UK, 1997 to 2013 (February 2014)*, Newport: Office for National Statistics, www.ons.gov.uk/ons/dcp171766_353368.pdf

Bozeman, B, 1987, *All organizations are public: Bridging public and private organization theories*, San Francisco, CA: Jossey-Bass

Britton, J, Chowdry, H, Dearden, L, 2014, *The 16 to 19 Bursary Fund impact evaluation – Interim report*, RR346, London: Department for Education

Buck, D, Dixon, A, 2013, *Improving the allocation of health resources in England: How to decide who gets what*, London: The King's Fund, www.kingsfund.org.uk/publications/improving-allocation-health-resources-england

Buck, D, Maguire, D, 2015, *Inequalities in life expectancy: Changes over time and implications for policy*, London: The King's Fund, www.kingsfund.org.uk/sites/files/kf/field/field_publication_file/inequalities-in-life-expectancy-kings-fund-aug15.pdf

Burchardt, T, 2013, *Re-visiting the conceptual framework for public/private boundaries in welfare*, Social Policy in a Cold Climate, Research Note 2, London: Centre for Analysis of Social Exclusion, London School of Economics and Political Science, http://sticerd.lse.ac.uk/dps/case/spcc/rn002.pdf

Burchardt, T, Hills, J, Propper, C, 1999, *Private welfare and public policy*, York: Joseph Rowntree Foundation, www.jrf.org.uk/report/private-welfare-and-public-policy

Burchardt, T, Obolenskaya, P, Vizard, P, 2015, *The coalition's record on adult social care: Policy, spending and outcomes 2010-2015*, Social Policy in a Cold Climate, Working Paper 17, London: Centre for Analysis of Social Exclusion, London School of Economics and Political Science, http://sticerd.lse.ac.uk/dps/case/spcc/WP17.pdf

Burton, M, 2015, Is the North/South divide history or current affairs?, *The Municipal Journal*, 22 January, www.themj.co.uk/Is-the-NorthSouth-divide-history-or-current-affairs/199384

Cabinet Office, ODPM (Office of the Deputy Prime Minister), 2011, *Opening doors, breaking barriers: A strategy for social mobility*, London: HM Government, www.gov.uk/government/publications/opening-doors-breaking-barriers-a-strategy-for-social-mobility

Cabinet Office, DETR (Department of the Environment, Transport and the Regions), 2002, *Your region, your choice: Revitalising the English regions*, London: DETR

Cameron, D, 2010, Transforming the British economy: Coalition strategy for economic growth, www.gov.uk/government/speeches/transforming-the-british-economy-coalition-strategy-for-economic-growth

Cameron, D, 2011a, Speech on public service reform, 17 January, www.newstatesman.com/uk-politics/2011/01/public-services-money-schools

Cameron, D, 2011b, Speech on Big Society, London, 14 February, www.gov.uk/government/speeches/pms-speech-on-big-society

Centre for Social Justice, 2009, *Breakthrough Britain: Dynamic benefits, towards welfare that works*, London: Centre for Social Justice, www.centreforsocialjustice.org.uk/UserStorage/pdf/Pdf%20reports/CSJ%20dynamic%20benefits.pdf

Centre for Social Justice, 2006, *Breakdown Britain: Executive summary*, London: Centre for Social Justice, www.centreforsocialjustice.org.uk/UserStorage/pdf/Pdf%20Exec%20summaries/Breakdown%20Britain.pdf

Chandler, D, Disney, R, 2014, Housing market trends and recent policies, in C Emmerson, P Johnson and H Miller (eds) *IFS green budget: February 2014*, London: Institute for Fiscal Studies, Chapter 5, www.ifs.org.uk/budgets/gb2014/gb2014_ch5.pdf

Chanfreau, J, Gowland, S, Lancaster, Z, Poole, E, Tipping, S, Toomse, M, 2011, *Maternity and paternity rights and Women Returners Survey 2009/10*, DWP Research Report, no 777 (January), London: Department for Work and Pensions, www.gov.uk/government/uploads/system/uploads/attachment_data/file/214367/rrep777.pdf

Cheshire, L, 2013, *Ending 15-minute care*, London: Leonard Cheshire Disability, www.leonardcheshire.org/sites/default/files/15%20min%20care%20report%20final.pdf

Chote, R, Crawford, R, Emmerson, C, Tetlow, G, 2010, *The public finances: 1997 to 2010*, 2010 Election Briefing Note No 6, IFS BN93, London: Institute for Fiscal Studies, www.ifs.org.uk/bns/bn93.pdf

CIH (Chartered Institute of Housing), 2014, *New approaches to fixed term tenancies*, Coventry: CIH

Civil Exchange, 2013, *The big society audit 2013*, London: Civil Exchange, www.civilexchange.org.uk/wp-content/uploads/2013/12/THE-BIG-SOCIETY-AUDIT-2013webversion.pdf

Clarke, A, William, P, Whitehead, C, 2014, *Housing associations and welfare reform: Facing up to the realities*, Cambridge: Centre for Housing & Planning Research, University of Cambridge, www.cchpr.landecon.cam.ac.uk/Projects/Start-Year/2009/Valuing-Planning-Obligations-in-England-2007-08/Housing-associations-welfare-reform-facing-up-to-the-realities

Connolly, S, Bevan, G, Mays, M, 2011, *Funding and performance of healthcare systems in the four countries of the UK before and after devolution*, London: The Nuffield Trust.

Conservative Party, The, 2010, *Conservative Liberal Democrat coalition negotiations agreements reached, 11 May 2010*, London: The Conservative Party, www.conservatives.com/~/media/Files/Downloadable%20Files/agreement.ashx?dl=true

Conservative Party, The, 2015, *Strong leadership, a clear economic plan, a brighter more secure future: The Conservative Party manifesto 2015*, London: The Conservative Party, https://issuu.com/conservativeparty/docs/ge_manifesto_low_res_bdecb3a47a0faf?e=16696947/12362115

Cooper, K, Stewart, K, 2013, *Does money affect children's outcomes? A systematic review*, York: Joseph Rowntree Foundation, https://www.jrf.org.uk/report/does-money-affect-children%E2%80%99s-outcomes

Corbyn, J, 2015, *Northern future*, https://d3n8a8pro7vhmx.cloudfront.net/jeremyforlabour/pages/103/attachments/original/1438626641/NorthernFuture.pdf?1438626641

CQC (Care Quality Commission), 2013, *A fresh start for the regulation and inspection of adult social care*, Newcastle upon Tyne: CQC, www.cqc.org.uk/sites/default/files/documents/20131013_cqc_afreshstart_2013_final.pdf

CQC, 2014, *The state of health care and adult social care in England 2013/14*, Newcastle upon Tyne: CQC, www.cqc.org.uk/sites/default/files/state-of-care-201314-full-report-1.1.pdf

CQC, 2015a, *The state of health care and adult social care in England 2014/15*, HC483, Newcastle upon Tyne: CQC, www.cqc.org.uk/sites/default/files/20151013_CQC_State_of_Care_Report_WEB.pdf

CQC, 2015b, *Hinchingbrooke Hospital: Quality report*. Date of inspection September 2014. Date of publication 9th Jan 2015, www.cqc.org.uk/sites/default/files/new_reports/AAAA2986.pdf

Crawford, R, Emmerson, C, 2012, *NHS and social care funding: The outlook to 2021/22*, Research report, London: Nuffield Trust, www.nuffieldtrust.org.uk/sites/files/nuffield/publication/120704_nhs-social-care-funding-outlook-2021-22.pdf

Crawford, C, Crawford, R, Jin, W, 2014a, *Estimating the public cost of student loans*, IFS Report 94, London: Institute for Fiscal Studies

Crawford, R, Emmerson, C, Keynes, S, 2014b, Public finances: Risks on tax, bigger risks on spending?, in *IFS green budget 2014*, London: Institute for Fiscal Studies, www.ifs.org.uk/budgets/gb2014/gb2014_ch2.pdf

Crisp, R, Mcamillan, R, Robinson, D, Wells, P, 2009, Continuity or change: What a future Conservative government might mean for regional, housing and welfare policies, *People, Place and Policy Online*, April, 58-74

Crowley, L, Balaram, B, Lee, N, 2012, *People or place – Urban policy in the age of austerity*, London: The Work Foundation, www.theworkfoundation.com/DownloadPublication/Report/321_Updated_People%20or%20Place_Urban%20Policy%20in%20the%20Age%20of%20Austerity.pdf

D'Arcy, C, Gardiner, L, 2015, *Just the job or a working compromise? The changing nature of self-employment, 2014*, London: The Resolution Foundation, www.resolutionfoundation.org/publications/just-the-job-or-a-working-compromise-the-changing-nature-of-self-employment/

Davis, A, Hirsch, D, Padley, M, 2014a, *A minimum income standard for the UK in 2014*, York: Joseph Rowntree Foundation, www.jrf.org.uk/report/minimum-income-standard-uk-2014

Davis, K, Stremikis, K, Schoen, C, Squires, D, 2014b, *Mirror, mirror on the wall: 2014 update, How the US health care system compares internationally*, New York: The Commonwealth Fund, www.commonwealthfund. org/~/media/files/publications/fund-report/2014/jun/1755_davis_ mirror_mirror_2014.pdf

DCLG (Department for Communities and Local Government), 2010a, *Rough sleeping in England: total street count and estimates 2010*, London: DCLG, www.gov.uk/government/statistics/rough-sleeping-in-england-total-street-count-and-estimates-2010

DCLG (2010b) *English indices of deprivation 2010*, www.gov.uk/ government/statistics/english-indices-of-deprivation-2010

DCLG (Department for Communities and Local Government), 2011, *Regeneration to enable growth: What the government is doing in support of community-led regeneration*, London: DCLG

DCLG, 2012a, *Live tables on homelessness*, www.gov.uk/government/ statistical-data-sets/live-tables-on-homelessness

DCLG, 2012b, *Live tables on rents, lettings and tenancies*, www.gov.uk/ government/statistical-data-sets/live-tables-on-rents-lettings-and-tenancies

DCLG, 2012c, *Government response to the House of Commons Communities and Local Government Committee Report of Session 2010-12: Regeneration*, Cm 8264, London: The Stationery Office

DCLG, 2012d, *Business plan 2012-2015*, London: DCLG, www. gov.uk/government/uploads/system/uploads/attachment_data/ file/7527/2154390.pdf

DCLG, 2012e, *Reinvigorating Right to Buy and one for one replacement*, London: DCLG, www.gov.uk/government/consultations/ reinvigorating-right-to-buy--2

DCLG (2014) *Live tables on housing market and house prices*, www.gov. uk/government/statistical-data-sets/live-tables-on-housing-market-and-house-prices

DCLG, 2015a, *Rough sleeping statistics England – Autumn 2014*, Official statistics, Homelessness Statistical Release, 26 February, London: DCLG, www.gov.uk/government/uploads/system/ uploads/attachment_data/file/407030/Rough_Sleeping_Statistics_ England_-_Autumn_2014.pdf

DCLG, 2015b, *English Housing Survey: Households 2013-14*, London: DCLG, www.gov.uk/government/uploads/system/uploads/ attachment_data/file/461439/EHS_Households_2013-14.pdf

DCLG (2015c) *English indices of deprivation 2015*, www.gov.uk/ government/statistics/english-indices-of-deprivation-2015'

DCSF (Department for Children, Schools and Families), 2007a, *The Children's Plan: Building brighter futures*, London: DCSF

DCSF, 2007b, *School workforce in England (including pupil: teacher ratios and pupil: adult ratios)*, January 2007 (Revised), http://webarchive.nationalarchives.gov.uk/20130401151655/http://www.education.gov.uk/researchandstatistics/statistics/statistics-by-topic/teachersandschoolworkforce/a00195587/dcsf-school-workforce-in-england-%28including-pupil-

DCSF, 2007c, *Schools, pupils and their characteristics: January 2007*, Statistical First Release, SFR 30/2007, http://webarchive.nationalarchives.gov.uk/20130401151655/http://media.education.gov.uk/assets/files/pdf/sfr302007v2pdf.pdf

DCSF, 2008, *Back on track: A strategy for modernising alternative provision for young people*, Cm 7410, London: The Stationery Office, www.gov.uk/government/uploads/system/uploads/attachment_data/file/328241/Back_on_Track.pdf

DCSF, 2009, School workforce in England (including Local Authority level figures), January 2009 (Revised). Statistical First Release 23/2009 http://webarchive.nationalarchives.gov.uk/20130401151655/http://www.education.gov.uk/researchandstatistics/statistics/statistics-by-topic/teachersandschoolworkforce/a00196163/school-workforce-%28including-pupil-

De Agostini, P, Hills, J, Sutherland, H, 2015, *Were we really all in it together? The distributional effects of the 2010-2015 UK coalition government's tax-benefit policy changes: An end-of-term update*, Social Policy in a Cold Climate, Working Paper 22, London: Centre for Analysis of Social Exclusion, London School of Economics and Political Science, http://sticerd.lse.ac.uk/dps/case/spcc/wp22.pdf

De Deken, J, 2013, Towards an index of private pension provision, *Journal of European Social Policy*, 23, 3, 270-86

DETR (Department of the Environment, Transport and the Regions), 2000, *Quality and choice: A decent home for all*, Housing Green Paper, London: DETR, http://webarchive.nationalarchives.gov.uk/20120919132719/http:/www.communities.gov.uk/documents/housing/pdf/138019.pdf

DfE (Department for Education), 2010a, *Provision for children under five years of age in England – January 2010*, London: DfE

DfE, 2010b, *Schools, pupils and their characteristics: January 2010*, Statistical First Release, SFR 09/2010, www.gov.uk/government/statistics/schools-pupils-and-their-characteristics-january-2010

DfE, 2010c, *Early years foundation stage profile attainment by pupil characteristics, England 2009/10*, Statistical First Release, SFR 39/2010, www.gov.uk/government/uploads/system/uploads/attachment_data/file/218832/sfr39-2010.pdf

DfE, 2010d, *Key Stage 2 attainment by pupil characteristics, in England 2009/10*, Statistical First Release, SFR 35/2010, www.gov.uk/government/uploads/system/uploads/attachment_data/file/218852/sfr35-2010.pdf

DfE, 2010e, *GCSE and equivalent attainment by pupil characteristics in England, 2009/10*, Statistical First Release, SFR 37/2010, www.gov.uk/government/uploads/system/uploads/attachment_data/file/218842/sfr37-2010.pdf

DfE, 2010f, *Early years foundation stage profile attainment by pupil characteristics, England 2009/10*, Statistical First Release, SFR 39/2010, www.gov.uk/government/uploads/system/uploads/attachment_data/file/218832/sfr39-2010.pdf

DfE, 2010h, *Key Stage 2 attainment by pupil characteristics, in England 2009/10*, Statistical First Release, SFR 35/2010, www.gov.uk/government/uploads/system/uploads/attachment_data/file/218852/sfr35-2010.pdf

DfE, 2010i, *GCSE and equivalent attainment by pupil characteristics in England, 2009/10*, Statistical First Release, SFR 37/2010, www.gov.uk/government/uploads/system/uploads/attachment_data/file/218842/sfr37-2010.pdf

DfE, 2011, *A new approach to child poverty: Tackling the causes of disadvantage and transforming families' lives*, London: DfE, www.education.gov.uk/publications/standard/publicationDetail/Page1/CM%208061

DfE, 2012, *School funding reform: Arrangements for 2013-14*, London: DfE, www.gov.uk/government/uploads/system/uploads/attachment_data/file/244364/school_funding_reform_-_final_2013-14_arrangements.pdf

DfE, 2012a, *Key Stage 2 attainment by pupil characteristics, in England 2011/12*, Statistical First Release, SFR 33/2012, www.gov.uk/government/uploads/system/uploads/attachment_data/file/219204/sfr19-2012.pdf

DfE, 2012b, *GCSE and equivalent attainment by pupil characteristics in England: 2010 to 2011.* SFR 03/2012, www.gov.uk/government/statistics/gcse-and-equivalent-attainment-by-pupil-DfE characteristics-in-england-2010-to-2011

DfE, 2012c, *EYFSP attainment by pupil characteristics in England: academic year 2011 to 2012*, released 21 November 2012, www.gov.uk/government/statistics/eyfsp-attainment-by-pupil-characteristics-in-england-academic-year-2011-to-2012

DfE, 2014a, *Academies/free schools*, www.gov.uk/government/uploads/system/uploads/attachment_data/file/416332/Master-indicator-23-25-Nov-2014.pdf

DfE, 2014b, *Childcare and Early Years Providers Survey 2013*, Statistical First Release SFR 33/2014

DfE, 2014c, *Children's Social Care Innovation Programme: The challenge*, www.gov.uk/government/uploads/system/uploads/attachment_data/file/342078/Children_s_Social_Care_Innovation_Programme_-_the_challenge.pdf

DfE, 2014d, *National curriculum assessments at Key Stage 2, 2014 (revised)*, Statistical First Release, SFR 50/2014, www.gov.uk/government/statistics-national-curriculum-assessments-at-key-stage-2-2014-revised

DfE, 2014e, Early years foundation stage profile attainment by pupil characteristics, England 2014, Statistical First Release, SFR 46/2014, www.gov.uk/government/uploads/system/uploads/attachment_data/file/376216/SFR46_2014_text.pdf

DfE, 2014f, *Section 251 outturn: 2013 to 2014 data: Table A, England Summary.* 16 December 2014, www.gov.uk/government/publications/section-251-outturn-2013-to-2014-data

DfE, 2015a, *Provision for children under five years old in England: January 2015*, London: DfE

DfE, 2015b, *School workforce in England: November 2014*, Statistical First Release, SFR 21/2015, www.gov.uk/government/uploads/system/uploads/attachment_data/file/440577/Text_SFR21-2015.pdf

DfE, 2015c, *Revised GCSE and equivalents results in England, 2013 to 2014*, Statistical First Release, SFR 02/2015, www.gov.uk/government/uploads/system/uploads/attachment_data/file/406314/SFR_02_2015-revised_GCSE_and_equivalents.pdf

DfE, 2015d, *Level 2 and 3 attainment by young people in England measured using matched administrative data: Attainment by age 19 in 2014*, Statistical First Release, SFR 11/2015, www.gov.uk/government/uploads/system/uploads/attachment_data/file/418381/SFR_11-2015.pdf

DfE, 2015e, *GCSE and equivalent attainment by pupil characteristics, 2013 to 2014 (revised)*, Statistical First Release, SFR 06/2015, www.gov.uk/government/uploads/system/uploads/attachment_data/file/399005/SFR06_2015_Text.pdf

DfE, 2015f, *Schools, pupils and their characteristics January 2015*. Statistical First Release No 16/2015. London: Department for Education

DfE, 2015g, *Participation in Education, Training and Employment by 16-18 year olds in England: End 2014*. Statistical First Release, SFR 19/2015., www.gov.uk/government/uploads/system/uploads/attachment_data/file/436526/Main_text_16-18_participation_SFR19_2015.pdf

DfE and BIS (Department for Business, Innovation and Skills), 2013, *Rigour and responsiveness in skills*, London: DfE and BIS

DfES (Department for Education and Skills), 2004, *Final report of the Working Group on 14-19 reform*, London: DfES, www.educationengland.org.uk/documents/pdfs/2004-tomlinson-report.pdf

DfES (2005) *Statistical first release, schools and pupils in England*, SFR 42/2005 http://webarchive.nationalarchives.gov.uk/20120504203418/http://education.gov.uk/rsgateway/DB/SFR/s000606/index.shtml

DH (Department of Health), 2008a, *Department of Health strategic framework*, London: DH, http://webarchive.nationalarchives.gov.uk/20130107105354/http:/www.dh.gov.uk/prod_consum_dh/groups/dh_digitalassets/@dh/@en/documents/digitalasset/dh_085932.pdf

DH, 2008b, *High quality care for all: NHS next stage review final report*, Cm 7432, London: DH, www.gov.uk/government/uploads/system/uploads/attachment_data/file/228836/7432.pdf

DH, 2009a, *Tackling health inequalities: 10 years on – A review of developments in tackling health inequalities in England over the last 10 years*, London: DH, http://webarchive.nationalarchives.gov.uk/20130107105354/http:/www.dh.gov.uk/prod_consum_dh/groups/dh_digitalassets/documents/digitalasset/dh_098934.pdf

DH, 2009b, *Valuing People Now: A new three-year strategy for people with learning disabilities*, http://webarchive.nationalarchives.gov.uk/20130107105354/http://www.dh.gov.uk/en/Publicationsandstatistics/Publications/PublicationsPolicyAndGuidance/DH_093377

DH, 2010, *Equity and excellence: Liberating the NHS*, White Paper, Cm 7881, London: The Stationery Office, www.gov.uk/government/uploads/system/uploads/attachment_data/file/213823/dh_117794.pdf

DH, 2010a, *The operating framework for the NHS in England 2011-12*, www.gov.uk/government/publications/the-operating-framework-for-the-nhs-in-england-2011-12

DH, 2011, *Resource allocation: weighted capitation formula, Seventh edition,* www.gov.uk/government/uploads/system/uploads/attachment_data/file/216320/dh_124947.pdf

DH, 2013a, *Draft national minimum eligibility threshold for adult care and support. A discussion document,* www.gov.uk/government/uploads/system/uploads/attachment_data/file/209595/National_Eligibility_Criteria_-_discussion_document.pdf

DH, 2013b, *Funding transfer from the NHS to social care 2013: Directions,* www.gov.uk/government/publications/funding-transfer-from-the-nhs-to-social-care-2013-to-2014-directions

DH, 2013c, *Exposition book public health allocations 2013-14 and 2014-15: Technical guide,* www.gov.uk/government/uploads/system/uploads/attachment_data/file/213324/Public-Health-Weighted-Capitation-FormulaTechnical-Guide-v0.13.pdf

DH, 2013d, Policy statement on care and support funding reform, www.gov.uk/government/uploads/system/uploads/attachment_data/file/217024/Policy-statement-on-funding-reform.pdf

DH and NHS England, 2014, *Achieving better access to mental health services by 2020,* London: DH and NHS England, www.gov.uk/government/uploads/system/uploads/attachment_data/file/361648/mental-health-access.pdf

DH, 2014, *HCHS Pay and Price Series 1975-76 to 2012-13,* Personal Communication with Dipesh Mistry (Assistant Analyst, Financial Planning Division, Department of Health)

DH and Treasury, 2015, *Department of Health's settlement at the Spending Review 2015,* www.gov.uk/government/news/department-of-healths-settlement-at-the-spending-review-2015

DIUS (Department for Innovation, Universities & Skills), 2008, *Innovation Nation.* London: The Stationery Office, www.gov.uk/government/uploads/system/uploads/attachment_data/file/238751/7345.pdf

Dorling, D, Rigby, J, Wheeler, B, Thomas, B, Fahmy, E, Gordon, D, Lupton, R, 2007, *Poverty, wealth and place in Britain 1968-2005,* Bristol: Policy Press for the Joseph Rowntree Foundation

Dorsett, R, Rolfe, H, George, A, 2011, *The Jobseeker's Allowance Skills Conditionality Pilot,* DWP Research Report 768, London: Department for Work and Pensions

Dowler, C, Calkin, S, 2014, 'Forward view: Unprecedented call for NHS funding growth', *Health Services Journal,* 23 October, www.hsj.co.uk/topics/finance-and-efficiency/forward-view-unprecedented-call-for-nhs-funding-growth/5076052.fullarticle

Dunhill, L, 2015, 'Exclusive: Stevens issues warning over government's NHS funding deal', *Health Services Journal*, 9th November, www.hsj.co.uk/news/finance/exclusive-stevens-issues-warning-over-governments-nhs-fundingdeal/5091783.article

DWP (Department for Work and Pensions), 2003, *Measuring child poverty*, London: Department of Work and Pensions

DWP, 2012a, *Evaluation of Mandatory Work activity*, Research Report 823, London: DWP, www.gov.uk/government/uploads/system/uploads/attachment_data/file/193330/rrep823.pdf

DWP, 2012b, *Households below average income – An analysis of the income distribution 1994/95 to 2012/13 (United Kingdom)*, London: DWP, www.gov.uk/government/uploads/system/uploads/attachment_data/file/325416/households-below-average-income-1994-1995-2012-2013.pdf

DWP, 2012c, *Impacts and costs and benefits of the Future Jobs Fund*, London: DWP, www.gov.uk/government/uploads/system/uploads/attachment_data/file/223120/impacts_costs_benefits_fjf.pdf

DWP, 2014, *Work Programme – Programme costs to 31st March 2014*, www.gov.uk/government/uploads/system/uploads/attachment_data/file/325995/Work_Programme_Costs_v7_2014-07-01.pdf

DWP, 2015a, *Benefit cap quarterly statistics: GB households capped to February 2015*, London: DWP

DWP, 2015b, *Work Programme official statistics to June 2015, September 2015 release*, London: DWP, www.gov.uk/government/statistics/work-programmes-statistical-summary-data-to-30-june-2015

DWP, 2015c, *Benefit expenditure and caseload tables 2015*, www.gov.uk/government/statistics/benefit-expenditure-and-caseload-tables-2015

DWP, 2015d, *Measuring child poverty*, London: DWP, www.bristol.ac.uk/poverty/downloads/keyofficialdocuments/Measuring%20child%20poverty%20DWP%202003.pdf

Edmiston, D, 2011, *The shifting balance of private and public welfare activity in the United Kingdom, 1979 to 2007*, CASEpaper 155, London: Centre for Analysis of Social Exclusion, London School of Economics and Political Science, http://sticerd.lse.ac.uk/dps/case/cp/CASEpaper155.pdf

Elming, W, Emmerson, C, Johnson, P, Chandler, C, 2015, *An assessment of the potential compensation provided by the new 'National Living Wage' for the personal tax and benefit measures announced for implementation in the current Parliament*, IFS Briefing Note BN175, London: Institute for Fiscal Studies, www.ifs.org.uk/uploads/publications/bns/BN175.pdf

Emerson, E, Hatton, C, 2008, *Estimating future need for adult social care services for people with learning disabilities in England*, Lancaster: Centre for Disability Research, http://eprints.lancs.ac.uk/21049/1/CeDR_2008-6_Estimating_Future_Needs_for_Adult_Social_Care_Services_for_People_with_Learning_Disabilities_in_England.pdf

Emmerson, C, Tetlow, G, 2015, Public finances under the coalition, in C Emmerson, P Johnson and R Joyce (eds) *IFS green budget 2015*, London: Institute for Fiscal Studies, Chapter 1, www.ifs.org.uk/publications/7554

Eurofound, 2014, *Access to healthcare in times of crisis*, Luxembourg: Publications Office of the European Union, www.eurofound.europa.eu/sites/default/files/ef_publication/field_ef_document/ef1442en.pdf

Eurostat (Online), *Eurostat statistics database*, http://ec.europa.eu/eurostat/data/database

Evandrou, M, Falkingham, J, 2009, Pensions and income security in later life, in J Hills, T Sefton and K Stewart (eds) *Towards a more equal society? Poverty, inequality and policy since 1997*, CASE Studies on Poverty, Place, and Policy, Bristol: Policy Press in association with the Joseph Rowntree Foundation

Fenton, A, 2013, *Small-area measures of income poverty*, CASEpaper 173, London: Centre for Analysis of Social Exclusion, London School of Economics and Political Science

Fernandez, J-L, Snell, T, Wistow, G, 2013, *Changes in the patterns of social care provision in England: 2005/6 to 2012/13*, PSSRU Discussion Paper 2867, Canterbury: Personal Social Services Research Unit, University of Kent, www.pssru.ac.uk/archive/pdf/dp2867.pdf

Ferrari, E, 2007, Housing market renewal in an era of new housing supply, *People, Place and Policy Online*, 1, 3, 124-35

Field, F, 2010, *The foundation years: Preventing poor children becoming poor adults: The Report of the Independent Review on Poverty and Life Chances*, London: Cabinet Office, http://webarchive.nationalarchives.gov.uk/20110120090128/http:/povertyreview.independent.gov.uk/media/20254/poverty-report.pdf

Finch, D, 2015, *Making the most of UC: Final report of The Resolution Foundation review of Universal Credit*, London: The Resolution Foundation, www.resolutionfoundation.org/publications/making-it-work-final-report-of-the-resolution-foundation-review-of-universal-credit/

Fitzgerald, A, Lupton, R, Brady, A-M, 2014, *Hard times, new directions? The impact of the local government spending cuts in three deprived neighbourhoods of London*, Social Policy in a Cold Climate, Working Paper 9, London: Centre for Analysis of Social Exclusion, London School of Economics and Political Science

Fitzpatrick, S, Pawson, H, Bramley, G, Wilcox, S, Watts, B, 2015, *The homelessness monitor: England 2015, The homelessness monitor 2011-2016*, London: Crisis, www.crisis.org.uk/data/files/publications/Homelessness_Monitor_England_2015_final_web.pdf

Foden, M, Fothergill, S, Gore, T, 2014, *The state of the coalfields: Economic and social conditions in the former mining communities of England, Scotland and Wales.* Sheffield: Centre for Regional Economic and Social Research

Forder, J, Fernandez, J, 2010, *The impact of a tightening fiscal situation on social care for older people*, PSSRU Discussion Paper 2723, Canterbury: Personal Social Services Research Unit, University of Kent, www.pssru.ac.uk/pdf/dp2723.pdf

Francis, B, 2011, *(Un)satisfactory? Enhancing life chances by improving 'satisfactory' schools*, London: RSA

Francis, R, 2010, *Independent Inquiry into Care provided by Mid Staffordshire NHS Foundation Trust: January 2005-March 2009 Volume 1*, HC375-I, London: The Stationery Office, http://webarchive.nationalarchives.gov.uk/20130107105354/http:/www.dh.gov.uk/prod_consum_dh/groups/dh_digitalassets/@dh/@en/@ps/documents/digitalasset/dh_113447.pdf

Francis, R, 2013, *Report of the Mid Staffordshire NHS Foundation Trust Public Inquiry*, London: The Stationery Office, http://webarchive.nationalarchives.gov.uk/20150407084003/http://www.midstaffspublicinquiry.com/report

Freeman, J, Gill, S, 2014, *Research on children's services spending and budgeting – Section 251 returns*, London: CIPFA (Chartered Institute of Public Finance and Accountancy)

Freud, D, 2007, *Reducing dependency, increasing opportunity options for the future of welfare to work: An independent report to the Department for Work and Pensions*, London: Department for Work and Pensions, www.dwp.gov.uk/publications/dwp/2007/welfarereview.pdf

FSA (Financial Services Authority), 2010, *Financial risk outlook 2010*, London: FSA, www.fsa.gov.uk/pubs/plan/financial_risk_outlook_2010.pdf

Fuller, A, Leonard, P, Unwin, L, Davey, G, 2015, *Does apprenticeship work for adults? The experiences of adult apprentices in England*, London: UCL Institute of Education

Gaffney, D, 2015, Retrenchment, reform, continuity: Welfare under the coalition, *National Institute Economic Review*, 231, 1, R 44-53

Gambaro, L, Stewart, KJ, Waldfogel, J, 2014, 'Introduction', in *An equal start? Providing quality early education and care for disadvantaged children*, Bristol: The Policy Press

Gardiner, L, Hussein, S, 2015, *As if we cared: The costs and benefits of a Living Wage for social care workers*, London: The Resolution Foundation, www.resolutionfoundation.org/wp-content/uploads/2015/03/As-if-we-cared.pdf

Glendinning, C, 2012, Home care in England: Markets in the context of under-funding, *Health and Social Care in the Community*, 20, 3, 292-9

Glennerster, H, 2015a, 'Health and long term care' in A Seldon and M. Finn (eds) *The coalition effect*, Cambridge: Cambridge University Press

Glennerster, H, 2015b, Personal communication with author

Goff, J, Hall, J, Sylva, K, Smith, T, Smith, G, Eisenstadt, N, Sammons, P, Evangelou, M, Smees, R, Chu, K, 2013, *Evaluation of Children's Centres in England (ECCE): Strand 3, Delivery of family services by children's centres*, London: Department for Education

Gregg, P, Harkness, S, 2003, Welfare reform and the employment of lone parents, in *The labour market under New Labour: The state of working Britain 2003*, Houndmills, Basingstoke and New York: Palgrave Macmillan

Gregg, P, Machin, S, Fernández-Salgado, M, 2014, Real wages and unemployment in the big squeeze, *The Economic Journal*, 124, 576, 408-32

Griffiths, R, 1988, *Community care: Agenda for action*, London: HMSO

Hall, I, 2011, The coalition and the UK housing market, *Politics*, 31, 2, 72-81

Hamnett, C, 2014, Shrinking the welfare state: The structure, geography and impact of British government benefit cuts, *Transactions of the Institute of British Geographers*, 39, 4, 490-503

Hancock, R, Wittenberg, R, Hu, B, Morciano, M, Comas-Herrera, A, 2013, *Long-term care funding in England: An analysis of the costs and distributional effects of potential reforms*, Canterbury: Personal Social Services Research Unit, University of Kent, www.lse.ac.uk/LSEHealthAndSocialCare/PDF/DP2857.pdf

Harker, R, 2011, NHS Funding and Expenditure, Standard Note SN/SG/724, House of Commons Library, http://researchbriefings.files.parliament.uk/documents/SN00724/SN00724.pdf

Harloe, M, 1995, *The people's home? Social rented housing in Europe and America*, Oxford: Wiley-Blackwell

Hastings, A, Bailey, N, Besemer, K, Bramley, G, Gannon, M, Watkins, D, 2013, *Coping with the cuts? Local government and poorer communities*, York: Joseph Rowntree Foundation

Hazell, R, Yong, B, 2015, *The politics of coalition: How the Conservative-Liberal Democrat government works*, Oxford: Hart Publishing

Health Survey for England, 2008, UKDA study number 6397. National Centre for Social Research and University College London. Department of Epidemiology and Public Health, Health Survey for England, 2008 [computer file]. 4th Edition. Colchester, Essex: UK Data Archive [distributor], August 2013. SN: 6397, http://dx.doi.org/10.5255/UKDA-SN-6397-2

Health Survey for England 2012, UKDA study number 7480. NatCen Social Research and University College London. Department of Epidemiology and Public Health, Health Survey for England, 2012 [computer file]. Colchester, Essex: UK Data Archive [distributor], April 2014. SN: 7480, http://dx.doi.org/10.5255/UKDA-SN-7480-1

HEFCE (Higher Education Funding Council for England), 2014, *Pressure from all sides: Economic and policy influences on part-time higher education*, London: HEFCE

Herden, E, Power, A, Provan, B, 2015, *Is welfare reform working? Impacts on working age tenants: A study of SW HAILO*, CASEreport 90, London: Centre for Analysis of Social Exclusion, London School of Economics and Political Science

Hickman, P, Reeve, K, Wilson, I, Green, S, Dayson, C, Kemp, P, 2014, *Direct payment demonstration projects: 12 month stage reports*, London: Department for Work and Pensions, www.shu.ac.uk/research/cresr/sites/shu.ac.uk/files/dwp-research-summary-dpdp-12-month-stage-reports.pdf

Hicks, J, 2015, Inequality, marketisation and the Left: Schools policy in England and Sweden, *European Journal of Political Research*, 54, 2, 326-42

Hills, J, 2007, *Ends and means: The future roles of social housing in England*, CASEreport 34, London: Centre for Analysis of Social Exclusion, London School of Economics and Political Science, http://eprints.lse.ac.uk/5568/1/Ends_and_Means_The_future_roles_of_social_housing_in_England_1.pdf

Hills, J, 2011, The changing architecture of the UK welfare state, *Oxford Review of Economic Policy*, 27, 4, 589-607

Hills, J, 2013, *Labour's record on cash transfers, poverty, inequality and the life cycle*, Social Policy in a Cold Climate, Working Paper 5, London: Centre for Analysis of Social Exclusion, London School of Economics and Political Science

Hills, J, 2015a, *The coalition's record on cash transfers, poverty and inequality 2010-2015*, Social Policy in a Cold Climate, Working Paper 11, London: Centre for Analysis of Social Exclusion, London School of Economics and Political Science

Hills, J, 2015b, *Good times, bad times: The welfare myth of them and us*, Bristol: Policy Press, www.policypress.co.uk/display. asp?K=9781447320036

Hills, J, 2015c, *New research evidence on social mobility and educational attainment, Social Policy in a Cold Climate, Summary July 2015*, http:// sticerd.lse.ac.uk/dps/case/spcc/socialmobility_summary.pdf

Hills, J, Stewart, K (eds), 2005, *A more equal society? New Labour, poverty, inequality and exclusion*, CASE Studies on Poverty, Place, and Policy, Bristol: Policy Press

Hills, J, Sefton, T, Stewart, K, 2009, *Towards a more equal society? Poverty, inequality and policy since 1997*, Bristol: Policy Press

Hills, J, Cunliffe, J, Obolenskaya, P, Karagiannaki, E, 2015a, *Falling behind, getting ahead: The changing structure of inequality in the UK, 2007-2013*, Social Policy in a Cold Climate, Research Report 5, London: London School of Economics and Political Science, http:// sticerd.lse.ac.uk/dps/case/spcc/RR05.pdf

Hills, J, Bastagli, F, Cowell, F, Glennerster, H, Karagiannaki, E, McKnight, A, 2015b, *Wealth in the UK: Distribution, accumulation, and policy*, Oxford: Oxford University Press

Hills, J, Brewer, M, Jenkins, S, Lister, R, Lupton, R, Machin, S, Mills, C, Modood, T, Rees, T, Riddell, S, 2010, *An anatomy of economic inequality in the UK – Report of the National Equality Panel*, CASEreport 60, London: London School of Economics and Political Science, http://eprints.lse.ac.uk/28344/1/CASEreport60.pdf

Hirsch, D, 2006, *What will it take to end child poverty? Firing on all cylinders*, York: Joseph Rowntree Foundation

HM Government, 2007, *World class skills: Implementing the Leitch Review of Skills in England*, London: HMSO

HM Government, 2008, *Putting people first: A shared vision and commitment to the transformation of adult social care*, http://webarchive. nationalarchives.gov.uk/20130107105354/http:/www.dh.gov.uk/ prod_consum_dh/groups/dh_digitalassets/@dh/@en/documents/ digitalasset/dh_081119.pdf

HM Government, 2010, *The coalition: Our programme for government*, London: Cabinet Office, www.gov.uk/government/uploads/system/uploads/attachment_data/file/78977/coalition_programme_for_government.pdf

HM Government, 2011a, *Laying the foundations: A housing strategy for England*, London: HM Government, www.gov.uk/government/uploads/system/uploads/attachment_data/file/7532/2033676.pdf

HM Government, 2011b, *Open public services*, White Paper, Cm 8145, London: The Stationery Office, www.gov.uk/government/uploads/system/uploads/attachment_data/file/255288/OpenPublicServices-WhitePaper.pdf

HM Government, 2012, *Opening doors, breaking barriers: A strategy for social mobility, Update on progress since April 2011*, www.dpm.cabinetoffice.gov.uk/sites/default/files_dpm/resources/HMG_SocialMobility_acc.pdf

HM Government, 2015, *Help to Buy (equity loan) scheme quarterly statistics, 3rd June 2015*, London: HM Government, www.gov.uk/government/statistical-data-sets/help-to-buy-equity-loan-scheme-monthly-statistics

HMRC (Her Majesty's Revenue and Customs), 2015, *Child and Working Tax Credits statistics: Finalised annual awards 2013 to 2014*, www.gov.uk/government/statistics/child-and-working-tax-credits-statistics-finalised-annual-awards-2013-to-2014

HM Treasury, 2003, *Every Child Matters*, Cm 5860, London: The Stationery Office, www.education.gov.uk/consultations/downloadableDocs/EveryChildMatters.pdf

HM Treasury, 2008a, *Pre-budget report 2008: Facing global challenges: supporting people through difficult times*. London: The Stationery Office, http://webarchive.nationalarchives.gov.uk/20100407010852/http://www.hm-treasury.gov.uk/prebud_pbr08_repindex.htm

HM Treasury, 2008b, *Budget 2008, Stability and opportunity: Building a strong, sustainable future*, Economic and fiscal strategy report and financial statement and budget report, March, London: The Stationery Office, www.gov.uk/government/uploads/system/uploads/attachment_data/file/250345/0388.pdf

HM Treasury, 2009a, *Budget 2009: Building Britain's future, Economic and fiscal strategy report and financial statement and budget report*, London: The Stationery Office

HM Treasury, 2009b, *Pre-budget report December 2009 – Securing the recovery growth and opportunity*, London: HM Treasury, www.gov.uk/government/publications/pre-budget-report-december-2009

HM Treasury, 2011, *Public expenditure statistical analyses 2011*, London: The Stationery Office, www.gov.uk/government/statistics/public-expenditure-statistical-analyses-2011'

HM Treasury, 2012, *Public expenditure statistical analyses 2012*, www.gov.uk/government/statistics/public-expenditure-statistical-analyses-2012

HM Treasury, 2013a, *Budget 2013*, London: HM Treasury, www.gov.uk/government/publications/budget-2013-documents

HM Treasury, 2013b, *Class (2013) 1: Sector classification*, London: HM Treasury, www.gov.uk/government/uploads/system/uploads/attachment_data/file/226420/PU1547_final.pdf

HM Treasury, 2013c, *Main supply estimates 2013-14*, London: HM Treasury

HM Treasury, 2014a, *Public expenditure statistical analyses 2014*, www.gov.uk/government/statistics/public-expenditure-statistical-analyses-2014

HM Treasury, 2014b, *Impact on households: distributional analysis to accompany Autumn Statement 2014*, www.gov.uk/government/uploads/system/uploads/attachment_data/file/293738/budget_2014_distributional_analysis.pdf

HM Treasury, 2015a, *Help to Buy: Mortgage Guarantee Scheme quarterly statistics: October 2013 to March 2015*, London: HM Treasury, www.gov.uk/government/uploads/system/uploads/attachment_data/file/431714/H2B_mortgage_guarantee_stats_030615.pdf

HM Treasury, 2015b, *Impact on households: Distributional analysis to accompany budget 2015*, London: HM Treasury, www.gov.uk/government/uploads/system/uploads/attachment_data/file/413877/distributional_analysis_budget_2015.pdf

HM Treasury, 2015c, *Public expenditure statistical analyses 2015*, www.gov.uk/government/statistics/public-expenditure-statistical-analyses-2015

HM Treasury, 2015d, *Summer budget 2015*, HC 264, London: The Stationery Office

HM Treasury, 2015e, *Whole of government accounts year ended March 2014*, HC 1091, London: HM Treasury, www.gov.uk/government/publications/whole-of-government-accounts-2013-to-2014

HM Treasury, 2015f, *GDP deflators at market prices, and money GDP: June 2015* (Quarterly National Accounts), www.gov.uk/government/statistics/gdp-deflators-at-market-prices-and-money-gdp-june-2015-quarterly-national-accounts

HM Treasury, Greater Manchester Combined Authority, 2014, *Greater Manchester Agreement: Devolution to the GMCA and transition to a directly elected mayor*, London: HM Treasury, www.gov.uk/government/uploads/system/uploads/attachment_data/file/369858/Greater_Manchester_Agreement_i.pdf

HMSO, 2001, *Statistics of education: Schools in England*, London: Her Majesty's Stationery Office

Hodkinson, S, 2011, The private finance initiative in English council housing regeneration: A privatisation too far?, *Housing Studies*, 26, 6, 911-32

Hodkinson, S, Robbins, G, 2013, The return of class war conservatism? Housing under the UK coalition government, *Critical Social Policy*, 33, 1, 57-77

Hodkinson, S, Watt, P, Mooney, G, 2013, Neoliberal housing policy – Time for a critical re-appraisal, *Critical Social Policy*, 33, 1, 3-16

Hoeckel, K, Cully, M, Field, S, Halász, G, Kis, V, 2009, *Learning for jobs: OECD reviews of vocational education and training: England and Wales*, Paris: OECD Publishing

Houghton, J, 2010, A job half done and half abandoned: New Labour's National Strategy for Neighbourhood Renewal 1999-2009, *International Journal of Neighbourhood Renewal*, 2, 2

House of Commons Children, Schools and Families Committee (2008) *Testing and assessment (Third Report 2007-08)*, London: The Stationery Office

House of Commons Children, Schools and Families Committee, 2010, *Training of teachers (Fourth report 2009-10)*, London: The Stationery Office

House of Commons Committee of Public Accounts, 2015a, *Financial sustainability of NHS bodies*, HC 736, London: The Stationery Office, www.publications.parliament.uk/pa/cm201415/cmselect/cmpubacc/736/736.pdf

House of Commons Committee of Public Accounts, 2015b, *School oversight and intervention: Thirty-second report of Session 2014-15*, London: The Stationery Office

House of Commons Communities and Local Government Committee, 2011, *Regeneration: Sixth report of Session 2010-12*, HC 1014, London: The Stationery Office

House of Commons Education Committee, 2014, *Underachievement in education by white working class children*, London: House of Commons

House of Commons Education Committee, 2015, *Academies and free schools: Fourth report of Session 2014-15*, HC258, London: The Stationery Office

HSCIC (Health and Social Care Information Centre) (nd) National Adult Social Care Intelligence Service (NASCIS) online analytical tool, https://nascis.hscic.gov.uk/Portal/Tools.aspx

HSCIC Online, HSCIC Indicator portal, https://indicators.ic.nhs.uk/webview/

HSCIC, 2012, *Abuse of vulnerable adults in England, Final Report 2010/11: Experimental Statistics*, www.hscic.gov.uk/pubs/abuseva1011

HSCIC, 2013a, *National gross current expenditure and national net current expenditure*, www.hscic.gov.uk/catalogue/PUB11644

HSCIC, 2013b, *Abuse of vulnerable adults in England, Final Report 2011/12: Experimental statistics*, www.hscic.gov.uk/catalogue/PUB10430/abus-vunr-adul-eng-11-12-fin-rep.pdf

HSCIC, 2014a, *Community care statistics, Social services activity, England – 2013-14, Final release*, www.hscic.gov.uk/article/2021/Website-Search?productid=16628&q=social+care+activity&sort=Relevance&size=10&page=1&area=both#top

HSCIC, 2014b, *Health Survey for England – 2013, Trend tables*, www.hscic.gov.uk/catalogue/PUB16077

HSCIC, 2014c, *PSS-EX1 return guidance*, http://www.hscic.gov.uk/media/13520/PSS-EX1-Guidance-2013-14/pdf/PSS-EX1_Guidance_2013-14_v1.0.pdf

HSCIC, 2014d, *Personal social services: Expenditure and unit costs, England – 2013-14, Final release*, www.hscic.gov.uk/catalogue/PUB16111

HSCIC, 2014e, *Abuse of vulnerable adults in England, Final Report 2012/13: Experimental Statistics*, www.hscic.gov.uk/catalogue/PUB13499/abus-vuln-adul-eng-12-13-fin-rep.pdf

HSCIC, 2014f, *Safeguarding adults return annual report, England 2013-14: Experimental statistics*, www.hscic.gov.uk/catalogue/PUB15671/sar-1314-rep.pdf

HSCIC, 2015a, *NHS workforce statistics in England, Summary of staff in the NHS – 2004-2014, Overview: National master tables*, London: NHS England, www.hscic.gov.uk/searchcatalogue?productid=17425&q=nhs+staff+non-medical&topics=0%2fWorkforce&sort=Most+recent&size=100&page=1#top

HSCIC, 2015b, *NHS outcomes framework*, 22 September, www.hscic.gov.uk/nhsof

HSCIC, 2015c, *NHS workforce statistics – June 2015*, Provisional statistics, www.hscic.gov.uk/searchcatalogue?productid=18679&topics=1%2fWorkforce%2fStaff+numbers&sort=Relevance&size=10&page=1#top

HSCIC, 2015d, *Measures from the adult social care outcomes framework, England 2014/15, Final release*, www.hscic.gov.uk/catalogue/PUB18657

HSCIC (2015e) *Personal social services: Expenditure and unit costs, England – 2014-15*, Provisional release: Detailed national expenditure (Excel), http://www.hscic.gov.uk/catalogue/PUB18445

Humphries, R, 2013, *Paying for social care beyond Dilnot*, London: The King's Fund, www.kingsfund.org.uk/sites/files/kf/field/field_publication_summary/social-care-funding-paper-may13.pdf

Huskinson, T, Kostadintcheva, K, Greevy, H, Salmon, C, Dobie, S, Medien, K, 2014, *Childcare and Early Years Survey of Parents 2012-13*, London: Department for Education

Hutchings, M, 2015, *Exam factories: The impact of accountability measures on children and young people*, London: National Union of Teachers

ICOF (Independent Commission on Fees), 2015, *Independent Commission on Fees 2015 final report*, London: ICOF

IMF (International Monetary Fund), 2013, *United Kingdom – 2013 Article IV consultation: Concluding statement of the mission*, Washington, DC: IMF, www.imf.org/external/np/ms/2013/052213.htm

Jerrim, J, 2012, The reliability of trends over time in international education test scores: Is the performance of England's secondary school pupils really in relative decline?, *Journal of Social Policy*, 42, 2, 259-79

Karagiannaki, E, Platt, L, 2015, *The changing distribution of individual incomes in the UK before and after the recession*, CASEPaper 192, London: Centre for Analysis of Social Exclusion, London School of Economics and Political Science, http://sticerd.lse.ac.uk/dps/case/cp/casepaper192.pdf

Kazimirski, A, Smith, R, Butt, S, Ireland, E, Lloyd, E, 2008, *Childcare and Early Years Survey 2007: Parents' use, views and experience*, Research Report DCSF-RR025, London: Department for Children, Schools and Families, http://roar.uel.ac.uk/1778/1/DCSF-RR025.pdf

Keep, E, 2008, *From competence and competition to the Leitch Review*, Working Paper 17, Brighton: Institute for Employment Studies

Keep, M, 2014, *Local government finance settlement 2014/15*, Commons Library Standard Note, SN06816, London: House of Commons Library

Kemeny, J, 2001, Comparative housing and welfare: theorising the relationship, *Journal of Housing and the Built Environment*, 16, 1, 53-70

Kennedy, S, 2014, *Child Poverty Act 2010: A short note*, House of Commons Library, Social Policy Section, Commons Briefing papers SN05585, http://researchbriefings.parliament.uk/ResearchBriefing/Summary/SN05585

Keogh, B, 2015, Letter from Bruce Keogh to Mr Simon Stevens, Chief Executive, NHS England, *Making waiting time standards work for patients*, London: NHS England, www.england.nhs.uk/wp-content/uploads/2015/06/letter-waiting-time-standards-sbk.pdf

King's Fund, The, 2005, *An independent audit of the NHS under Labour (1997-2005)*, Briefing Paper, London: The King's Fund and *Sunday Times*, www.kingsfund.org.uk/sites/files/kf/field/field_publication_file/independent-audit-nhs-under-labour-1997%E2%80%932005-sunday-times-march-2005.pdf

King's Fund, The, 2006, *Wanless social care review. securing good care for older people: Taking a long term view*, www.kingsfund.org.uk/sites/files/kf/field/field_publication_file/securing-good-care-for-older-people-wanless-2006.pdf

Lafond, S, Sandeepa, A, Charlesworth, A, McKeon, A, 2014, *Into the red? The state of the NHS' finances. An analysis of NHS expenditure between 2010 and 2014*, Research Report, London: Nuffield Trust, www.nuffieldtrust.org.uk/sites/files/nuffield/publication/into_the_red.pdf

LaingBusson, 2014, *Healthcare market review 2013-2014*, 26th edn, www.laingbuisson.co.uk/MarketReports/LatestMarketReports/tabid/570/ProductID/605/Default.aspx

Lane, P, Foster, R, Gardiner, L, Lanceley, L, Purvis, A, 2013, *Work Programme evaluation: Procurement, supply chains and implementation of the commissioning model*, London: The Stationery Office, http://socialwelfare.bl.uk/subject-areas/services-activity/employment/departmentforworkandpensions/145588rrep832.pdf

Larkin, K, 2009, *Public sector cities: Trouble ahead*, London: Centre for Cities, http://centreforcities.customer.meteoric.net/assets/files/09-07-16%20Public%20sector%20cities.pdf

Le Grand, J, 2013, *The Public Service Mutual: A revolution in the making? The ownership revolution that Britain needs*, ResPublica, www.respublica.org.uk

Leitch Review of Skills, 2006, *Prosperity for all in the global economy – World class skills: The Leitch Review of Skills*, London: HMSO

LGA (Local Government Association), 2014a, *Adult Social Care Efficiency Programme – The final report*, London: LGA, www.local.gov.uk/documents/10180/11779/LGA+Adult+Social+Care+Efficiency+Programme+-+the+final+report/8e042c7f-7de4-4e42-8824-f7dc88ade15d

LGA, 2014b, *Future funding outlook 2014*, www.local.gov.uk/documents/10180/5854661/L14-340+Future+funding+-+initial+draft.pdf/1854420d-1ce0-49c5-8515-062dccca2c70

LGA, 2015, *Future funding outlook for councils 2019/20, Interim 2015 update*, London: LGA, www.local.gov.uk/documents/10180/11531/Future+Funding+Outlook+interim/39ad19fb-e5d8-4a2b-81a8-bf139497782d

Liberal Democrat Party, 2010, *Change that works for you: Liberal Democrat manifesto 2010*, www.politicsresources.net/area/uk/ge10/man/parties/libdem_manifesto_2010.pdf

Lupton, R, 2003, *Poverty Street: The dynamics of neighbourhood decline and renewal*, Bristol: Policy Press

Lupton, R, 2011, "No change there then!" The onward march of school markets and competition, *Journal of Educational Administration and History*, 43, 4, 309-23

Lupton, R, 2013, What is neighbourhood renewal policy for?, *People, Place and Policy*, 7, 2, 66-72

Lupton, R, Fitzgerald, A, 2015, *The coalition's record on area regeneration and neighbourhood renewal 2010-2015*, Social Policy in a Cold Climate, Working Paper 19, London: Centre for Analysis of Social Exclusion, London School of Economics and Political Science

Lupton, R, Obolenskaya, P, 2013, *Labour's record on education: Policy, spending and outcomes 1997-2010*, Social Policy in a Cold Climate, Working Paper 3, London: Centre for Analysis of Social Exclusion, London School of Economics and Political Science

Lupton, R, Thomson, S, 2015a, *The coalition's record on schools: Policy, spending and outcomes 2010-2015*, Social Policy in a Cold Climate, Working Paper 13, London: Centre for Analysis of Social Exclusion, London School of Economics and Political Science

Lupton, R. and Thomson, S, 2015b, 'Socio-economic inequalities in English schooling under the Coalition Government 2010–2015', *London Review of Education*, 13(2), pp 4-20

Lupton, R, Fenton, A, Fitzgerald, A, 2013a, *Labour's record on neighbourhood renewal in England: Policy, spending and outcomes 1997-2010*, Social Policy in a Cold Climate, Working Paper 6, London: Centre for Analysis of Social Exclusion, London School of Economics and Political Science

Lupton, R, Unwin, L, Thomson, S, 2015a, *The coalition's record on further and higher education and skills 2010-2015*, Social Policy in a Cold Climate, Working Paper 14, London: Centre for Analysis of Social Exclusion, London School of Economics and Political Science

Lupton, R, Burchardt,T, Fitzgerald, A, Hills, J, McKnight, A, Obolenskaya, P, Stewart, K, Thomson, S, Tunstall, R, Vizard, P, 2015b, *The Coalition's social policy record: Policy spending and outcomes 2010-2015*, Social Policy in a Cold Climate, Research Report 4, London: Centre for Analysis of Social Exclusion, London School of Economics and Political Science

Lupton, R, Hills, J, Stewart, K, Vizard, P, 2013b, *Labour's social policy record: Policy, spending and outcomes 1997-2010*, Research Report RR01, Social Policy in a Cold Climate, London: Centre for Analysis of Social Exclusion, London School of Economics and Political Science

MacInnes, T, Aldridge, H, Bushe, S, Tinson, A, Born, TB, 2014, *Monitoring poverty and social exclusion 2014*, York: Joseph Rowntree Foundation, http://npi.org.uk/files/8214/1658/1400/Monitoring_Poverty_and_Social_Exclusion_2014.pdf

McKnight, A, 2009, More equal working lives? An assessment of New Labour policies, in J Hills, T Sefton and K Stewart (eds) *Towards a more equal society? Poverty, inequality and policy since 1997-2009*, Bristol: Policy Press, pp 91-114, www.policypress.co.uk/display.asp?k=9781847422019

McKnight, A, 2014, *Disabled people's financial histories: Uncovering the disability wealth-penalty*, CASEPaper, London: Centre for Analysis of Social Exclusion, London School of Economics and Political Science, http://sticerd.lse.ac.uk/dps/case/cp/casepaper181.pdf

McKnight, A, 2015, *The coalition's record on employment: Policy, spending and outcomes 2010-2015*, Social Policy in a Cold Climate, Working Paper 15, London: Centre for Analysis of Social Exclusion, London School of Economics and Political Science

McKnight, A, Gardiner, L, 2015, Paying up: Who's been getting pay rises and who hasn't, and will that change?, in *Securing a pay rise: The path back to shared wage growth*, London: The Resolution Foundation, pp 17-22, www.resolutionfoundation.org/publications/securing-a-pay-rise-the-path-back-to-shared-wage-growth/

Maisey, R, Poole, E, Chanfreau, J, Fry, A, 2015, *Children's Centres Evaluation in England. Strand 2: Longitudinal survey of families using children's centres in the most disadvantaged areas*, Research Report DFE-RR434, London: Department for Education, www.gov.uk/government/uploads/system/uploads/attachment_data/file/407074/RR434_-_Evaluation_of_children_s_centres_in_England_follow-up_survey_of_families.pdf

Marmot, M, 2010, *Fair society, healthy lives: Strategic review of health inequalities in England post 2010*, London: The Marmot Review, www.instituteofhealthequity.org/projects/fair-society-healthy-lives-the-marmot-review

Marshall, A, 2008, *The future of regional development agencies*, London: Centre for Cities

Martin, R, 2015, Rebalancing the spatial economy: The challenge for regional theory, *Territory, Politics, Governance*, 3, 3, 235-72

Martin, R, Pike, A, Tyler, P, Gardiner, B, 2015, *Spatially rebalancing in the UK economy: The need for a new policy model*, Seaford: Regional Studies Association, www.regionalstudies.org/uploads/documents/SRTUKE_v16_PRINT.pdf

Mayhew, K, Keep, E, 2014, *Industrial strategy and the future of skills policy: The high road to sustainable growth*, CIPD Research Insight, London: Chartered Institute of Personnel and Development, www.cipd.co.uk/binaries/industrial-strategy-and-the-future-of-skills-policy_2014.pdf

Mays, N, Dixon, A, 2011, Assessing and explaining the impact of New Labour's market reforms, in A Dixon, N Mays and L Jones (eds) *Understanding New Labour's market reforms of the English NHS*, London: The King's Fund, pp 124-142, www.kingsfund.org.uk/publications/understanding-new-labours-market-reforms-english-nhs

Messenger, C, Molloy, D, 2014, *Getting it right for families: A review of integrated systems and promising practice in the early years*, London: Early Intervention Foundation

Mitchell, A, 2012, The time is right to revive the campaign for northern devolution, *The Guardian*, 7 March, www.theguardian.com/uk/the-northerner/2012/mar/07/austin-mitchell-north-hannah-mitchell-foundation

Monitor, 2013, *Closing the NHS funding gap: How to get better value health care for patients*, IRREP 22/13, London: Monitor, www.gov.uk/government/uploads/system/uploads/attachment_data/file/284044/ClosingTheGap091013.pdf

Monitor, 2015, *Performance of the foundation trust sector: 3 months ended 30 June 2015*, London: Monitor, www.gov.uk/government/uploads/system/uploads/attachment_data/file/466705/To_publish_-_Performance_of_the_NHS_Foundation_Trust_Sector-_3_monts_ended_30_June_-_report.pdf

Morgan, D, Astolfi, R, 2013, *Health spending growth at zero: Which countries, which sectors are most affected?*, OECD Health Working Papers No. 60, Paris: OECD Publishing, www.oecd-ilibrary.org/docserver/download/5k4dd1st95xv.pdf?expires=1454674136&id=id&accname=guest&checksum=66BB5A7ACF1934C040AFF649E418119D

Morgan, D, Astolfi, R, 2014, *Health spending continues to stagnate in many OECD countries*, OECD Health Working Papers No. 68, Paris: OECD Publishing, www.oecd.org/officialdocuments/publicdisplaydocumentpdf/?cote=DELSA/HEA/WD/HWP%282014%291&docLanguage=En

Munro, E, 2011, *The Munro Review of child protection: Final report: A child-centred system*, Cm 8062, London: The Stationery Office, www.gov.uk/government/uploads/system/uploads/attachment_data/file/175391/Munro-Review.pdf

NAO (National Audit Office), 2002, *Individual learning accounts*, London: The Stationery Office

NAO, 2009, *Train to Gain: Developing the skills of the workforce*, London: The Stationery Office

NAO, 2010, *Tackling inequalities in life expectancy in areas with the worst health and deprivation*, HC186, London: NAO, https://www.nao.org.uk/wp-content/uploads/2010/07/1011186.pdf

NAO, 2012, *Managing the expansion of the academies programme*, London: NAO

NAO, 2013, *Savings from operational PFI contracts*, London: NAO, www.nao.org.uk/wp-content/uploads/2013/11/Savings-from-operational-PFI-contracts_final.pdf

NAO, 2014a, *Impact of funding reductions on local authorities*, London: NAO, www.nao.org.uk/wp-content/uploads/2014/11/Impact-of-funding-reductions-on-local-authorities.pdf

NAO, 2014b, *The financial sustainability of NHS bodies*, HC 722, London: NAO, www.nao.org.uk/wp-content/uploads/2014/11/The-financial-sustainability-of-NHS-bodies.pdf

NAO, 2014c, *The Help to Buy equity scheme*, London: NAO

NAO, 2014d, *The Work Programme*, London: NAO, www.nao.org.uk/wp-content/uploads/2014/07/The-work-programme.pdf

NAO, 2015, *Funding for disadvantaged pupils*, London: NAO

NatCen (National Centre for Social Research), 2015, *British Social Attitudes 32*, London: NatCen, www.bsa.natcen.ac.uk/media/38972/bsa32_fullreport.pdf

National Assembly for Wales, 2013, *Public services reform: Timeline of local government developments*, Research Paper 13/052, Cardiff: National Assembly for Wales, www.assembly.wales/Research%20Documents/Public%20services%20reform%20timeline%20of%20local%20government%20developments%20-%20Research%20paper-11072013-248000/13-052-English.pdf

Nationwide, 2015, House price index data. www.nationwide.co.uk/about/house-price-index/download-data#xtab:affordability-benchmarks

NCVO (National Council of Voluntary Organisations), 2015, *UK civil society almanac 2015*, http://data.ncvo.org.uk/a/almanac15/introduction-2/

NESS (National Evaluation of Sure Start), 2005, *Early impacts of Sure Start local programmes on children and families*, Research Report NESS/2005/FR/013, London: HMSO, www.ness.bbk.ac.uk/impact/documents/1183.pdf

NESS, 2008, *The impact of Sure Start local programmes on three year olds and their families*, Research Report NESS/2008/FR/027, Nottingham: Department for Education and Skills, www.ness.bbk.ac.uk/impact/documents/41.pdf

NESS, 2012, *The impact of Sure Start local programmes on seven year olds and their families*, Research Report DFE-RR220, London: Department for Education, www.gov.uk/government/uploads/system/uploads/attachment_data/file/184073/DFE-RR220.pdf

Newton, B, Speckesser, S, Nafilyan, V, Maguire, S, Devins, D, Bickerstaffe, T, 2014, *The youth contract for 16-17 year olds not in education, employment or training evaluation: Research report*, London: Department for Education

Newton, B, Meager, N, Bertram, C, Corden, A, Lalani, M, Metcalf, H, Rolfe, H, Sainsbury, R, Weston, K, 2012, *Work Programme evaluation: Findings from the first phase of qualitative research on programme delivery*, DWP Research Report No 821, London: Department for Work and Pensions, www.gov.uk/government/uploads/system/uploads/attachment_data/file/193323/rrep821.pdf

NHS, 2009, *The handbook to the NHS Constitution*, http://webarchive.nationalarchives.gov.uk/20130107105354/http://www.dh.gov.uk/prod_consum_dh/groups/dh_digitalassets/@dh/@en/@ps/@sta/@perf/documents/digitalasset/dh_109785.pdf

NHS England, 2013a, *Allocation of resources to NHS England and the commissioning sector for 2014/15 and 2015/16*, Paper NHSE121305, https://www.england.nhs.uk/wp-content/uploads/2013/12/bm-item7.pdf

NHS England, 2013b, *Fundamental review of allocations policy – Annex C: Technical guidance to weighted capitation formula for clinical commissioning groups, 2013*, www.england.nhs.uk/wp-content/uploads/2013/08/ann-c-tech-guid.pdf

NHS England, 2013c, *News: NHS England publishes CCG funding allocations for next two years following adoption of new formula*, https://www.england.nhs.uk/2013/12/18/ccg-fund-allocs/

NHS England, 2014a, *Allocation of resources to NHS England and the commissioning sector for 2014/15 and 2015/16*, Board Paper NHSE121305, www.england.nhs.uk/wp-content/uploads/2013/12/bm-item7.pdf

NHS England, 2014b, *Delayed transfers of care statistics*, www.england.nhs.uk/statistics/wp-content/uploads/sites/2/2013/04/Annual-DTOC-report-2013-14-v2.pdf

NHS England, 2014c, *Five year forward view*, www.england.nhs.uk/wp-content/uploads/2014/10/5yfv-web.pdf

NHS England, 2015a, *Consultant-led referral to treatment waiting times data 2015-16*, RTT overview timeseries (to Jul 2015), www.england.nhs.uk/statistics/statistical-work-areas/rtt-waiting-times/rtt-data-2015-16/

NHS England, 2015b, *GP patient survey – National summary report*, http://gp-survey-production.s3.amazonaws.com/archive/2015/July/July%202015%20National%20Summary%20Report.pdf

NHS England, 2015c, *Overall patient experience scores: 2014 adult inpatient survey update, Overall results tables – England*, www.england.nhs.uk/statistics/2015/05/21/overall-patient-experience-scores-2014-adult-inpatient-survey-update/

NHS England, 2015d, *A&E attendances and emergency admissions 2015-16, Quarterly time Series 2004-05 onwards with Annual (03.07.15)*, www.england.nhs.uk/statistics/statistical-work-areas/ae-waiting-times-and-activity/statistical-work-areasae-waiting-times-and-activityae-attendances-and-emergency-admissions-2015-16-monthly-3/

NHS England, 2015e, *Cancer waiting times – National time series Q4 2008-09 to Q1 2015-16 (provider based)*, www.england.nhs.uk/statistics/statistical-work-areas/cancer-waiting-times/

NHS Trust Development Authority, 2015, *NHS trusts – Financial position for Q1 of 2015/16*, www.ntda.nhs.uk/blog/2015/10/09/nhs-trusts-financial-position-for-q1-of-201516/

NRU (Neighbourhood Renewal Unit), 2008, *Departmental floor targets*, http://webarchive.nationalarchives.gov.uk/20060530091128/http://neighbourhood.gov.uk/page.asp?id=585

The Nuffield Trust, The Health Foundation and The King's Fund, 2015, *The Spending Review: what does it mean for health and social care?*, www.kingsfund.org.uk/sites/files/kf/field/field_publication_file/Spending-Review-Nuffield-Health-Kings-Fund-December-2015_0.pdf

Nutbrown, C, 2012, *Foundations for quality: The independent review of early education and childcare qualifications, Final report,* www.gov.uk/government/uploads/system/uploads/attachment_data/file/175463/Nutbrown-Review.pdf

Obolenskaya, P, Burchardt, T, 2016, *Trends in public and private welfare 1979-80 to 2013-14,* CASEpaper 193, London: Centre for Analysis of Social Exclusion, London School of Economics and Political Science

Obolenskaya, P, Lupton, R, Provan, B, 2016, *Pulling in the same direction? Economic and social outcomes in London and the North since the recession,* Social Policy in a Cold Climate, Working Paper 23, London: London School of Economics, http://sticerd.lse.ac.uk/dps/case/spcc/wp23.pdf

OBR (Office for Budget Responsibility), 2011, *Fiscal sustainability report: July 2011,* http://budgetresponsibility.org.uk/wordpress/docs/FSR2011Annexes.pdf

OBR, 2012, *Fiscal sustainability report: July 2012,* http://budgetresponsibility.org.uk/fiscal-sustainability-report-july-2012/

OBR, 2013, *Fiscal sustainability report: July 2013,* London: The Stationery Office, http://budgetresponsibility.org.uk/wordpress/docs/2013-FSR_OBR_web.pdf

OBR, 2014, *Welfare trends report,* London: The Stationery Office, http://budgetresponsibility.org.uk/wordpress/docs/Welfare_trends_report_2014_dn2B.pdf

ODPM (Office of the Deputy Prime Minister), 2005, *Sustainable communities: Homes for all: A five year plan from the Office of the Deputy Prime Minister,* London: ODPM

ODPM, 2015, *Social mobility indicators, 25 March 2015 update,* London: HM Government, www.gov.uk/government/publications/social-mobility-indicators/social-mobility-indicators

OECD (Organisation for Economic Co-operation and Development), 2010, *Education at a Glance 2010,* Paris: OECD, www.oecd-ilibrary.org/content/book/eag-2010-en

OECD, 2011, *Health at a Glance 2011: OECD indicators,* Paris: OECD Publishing, www.oecd.org/els/health-systems/49105858.pdf

OECD, 2014, *Health at a Glance: Europe 2014,* Paris: OECD Publishing, http://ec.europa.eu/health/reports/docs/health_glance_2014_en.pdf

OECD, 2015a, *Focus on health spending: OECD health statistics 2015,* Paris: OECD Publishing, www.oecd.org/health/health-systems/Focus-Health-Spending-2015.pdf

OECD, 2015b, *OECD health statistics 2015, Frequently requested data,* www.oecd.org/health/health-systems/OECD-Health-Statistics-2015-Frequently-Requested-Data.xls

OECD.Stat (Online), *OECD statistics*, online database, http://stats. oecd.org/

O'Hara, M, 2014, *Austerity bites*, Bristol: Policy Press

ONS (Office for National Statistics), 2010a, *Business Register and Employment Survey (BRES)*, Newport: ONS, www.ons.gov.uk/ons/ rel/bus-register/business-register-employment-survey/2008/index. html

ONS, 2010b, *General Lifestyle Survey, 2008 report, Reference tables*, Newport: ONS, www.ons.gov.uk/ons/publications/re-reference-tables.html?edition=tcm%3A77-49408&format=hi-vis

ONS, 2011, *Population estimates for UK, England and Wales, Scotland and Northern Ireland, Population Estimates Timeseries 1971 to Current Year*, http://www.ons.gov.uk/ons/rel/pop-estimate/population-estimates-for-uk--england-and-wales--scotland-and-northern-ireland/ population-estimates-timeseries-1971-to-current-year/index.html

ONS, 2012, *Public sector classification guide, September 2012*, Newport: ONS, www.ons.gov.uk/ons/publications/re-reference-tables. html?edition=tcm%3A77-277291

ONS, 2013a, *Opinions and Lifestyle Survey, smoking habits amongst adults, 2012*, Newport: ONS, www.ons.gov.uk/ons/publications/ re-reference-tables.html?edition=tcm%3A77-315987

ONS, 2013b, *Providing unpaid care may have an adverse affect on young carers' general health*, Newport: ONS, www.ons.gov.uk/ons/rel/ census/2011-census-analysis/provision-of-unpaid-care-in-england-and-wales--2011/sty-unpaid-care.html

ONS, 2013c, *Population estimates for UK, England and Wales, Scotland and Northern Ireland, mid-2001 to mid-2010 revised*, www.ons.gov. uk/ons/rel/pop-estimate/population-estimates-for-uk--england-and-wales--scotland-and-northern-ireland/mid-2001-to-mid-2010-revised/index.html

ONS, 2013d, *National population projections, 2012-based projections*, Table A2-4, Principal Projection - England Population in Age Groups, 2012-based (Excel sheet), www.ons.gov.uk/ons/publications/re-reference-tables.html?edition=tcm%3A77-318453

ONS, 2013e, *Release edition reference tables: Population estimates for UK, England and Wales, Scotland and Northern Ireland, mid-2011 and mid-2012*, www.ons.gov.uk/ons/publications/re-reference-tables. html?edition=tcm%3A77-319259

ONS, 2014a, *Life expectancy at birth and at age 65 by local areas in England and Wales, 2011-13*, Newport: ONS, www.ons.gov.uk/ons/ publications/re-reference-tables.html?edition=tcm%3A77-370972

ONS, 2014b, *Self-employed workers in the UK – 2014*, Newport: ONS, www.ons.gov.uk/ons/dcp171776_374941.pdf

ONS, 2014c, *UK wages over the past four decades – 2014*, Newport: ONS, www.ons.gov.uk/ons/dcp171776_368928.pdf

ONS, 2014d, *Opinions and Lifestyle Survey, adult smoking habits in Great Britain, 2013*, Newport: ONS, www.ons.gov.uk/ons/publications/re-reference-tables.html?edition=tcm%3A77-380033

ONS 2014e *Overcrowding and under-occupation in England and Wales*, www.ons.gov.uk/ons/rel/census/2011-census-analysis/overcrowding-and-under-occupation-in-england-and-wales/index.html

ONS, 2015a, *Inequality in healthy life expectancy at birth by national deciles of area deprivation: England, 2011 to 2013*, Newport: ONS, www.ons.gov.uk/ons/publications/re-reference-tables.html?edition=tcm%3A77-392673

ONS, 2015b, *Public service productivity estimates: Healthcare, 2012*, Newport: ONS, www.ons.gov.uk/ons/rel/psa/public-sector-productivity-estimates--healthcare/2012/index.html

ONS, 2015c, *The effects of taxes and benefits on household income, 2013/14*, Newport: ONS, www.ons.gov.uk/ons/dcp171778_367431.pdf

ONS, 2015d, *The effects of taxes and benefits on household income, historical data, 1977 to financial year ending 2014*, Newport: ONS, www.ons.gov.uk/ons/rel/household-income/the-effects-of-taxes-and-benefits-on-household-income/historical-data--1977-2013-14/index.html

ONS, 2015e, *Suicides in the United Kingdom, 2013 registrations*, reference tables, Newport: ONS, www.ons.gov.uk/ons/publications/re-reference-tables.html?edition=tcm%3A77-385245

ONS, 2015f, *Measuring national well-being, life in the UK, 2015*, Newport: ONS, www.ons.gov.uk/ons/publications/re-reference-tables.html?edition=tcm%3A77-391358

ONS, 2015g, *Labour market statistics, September 2015*, Newport: ONS, www.ons.gov.uk/ons/rel/lms/labour-market-statistics/september-2015/index.html

ONS, 2015h, *Sustainable development indicators, July 2015*. 13th July 2015.

ONS, 2015i, *Population estimates for UK, England and Wales, Scotland and Northern Ireland, mid-2014*. Published 25 June 2015. Text. http://ons.gov.uk/ons/publications/re-reference-tables.html?edition=tcm%3A77-368259

ONS, 2015j, *Suicides in the United Kingdom, 2013 registrations*, Statistical Bulletin, Newport: ONS, www.ons.gov.uk/ons/dcp171778_395145.pdf

ONS, 2015k, *Regional household income, regional gross disposable household income (GDHI) 2013*, Reference tables, www.ons.gov.uk/ons/publications/re-reference-tables.html?edition=tcm%3A77-386452

ONS, 2015l, *Regional labour market statistics* (reference tables), December 2015, www.ons.gov.uk/ons/rel/subnational-labour/regional-labour-market-statistics/december-2015/index.html

Pawson, H, Wilcox, S, 2013, *UK housing review 2013*, Coventry: Chartered Institute of Housing, www.cih.org/resources/PDF/Policy%20free%20download%20pdfs/UKHR%202013%20Briefing%20Paper.pdf

Perry, J, Williams, M, Sefton, T, Haddad, M, 2014, *Emergency use only: Understanding and reducing the use of food banks in the UK*, London: Child Poverty Action Group, Church of England, Oxfam GB and The Trussell Trust, www.trusselltrust.org/resources/documents/press/foodbank-report.pdf

Pesch, U, 2005, *The predicaments of publicness*, Delft: Eburon

Pickard, L, 2015, A growing care gap? The supply of unpaid care for older people by their adult children in England to 2032, *Ageing & Society*, 35, 1, 96–123

Poverty Site, The, nd, *UK: Overcrowding*, www.poverty.org.uk/82/index.shtml

Powell, M, Miller, R, 2013, Privatizing the English National Health Service – an irregular verb?, *Journal of Health Politics, Policy and Law*, 38, 5, 1051-9

Powell, M, Miller, R, 2014, Framing privatisation in the English National Health Service, *Journal of Social Policy*, 43, 3, 575-94

Power, A, Provan, B, Herden, E, Serle, N, 2014, *The impact of welfare reform on social landlords and tenants*, Report by LSE Housing and Communities for the Joseph Rowntree Foundation, York: Joseph Rowntree Foundation, www.jrf.org.uk/report/impact-welfare-reform-social-landlords-and-tenants

Prime Minister's Office, 2014, *Growth deals: Firing up local communities*, 7 July

Pring, R, Hayward, D, Hodgson, A, Johnson, J, Keep, E, Oancea, A, Rees, G, Spours, K, Wilde, S, 2009, *Education for all: The future of education and training for 14-19 year olds*, London: Routledge

Prisk, M, 2012, Speech at the Council of Mortgage Lenders Conference, London, 11 July, www.gov.uk/government/speeches/council-of-mortgage-lenders-conference

Prisk, M, 2013a, Keynote speech at the Chartered Institute of Housing Conference, Manchester, 27 June, www.gov.uk/government/speeches/housing-speech-by-mark-prisk

Prisk, M, 2013b, Speech to the Home Builder's Federation Annual Policy Conference 2013, London, 3 December, www.gov.uk/government/speeches/home-builders-federation-conference-2013

Raco, M, 2013, *State-led privatisation and the demise of the democratic state: Welfare reform and localism in an era of regulatory capitalism*, New edition, Aldershot: Ashgate

Rawnsley, A, 2010, *The end of the party: The rise and fall of New Labour*, London: Penguin

Reed, H, Portes, H, 2014, Cumulative Impact Assessment: A Research Report by Landman Economics and the National Institute of Economic and Social Research (NIESR) for the Equality and Human Rights Commission, Equality and Human Rights Commission Research report 94, Manchester: EHRC, www.equalityhumanrights. com/sites/default/files/publication_pdf/Cumulative%20Impact%20 Assessment%20full%20report%2030-07-14.pdf

Riley, J, Chote, R, 2014, *Crisis and consolidation in the public finances*, Working Paper No 7, London: Office for Budget Responsibility, http://budgetresponsibility.org.uk/wordpress/docs/WorkingPaper7a. pdf

Roberts, A, Marshall, L, Charlesworth, A, 2012, *A decade of austerity? The funding pressures facing the NHS from 2010/11 to 2021/22*, Research report, London: Nuffield Trust, www.nuffieldtrust.org.uk/ sites/files/nuffield/121203_a_decade_of_austerity_full_report.pdf

Roberts, N, Stewart, KJ, 2015, 'Plans to axe child poverty measures contradict the vast majority of expert advice the government received', LSE Politics and Policy blog, November 17th 2015. http://blogs.lse. ac.uk/politicsandpolicy/plans-to-axe-child-poverty-measures-have-no-support-among-experts/

Rugg, J, Rhodes, D, 2008, *The private rented sector: Its contribution and potential*, York: Centre for Housing Policy, University of York, www. york.ac.uk/media/chp/documents/2008/prsreviewweb.pdf

Rutter, J, 2015, *Childcare costs survey 2015*, London: Family and Childcare Trust

Salmond, A, 2008, *On delivering more effective government*, Edinburgh, 30 January, www.gov.scot/News/Speeches/Speeches/First-Minister/ simplifyingpublicservices

Sefton, T, Hills, J, Sutherland, H, 2009, Poverty, inequality and redistribution, in *Towards a more equal society? Policy, inequality and policy since 1997*, Bristol: Policy Press, pp 21-45

Seldon, A, Finn, M (eds), 2015, *The coalition effect, 2010-2015*, Cambridge: Cambridge University Press

Sellick, C, 2011, Privatising foster care: The UK experience within an international context, *Social Policy and Administration*, 45, 7, 788-805

SEU (Social Exclusion Unit), 2001, *A new commitment to neighbourhood renewal: National strategy action plan*, London: SEU

SFA (Skills Funding Agency) (2014) *Further education and skills: statistical first release – learner participation, outcomes and level of highest qualification,* www.gov.uk/government/uploads/system/uploads/attachment_data/file/362086/learner-participation-outcomes-and-level-of-highest-qualification-release-june14-sept-update.pdf

SFA (2015) *Further education and skills: statistical first release - learner participation, outcomes and level of highest qualification,* www.gov.uk/government/uploads/system/uploads/attachment_data/file/457619/SFR_commentary_June_2015.pdf

Shale, J, Balchin, K, Rahman, J, Reeve, R, Rolin, M (eds.) (2014) *Households below average income: An analysis of the income distribution 1994/95–2012/13.* July 2014 (United Kingdom). London, Department for Work and Pensions.

Shale, J, Balchin, K, Rahman, J, Reeve, R, Rollin, M (2015) *Households below average income: An analysis of the income distribution 1994/95-2013/14.* June 2015 (United Kingdom). London: Department for Work and Pensions, www.gov.uk/government/statistics/households-below-average-income-19941995-to-20132014

Shapps, G, 2010, Speech at the National Housing Federation Annual Conference, 22 September, International Convention Centre, Birmingham National, www.gov.uk/government/speeches/national-housing-federation-annual-conference-2010

Shapps, G, 2011, Role of building societies, Speech, 20 October, Savoy Place, London, www.gov.uk/government/speeches/role-of-building-societies--2

Sibieta, L, 2015, School spending in England 2010-15, *Fiscal Studies*, 36, 3, 283-302

Sibieta, L, Chowdry, H, Muriel, A, 2008, *Level playing field? The implications of school funding*, Reading: CfBT Education Trust, www.cfbt.com/evidenceforeducation/pdf/LevelPlayingFieldReport_FINAL.pdf

Skills for Care (2012) *The size and structure of the adult social care sector and workforce in England, 2012*, www.skillsforcare.org.uk/NMDS-SC-intelligence-research-and-innovation/NMDS-SC/Workforce-intelligence-publications/The-state-of-the-adult-social-care-sector-and-workforce-in-England,-2012.aspx

Slocock, C, 2015, *Whose society? The final big society audit*, Civil Exchange, www.civilexchange.org.uk/wp-content/uploads/2015/01/Whose-Society_The-Final-Big-Society-Audit_final.pdf

Smithies, R, 2005, *Public and private welfare activity in the United Kingdom, 1979 to 1999*, CASEpaper 93, London: Centre for Analysis of Social Exclusion, London School of Economics and Political Science, http://sticerd.lse.ac.uk/dps/case/cp/CASEpaper93.pdf

Smith, M, Jones, R, 2015, From Big Society to small state: Conservatism and the privatisation of government, *British Politics*, 10, 2, 226-48

Smith, R, Poole, E, Perry, J, Wollny, I, Reeves, A, Coshall, C, d'Souza, J, 2010, *Childcare and Early Years Survey of Parents 2009*, DFE-RR054, London: Department for Education, www.education.gov.uk/publications/RSG/Earlyyearsandchildcareworkforce/Page1/DFE-RR054

Social Mobility and Child Poverty Commission, 2014, *State of the Nation 2014: Social mobility and child poverty in Great Britain*, www.gov.uk/government/uploads/system/uploads/attachment_data/file/365765/State_of_Nation_2014_Main_Report.pdf

Stephens, M, Whitehead, C, Munro, M, 2005, *Lessons from the past, challenges for the future for housing policy: An evaluation of English housing policy 1975-2000*, London: Office of the Deputy Prime Minister, www.ahuri.edu.au/downloads/2005_Events/Christine_Whitehead/UK_Housing_Policy_1975_2000.pdf

Stevens, S, 2015, 'The next five years for the NHS', speech, 18 May 2015, West Midlands, www.england.nhs.uk/2015/05/fit-for-future/#full-speech

Stewart, K, 2009, A scar on the soul of Britain: Child poverty and disadvantage under New Labour, in J Hills, T Sefton and K Stewart (eds) *Towards a more equal society? Policy, inequality and policy since 1997*, Bristol: Policy Press, pp 47–70

Stewart, K, 2013, *Labour's record on the under-fives: Policy spending and outcomes 1997-2010*, Social Policy in a Cold Climate, Working Paper 4, London: Centre for Analysis of Social Exclusion, London School of Economics and Political Science, http://sticerd.lse.ac.uk/dps/case/spcc/wp04.pdf

Stewart, K, Obolenskaya, P, 2015, *The coalition's record on the under fives: Policy, spending and outcomes 2010-2015*, Social Policy in a Cold Climate, Working Paper 12, London: Centre for Analysis of Social Exclusion, London School of Economics and Political Science

Sutherland, H, 1999, *With respect to old age: Long term care – Rights and responsibilities*, London: HMSO, http://webarchive.nationalarchives. gov.uk/+/www.dh.gov.uk/en/Publicationsandstatistics/Publications/ PublicationsPolicyAndGuidance/DH_4008520

Sutherland, H, Figari, F, 2013, EUROMOD: The European Union tax-benefit microsimulation model, *International Journal of Microsimulation*, 6, 1, 4-26

Sylva, K, Goff, J, Eisenstadt, N, Smith, T, Hall, J, Evangelou, M, Smith, G, Sammons, P, 2015, *Organisation, services and reach of children's centres: Evaluation of Children's Centres in England (ECCE Strand 3)*, London: Department for Education

Tallon, A, 2010, *Urban regeneration in the UK*, 2nd edn, London and New York: Routledge

Tanner, E, Agur, M, Hussey, D, 2012, *Evaluation of Children's Centres in England (ECCE) Strand 1: First survey of children's centre leaders in the most deprived areas*, London: Department for Education, www. education.gov.uk/publications/standard/publicationDetail/Page1/ DFE-RR230

Taylor-Gooby, P, 2012, Root and branch restructuring to achieve major cuts: The social policy programme of the 2010 UK coalition government, *Social Policy & Administration*, 46, 1, 61-82

Taylor-Gooby, P, 2013, Public policy futures: A left trilemma?, *Critical Social Policy*, 33, 3, 403-26

Telegraph, The, 2010, Middle classes told to stop using Sure Start, 8 November, www.telegraph.co.uk/news/politics/david-cameron/7937248/Middle-classes-told-to-stop-using-Sure-Start. html

Thalen, K, Streeck, W (eds) (2005) *Beyond continuity: Institutional change in advanced political economies*, Oxford: Oxford University Press

Thorlby, R, Maybin, J, 2010, *A high performing NHS? A review of progress 1997-2010*, London: The King's Fund, www.kingsfund.org.uk/sites/ files/kf/High-Performing-NHS-progress-review-1997-2010-Ruth-Thorlby-Jo-Maybin-Kings-Fund-April-2010.pdf

Tickell, C, 2011, *The early years: Foundations for life, health and learning: An independent report on the Early Years Foundation Stage to Her Majesty's Government*, London: The Stationery Office, www.educationengland. org.uk/documents/pdfs/2011-tickell-report-eyfs.pdf

Timmins, N, 2015, Welfare, in A Seldon and M Finn (eds) *The coalition effect, 2010-2015*, Cambridge: Cambridge University Press, pp 317-344

Townsend, P, Davidson, N, Whitehead, M, 1992, *Inequalities in health: The Black Report and the health divide*, Harmondsworth: Penguin Books

Triggle, N, 2014, 'NHS needs extra cash and overhaul, say health bosses', BBC News, 23 October 2014, www.bbc.co.uk/news/health-29726934

Tunstall, R, 2015, *The coalition's record on housing: Policy, spending and outcomes 2010-2015*, London: Centre for Analysis of Social Exclusion, London School of Economics and Political Science

UCAS, 2014, *Analysis note 2014/02*, Figure 1, www.ucas.com/sites/default/files/analysis-note-2014-02-fsm.pdf

UKCES (United Kingdom Commission for Employment and Skills), 2009, *Towards ambition 2020: Skills, jobs, growth*, Wath-Upon-Dearne: UKCES

UKCES, 2011, *Employer ownership of skills*, London: UKCES

UNICEF Office of Research, 2014, *Children of the recession: The impact of the economic crisis on child well-being in rich countries*, Florence: UNICEF, www.unicef-irc.org/publications/733

Universities UK, 2014, *Trends in undergraduate recruitment*, London: Universities UK

Unwin, L, Fuller, A, Turbin, A, Young, M, 2004, *What determines the impact of vocational qualifications? A literature review*, DfES Research Report 522, Nottingham: Department for Education and Skills, http://webarchive.nationalarchives.gov.uk/20130401151715/http://www.education.gov.uk/publications/eOrderingDownload/RR522.pdf

Valuation Office Agency, 2011, *Private rental market statistics – England only*, http://webarchive.nationalarchives.gov.uk/20140712003745/http://www.voa.gov.uk/corporate/statisticalReleases/110929_PrivateResidentialRentalMarketStatistics.html

Vizard, P, Obolenskaya, P, 2013, *Labour's record on health: Policy spending and outcomes 1997-2010*, Social Policy in a Cold Climate, Working Paper 2, London: Centre for Analysis of Social Exclusion, London School of Economics and Political Science, http://sticerd.lse.ac.uk/dps/case/spcc/wp02.pdf

Vizard, P, Obolenskaya, P, 2015, *The coalition's record on health: Policy spending and outcomes 2010-2015*, Social Policy in a Cold Climate, Working Paper 16, London: Centre for Analysis of Social Exclusion, London School of Economics and Political Science, http://sticerd.lse.ac.uk/dps/case/spcc/WP16.pdf

Vizard, P, Karagiannaki, E, Cunliffe, J, Fitzgerald, A, Obolenskaya, P, Thomson, S, Grollman, C, Lupton, R, 2015, *The changing anatomy of economic inequality in London (2007-2013)*, Social Policy in a Cold Climate, Research Report 6, London: Centre for Analysis of Social Exclusion, London School of Economics and Social Exclusion, http://sticerd.lse.ac.uk/dps/case/spcc/RR06.pdf

Vlachantoni, A, Shaw, R, Evandrou, M, Falkingham, J, 2015, The determinants of receiving social care in later life in England, *Ageing and Society*, 35, 2, 321-45

Vlachantoni, A, Shaw, R, Willis, R, Evandrou, M, Falkingham, J, Luff, R, 2011, *Measuring unmet need for social care amongst older people*, Population Trends No 145, Autumn, Newport: Office for National Statistics, www.palgrave-journals.com/pt/journal/v145/n1/pdf/pt201117a.pdf

Waldfogel, J, 2006, *What children need*, Cambridge, MA: Harvard University Press

Wanless, D, 2002, *Securing our future health: Taking a long-term view, Final report*, London: HM Treasury, http://si.easp.es/derechosciudadania/wp-content/uploads/2009/10/4.Informe-Wanless.pdf

West, A, Nikolai, R, 2013, Welfare regimes and education regimes: Equality of opportunity and expenditure in the EU (and US), *Journal of Social Policy*, 42, 3, 469-93

Whalley, R, 2012, Social care: Need for and receipt of help, in Health and Social Care Information Centre (ed) *Health Survey for England 2012*, Volume 1, Chapter 8, www.hscic.gov.uk/catalogue/PUB13218/HSE2012-Ch8-Social-care-need.pdf

Whitehead, C, Williams, P, 2011, Causes and consequences? Exploring the shape and direction of the housing system in the UK post the financial crisis, *Housing Studies*, 26, 7-8, 1157-69

Wilcox, S, 2014, *Housing Benefit size criteria: Impacts for social sector tenants and options for reform*, York: Joseph Rowntree Foundation

Wilcox, S, Perry, J, William, P, 2015, *UK housing review, Briefing 2014*, Coventry: Chartered Institute of Housing, www.cih.org/resources/PDF/Policy%20free%20download%20pdfs/UKHR%20Briefing%202014%20bookmarked.pdf

Wilson, W, 2014, *Housing Benefit: Discretionary Housing Payments (DHPs) – Commons Library Standard Note, 22 September 2014*, Standard Notes SN06899, London: House of Commons Library, http://researchbriefings.parliament.uk/ResearchBriefing/Summary/SN06899

Wilson, W, 2015a, *Rent setting for social housing tenancies (England) – Commons Library Standard Note 1090, January 2015*, Standard Notes SN/SP/1090, London: House of Commons Library, http://researchbriefings.parliament.uk/ResearchBriefing/Summary/SN01090

Wilson, W, 2015b, *The New Homes Bonus scheme, Commons Library Standard Note 26, November 2014, Standard Notes SN05724*, London: House of Commons Library, http://researchbriefings.parliament.uk/ResearchBriefing/Summary/SN05724

Wolf, A, 2007, Round and round the houses: The Leitch Review of Skills, *Local Economy*, 22, 2, 111-17

Wolf, A. (2011) *Review of vocational education: The Wolf Report*. London: Department for Education

Wong, C, Gibb, K, McGreal, S, Webb, B, Leishman, C, Blair, N, Hinks, S, MacIntyre, S, 2011, *Housing and neighbourhoods monitor 2011: Fragility and recovery*, York: Joseph Rowntree Foundation, http://eprints.gla.ac.uk/60452/1/60452.pdf

Wood, J, Heath, S, 2014, Clinical Commissioning Group (CCG) funding, SN06779, House of Commons Library, http://researchbriefings.files.parliament.uk/documents/SN06779/SN06779.pdf

Wren-Lewis, S, 2013, 'Aggregate fiscal policy under the Labour government 1997-2010', *Oxford Review of Economic Policy*, 29(1), pp 25-46.

Wren-Lewis, S, 2015, 'The Macroeconomic Record of the Coalition Government', *National Institute Economic Review*, 23(1): R5-16.

Index

Page references for tables, figures and boxes are given in *italics*; those for notes are followed by n